Specification Analysis in the Linear Model

Specification Analysis in the Linear Model

(In Honour of Donald Cochrane)

Edited by
Maxwell L. King and David E. A. Giles
Department of Econometrics and Operations Research, Monash University
and Department of Economics and Operations Research, University of Canterbury

Routledge & Kegan Paul
London and New York

First published in 1987 by
Routledge & Kegan Paul Ltd
11 New Fetter Lane, London EC4P 4EE

Published in the USA by
Routledge & Kegan Paul Inc.
in association with Methuen Inc.
29 West 35th Street, New York, NY 10001

Set in Times, 10 on 12pt.
by Columns, Reading
and printed in Great Britain
by Billing and Sons Ltd.
Worcester

Library of Congress Cataloging in Publication Data

Main entry under title:
Specification analysis in the linear model.
Includes index.
1. Econometric models—Addresses, essays, lectures.
2. Econometrics—Addresses, essays, lectures.
3. Cochrane, Donald, d. 1983. I. Cochrane, Donald, d.
1983. II. King, Maxwell L. III. Giles, David E.A.,
1949–
HB141.S65 1985 330'.028 85-2117

ISBN 0-7102-0614-3

Contents

Preface

This volume has been prepared by the editors and contributors to honour Donald Cochrane, who died in March 1983. Cochrane was a graduate of the Universities of Melbourne and Cambridge, and was foundation Dean of Economics and Politics at Monash University until his premature retirement in December 1981. As Dean, he provided an academic environment within which teaching and research in economics, and its various areas of specialisation, were able to flourish. Econometrics was one such area. During a long and distinguished academic and public career as an economist and educator, Donald Cochrane made many lasting contributions, and in recognition of these he received various honours, including the first Honorary Doctorate in Economics to be awarded by Monash University. In this book, however, some of Cochrane's former colleagues pay tribute to just one aspect of his work – that in the discipline of econometrics.

In 1949, Donald Cochrane and Guy Orcutt published two path-breaking articles (reproduced in the Appendix to this book) discussing various statistical issues which arise when estimating economic relationships, which may be simultaneous in nature, and in which the regression errors follow an autoregressive process rather than being serially independent. These papers illustrated that when working with economic time-series data there is a high probability that the errors in regression relationships are positively autocorrelated; they investigated the extent to which such a specification could reduce the efficiency of the least squares estimator and predictor; they considered the need to modify this estimator when this more general error specification prevails; and they suggested a simple transformation of the data and a correspondingly modified least squares estimator for the parameters of such a relationship. The merits of this 'Cochrane-Orcutt transformation' were investigated by means of a simulation experiment, and today this technique (and various refinements of it) is as widely used and well known as any of the various devices used in econometrics to deal with generalisations of the specification of the linear statistical model.

These fundamental contributions to our understanding of the importance of the specification of the error term in a regression relationship, and this early attempt to provide a pragmatic but statistically sound solution to an important specification 'problem', are excellent illustrations of the objectives and contributions of econometrics in its fifty years as a recognised field of study. In a narrow sense, much of the statistical (as opposed to mathematical economic) content of econometrics rests with the analysis of specification and mis-specification problems associated with the linear model. What are the consequences for conventional estimators, predictors and tests when the assumptions of this model (on which these inferential procedures are based) are violated? What statistical costs are incurred if we use an estimator or test in an inappropriate situation? To what extent can we test the validity of the assumptions on which our inferential procedures are based? In what ways should our estimators, tests and predictors be modified to take account of more general underlying conditions than usually are assumed to prevail?

These, and other related questions, are central to both the theory and application of econometrics. Indeed, it could be argued that much of what distinguishes this discipline from other 'metrics' is its emphasis on such specification issues, especially as they relate to model simultaneity, measurement errors, non-scalar error covariance structures, and dynamic adjustment mechanisms. With these distinctive features of econometrics in mind, and given that Donald Cochrane's own work was so central to a generation of effort devoted to various aspects of specification and misspecification in empirical economics, it is fitting that the attention of this volume should be focussed upon specification analysis in the linear statistical model.

The editors are especially pleased that this volume includes papers written by Guy Orcutt and by some of Donald Cochrane's other associates during his time at the University of Cambridge. Richard Stone was, of course, central to this group, and also supervised Cochrane's doctoral thesis; and Geoffrey Watson had even earlier connections with Cochrane through the University of Melbourne. More recent colleagues, and graduates of the Faculty of Economics and Politics at Monash University are well represented among the contributors to this book, as are econometricians who have held visiting appointments in this Faculty in recent years and have shared in the healthy academic environment that Donald Cochrane helped to promote. We hope that this collection of papers is a fitting recognition of Donald Cochrane's own contributions to econometrics.

The preparation of this volume would not have been possible without the assistance of a number of people. Generous financial support was given by Monash University, and in this regard we are particularly grateful to our Vice Chancellor, Professor R. L. Martin; our Dean of Economics and Politics, Professor W. A. Sinclair; and the Monash University Publications Committee for the special interest that they showed in this project. The contributors themselves, and a number of our colleagues, generously participated in a most valuable informal refereeing of the preliminary draft of the manuscript. We are most grateful to the American Statistical Association, the Colston Research Society, P. E. Hart, G. Mills, J. K.

Whitaker, Guy Orcutt and Denis Sargan for granting permission to reproduce the material in the Appendix. Finally, we would like to thank Mrs Mary Englefield and Mrs Carol Clark for their assistance in the preparation of this volume, and especially for their excellent typing of much of the manuscript.

Maxwell L. King
David E. A. Giles
Melbourne, Australia
September, 1984

1 Introduction

Maxwell L. King and David E. A. Giles

The basis for this book is a collection of fifteen original articles prepared by a number of Donald Cochrane's colleagues and associates. These articles develop the general specification analysis theme in various ways. However, there is a particular emphasis on specification issues arising in the context of autocorrelated errors in the regression model, and this emphasis links the book closely to the early contribution of Cochrane and Orcutt (1949) and Orcutt and Cochrane (1949). These papers, and part of an article by Sargan (1964) which has direct bearing on the computational aspects of the Cochrane-Orcutt work, are reproduced as Appendixes to this book. Special features of the volume are the inclusion of major survey chapters, and the balance between theoretical and applied econometrics in the various articles. Indeed, it is the editors' hope that this book will contain much that is of practical help and interest to applied researchers, as well as to students and researchers whose interests lie more with the underlying statistical theory of econometrics.

The first part of the book comprises six chapters which deal with various aspects of regression analysis when the model errors are autocorrelated. This section begins with two survey papers. In Chapter 2, Ted Hannan appraises the original Cochrane-Orcutt work from the present perspective. He discusses spectral methods for regression and considers a link between this approach and the Cochrane-Orcutt transformation in the handling of autocorrelated disturbances. Hannan notes that the models discussed by those authors are of the ARMAX type and he stresses the need for a careful interaction of prior and sample information in the fitting of such models, noting that a useful benefit of such interaction may be to constrain the problem to one of manageable size.

Chapter 3, by Maxwell King provides a comprehensive survey of the literature on testing for various forms of autocorrelation in regression disturbances. King links the early work of Cochrane and Orcutt on the consequences of, and estimation under, autocorrelated errors, to the work of Durbin and Watson (1950, 1951) on testing the hypothesis of serial independence against the alternative of a first-order autoregressive process. The emphasis of the survey is on the power properties of various tests, and one of King's conclusions is that care must be taken not to place too much faith in Likelihood Ratio and Lagrange Multiplier tests unless their power properties have been adequately explored in finite samples. King proposes a general strategy for constructing tests against composite alternative hypotheses which will hopefully receive further attention in the literature.

Chapters 4 to 7 discuss various specific aspects of regression analysis with autocorrelated errors. In the first of these four papers Grant Hillier and Maxwell King obtain bounds on the value that may be taken by any linear combination of the elements of the best linear unbiased estimator of the coefficient vector in the model when the errors have a non-scalar covariance matrix. This situation arises, for example, when the disturbances are autocorrelated. Hillier and King use these bounds to investigate the range of values which may be taken by the statistic for testing simple restrictions on the coefficient vector when the true form of the error covariance matrix is taken into account. Their results indicate the extent to which our inferences may be sensitive to departures from the usual scalar error covariance assumption.

In Chapter 5, Lonnie Magee, Aman Ullah and Viren Srivastava provide some important analytical evidence on the sampling properties of the two-step Cochrane-Orcutt estimator when an estimate of the autocorrelation parameter is used. The estimator (and the closely associated procedure suggested by Prais and Winsten (1954)) is shown to be unbiased under quite general conditions. The efficiencies of these two estimators are compared by numerically evaluating certain large-sample approximations to their covariance matrices in a variety of finite-sample situations.

David Giles and Murray Beattie consider the problem of estimating a dynamic regression model when the disturbances are autocorrelated and when a sequential strategy is adopted. Using a Monte Carlo experiment they investigate the finite-sample risks of various preliminary-test estimators, where the test in question is of the hypothesis that the disturbances are serially independent. The study illustrates some of the consequences of such pre-testing and suggests which tests and estimators may lead to relatively low risk in this context.

This first part of the book is completed with a paper by Peter Praetz, who considers several specification issues which relate closely to the work of Cochrane and Orcutt. Praetz considers the effects on the Durbin-Watson test of falsely omitting variables from a linear regression model; the extent to which this test statistic is biased when the functional form of the model is mis-specified; and the bias induced in other conventional tests and summary measures when the errors in fact follow a first-order autoregressive scheme. One interesting aspect of Praetz's results is that model mis-specification may bias a statistic which is itself used to test for some form of mis-specification. This suggests a danger in placing too much emphasis on single specification errors, and as Praetz points out, many interesting combinations of model mis-specification remain to be studied.

Part II of the volume is devoted to some more general specification problems. The question of overall model specification is approached at a fundamental level by Guy Orcutt in Chapter 8. In this paper Orcutt makes the distinction between two broad types of structural modelling: that encountered in macroeconomic time-series models, where the equations may be either simultaneous or recursive in nature; and that used to describe micro activity, where a joint conditional probability function is introduced and represented by complete sets of recursive regressions (one set for the members of each micro-group). This second type of structural modelling is emphasised and supported by Orcutt in this chapter, and he argues that such microanalytic models are the most general of those usually encountered in empirical economic analysis. The author makes a convincing case for microentity-oriented joint conditional probability functions, and the use of recursive regressions for specification and estimation purposes.

The second paper in this section surveys the literature on testing separate (non-nested) regression models. In this chapter Michael McAleer discusses the links between some of the recent tests of this type, and some of the more established tests for various forms of model mis-specification. He also offers a unified presentation of those specification tests which have been developed from the likelihood ratio principle, and those which are founded on the fitting of artificial regressions. This survey points out some directions for future research in an area which has undergone rapid development in recent years, and which addresses the fundamental issues of model specification in econometrics.

This part of the volume concludes with a discussion of functional forms in duality theory, by Keith McLaren and Russel Cooper. This chapter deals with the specification of econometric relationships in a broad sense, namely in terms of the form of the estimating equation and the restrictions on the parameters implied by the underlying economic theory. The authors concentrate on the problem of generating functional forms which are consistent with the implications of intertemporal duality in the theory of the firm and in consumer theory. Some practical approaches are suggested. This paper serves to remind us that the question of model specification begins with the economic theory that underlies our estimating equations.

The third part of the book contains two chapters dealing with statistical issues of direct concern to econometricians. In Chapter 11 Geoffrey Watson considers the problem of estimating the spectral form of a population cross-product matrix from the eigenvalues and eigenvectors of the corresponding sample moment matrix. Alternative asymptotic approaches are discussed and compared. The techniques described in this paper are potentially applicable to other estimators of interest to econometricians such as the limited information maximum likelihood estimator for linear simultaneous equations.

The second study in this part of the volume deals with the problem of prediction from a regression model when the regressors are themselves random in nature. This situation arises frequently in econometrics, and raises some important specification issues. Clearly, a mis-specification problem arises if the random nature of the regressors is ignored either at the estimation stage of the analysis, or when the model is used to generate predictions. Here, Arnold Zellner and Soo-Bin Park analyse this situation from the Bayesian viewpoint, and take account of the uncertainty associated with the future values of the regressors in obtaining the full, unconditional, predictive density for the model's dependent variable. The authors illustrate the consequences of failing to adequately take account of the randomness of the regressors – in an application they find that misleadingly precise predictive inferences arise. This study is a good example of the way in which the Bayesian approach in statistics offers powerful and flexible solutions to inference problems in econometrics.

The volume concludes with a section comprising three chapters devoted to data issues and applied econometric studies. In the first of these, Richard Stone considers systems of national income accounts, and in particular adjusting the entries so that the accounts balance without the introduction of residual errors, unidentified items and other balancing entries. The technique of making such adjustments by the method of least squares, proposed earlier by Stone and others, is reviewed. The author then discusses the important issue of the absolute accuracy of the national income account entries before and after adjustment.

In Chapter 14 Kenneth Clements and John Taylor use a portfolio approach to model the holdings of financial assets by Australian households. This study illustrates, among other things, the testing and implementation of restrictions from the underlying economic theory when specifying and estimating a structural econometric model. This structural modelling approach is compared with two alternatives: a Markov chain model, and the application of a logistic growth model to one of the assets in question. Maximum likelihood estimation is used to fit the logistic curve, and the results are found to accord well with the relevant findings from the structural modelling exercise.

The final chapter in the collection of original papers reports on an empirical study by Ross Williams, who models dwelling commencements in Australia. The emphasis of the study clearly is on model specification, especially with regard to the inter-related issues of lag structure and error autocorrelation. Williams takes the relevant part of the NIF-10 model of the Australian economy and investigates the consequences of modifying its specification in various ways. This study illustrates the need for a careful treatment of systematic and error dynamics when specifying and estimating econometric models, and the implications for policy-makers who may use the forecasts that these models generate.

The volume is completed with the inclusion of Appendixes which reproduce the two original articles written by Donald Cochrane and Guy

Orcutt. These pieces are included to put directly before the reader the basic material which has stimulated a considerable amount of important work on model specification in econometrics. Obviously, these contributions are of direct relevance to the other papers in this book. Also reproduced there is an appendix to an important article by Denis Sargan. This piece is included because it provides a formal discussion of an iterative procedure which is directly relevant to the estimation of the parameters of a regression model after the 'Cochrane-Orcutt transformation' has been applied.

From this brief description of the contents of this volume it will be clear that the general theme of specification analysis in econometrics is developed in a variety of ways in the papers collected here. There is a heavy emphasis on the specification of the error term in regression analysis, which places these studies well within the spirit of the early econometric work to which Donald Cochrane contributed. At the same time, new issues are taken up, such as the testing of non-nested models, and pre-test estimation. There are numerous results and conclusions in these papers that point out new directions for further research, and offer practical guidance for applied researchers. Hopefully, this volume will stimulate further work on the many problems which remain unexplored in the general area of model specification and mis-specification in econometrics.

References

Cochrane, D. and Orcutt, G. H. (1949), 'Application of Least Squares Regression to Relationships Containing Auto-Correlated Error Terms', *Journal of the American Statistical Association*, 44, 32-61.

Durbin, J. and Watson, G. S. (1950), 'Testing for Serial Correlation in Least Squares Regression I', *Biometrika*, 37, 409-28.

Durbin, J. and Watson, G. S. (1951), 'Testing for Serial Correlation in Least Squares Regression II', *Biometrika*, 38, 159-78.

Orcutt, G. H. and Cochrane, D. (1949), 'A Sampling Study of the Merits of Autoregressive and Reduced Form Transformations in Regression Analysis', *Journal of the American Statistical Association*, 44, 356-72.

Prais, S. J. and Winsten, C. B. (1954), 'Trend Estimators and Serial Correlation', mimeographed, Chicago: Cowles Commission.

Sargan, J.D. (1964), 'Wages and Prices in the United Kingdom: A Study in Econometric Methodology', in *Econometric Analysis for National Economic Planning*, eds. P.E. Hart, G. Mills and J.K. Whitaker, London: Butterworths, 25-63.

Part I
Linear regression with autocorrelated errors

2 The Cochrane and Orcutt papers

E. J. Hannan

1 The first paper

In 1949 two papers by D. Cochrane and G.H. Orcutt introduced a range of problems connected with dynamic, linear models that are still being studied. Avoiding such hyperbole as the occasion might induce it may fairly be said that the papers were important. The papers dealt with two problems, namely that arising from the fact that there may be many endogenous variables (or outputs) connected by as many simultaneous relations, and that arising from autocorrelation of the disturbances in the equations. A third problem, mentioned but not discussed, is that of errors of measurement in the exogenous variables (inputs). We shall discuss this only briefly.

The first paper, Cochrane and Orcutt (1949), we shall refer to as CO. This dealt with autocorrelation in the disturbances u_t in a single equation

$$Y_t = \mu + \sum_1^m \beta_j X_{j,t} + u_t, \qquad t=1, \ldots, n. \tag{1}$$

The method of investigation was substantially by simulation, the model for u_t being of ARMA type

$$\sum_0^p \phi_j u_{t-j} = \sum_0^q \psi_j \varepsilon_{t-j}, \quad \phi_0 = \psi_0 = 1, \quad E(\varepsilon_s \varepsilon_t) = \delta_{st}\, \sigma^2. \tag{2}$$

Here the ε_t are the linear innovations or prediction errors for u_t from its past. In fact in CO, p and q were 1 or 2 and one zero of $\phi(z)$, where $\phi(z) = \Sigma\, \phi_j z^i$, $\psi(z) = \Sigma\, \psi_j z^i$, was sometimes allowed to be unity. This zero can, of course, be removed by differencing the data. Apart from that the other zero lay outside of $|z| = 1$.

CO dealt with evidence from experience for autocorrelation in the u_t, with testing for this and with the effectiveness of the Cochrane-Orcutt transformation (COT) in regaining lost efficiency due to ignoring the autocorrelation. In general terms we mean by the COT the 'autoregressive' transformation

$$Y_t \rightarrow \Sigma\, b_j\, Y_{t-j}; \quad X_{k,t} \rightarrow \Sigma b_j\, X_{k,t-j}, \quad k=1, \ldots, m.$$

The b_j are chosen so that $b(z) = \Sigma\, b_j\, z^i$ will be near to $\psi(z)^{-1}\, \phi(z)$, which is however unknown. CO considered in detail the case of where $\psi(z) = 1$, $\phi(z) = 1 - \varrho z$, so that $b(z) = 1 - \varrho z$ is an optimal choice. They introduced an iterative procedure whereby ordinary least squares (OLS) is used to estimate (1), after which $\hat{u}_t = Y_t - \Sigma\, \hat{\beta}_k X_{k,t}$, $t=1, \ldots, n$, are used to estimate ϱ by means of their first (sample) autocorrelation

$$\hat{\varrho} = \sum_{1}^{T-1} \hat{u}_t \hat{u}_{t+1} / \sum_{1}^{T} \hat{u}_t^2 .$$

The COT is then applied and the transformed quantities used to estimate the β_j . CO commented on the bias towards zero in $\hat{\varrho}$ and rejected the procedure arguing instead for the use of $b(z) = 1 - z$ on the grounds that ϱ will often be near to unity. It is well known that differencing (i.e. $\varrho = 1$) may be very inadvisable as it may 'throw the baby out with the bath water' by eliminating the main source of variation in the input as well as in the output. An example is the estimation of a trend.

Almost immediately after these two papers came two by Durbin and Watson (1950, 1951) which dealt with testing whether the u_t were serially independent. We shall not discuss this here save to say that the bounds test there introduced no longer seems necessary as the level at which the observed statistic is just significant can fairly easily be calculated. (See Hannan, 1970, pp. 459-60.) Of course the bounds test may first be used and the precise significance point located only if that is inconclusive. There is a tendency in modern time series literature to replace hypothesis testing by model fitting procedures wherein (1), (2) would be, for example, considered as prescribing the model and would be estimated along with p,q. It is not thought that there is any true model but some criterion is optimised that balances a measure of goodness of fit against the 'cost' in terms of parameters estimated. It may be that these procedures are more suitable for 'large' n (say $n=100$ or more) and in economics a more cautious diagnostic procedure is called for to economise on parameters, with the smaller samples met in that field.

The loss of efficiency in least squares due to autocorrelated residuals was extensively investigated in the 10 years after CO. A survey with references may be found in Hannan (1970, Chapter VII). The effectiveness of the COT has been queried by Maeshiro (1976). The case $\psi(z) = 1$, $\phi(z) = 1 - \varrho z$, $m=1$ is considered and the true ϱ is used in the COT, which serves to increase the surprise felt at the results. The *true* variances of COT and OLS are calculated for cases where $X_{1,t}$ is trending, e.g. $X_{1,t}=\lambda^t$, Bt or real GNP in USA. For $\varrho > 0$ in these cases Var(OLS)/Var(COT) < 1 at $n=20$ (the CO sample size), values less than 0.8 are common and there are some very low values at $\lambda < 1$. Part of the reason is that some of the $X_{1,t}$ series have most of their variation accounted for by very low frequencies. (See the next section and particularly (5)). Indeed for *Bt* it is known (Hannan, 1960, p. 115) that OLS is asymptotically efficient. But then so would be COT. However a major part of the effect is due to the fact that COT uses only the observation pairs $(X_{1,t} - \varrho X_{1,t-1}, Y_t - \varrho Y_{t-1})$, $t=2, \ldots, 20$ and omits $X_{1,1}, Y_1$. In the cases listed above, and particularly for $\lambda < 1$, this last pair may provide a point in the scatter diagram far from the centroid and hence there may be a considerable loss of information in neglecting it. Maeshiro's results should not be taken too seriously as some of his examples are rather extreme but they show that asymptotic theory must be used with care. One alternative, with n small, is to try to conserve information by using an *exact* likelihood. We go on to discuss ways of constructing that.

2 Spectral methods in estimation

Spectral methods in inference were probably first introduced in Whittle (1951). They were developed for regression in Hamon and Hannan (1963), and Hannan (1963). The justification is as follows. Let u_t, $t=1, \ldots, n$, be replaced by the new random variables, got by a fixed orthogonal transformation

$$c_u(j) = \left(\frac{2}{n}\right)^{\frac{1}{2}} \sum_1^n u_t \cos t\omega_j, \qquad s_u(j) = \left(\frac{2}{n}\right)^{\frac{1}{2}} \sum_1^n u_t \sin t\omega_j,$$

$$j = 1, 2, \ldots, \left[\frac{n-1}{2}\right];$$

$$c_u(0) = n^{-\frac{1}{2}} \sum_1^n u_t; \qquad c_u(n/2) = n^{-\frac{1}{2}} \sum_1^n (-)^t u_t, \qquad n \text{ even.}$$

Here $\omega_j = 2\pi j/n$ and $[x]$ is the integer part of x. It is convenient to introduce

$$w_u(\omega_j) = 2^{-\frac{1}{2}}\{c_u(j) + is_u(j)\}, \quad j=1, \ldots, \left[\frac{n-1}{2}\right],$$

$$w_u(0) = c(0), \; w_u(\pi) = c(n/2).$$

Thus the $w_u(\omega_j)$ are got by a fixed unitary transformation from the u_t. If the spectral density ('spectrum'), $f_u(\omega)$ is

$$2\pi f_u(\omega) = \Sigma\, \gamma_u(j) e^{ij\omega}, \; \gamma_u(j) = \mathrm{E}(u_t u_{t+j})$$

then under rather general conditions the random variables $c_u(j)$, $s_u(j)$ have a covariance matrix that converges, uniformly in the elements, to a diagonal matrix with elements $2\pi f_u(\omega_j)$ in the diagonal corresponding to both $c_u(j)$ and $s_u(j)$. Thus an approximation to $2n^{-1}$ log likelihood is (up to an additive constant)

$$\frac{1}{n}\sum_j \log\{2\pi f_u(\omega_j)\} + \frac{1}{n}\sum_j \frac{c_u(j)^2 + s_u(j)^2}{2\pi f_u(\omega_j)}$$

$$= \frac{1}{n}\sum_{\omega_j} \log\{2\pi f_u(\omega_j)\} + \frac{1}{n}\sum_j \frac{|w_u(\omega_j)|^2}{2\pi f_u(\omega_j)} \qquad (3)$$

where in the latter form the sum is over $-\pi < \omega_j \leqslant \pi$. An approximation to this is

$$\log \sigma^2 + \frac{1}{2\pi}\int_{-\pi}^{\pi} \frac{|w_u(\omega)|^2}{2\pi f_u(\omega)}\, d\omega \quad . \qquad (4)$$

These formulae are due to Whittle (1951). Their use in connection with the procedures of Section 1 is through putting $w_u(\omega) = w_y(\omega) - \Sigma\, \beta_k w_k(\omega)$, where $w_k(\omega)$ is formed from $X_{k,t}$, and $2\pi f_u(\omega) = |\phi(\exp i\omega)|^{-2}|\psi(\exp i\omega)|^2\sigma^2$. In particular, for the vector β composed of the β_j we are led to the estimate

$$\tilde{\beta} = \{\sum_{\omega_j} \tilde{f}(\omega_j)^{-1} w_x(\omega_j) w_x(\omega_j)^*\}^{-1}\{\sum_{\omega_j} \tilde{f}(\omega_j)^{-1} w_x(\omega_j) w_j(\omega_j)^*\}. \qquad (5)$$

Here $\tilde{f}$ is computed from the estimates of ϕ,ψ. The covariance matrix is estimated as 2π by the first factor. The estimation could be by an iterative procedure where first $\tilde{\beta}^{(1)}$ is formed using $\tilde{f} \equiv$ constant, then $\tilde{f}_u{}^{(1)}$ is estimated using $\tilde{w}_u = w_y - \Sigma\, \tilde{\beta}_k{}^{(1)} w_k$ in (3), then $\tilde{\beta}^{(2)}$ is formed using this $\tilde{f}_u{}^{(1)}$ in (5) and so on.

There has recently been some resurgence of interest in (3), (4). (See also Hannan, 1970, Chapters III and VII.) However, they must be used with care for the following reasons.

(i) The equation (3) is equivalent to saying that the u_t are Gaussian with a covariance matrix that is a circulant, so that $\gamma_u(j) = \gamma_u(n-j)$. The Guassian assumption is not critical but the circular assumption can produce bad effects in small samples, though the effects are asymptotically very small.

(ii) The equation (4) is not a valid likelihood as the implied covariance matrix of the data is A^{-1} where A has elements

$$a_{jk} = \int_{-\pi}^{\pi} \frac{1}{f(\omega)}\, e^{i(j-k)\omega}\, d\omega.$$

However $-\, n^{-1} \log \det A \neq \sigma^2$, though the error goes to zero as $n \to \infty$. Also A^{-1} is not, of course, the correct covariance matrix.

It can be shown that all effects mentioned above disappear asymptotically. However, they may be of importance in small samples. The formula (5) also has virtues because the summations, over $-\pi < \omega_j \leq \pi$, may be reduced to cover a smaller range of frequencies (symmetric with respect to $\omega = 0$) so as to avoid frequencies (for example those near $\pm\pi$) where measurement errors in the $X_{k,t}$ may be relatively large. Measurement error is likely to have a near to uniform spectrum while the $X_{k,t}$ are likely to have spectra concentrated near $\omega = 0$. Hence the error will be relatively large near π. Formula (5) could also be used without the model (2) by constructing a smoothed estimate of the spectrum via the $\tilde{\omega}_u$.

However, it may be preferable in some circumstances to work with a more 'exact' likelihood. (Of course no likelihood is truly exact as knowledge needed for the construction of that is never available.) We go on in Section 4 to discuss this in relation to the second Cochrane and Orcutt paper (Orcutt and Cochrane, 1949), which we henceforth refer to as OC.

3 The second paper

In OC a two output model is considered

$$Y_{1,t} = \mu_1 + \gamma_1 Y_{2,t} + u_{1,t}\,, \tag{6a}$$

$$Y_{2,t} = \mu_2 + \gamma_2 Y_{1,t} + u_{2,t}, \tag{6b}$$

$$u_{j,t} = \mu_{j,t-1} + \varepsilon_{j,t}\,,\quad j=1,2;\ \mathrm{E}\{\varepsilon_{j,s}\,\varepsilon_{k,t}\} = 0,\ s \neq t\,.$$

In OC the values $\gamma_1 = 1$, $\gamma_2 = 0.4$ are used. Among other methods they use first differences, $\eta_{j,t} = Y_{j,t} - Y_{j,t-1}$ so that, putting η_t for the vectors composed of the $\eta_{j,t}$, $j=1,2$, and similarly for ε_t,

$$\eta_t = \begin{bmatrix} -\gamma_1\gamma_2 & 0 \\ -\gamma_2 & 0 \end{bmatrix} \eta_{t-1} + \varepsilon_t\,. \tag{7}$$

This is the differenced form of what OC call the reduced form. The most surprising result in their simulations is that, when $\mathrm{E}\{\varepsilon_{1,t}\,\varepsilon_{2,t}\} = 0$, then using the differenced form of (6a) and OLS the results are better, for $n=20$, than those obtained from (7). Of course OLS applied to (7) is asymptotically efficient while the other method is inconsistent, since $Y_{2,t} - Y_{2,t-1}$ is not independent of $\varepsilon_{1,t}$. Some of the effect may be due to the method applied to (7) being non-maximum likelihood (though asymptotically equivalent) but much may be due to a trade of a small increase in bias for a larger reduction in variance, due to the single equation method based on (6a). Again the near irrelevance of asymptotic criteria in small samples is seen.

The final conclusion of OC is that 'unless it is possible to specify with some accuracy the interconnection between error terms' and 'unless it is possible to choose approximately the correct autoregressive transformation' the feasibility of estimating such structures from only 20 true points is in doubt. 'This scepticism will be considerably increased' if one has to choose the variables involved and their lags.

Of course $n=20$ is very small, even in econometrics, by the standards of today. All of the OC models are of the form, for s outputs, as components of Y_t and m inputs as components of X_t ,

$$\sum_0^p \Phi(j) Y_{t-j} = \sum_1^r \Delta(j) X_{t-j} + \sum_0^q \psi(j)\varepsilon_{t-j}; \quad \mathrm{E}\{\varepsilon_s\varepsilon_t'\} = \delta_{st}\Omega, \quad \Phi(0) = \psi(0) \ , \tag{8}$$

and in all cases, at least after differencing,

$$\phi(z) = \Sigma\, \Phi(j)z^j \ , \ \psi(z) = \Sigma\, \Psi(j)z^j \ , \ \delta(z) = \Sigma\, \Delta(j)z^j$$

satisfy det $\phi(z)$, det $\psi(z) = 0$, $|z| \leq 1$. We henceforth assume this but do not assume that the lag structure is known, and go on to discuss modern methods for estimating (8) and their relevance to the questions OC raised.

4 Armax models

We have previously considered the ARMAX model when s=1, via (1), (2) and have considered maximum likelihood (ML) via (3), (4). We now consider (8) in general via an exact Gaussian likelihood. We shall later discuss the relevance of these ideas for econometrics in the light of the findings in OC discussed in Section 3. There are at least two problems to be faced. The first is the coordinatisation of (8) for $s > 1$. It can easily be shown (Hannan, 1971) that if $k(z) = \phi(z)^{-1}\psi(z)$, $l(z) = \phi(z)^{-1}\delta(z)$ then k, l, Ω are uniquely determined by the requirements on the zeros of det ϕ, det ψ together with $\Phi(0) = \psi(0)$. However, the factorisations, $k = \phi^{-1}\psi$, $l = \phi^{-1}\delta$, are far from unique. For a unique parameterisation we must in some sense or other specify maximum lags. The second problem is the construction and optimisation of the likelihood. This necessarily waits upon the solution of the first problem. We now discuss that. The discussion must be brief and heuristic because the subject is not easy. (See Deistler and Hannan, 1981, for some references.) Let us put

$$k(z) = \sum_0^\infty K(j)z^j \ , \quad l(z) = \sum_1^\infty L(j)z^j \ .$$

Then

$$Y_t = \sum_0^\infty K(j)\varepsilon_{t-j} + \sum_1^\infty L(j)X_{t-j} \ , \quad K(0) = I_s \ .$$

Define the predictors

$$Y(t+u|t) = \sum_u^\infty K(j)\varepsilon_{t+u-j} + \sum_u^\infty L(j)X_{t+u-j} \ .$$

We apologise for the change of notation, so that the time parameter is now an argument variable, in parentheses, but this is needed for a manageable notation. $Y_j(t+u|t)$, which is the jth component of $Y(t+u|t)$, can be regarded as the best linear predictor of $Y_{j,t+u}$, from observations to time t. (It is not *the* best linear predictor because we have not used knowledge of any autocorrelation in the X_t sequences. $Y(t+u|t)$ is a theoretical quantity and is not computed.) It is a consequence of (8), and indeed equivalent to (8), that the rank of the collection of all $Y_j(t+u,t)$; $j=1, \ldots, s$; $u=1,2, \ldots,$ is finite. This rank, called the order of the system or the McMillan degree, will be indicated by ν. Thus we can find ν among the $Y_j(t+u|t)$ in terms of which all others can be expressed linearly. These ν can always be chosen, for appropriate ν_j, in the form

$$Y_j(t+u,t)\ ,\ u=1, \ldots, \nu_j;\ j=1, \ldots, s\ .\ \Sigma\, \nu_j = \nu\ . \tag{9}$$

As a consequence of the definition of the $Y(t+u|t)$ we have the following relations

$$\begin{aligned} Y_j(t+u|t) &= Y_j(t+u|t-1) + \sum_1^s \varkappa_{jk}(u)\varepsilon_{k,t} + \sum_1^n \lambda_{jk}(u)X_{k,t}\ , \\ &\qquad u=1, \ldots, \nu_j-1, \\ Y_j(t+\nu_j|t) + \sum_{k=1}^s \sum_{v=1}^k \alpha_{jk}(v-1)Y_k(t+v-1|t-1) &= \sum_1^s \varkappa_{jk}(\nu_j)\varepsilon_{k,t} \\ &\quad + \sum_1^m \lambda_{jk}(\nu_j)X_{k,t}\ . \end{aligned} \tag{10}$$

Here $\varkappa_{jk}(u)$, $\lambda_{jk}(u)$ are typical elements, respectively, of $K(u)$, $L(u)$. Let $x(t+u|t)$ be composed of the $Y_j(t+u|t)$ in (9). Then it follows easily that

$$\begin{aligned} x(t+1|t) &= Fx(t|t-1) + LX_t + K\varepsilon_t \\ Y_t &= Hx(t|t-1) + L(0)X_t + \varepsilon_t\ . \end{aligned} \tag{11}$$

Here, F,K,L are composed respectively of

$$\begin{aligned} &\alpha_{jk}(v),\ v=0,1, \ldots, \nu_j-1; \quad j,k=1, \ldots, s\ . \\ &\varkappa_{jk}(v),\ v=1,2, \ldots, \nu_k\ ; \quad j,k=1, \ldots, s\ . \\ &\lambda_{jk}(v),\ v=1,2, \ldots, \nu_k\ ; \quad j=1, \ldots, s;\ k=1, \ldots, m. \end{aligned} \tag{12}$$

The matrix F also has most elements zero and some unity. We leave the reader to discern its form, from (10). The $\nu(2s+m)$ quantities listed in (12) coordinatise the set, $U(\{\nu_j\})$, of all ARMAX structures for which the random variables listed in (9) form a basis for the predictors. The matrix H is of the form $[I_s,0]$ if $\nu_j \geq 1$, $j=1, \ldots, s$ (the standard case) and if we order the elements of $x(t|t-1)$ first according to u and then j . If $M(\nu)$ is the set of all ARMAX structures of order ν then the sets $U(\{\nu_j\})$ are open and dense in $M(\nu)$ (in a natural topology) for all choices of ν_j , $\Sigma\,\nu_j = \nu$. Thus they intersect. This can be avoided, at the cost of some arbitrariness, by requiring the set (9) to be the first linearly independent set met as the $Y_j(t+u|t)$ are examined in the order determined by taking u first and then j. Call the set of ARMAX structures, for which (9) is such a first linearly independent set, $V(\{\nu_j\})$. Then $V(\{\nu_j\} \subset U(\{\nu_j\})$. Also for $V(\{\nu_j\})$

$$\alpha_{jk}(\nu) = 0,\ \nu > \nu_j;\ \alpha_{jk}(\nu_j) = 0\ ,\ j < k\ . \tag{13}$$

The ν_j prescribe a lag structure in the sense that they prescribe a maximum lag in each row of the ARMAX system. They are, when (13) holds, called dynamical indices or Kronecker indices. Thus we could set out to estimate the ARMAX system by constructing the likelihood via (11), using (12) or (12),(13) as parameters. We would also have to determine ν or the ν_j . One procedure could be to recognise that we need only examine one $U(\{\nu_j\})$ for each $\nu = \Sigma\nu_j$ because each is open and dense in $M(\nu)$. We might choose the ν_j as follows.

$$\nu = ps+r,\ 0 \le r < s\ ;\ \nu_j = p+1,\ j=1,\ .\ .\ .\ ,\ r;\ \nu_j = p,\ j=r+1,\ .\ .\ .\ ,\ s. \tag{14}$$

In this case (only) $U(\{\nu_j\}) = V(\{\nu_j\})$. Thus we then have only to determine ν , and the $\alpha_{jk}(\nu)$, $\varkappa_{jk}(\nu)$, $\lambda_{jk}(\nu)$ prescribed by (12), (13) for these ν_j as well as Ω. For each ν we maximise the Gaussian likelihood and find Ω_ν , i.e. the ML estimator of Ω at ν . Then choose ν by minimising

$$\log \det \Omega_\nu + \nu(2s+m)C(n)/n\ ,\quad n \le V(n). \tag{15}$$

If $C(n) = \log n$ and $V(n)$ increases with n say as $(\log n)^a$, $a < \infty$ then the estimate $\hat{\nu}$ will converge to ν . It remains to show how to calculate the likelihood. We may do this, as is well known, via the Kalman filter. This constructs vectors e_t that are *finite* past prediction errors (i.e. errors in predicting Y_{t+1} from Y_s, X_s, $s=1,\ .\ .\ .\ ,\ t$.) together with the estimate Ω_ν. The formulae are well known and readily available (Anderson and Moore, 1979) and are not reproduced here. Then $-2n^{-1}$ log likelihood is, up to a constant,

$$\frac{1}{n}\sum_1^n \log\det(\Omega_t) + \frac{1}{n}\,\Sigma\, e_t'\Omega_t^{-1}e_t. \tag{16}$$

Of course e_t , Ω_t are functions of the parameters specified by (12), (13) as well as Ω. Thus initial values have to be found for these and then (16) optimised iteratively. The Kalman filter may be used to calculate derivatives.

This program gives a more or less complete answer to the problem of estimating (8). Returning to (11),

$$k(z) = H\{Iz^{-1}-F\}^{-1}K + I_s\ ,\ l(z) = H\{Iz^{-1}- F\}^{-1}L + L(0)\ ,$$

which shows how the transfer functions are constructed from the estimates of (11). The function $\phi(z)$ corresponding to $U(\{n_j\})$ is formed so that $\Phi(v)$ has $\alpha_{jk}(v_j-v)$ in the (j,k)th place, $v=0,1,\ldots,\max v_j$. (All $\alpha_{jk}(v)$ not listed in (12) are null and for (14) we must take account of (13)). Then $\psi(z) = \phi(z)k(z)\ ,\ \delta(z) = \phi(z)\ l(z)$.

This approach to the estimation of ARMAX systems appears to accord with that put forward by R.E. Kalman (1983), who is an originator of many of the ideas put forward in this section. Kalman was not concerned with the detailed procedure of estimation described nor with the proposition that only the neighbourhoods $U(\{v_j\})$ for the v_j in (14) be considered nor with the use of (15), but it is in the general spirit of his approach. However, there are problems associated with it. Some of these are of a statistically technical and algorithmic nature and can be overcome (e.g. how to initiate the iterative optimisation of (16)). The ones we discuss here relate to the appropriateness of the overall approach for econometrics and in turn relate to the findings in OC discussed in Section 3.

There may well be a range of situations where the procedures just described will work. These would be cases where s and m are small. Indeed otherwise the number of parameters is likely to be too large in relation to the amount of data available. Apart from Ω there are $(ps+r)(2s+m) = 2ps^2 + psm + r(2s+m)$ parameters. The integer $p+1$ is the maximum lag ($r > 0$). If $s=5$, $m=3$, $p=3$, $r=0$ then $(ps+r)(2s-m) = 234$. If one had $n = 80$ (which is quite large in econometrics) then one has 640 numbers initially and, adding the 10 covariance estimates, 244 numbers finally, which is a very ineffective data reduction. Moreover one does not know n (i.e. p,r) so that this understates the difficulty. There are other considerations. We have mentioned measurement noise in relation to (5). Another problem relates to time varying parameter and nonlinear characteristics of the system. Adaptive methods, that change the model as time progresses, for example on the basis of a comparison of previous predictions with the actual history, may help here. In general all of this confirms the OC findings of 35 years ago that in an economic context the possibility of using general modelling techniques will be very limited unless reliable prior information is available sufficient in quantity to reduce the problem to manageable proportions.

The final conclusion is that the Cochrane and Orcutt papers were far seeing and relate well to current problems in econometrics.

References

Anderson, B.D.O., and Moore, J.B. (1979) *Optimal Filtering*, New York: Prentice Hall.

Cochrane, D., and Orcutt, G.H. (1949), 'Application of Least Squares Regression to Relationships Containing Auto-Correlated Error Terms', *Journal of the American Statistical Association*, 44, 32-61.

Deistler, M., and Hannan, E.J. (1981), 'Some Properties of the Parameterization of ARMA Systems with Unknown Order', *Journal of Multivariate Analysis*, 11, 474-84.

Durbin, J., and Watson, G.S. (1950), 'Testing for Serial Correlation in Least Squares Regression I', *Biometrika*, 37, 409-28.

Durbin, J., and Watson, G.S. (1951), 'Testing for Serial Correlation in Least Squares Regression II', *Biometrika*, 38, 159-78.

Hamon, B.V., and Hannan, E.J. (1963), 'Estimating Relations Between Time Series', *Journal of Geophysical Research*, 21, 6033-41.

Hannan, E.J. (1960) *Time Series Analysis*, London: Methuen.

Hannan, E.J. (1963), 'Regression for Time Series', in *Time Series Analysis*, ed. M.R. Rosenblatt, New York: Wiley, 17-37.

Hannan, E.J. (1970) *Multiple Time Series*, New York: Wiley.

Hannan, E.J. (1971), 'The Identification Problem for Multiple Equation Systems with Moving Average Errors', *Econometrica*, 39, 751-66.

Kalman, R.E. (1983), 'Identifiability and Problems of Model Selection in Econometrics', in *Advances in Econometrics*, ed. W. Hildenbrand, Cambridge: Cambridge University Press, 169-207.

Maeshiro, A. (1976), 'Autoregressive Transformation, Trended Independent Variables and Autocorrelated Disturbance Terms', *Review of Economics and Statistics*, 58, 497-500.

Orcutt, G.H., and Cochrane, D. (1949), 'A Sampling Study of the Merits of Autoregressive and Reduced Form Transformation in Regression Analysis', *Journal of the American Statistical Association*, 44, 356-72.

Whittle, P. (1951) *Hypothesis Testing in Time Series Analysis*, Uppsala: Almqvist and Wiksells.

3 Testing for autocorrelation in linear regression models: a survey

Maxwell L. King[1]

1 Introduction

The seminal work of Cochrane and Orcutt (1949) did much to alert econometricians to the difficulties of assuming uncorrelated disturbances in time series applications of the general linear model. Because the neglect of correlation between regression disturbances can lead to inefficient parameter estimates, misleading inferences from hypothesis tests and inefficient predictions, the desirability of testing for the presence of such correlation is widely accepted. This paper attempts to survey the vast and varied literature concerned with testing for autocorrelation in the context of the linear regression model. This particular testing problem must surely be the most intensely researched testing problem in econometrics. We will therefore be interested to see what lessons concerning hypothesis testing in econometrics can be learnt from the study of this literature.

Throughout, our main interest will be in the power properties of the competing test procedures. Computational convenience is of secondary concern because of recent and likely future advances in computer technology. To save space, some important sections of the literature are not considered. These include pre-test considerations [see for example, Judge and Bock (1978, ch. 7), Nakamura and Nakamura (1978), Fomby and Guilkey (1978), King and Giles (1984), Griffiths and Beesley (1984) and Giles and Beattie (1987)], testing for serial correlation in the disturbances of a simultaneous equation model [see for example, Durbin (1957), Guilkey (1974, 1975), Godfrey (1976), Maritz (1978), Smith (1978), Harvey and Phillips (1980, 1981), Breusch and Godfrey (1981) and Owen (1981)], testing jointly for serial correlation and other forms of mis-specification [see for example, Savin and White (1978b), Jarque and Bera (1980), Bera and Jarque (1981, 1982), King and Evans (1984), King and Skeels (1984) and Praetz (1987)] and testing for one form of serial correlation against another form [see for example, Sargan (1964), Godfrey (1978c), King (1983a) and King and McAleer (1984)].

Briefly, the plan of the remainder of this paper is as follows. Section 2 reviews developments on testing for serial correlation prior to Durbin and Watson (1950) while Section 3 discusses the seminal contributions of Cochrane and Orcutt (1949) and Durbin and Watson (1950, 1951). The large body of literature on the Durbin-Watson (DW) test is surveyed in Section 4. Sections 5, 6 and 7, respectively, consider tests based on transformed residuals, non-parametric tests and tests which have optimal power in a particular neighbourhood of the parameter space under the alternative hypothesis. Section 8 surveys tests for first-order Autoregressive (AR(1)) disturbances in the linear regression model not discussed in earlier sections. The literature on robustness properties of tests for AR(1) disturbances is reviewed in Section 9 while Section 10 is concerned with testing when a lagged dependent variable is a regressor. Section 11 surveys test procedures designed to detect certain non-AR(1) forms of serial correlation. Some concluding remarks may be found in the final section.

2 Early Contributions

Mauchly (1940) was perhaps the first to propose a formal test for independence in a normal n-variate population although he assumed the availability of repeated observations. Then followed the influential work of von Neumann which began with a paper by von Neumann, Kent, Bellinson and Hart (1941), the main purpose of which was to propose an efficient estimator of the variance of a time series whose mean is slowly changing. Later papers (von Neumann, 1941, 1942) considered the distribution of the ratio of the mean squared successive difference to the sample variance for a Gaussian time series. This ratio is of the form

$$\eta = \delta^2/s^2 ,$$

where

$$\delta^2 = \sum_{t=1}^{n-1} (x_{t+1} - x_t)^2/(n-1), \quad s^2 = \sum_{t=1}^{n} (x_t - \bar{x})^2/n, \; \bar{x} = \sum_{t=1}^{n} x_t/n,$$

and $x_1, \ldots, x_n$ are n observations from a $N(\xi,\sigma^2)$ distribution. η was proposed as a test statistic for a test of independence of the x_t's. Young (1941) had earlier proposed the use of a related statistic for this problem while Williams (1941) determined the moments of η by an alternative method to that of von Neumann. Hart (1942a, 1942b) tabulated the distribution function and critical values of η assuming independent x_t's.

With econometric applications in mind, Koopmans (1942) explicitly considered the AR(1) process

$$x_t = \varrho x_{t-1} + \varepsilon_t , \quad \varepsilon_t \sim IN(0,\sigma^2), \quad t = 1, \ldots, n,$$

and the problem of testing $\varrho = 0$ in such a model. For this purpose he studied the distribution of the first-order autocorrelation coefficient,

$$\sum_{t=1}^{n-1} x_t x_{t-1} \bigg/ \sum_{t=1}^{n} x_t^2 ,$$

which is closely related to von Neumann's ratio. R. L. Anderson (1942) focused attention on the case in which the covariance matrix of $x = (x_1, \ldots, x_n)'$ is circular and examined the distribution of the circular correlation coefficient of various lags. This work was extended by Dixon (1944), Rubin (1945), Madow (1945), Hsu (1946) and Leipnik (1947). With respect to testing $H_0 : \varrho = 0$ in the circular AR(1) model with unknown mean,

$$(x_t - \xi) = \varrho(x_{t-1} - \xi) + \varepsilon_t , \quad x_0 = x_n , \quad \varepsilon_t \sim \mathrm{IN}(0,\sigma^2) ,$$

Lehmann (1947) proved that rejecting H_0 for large values of the circular correlation coefficient,

$$\sum_{t=1}^{n} (x_t - \bar{x})(x_{t-1} - \bar{x}) \bigg/ \sum_{t=1}^{n} (x_t - \bar{x})^2 ,$$

is a Uniformly Most Powerful (UMP) similar test against $H_a^+ : \varrho > 0$ and that for the two-sided problem a type B_1 test exists.[2]

T.W. Anderson (1948) made an early and important contribution to the problem of testing for serial correlation in the linear regression model,

$$y = X\beta + u , \tag{2.1}$$

where y is $n \times 1$, X is an $n \times k$ nonstochastic[3] matrix of rank $k < n$, β is a $k \times 1$ vector of parameters and u is an $n \times 1$ disturbance vector. He considered the problem of testing $H_0 : \lambda = 0$ assuming

$$u \sim \mathrm{N}(0,\sigma^2[I_n + \lambda\Theta]^{-1}), \tag{2.2}$$

where σ^2 and λ are unknown scalars and Θ is a known $n \times n$ matrix such that $[I_n + \lambda\Theta]$ is positive definite.[4] By restricting attention to similar tests and applying Neyman-Pearson theory, he showed that if the column space of X is spanned by k eigenvectors of Θ, rejecting H_0 for small values of

$$r = e'\Theta e/e'e , \tag{2.3}$$

where e is the Ordinary Least Squares (OLS) residual vector from (2.1), is a UMP similar test against $H_a^+ : \lambda > 0$. For the same class of X matrices, an appropriately defined two-sided critical region based on (2.3) is a B_1 test of H_0 against $H_a : \lambda \neq 0$. He also showed that no UMP similar test of H_0 against H_a^+ exists if the disturbances of (2.1) follow a stationary AR(1) process or if they follow a nonstationary AR(1) process with $u_0 = 0$, although in the case of circular AR(1) disturbances, a UMP similar test does exist for certain X matrices.

Moran (1950b) found the first two moments of the circular autocorrelation coefficient for residuals from a regression with an intercept and one independent variable. He suggested the use of a normal approximation for finding the critical value in this case. R. L. Anderson and T. W. Anderson (1950) showed that the results of R. L. Anderson (1942) could be used to find the exact critical value of a test based on the circular autocorrelation coefficient when one is testing the residuals of a regression on a Fourier series.

3 The Cambridge School and the Durbin-Watson Test

With the creation of a system of national accounts for the British economy, Keynes successfully argued for a Department of Applied Economics to be set up at Cambridge University. Richard Stone, who had worked with Keynes on the national accounts, was appointed director. Stone was soon able to attract to his new department a number of talented young researchers whose work was to have a great impact on the practice of econometrics.

There was the work of Cochrane and Orcutt (1949)[5] which succeeded in bringing the serial correlation problem to the attention of econometricians. Donald Cochrane was a PhD student in the Department, while Guy Orcutt joined the staff in 1946 as a senior research worker. At about this time, Klein (1947) published an econometric model of the U.S. economy and used the von Neumann ratio to test the independence of its disturbances. His testing revealed evidence of lack of independence in very few equations. Cochrane and Orcutt argued that it is likely that the disturbances of econometric models are positively correlated. They gave a number of theoretical reasons to support their case, and examined the results of the application of the von Neumann ratio to the estimated residuals from four econometric models including two of Klein's models. They also performed a small simulation experiment which cast doubt on the reliability of the von Neumann ratio as a test for correlated disturbances in econometric models. For the particular models they considered, their experiment showed the von Neumann ratio to be biased towards accepting randomness and that this bias increases with the number of regressors.

Cochrane and Orcutt also discussed the cost of ignoring serial correlation, thus highlighting the need for a reliable test for correlated disturbances. Their 'tentative' method of dealing with AR(1) disturbances, now known as the Cochrane-Orcutt transformation, became widely used. In 1950, two of their Cambridge colleagues published a solution to the testing problem that Cochrane and Orcutt posed.

In the late 1940's James Durbin was a postgraduate student studying mathematical statistics at Cambridge. Because he had expressed an interest in economic applications, he was attached to the Department of Applied Economics. At about this time, T. W. Anderson was a short term visitor to the Department and Geoffrey Watson was a PhD student at North Carolina under R. L. Anderson's guidance. R. L. Anderson had suggested to Watson that he consider deriving the null distribution of the von Neumann ratio applied to OLS regression. Watson joined the Department of Applied Economics in 1949 and collaborated with Durbin on this project while the latter was employed as a research worker in the Department. Their collaboration continued for a time after Durbin took up an appointment at the London School of Economics.

The work of Durbin and Watson (1950, 1951)[6] has undoubtedly been most influential. They considered the problem of testing $H_0 : \varrho = 0$ in the linear regression model (2.1) where the disturbances are generated by the stationary AR(1) process

$$u_t = \varrho u_{t-1} + \varepsilon_t, \quad |\varrho| < 1, \quad \varepsilon_t \sim \mathrm{IN}(0,\sigma^2). \tag{3.1}$$

T. W. Anderson's (1948) findings led them to examine the distribution of

$$r = e'Ae/e'e = u'MAMu/u'Mu \; ,$$

where $e = My = Mu$ is the OLS residual vector from (2.1), A is any real symmetric matrix and $M = I_n - X(X'X)^{-1}X'$. A central result is the following lemma which has become known as the Durbin-Watson Lemma.

Lemma: There exists an orthogonal transformation, $u = H\zeta$, such that

$$r = \sum_{i=1}^{n-k} \nu_i \zeta_i^2 \Big/ \sum_{i=1}^{n-k} \zeta_i^2 \; ,$$

where $\nu_1, \nu_2, \ldots, \nu_{n-k}$ are the eigenvalues of MA other than k zero roots. If s of the columns of X are linear combinations of s of the eigenvectors of A, and if $\lambda_1 \leqslant \lambda_2 \leqslant \ldots \leqslant \lambda_{n-s}$ are the eigenvalues of A associated with the remaining $n-s$ eigenvectors then

$$\lambda_i \leqslant \nu_i \leqslant \lambda_{i+k-s}, \qquad i = 1, \ldots, n-k \; .$$

Corollary:

$$r_L \leqslant r \leqslant r_U \tag{3.2}$$

where

$$r_L = \sum_{i=1}^{n-k} \lambda_i \zeta_i^2 \Big/ \sum_{i=1}^{n-k} \zeta_i^2 \quad \text{and} \quad r_U = \sum_{i=1}^{n-k} \lambda_{i+k-s}\, \zeta_i^2 \Big/ \sum_{i=1}^{n-k} \zeta_i^2.$$

Observe that because H is orthogonal, $u \sim \mathrm{N}(0,\sigma^2 I_n)$ implies $\zeta \sim \mathrm{N}(0,\sigma^2 I_n)$.

Durbin and Watson (1950) studied the distribution of r under this assumption and concluded that there is 'no elementary expression for its density' (p.418). They discussed approximating the distribution by a beta distribution and gave expressions for the first four moments of r under H_0.

Their particular choice of A for their test statistic drew heavily on the work of T. W. Anderson (1948). The joint density of u under (2.1) and (3.1) is of the form

$$\alpha \exp\left[-\frac{1}{2\sigma^2}\left\{(1-\varrho)^2 u'u + \varrho u'A_1 u + \varrho(1-\varrho)u'C_1 u\right\}\right], \tag{3.3}$$

where A_1 is the $n \times n$ first-differencing matrix,

$$A_1 = \begin{bmatrix} 1 & -1 & 0 & \cdots & \cdot & 0 \\ -1 & 2 & -1 & & & 0 \\ 0 & -1 & 2 & & & 0 \\ \cdot & & \cdot & & & \cdot \\ \cdot & & & \cdot & & \cdot \\ \cdot & & & & \cdot & \cdot \\ \cdot & & & & 2 & -1 \\ 0 & 0 & 0 & \cdots & -1 & 1 \end{bmatrix},$$

C_1 = diag(1,0,0, . . . ,0,1) and α is a positive scalar. Durbin and Watson considered approximating (3.3) either by

$$\alpha \exp\left[-\frac{1}{2\sigma^2}\left\{(1-\varrho)^2\, u'u + \varrho u'A_1 u\right\}\right] \tag{3.4}$$

or by

$$\alpha \exp\left[-\frac{1}{2\sigma^2}\left\{(1-\varrho)^2 u'u + \varrho u'(A_1+C_1)u\right\}\right]. \tag{3.5}$$

For computational convenience and because of the similarity of the resultant test statistic to the von Neumann ratio, they chose (3.4) which gives rise to the DW test statistic,

$$d = e'A_1e/e'e = \sum_{t=2}^{n} (e_t - e_{t-1})^2 \,/\, \sum_{t=1}^{n} e_t^2 .$$

Anderson's (1948) result implies that for testing H_0 against $H_a^+ : \varrho > 0$, rejecting H_0 for small values of d is approximately UMP similar when the column space of X is spanned by k eigenvectors of A_1.

In their second paper, Durbin and Watson emphasized some of the more practical aspects of their test. As the DW Lemma shows, the distribution of d under H_0 depends on the design matrix, X. In order to partially overcome this problem, they presented tables of bounds for the 0.05, 0.025 and 0.01 significance points of d for regressions with an intercept. Against $H_a^+ : \varrho >$ 0, H_0 is rejected if the observed value of d is less than the lower bound, d_L, while H_0 is accepted if the observed d is greater than the upper bound, d_U.

Otherwise, the test is inconclusive. Against $H_a^-: \varrho < 0$, $4-d$ may be used in place of d in the above procedure. For a regression fitted through the origin, Durbin and Watson suggested re-estimation with an intercept term included to enable the use of their tabulated bounds. In the case of an inconclusive result from the use of their bounds, they recommended an approximate procedure based on fitting a beta distribution with the mean and variance of the null distribution of $d/4$.

4 Further developments concerning the DW test procedure

In this section we review various extensions and refinements to the DW test procedure for the original problem of testing H_0 in (2.1) and (3.1). Generalizations of the DW procedure to other related hypothesis testing problems are considered in later sections.

4.1 Approximations to the DW critical value

Procedures for approximating the true critical value of d for use when the DW test is inconclusive have been reviewed by Durbin and Watson (1971), Harrison (1972) and Maddala (1977, p. 285). The six approximations considered by Durbin and Watson are:

(i) The beta approximation. This is the procedure, originally suggested by Durbin and Watson (1951), discussed above.

(ii) The Jacobi approximation. This was used by Durbin and Watson (1951) to compute the significance points of d_L and d_U. It is based on fitting a distribution whose density is the beta density times a weighted sum of Jacobi polynomials, to the null distribution of d using the first four moments. A version of this method that does not assume knowledge of the smallest and largest non-zero eigenvalues of MA_1 is described in Durbin and Watson (1971).

(iii) The d_U approximation. Hannan (1957) observed that for orthogonal polynomial regressors, the d_U critical value is an approximation of the order n^{-2} to the true DW critical value. [Also see McGregor (1960)]. Hannan and Terrell (1968) showed that this approximation is good whenever the spectrum of the regressors is relatively concentrated near the origin, which some authors have argued to often be the case in economic applications.

(iv) The Theil-Nagar approximation. For slowly changing regressors, Theil and Nagar (1961) tabulated approximate critical values which do not depend on X. Hannan and Terrell (1968) suggested that d_U critical values give a better approximation for the class of regressors considered by Theil and Nagar.

(v) The Henshaw approximation. Henshaw's (1966) approximation is based on fitting a beta distribution with the correct first four moments to the null distribution of $d/4$.

(vi) The $a+bd_U$ approximation. Durbin and Watson (1971) suggested approximating the true critical value of d by $a+bd_U^0$ where d_U^0 is the tabulated critical value of d_U and a and b are chosen so that the first two moments of $a+bd_U$ and d are the same under H_0.

Durbin and Watson (1971) compared the accuracy of the above approximations for a variety of significance levels using four design matrices from economic applications. They found that the Henshaw and Jacobi approximations are the most accurate, no doubt because they both use the first four moments of d. The DW beta and $a+bd_U$ approximations were found to be accurate enough for most practical applications except possibly when n is small and k is large. It would seem advisable to use the beta approximation for regressors which are not 'smoothly evolving'. The accuracy of the d_U and Theil-Nagar approximations were found to be similar and generally unacceptably poor.

More recently, Fuller (1976, pp.243-4) observed that for $n > 10$, the significance points of the t statistic associated with the AR(1) coefficient computed from the von Neumann ratio closely approximate those of the Student's t distribution with $n + 3$ degrees of freedom. This led Fuller (p. 402) to suggest the use of the Student's t distribution with $n - k + 4$ degrees of freedom in an approximation to the null distribution of the DW test statistic. However, as Fuller himself remarks, 'there is little reason to believe that the resulting approximation would be as accurate as the beta approximation suggested by Durbin and Watson.'

There is also the normal approximation which Maddala (1977, p. 286) attributes to an unpublished paper by Blattberg. This involves treating $\{d - E(d)\}/\{Var(d)\}^{\frac{1}{2}}$ as a N(0,1) variate under H_0 where

$$E(d) = \text{trace}(MA_1)/(n - k)$$

and

$$Var(d) = 2\{\text{trace}(MA_1)^2 - (n-k)[E(d)]^2\}/\{(n-k)(n-k+2)\}.$$

Ali (1983, 1984) suggested approximating the distribution of d by the four-parameter Pearson distribution. He empirically compared the accuracy of his approximation with that of the normal approximation for the four data sets used by Durbin and Watson (1971) and found his approximation to be more accurate for smaller sample sizes ($n \leqslant 21$).

A more comprehensive empirical study was conducted by Evans and King (1985a) who compared the accuracy of the normal, two moment beta and four moment beta approximations to the critical values of a variety of tests for non-spherical disturbances in (2.1) including the DW test. They found that overall, the three approximations provide reasonably accurate critical values, with the four moment beta and normal approximations being the most and least accurate, respectively. Skewness is found to be a determining factor with respect to accuracy and leads to the suggestion that if the test statistic's coefficient of skewness exceeds 0.14 in absolute value, one should think twice about using the two moment beta and normal approximations. They conclude that the normal approximation can be used with confidence to compute DW critical values whenever $n \geq 100$. Mention should also be made of Jeong's (1985) more accurate alternative to the $a + bd_U$ approximation and Theil and Shonkwiler's (1986) suggestion of a Monte Carlo based approximation.

4.2 Calculation of the true DW critical value

From the DW Lemma, it follows that the α level DW critical value, d^*_α, can be found by solving

$$\Pr\left[\sum_{i=1}^{n-k} (\nu_i - d^*_\alpha)\xi_i^2 < 0\right] = \alpha \tag{4.1}$$

for d^*_α, where $\nu_1, \ldots, \nu_{n-k}$ are the eigenvalues of MA_1 other than k zeros and $\xi_i \sim \mathrm{IN}(0,1)$. Abrahamse and Koerts (1969) suggested the use of Imhof's (1961) algorithm for evaluating the LHS of (4.1) for a given d^*_α value and in their book, Koerts and Abrahamse (1969, pp. 159-60) presented a Fortran subroutine called FQUAD which evaluates

$$\Pr\left[\sum_{i=1}^{m} \lambda_i\xi_i^2 < \eta\right],$$

where λ_i and η are fixed and $\xi_i \sim \mathrm{IN}(0,1)$. Given that the eigenvalues, ν_i, have been computed using a standard algorithm, d^*_α may be found using FQUAD to evaluate the LHS of (4.1) and an iterative procedure such as Lagrangian interpolation or the secant method to solve (4.1). A slower but more reliable version of Imhof's algorithm has been coded in Algol by Davies (1980) while Palm and Sneek (1984) have suggested modifications which eliminate the need to compute eigenvalues.

A second method of calculating d^*_α is discussed by Durbin and Watson (1971) and Farebrother (1980a, 1984a). It is based on a method suggested by Pan (1968) for calculating the distribution function of a ratio of quadratic forms in normal variables. Durbin and Watson report that in their experience, it is faster for small sample sizes than Koerts and Abrahamse's version of Imhof's algorithm while for larger sample sizes, the latter is much quicker. Farebrother (1980a) gives an Algol version of Pan's algorithm.[7] L'Esperance, Chall and Taylor (1976) discuss a third alternative which involves using complex arithmetic rather than real-valued versions of complex integration favoured by Imhof and Pan.

As Hannan (1970, p. 459) and L'Esperance and Taylor (1975) observe, in practice it is not necessary to solve (4.1) for d^*_α in order to apply the DW test exactly. Instead one can evaluate the LHS of (4.1) with the observed value of d in place of d^*_α. Against H^+_a, H_0 is rejected if the resultant probability, sometimes called the p-value, is less than α, the desired significance level.

Tables of exact critical values of d for certain X matrices have been published. King (1980b, 1981c, 1983b) presented critical values of d for regressions which involve a constant plus trend and/or quarterly or monthly seasonal dummy variables. DW critical values for polynomial trend regressions of degree ranging from one to five have been tabulated by Bartels, Bornholt and Hanslow (1982).

4.3 The DW test for regressions through the origin

As noted above, in order to test H_0 with respect to a regression fitted through the origin, Durbin and Watson (1951) suggested re-estimating the equation with a superfluous intercept term so that their tabulated bounds can be used. Kramer (1971) provided an alternative method of dealing with this case when he published tables of bounds appropriate for testing regressions through the origin against H^+_a. King (1981a) observed that Durbin and Watson's approach circumvents the problem of pre-test bias that occurs if the decision to fit through the origin has been made with the aid of regression data. He compared the powers of Durbin and Watson's and Kramer's procedures for selected design matrices and found the latter to be more powerful, surprisingly so for small (n = 15) samples.

4.4 Tables of bounds for the DW test

The original DW tables were computed by hand using mechanical calculating machines. Koerts and Abrahamse (1969, Tables 22a, b, c) used their computer based methods for finding d^*_α, to recalculate the original DW tables to three-decimal-place accuracy. Savin and White (1977) extended the one and five per cent significance tables to cover values of n from 6 to 200 and k from 2 to 21 while King (1983b, Tables 1, 2) with monthly data in mind, tabulated further one and five per cent bounds for sample sizes up to 300.

Let $d^0_{L\alpha}$ and $d^0_{U\alpha}$ denote the lower and upper bounds, respectively, of d^*_α for a regression through the origin and let $d^1_{L\alpha}$ and $d^1_{U\alpha}$ denote the corresponding bounds for a regression with an intercept.

Kramer (1971) showed that

$$d^0_{L\alpha} < d^1_{L\alpha}$$

and

$$d^0_{U\alpha} = d^1_{U\alpha} \,. \tag{4.2}$$

He tabulated values of $d^0_{L\alpha}$ with $\alpha = 0.01, 0.05$ for testing H_0 against H_a^+. For a regression with an intercept, one can use

$$d^1_{L(1-\alpha)} = 4 - d^1_{U\alpha} \quad \text{and} \quad d^1_{U(1-\alpha)} = 4 - d^1_{L\alpha}$$

when testing against[8] $H_a^- : \varrho < 0$. These relationships do not hold for regressions without an intercept. (4.2) implies that $d^0_{U(1-\alpha)} = 4 - d^1_{L\alpha}$ and selected values of $d^0_{L(1-\alpha)}$ for $\alpha = 0.05, 0.01$, have been tabulated by King (1979, 1981a). Kramer's and King's tables of bounds have been extended to cover a wider range of n and k values by Farebrother (1980b) who also provided corrections to the Savin and White tables.

Obviously it is desirable that the size of the inconclusive region be small. Regrettably, it grows rapidly as k increases, although the more regressors that can be explicitly accounted for when the bounds are computed, the smaller the resultant inconclusive region. With this in mind, King (1981c) considered the class of regression models (2.1) whose design matrices can be partitioned as $X = [X_1 \vdots X_2]$, where X_1 is $n \times s$ and X_2 is $n \times (k - s)$, and which share the same column space of X_1. For example, X_1 could be the $n \times 4$ matrix of observations on a full set of quarterly seasonal dummy variables. He proved the following extension to the DW Lemma.

Lemma: If $\nu_1 \leqslant \nu_2 \leqslant \ldots \leqslant \nu_{n-k}$ are the eigenvalues of MA other than k zero roots and if $\lambda_1 \leqslant \lambda_2 \leqslant \ldots \leqslant \lambda_{n-s}$ are the eigenvalues of M_1A other than s zero roots, where A is any $n \times n$ real symmetric matrix and $M_1 = I_n - X_1(X_1'X_1)^{-1}X_1'$, then

$$\lambda_i \leqslant \nu_i \leqslant \lambda_{i+k-s} \,.$$

Corollary:

$$r_L^* \leqslant r \leqslant r_U^* \,,$$

where

$$r_L^* = \sum_{i=1}^{n-k} \lambda_i \zeta_i^2 \,/\, \sum_{i=1}^{n-k} \zeta_i^2 \,, \quad r_U^* = \sum_{i=1}^{n-k} \lambda_{i+k-s} \zeta_i^2 \,/\, \sum_{i=1}^{n-k} \zeta_i^2 \,,$$

and under $H_0 : u \sim N(0,\sigma^2 I_n)$, $\zeta \sim N(0, I_{n-k})$.

King (1980b, 1981c) used this result to tabulate 0.01, 0.05, 0.95, 0.99 significance points of lower and upper bounds of the DW test statistic, d, for regressions with (i) a full set of quarterly seasonal dummy variables, (ii) an intercept and a linear trend variable, (iii) a full set of quarterly seasonal dummy variables and a linear trend regressor. A later paper (King, 1983b) gives analogous tables for monthly data.

4.5 Further optimal power properties of the DW test

In their 1971 paper, Durbin and Watson declared their preference for a theory of invariance approach to the problem of testing H_0 against H_a^+ (or H_a^-) in (2.1) and (3.1) as opposed to the similar region approach used previously by Anderson (1948) and themselves in 1950. They observed that the testing problem remains invariant under transformations of the form

$$y^* = \gamma_0 y + X\gamma , \tag{4.3}$$

where γ_0 is a positive scalar and γ is a $k \times 1$ vector. They used Lehmann's (1959, ch.6) method to show that against H_a^+ (H_a^-) rejecting H_0 for small (large) values of d is approximately UMP Invariant (UMPI) when the column space of X is spanned by k eigenvectors of A_1 and that for any X matrix, it is approximately Locally Best Invariant (LBI) [or locally Most Powerful Invariant (MPI) in the neighbourhood of $\varrho = 0$]. Alternative proofs of these results are given by Kariya (1977, 1980) and King (1980a). A general result proved by Kariya (1977) implies that when the column space of X is spanned by k eigenvectors of A_1, against $H_a : \varrho \neq 0$, an appropriate unbiased critical region of the form $d < d_1$ or $d > d_2$, is a UMP unbiased invariant test.

4.6 The DW power function

Abrahamse and Koerts (1969) suggested the following method of computing the power of the DW test for a given X matrix. Previously, they (Koerts and Abrahamse, 1968) used the Monte Carlo (MC) method. For any given critical valude d^*, the power of the critical region $d < d^*$ under (2.1) and (3.1) is

$$\begin{aligned} \Pr\,(d < d^*) &= \Pr\,[u'M(A_1 - d^*I_n)Mu < 0] \\ &= \Pr\,[\zeta'(\Sigma^{1/2})'M(A_1 - d^*I_n)M\Sigma^{1/2}\zeta < 0] \\ &= \Pr\,\left[\sum_{i=1}^{n-k} \gamma_i\zeta_i^2 < 0\right], \end{aligned} \tag{4.4}$$

where $\Sigma^{1/2}$ is any matrix such that

$$\Sigma^{1/2}(\Sigma^{1/2})' = \begin{bmatrix} 1 & \varrho & \varrho^2 & \cdots & \varrho^{n-1} \\ \varrho & 1 & \varrho & & \cdot \\ \varrho^2 & \varrho & 1 & & \cdot \\ \cdot & & & \cdot & \cdot \\ \cdot & & & \cdot & \cdot \\ \cdot & & & \cdot & \cdot \\ \cdot & & & \cdot & \cdot \\ \varrho^{n-1} & \cdot & \cdots & \cdot & 1 \end{bmatrix}, \tag{4.5}$$

γ_i are the eigenvalues of $(\Sigma^{1/2})'M(A_1 - d^*I_n)M\Sigma^{1/2}$ excluding k zero roots and $\zeta_i \sim \text{IN}(0,1)$. Thus Koerts and Abrahamse's (1969) FQUAD subroutine can be applied to compute the power of any test whose statistic reduces to a ratio of quadratic forms in u for any form of serial correlation (and/or heteroscedasticity).

A number of authors have computed the power of the DW test against AR(1) disturbances for various X matrices. Those who have favoured the MC method include Habibagabi and Pratschke (1972), Dent (1973), Harrison (1975), Schmidt and Guilkey (1975) and Weber and Monarchi (1982). Abrahamse and Koerts's approach has been used by Abrahamse and Louter (1971), Dubbelman (1972, 1978), Berenblut and Webb (1973), Phillips and Harvey (1974), L'Esperance and Taylor (1975), Tillman (1975), Fraser, Guttman and Styan (1976), Smith (1977), Dent and Styan (1978), Dent and Cassing (1978), King (1979, 1981a, 1985a), Cassing and White (1983) and others.

Dent (1974) proposed an analytic approximation to the distribution of d under $\text{H}_\text{a} : \varrho \neq 0$. For design matrices comprised of linear combinations of the eigenvectors corresponding to the k smallest eigenvalues of A_1, it appears to be a reasonably good approximation. Its accuracy for other design matrices is much less certain. An alternative approximation based on the four-parameter Pearson distribution is discussed by Ali (1984).

Tillman (1975) studied the power of the DW test assuming the covariance matrix of u is proportional to

$$[(1 - \varrho)^2 I_n + \varrho A_1]^{-1} \tag{4.6}$$

rather than (4.5). He found an upper bound and an attainable lower bound for γ_i in (4.4) and hence was able to compute bounds for the DW power function that are independent of the X matrix. For regressions with an intercept, these bounds can be tightened by taking account of the constant regressor. Tillman also computed the DW power for Watson's X matrix.[9] He observed that for Watson's X matrix without an intercept, the power of the DW test tends to zero as ϱ tends to one. More recently, Krämer (1985) showed that in a regression without an intercept, the limit of the DW test's power as ϱ tends to one can take only the value zero or one. Which value it takes depends on the X matrix.

Two measures of how close the column space of X is to being spanned by k of the eigenvectors of A_1 are given by Cassing and White (1983). Unfortunately these measures appear to be only vaguely related to the distance between the DW power curve and the ceiling of the power envelope.

4.7 Durbin and Watson's choice of test statistic

As noted in Section 3, when Durbin and Watson (1950) made their choice of test statistic, they considered approximating the density of u, given by (3.3), with either (3.4) or (3.5). Their choice of (3.4) resulted in their test statistic being d. Had they chose (3.5), the DW test statistic might well have been

$$d' = e'A_0e/e'e = d + (e_1^2 + e_n^2)/e'e ,$$

where A_0 is A_1 with 2 instead of 1 as the top left and bottom right elements. Rejecting H_0 for small (large) values of d' provides an approximately UMP similar test as well as an approximately UMPI test against H_a^+ (H_a^-) when the column space of X is spanned by k eigenvectors of A_0.

King (1981b) studied the theoretical and empirical power properties of a test based on d' and found this test to be a true[10] LBI test against H_a^+ (H_a^-). He also found it to be more powerful than the DW test against H_a^- and generally for $\varrho < 0.5$ against H_a^+ but less powerful, as a rule, for $\varrho > 0.5$. Using the extension to the DW Lemma discussed in Section 4.4, he tabulated bounds for 0.05 and 0.95 critical values of d' for regressions with an intercept. As Dufour and Dagenais (1985) point out, one can obtain approximate or exact critical values of d' by the application of existing algorithms for the DW test. This can be done by applying such an algorithm to the artificial regression obtained by extending the sample back one period and forward one period using zeros if necessary and including two dummy variables whose only non-zero values are for the first and last new observations, respectively.

5 Tests based on LUS and LUF residuals

A large proportion of the literature on testing for AR(1) disturbances in (2.1) has been concerned with the problem of the inconclusive region of the DW test. This region results from the OLS residual vector, e, being distributed $N(0,\sigma^2 M)$ under H_0. In order to overcome this difficulty, Theil (1965, 1968) proposed the use of residuals whose joint distribution is independent of the design matrix, in tests for AR(1) disturbances. He defined the Linear Unbiased with Scalar covariance matrix (LUS) residual vector and showed[11] that a necessary and sufficient condition for an $m \times 1$ residual vector to be LUS is that it can be written in the form

$$v = B'y \tag{5.1}$$

with B, an $n \times m$ nonstochastic matrix, satisfying

$$B'X = 0 \tag{5.2}$$

and

$$B'B = I_m . \tag{5.3}$$

In addition, Theil showed that m cannot exceed $n - k$.

The following alternative condition was suggested by Koerts (1967) and proven in King (1979).

Theorem: A necessary and sufficient condition that an $(n - k) \times 1$ residual vector is LUS is that it can be written in the form (5.1), where B is an $n \times (n - k)$ nonstochastic matrix whose columns are orthonormal eigenvectors corresponding to the unit eigenvalues of M.

Corollary: Let B_0 be any given $n \times (n - k)$ nonstochastic matrix such that (5.2) and (5.3) hold. A necessary and sufficient condition that an $(n - k) \times 1$ residual vector, v, is LUS is that it can be written in the form $v = GB_0'y$, where G is an $(n - k) \times (n - k)$ orthogonal matrix.

Godolphin and de Tullio (1978) show a result rather similar to the above corollary and they also prove the following theorem.

Theorem: Let $X = [X_k' \vdots X_*']'$, where X_k is $k \times k$ and non-singular and let B be an $n \times (n - k)$ nonstochastic matrix. Then (5.2) and (5.3) are satisfied if and only if $BB' = M$.

As Koerts (1967) notes, LUS residuals can also be thought of as a rotation of OLS residuals. Let B and C be the $n \times (n - k)$ and $n \times k$ matrices whose columns are orthonormal eigenvectors corresponding to the unit and zero eigenvalues of M, respectively, and let $D = [B \vdots C]$. Then

$$D'MD = \begin{bmatrix} I_{n-k} & 0 \\ 0 & 0 \end{bmatrix},$$

$DD' = D'D = I_n$ and hence $BB' = M$, $B'M = B'$ and $C'M = 0$. D' is an orthogonal matrix which rotates the OLS residual vector to an $(n - k) \times 1$ LUS residual vector, $B'y$, and a $k \times 1$ zero vector as follows:

$$D'e = \begin{bmatrix} B'u \\ 0 \end{bmatrix} = \begin{bmatrix} B'y \\ 0 \end{bmatrix}.$$

Clearly there are an infinite number of LUS residual vectors. Theil defined the Best LUS (BLUS) residual vector to be that which minimizes the expected sum of squared estimation errors for a selected $n - k$ disturbances.[12] This leads to the problem of which $n - k$ disturbances to estimate. For the serial correlation testing problem, Theil suggested $n - k$ consecutive disturbances with the above rule to decide which end disturbances not to estimate. This can require a lot of computation, especially when k is large. Other choice criteria have been proposed by Koerts and Abrahamse (1969), Ramsey (1969), Godolphin and de Tullio (1978) and Evans (1983).

Theil (1965) suggested the use of BLUS residuals in the von Neumann ratio, η, as an alternative to the DW test. For this purpose, Koerts and Abrahamse (1969, Table 1) tabulated selected significance points of $(n - k - 1)\eta/(n - k)$. However, Press (1969) noted that the modified von Neumann ratio, $\eta_* = v'A_1v/v'v$, where A_1 is defined in Section 3, is a more appropriate test statistic because BLUS residuals have an expected value of zero. Press and Brooks (1969) computed selected significance points of η_* and their tables have been reproduced in Theil (1971).

A number of authors followed Theil's lead and also proposed tests based on residuals which are independent of X. Golub and Styan (1973) showed that Golub's (1965) LUSH residual vector has a scalar covariance matrix and hence can be used in the modified von Neumann ratio.[13] Phillips and Harvey (1974) proposed a simple test against AR(1) disturbances based on recursive residuals which also are LUS. More recently, Dent and Styan (1978) suggested the use of Tiao and Guttman's (1967) Augmented Unbiased with Scalar covariance matrix (AUS) residuals in η_*. Tiao and Guttman's $n \times 1$ Best AUS (BAUS) residual vector is of the form

$$X(X'X)^{-1/2}\,w + e\ ,$$

where w is a $k \times 1$ vector such that $w \sim N(0,\sigma^2 I_k)$ and $E(uw') = 0$. In practice, because σ^2 is unknown, Dent and Styan suggested it be replaced by an unbiased estimate, resulting in an approximate BAUS residual vector.

What of the relative power properties of the above tests? Koerts and Abrahamse (1969) concluded that Theil's BLUS test generally has lower power than the DW test using the exact critical value. This conclusion has been verified by a number of studies including those of Dubbelman (1972, 1978), L'Esperance and Taylor (1975), Fraser, Guttman and Styan (1976) and Dubbelman, Louter and Abrahamse (1978). Fraser *et al.* also found that the power of the BLUS test is sometimes less than that of tests based on LUSH residuals. Savin and White (1978a) report that Ward (1973) draws a similar conclusion. Phillips and Harvey (1974) found little to choose between tests based on recursive residuals and BLUS residuals, in terms of power. They favoured the former residuals on the grounds of computational simplicity. Dent and Styan (1978) report a similar finding regarding the relative power properties of tests based on BLUS and their BAUS residuals.

Others have suggested tests based on Linear Unbiased with Fixed covariance matrix (LUF) residual vectors.[14] For example, Durbin (1970b) constructed a test based on the DW statistic calculated using residuals which have the same distribution as residuals from a regression on the eigenvectors corresponding to the smallest k eigenvalues of A_1. This enables the tabulated significance points of the DW upper bound to be used as critical values. An unattractive feature of this test is that it is not invariant to transformations of the form (4.3). Sims (1975) suggested a modification to this test in order to improve its properties.

Abrahamse and Koerts (1969, 1971) hypothesised that the poor power of the BLUS test is due to the scalar covariance restriction. They (1971) considered LUF residuals of the form

$$\bar{v} = C'y\ ,$$

where C is an $n \times n$ matrix such that $C'X = 0$, $C'C = \Omega$, and Ω is an $n \times n$ covariance matrix fixed *a priori*. Ω is required to be idempotent with rank $n - k$. The Abrahamse-Koerts (AK) Best LUF (BLUF) residual vector[15] is that with C chosen to minimise $E[(\bar{v} - u)' (\bar{v} - u)]$. Their test is based on the use of BLUF residuals in the DW statistic with Ω chosen so that $\bar{v}$ has the same null distribution as Durbin's (1970b) residuals and hence the DW upper bound tables provide the appropriate critical values. Their particular choice of Ω is based on a desire for $\bar{v}$ to closely approximate e for 'typical' economic design matrices. Dubbelman, Abrahamse and Koerts (1972) discussed a more general AK procedure. Among other things, they dropped the requirement that Ω be idempotent and generalized the criterion used to choose the 'best' LUF residual vector.

Power studies by Abrahamse and Louter (1971), Dubbelman (1972, 1978), Dubbelman, Louter and Abrahamse (1978) and Dent and Cassing (1978) suggest that, for a number of economic applications, the AK test has similar power to the DW test and is superior in this regard to the BLUS and Durbin's LUF tests. These studies have also identified design matrices for which the AK test has relatively poor power. In an attempt to find a solution to this problem, Dubbelman (1972, 1978) investigated a test procedure which involves a range of AK type tests, but each with a different Ω matrix, and a selection criterion which has regard to the design matrix when the choice of test statistic is made. From the empirical evidence presented by Dubbelman (1972, 1978) and Dubbelman, Louter and Abrahamse (1978) it appears that Dubbelman's procedure does have reasonably good power relative to the DW test. Unfortunately, this procedure can only be regarded as a serious alternative to the DW test for small n and k because for large n or k, an unmanageable number of significance points need to be tabulated.

Evans (1983, 1986) considered the problem of constructing a LUF test for seasonal economic time series regressors, both with and without seasonal dummies. She proposed two LUF tests, one based on the spectral analysis of 'typical' seasonal data and the other designed to utilize King's (1981c, 1983b) DW bounds for regressions with seasonal dummy variables.

Under (2.1) and (3.1), $y \sim N(X\beta, \sigma_u^2\Sigma)$, where $\sigma_u^2 = \sigma^2/(1-\varrho^2)$ and Σ is given by (4.5). Therefore a LUS residual vector, v, defined by (5.1), (5.2) and (5.3) has a $N(0, \sigma_u^2 B'\Sigma B)$ distribution. Kadiyala (1970) noted that for a fixed value of ϱ under H_a^+ (or H_a^-), say ϱ_1, B can be chosen to diagonalize Σ so that under $H_1 : \varrho = \varrho_1$, $v \sim N(0, \sigma_u^2 D)$, where D is a diagonal matrix. Without discussing how such B matrices might be found in practice, he proposed two LUS residual tests. The first is the use of v in the modified von Neumann ratio, a rather strange choice of test statistic in view of the form of D under H_1. The second test is based on rejecting H_0 for large absolute values of

$$s_3 = b_2'v / b_1'v \ ,$$

where b_1 and b_2 are two $(n - k) \times 1$ vectors of unit length such that $b_1'b_2 = 0$. Under H_0 s_3 has a Cauchy distribution.

In all, it does seem that the large literature on LUS and LUF tests has not been particularly fruitful. One reason would seem to be the inappropriate choice of test statistic. King (1979) showed that for each test based on LUF residuals, there exists an exactly equivalent test with a different test statistic based on LUS residuals. Hence we can limit our discussion to LUS residual tests.

King (1979, 1980a) also proved that if $\varrho \neq 0$ is known under H_a^+ (or H_a^-), a MPI test is to reject H_0 for small values of

$$v'(B'\Sigma B)^{-1}v/v'v \,. \tag{5.4}$$

As we shall see in Section 7, this test also has good power when ϱ is unknown under H_a^+ and the ϱ in Σ is fixed at a middle value of ϱ under H_a^+ such as 0.5. Such a test is clearly different to the use of v in the modified von Neumann ratio, thus explaining the poor power of many of the LUS based tests discussed above.

However, since B depends on X through (5.2), the use of (5.4) clearly defeats the purpose of using LUS residuals; that is to use a test whose critical values can be tabulated. One alternative is to set $B = B_*$ in (5.4) and then to choose the B of (5.1) to be as 'close' as possible to B_*. In particular, when the columns of B_* are chosen to be the eigenvectors corresponding to the $n - k$ largest eigenvalues of A_1 and $\Sigma/(1 - \varrho^2)$ is approximated by (4.6), King (1979) showed that the resultant test is equivalent to the AK test. Furthermore, when the column space of X is spanned by the remaining eigenvectors of A_1, this test is also equivalent to the DW test and is approximately UMPI.

6 Nonparametric tests

A simple solution to the problem of testing for serial correlation in the disturbances of (2.1) is to apply a nonparametric test of randomness to the OLS residuals. This approach, which Malinvaud (1966, p. 422) and Johnston (1972, p. 250) briefly discussed, was no doubt favoured in the past by researchers who were computerless or who found it a useful way of resolving the inconclusiveness of the DW test. However, in recent years, computer advances and better knowledge of the poor power of such procedures relative to the DW test have made them much less attractive.

The following are some examples of such tests.[16]

(i) Let v be the number of runs of consecutive positive or negative residuals. Cumulative probabilities of the null distribution of v when n is small and the process is random have been tabulated by Swed and

Eisenhart (1943). A normal approximation can be used for large samples.

(ii) Let μ be the number of turning points in consecutive residuals. For a random process, Kendall (1976) gives the first four moments of μ and suggests the use of a normal approximation with mean $2(n - 2)/3$ and variance $(16n - 29)/90$.

(iii) Let τ be the number of sign changes in consecutive residuals. For a random process, τ has a binomial distribution with parameters $\frac{1}{2}$ and $(n - 1)$. Note that $\tau = \nu - 1$. See Geary (1970) for further details.

(iv) Let a_1 denote the frequency with which both e_t and e_{t+1} are positive, a_2 the frequency with which $e_t > 0$ and $e_{t+1} < 0$, a_3 the frequency with which $e_t < 0$ and $e_{t+1} > 0$ and a_4 the frequency with which both e_t and e_{t+1} are negative. The test based on

$$\eta = (n - 1)(a_1a_4 - a_2a_3)^2/\{(a_1 + a_2)(a_1 + a_3)(a_2 + a_4)(a_3 + a_4)\}$$

being distributed approximately $\chi^2(1)$ in large samples under H_0 is known as the sign reversal test. It was first proposed in the regression context by Griliches *et al.* (1962) because of its robustness to outliers, a property not shared by the DW test.

The significance levels of the above tests are not exact, often for more than one reason. The tests are applied as if the OLS residuals are true disturbances and hence uncorrelated under H_0. As a consequence of OLS regression, the restriction $X'e = 0$ is imposed on the residuals. It implies that there are always k linear dependencies amongst the residuals and hence they are never uncorrelated. With reasonably weak conditions on X, however, the residuals converge in probability to the corresponding disturbances as n increases and, therefore, the tests are asymptotically valid. The use of normal or $\chi^2(1)$ approximations are a further cause of inexact significance levels.

Over the past decade, test (iii), the Sign Change (SC) test, has received a fair degree of attention in the literature. Habibagahi and Pratschke (1972) used the MC method to compare its power with that of the DW test when the lower bound is used as the critical value, in a simple trend regression model. They found the DW test to be the more powerful test. Belsley (1973, 1974) argued that a positive feature of the SC test is that it is a general test for serial correlation and, unlike the DW test, might be expected to have good power against second or higher order autoregressive disturbances. This claim was disputed by Tillman (1974) while Smith's (1976) MC experiment showed that against a variety of second-order Autoregressive (AR(2)) disturbances, the DW test is more powerful than the SC test. Harrison (1975) and Schmidt and Guilkey (1975) separately were critical of various aspects of Habibagahi and Pratschke's experiment, especially the use of the DW lower bound. They presented their own power calculations and concluded that the DW test is more powerful than the SC test. More recently, Schmidt and Guilkey (1982) suggested a modification to the SC test designed to improve control over the test's true significance level.[17]

7 Locally optimal tests

Recent advances in computer software and hardware have caused a change of emphasis in the literature away from test procedures which are computationally simple to apply or which overcome the inconclusiveness of the DW test, towards tests which have relatively high power. In this section we review a number of tests which have optimal power at least in a particular neighbourhood of the parameter space under the alternative hypothesis. As a consequence, such tests are typically more powerful than the DW test, at least for some values of ϱ under H_a^+.

Kadiyala (1970) considered the problem of testing for serial correlation in (2.1) by first investigating the simpler problem of testing $H_0 : u \sim N(0,\sigma^2 I_n)$ against $H_1 : u \sim N(0,\sigma^2\Omega)$, where Ω is a known $n \times n$ positive definite matrix. He noted that u is not directly observable and proposed that his analysis should start with an observable random vector. His choice of the OLS residual vector enabled him to show, using a result from Lehmann and Stein (1948), that a most powerful test with respect to his transformed problem is to reject H_0 for small values of

$$v'(B'\Omega B)^{-1}v/v'v \ , \tag{7.1}$$

where v and B are defined by (5.1), (5.2) and (5.3). King (1980a, Lemma 2) shows that (7.1) also is of the form

$$\hat{u}'\Omega^{-1}\hat{u}/e'e \ , \tag{7.2}$$

where $\hat{u}$ is the Generalized Least Squares (GLS) residual vector assuming covariance matrix Ω.

Durbin and Watson (1971, pp. 9-10) attempted to derive a MPI test of H_0 against H_1 where invariance is with respect to (4.3). Webb (1973) pointed out a mistake in their proof.[18] Consequently, the test they finally obtain is not MPI in all cases, the only exception being when $\hat{u}$ and e coincide. Because their conclusions regarding optimal power properties of the DW test concern situations where $\hat{u}$ and e coincide, these conclusions are unaffected.

As an alternative to the DW test, Berenblut and Webb (1973) proposed the use of the statistic,

$$g = y'(B_1 - B_1X(X'B_1X)^{-1}X'B_1)y/y'My \ ,$$

where B_1 is the $n \times n$ matrix A_1 defined in Section 3 with the top left element being 2 instead of 1. They considered both stationary AR(1) disturbances as defined by (3.1) and nonstationary AR(1) disturbances generated as

$$u_t = \varrho u_{t-1} + \varepsilon_t\ , \quad u_1 = \varepsilon_1\ , \quad \varepsilon_t \sim \text{IN}(0,\sigma^2)\ , \qquad (7.3)$$

where ϱ can take any value. Note that their test statistic, g, is of the form (7.2) when, under H_1, u is generated by (7.3) with $\varrho = 1$.

They showed[19] that rejecting H_0 for small values of g is an approximately UMPI test against H_a^+ with respect to (3.1) when the column space of X is spanned by k eigenvectors of A_1 including the eigenvector $l = (1, 1, \ldots, 1)'$. The same test was shown to be locally MPI in the neighbourhood of $\varrho = 1$, provided l is included as a regressor. Against H_a^+ with respect to the nonstationary process (7.3), they demonstrated that their test is approximately UMPI when the column space of X is spanned by some k eigenvectors of B_1. They also showed it to be locally MPI in the neighbourhood of $\varrho = 1$ against the same alternative hypothesis for any X matrix. Using empirical methods, they compared the power of their test against that of the DW test for a limited range of X matrices under both (3.1) and (7.3). They concluded that in both cases their test has greater power than the DW test for large values of ϱ.

Fraser, Guttman and Styan (1976) considered the problem of testing H_0 against H_a^+ in (2.1) and (3.1) from the viewpoint of the probability distribution of $z = u/\sigma$. By factoring this distribution into a distribution of what is observed concerning z and a conditional distribution of what is not observed, and by applying Neyman-Pearson theory, Fraser *et al.* constructed a test which they call the Likelihood Ratio Observable (LRO) test. For the problem of testing H_0 against H_1 considered by Kadiyala (1970), the LRO test rejects H_0 for small values of (7.1) (or equivalently (7.2)) and hence corresponds to Kadiyala's test. Against H_a^+, they proposed two operational versions of their LRO test; that based on (7.1) (or (7.2)) with Ω replaced by $R(\varrho) = \Sigma/(1 - \varrho^2)$ evaluated at $\varrho = 0.5$, where Σ is given by (4.5) and the limit of such LRO tests as ϱ in $R(\varrho)$ tends to zero. This latter test, which they call the LMPZ test, is equivalent to the LBI test against H_a^+ discussed in Section 4.7. They call the former test the LRO(ϱ_1=0.5) test.

For four design matrices, Fraser *et al.* compared the power of their tests with those of the DW, BLUS and LUSH tests. They found the LRO(ϱ_1=0.5) test generally to be slightly more powerful than the DW test with the LMPZ test being the most powerful test for $\varrho = 0.2$ but being slightly less powerful than the DW test for $\varrho \geqslant 0.6$. The BLUS and LUSH tests were found to have relatively poor power.

Using an alternative method to that used by Durbin and Watson (1971), King (1980a, Theorem 3) proved that for testing H_0 against H_1, Kadiyala's test based on (7.1) (or (7.2)) is MPI. In a later paper (1985a) he investigated the problem of testing H_0 against H_a^+ (or H_a^-) with respect to (2.1) and (3.1) and studied the small sample power properties of this test with Ω replaced by $R(\varrho_1)$, where $\varrho_1 \neq 0$ is known and fixed. This test, which rejects H_0 for small values of

$$s(\varrho_1) = \hat{u}'R^{-1}(\varrho_1)\hat{u}/e'e\ , \tag{7.4}$$

where $\hat{u}$ is the GLS residual vector assuming covariance matrix $R(\varrho_1)$, is an operational version of the Fraser *et al.* LRO test and, by construction, is locally MPI in the neighbourhood of $\varrho = \varrho_1$. It is also approximately UMPI against H_a^+ (H_a^-) when the column space of X is spanned by k of the eigenvectors of $R(\varrho_1)$ and provided $\varrho_1 > 0$ ($\varrho_1 < 0$).

The statistic, $s(\varrho_1)$, can be calculated as a ratio of two sums of squared OLS residuals since the numerator is the sum of squared residuals from the transformed model,

$$(1 - \varrho_1^2)^{1/2}y_1 = (1 - \varrho_1^2)^{1/2}x_1'\beta + (1 - \varrho_1^2)^{1/2}u_1\ ,$$

$$y_t - \varrho_1 y_{t-1} = (x_t - \varrho_1 x_{t-1})'\beta + u_t - \varrho_1 u_{t-1}\ , \quad t = 2, \ldots, n,$$

where x_t' is a $1 \times k$ vector representing the tth row of X. As is the case for the DW test, finding the critical value of (7.4) requires a degree of computational effort. King showed that (7.4) can be written as

$$s(\varrho_1) = \sum_{i=1}^{m} \lambda_i \xi_i^2 \Big/ \sum_{i=1}^{m} \xi_i^2\ ,$$

where $m = n - k$, $\lambda_1, \ldots, \lambda_m$ are the reciprocals of the non-zero eigenvalues of $R(\varrho_1)M$ and under H_0, $\xi_i \sim IN(0,1)$. This form of $s(\varrho_1)$ allows the critical value of (7.4) to be calculated using the methods for finding d_α^* discussed in Section 4.2. It also allowed King (1985a) to tabulate attainable bounds for the test's critical values for regressions with an intercept.

As a general rule, King suggested the use of $\varrho_1 = 0.5$ in (7.4). He made this choice after conducting an empirical power experiment which compared the power of the DW, LBI (d'), $s(0.5)$, $s(0.75)$ and g tests for a range of X matrices against H_a^+. In terms of power, the $s(0.5)$ test was found to dominate the DW test and the $s(0.75)$ test was found to dominate the g test, almost always. For the majority of economic design matrices, the difference in power is small, but in some cases there is a very clear power advantage to be gained from using the $s(0.5)$ test instead of the DW test. This is especially true for Watson's X matrix.[20] Thus, it seems to be advantageous to use the $s(0.5)$ test in preference to the DW test for although the power advantage may be limited for most economic applications, there is always the chance that one may encounter a design matrix for which the power advantage is reasonably substantial. Furthermore, such cases seem likely to be those for which the OLS estimator is relatively inefficient under H_a^+ and a powerful test is needed most.

8 Other tests for AR(1) disturbances

This section reviews further tests for AR(1) disturbances in (2.1) not discussed in previous sections. We begin by considering the application of three methods of test construction which, more recently, have attracted a great deal of interest in the econometrics literature. They are the Likelihood Ratio (LR) test, the Wald test and the Lagrange Multiplier (LM) test.

There is surprisingly little written on the use of the LR and Wald tests against AR(1) disturbances in non-dynamic regression models. For the two-sided[21] problem of testing H_0 against $H_a : \varrho \neq 0$, Dent (1973) used the MC method to compare the power of the DW test, Theil's BLUS test, Dent and Styan's BAUS test and two Wald-type tests based on normal and beta approximations to the null distribution of the Maximum Likelihood Estimator (MLE) of ϱ in (3.1). He found that the DW test (using the Theil-Nagar approximate critical value) has the best power overall while the Wald-type tests and the LR test have relatively poor power, especially for small samples and against $\varrho > 0$. The relatively poor performance of the LR test in small samples has been confirmed by the author in an unpublished power comparison of the DW, $s(\varrho_1)$ and LR tests using exact critical values. It appears that for smoothly evolving regressors, the LR test has relatively poor power against $\varrho > 0$ but is generally more powerful than the DW test against $\varrho < 0$. The reverse seems to be the case for rapidly changing regressors. These effects appear to be caused by the small-sample bias of the MLE of ϱ.

Schmidt and Guilkey (1975) examined the power against H_a^+ of a Wald-type test based on a Student's t (with $n - k$ degress of freedom) approximation of the null distribution of a least squares estimate of ϱ,

$$\varrho^* = \sum_{t=2}^{n} e_t e_{t-1} \Big/ \sum_{t=1}^{n-1} e_t^2 ,$$

where e is the OLS residual vector. In a very limited MC power comparison, they found it to be rather less powerful than the DW test but generally more powerful than the SC test.

Against H_a^+, the LBI d' test can be shown to be equivalent to the one-sided exact LM test for this problem [see King and Hillier (1985)]. Some econometricians argue that the asymptotic two-sided LM test based on the statistic

$$n(1-\tfrac{1}{2}d')^2 = n\Big(\sum_{t=2}^{n} e_t e_{t-1} \Big/ \sum_{t=1}^{n} e_t^2\Big)^2 \qquad (8.1)$$

is a useful test. Under H_0 , (8.1) has an asymptotic chi-squared distribution with one degree of freedom. As one can readily see this test is equivalent to a two-sided d' test and so does not allow one to exploit information about the sign of ϱ one typically has in economic situations. Furthermore, King's (1981b) tables of bounds on the critical values of d' suggest that asymptotic critical values may be rather unreliable, at least for small to moderate sized samples and/or a reasonable number of regressors. On the other hand, it does have the advantage of being easily computed, particularly in non-standard situations; see for example Pagan and Hall (1983), Lee (1984), Evans and Patterson (1985), Robinson (1985) and Robinson, Bera and Jarque (1985).

Ogawara (1951) constructed an exact test of $H_0 : \varrho = 0$ in the AR(1) process

$$(x_t - \xi) = \varrho(x_{t-1} - \xi) + \varepsilon_t\,, \quad \varepsilon_t \sim \mathrm{IN}(0,\sigma^2),$$

by considering the conditional distribution of x_{2t} for fixed values of x_{2t-1}. He showed that $b = 2\varrho(1 - \varrho^2)^{-1}$ is the regression coefficient of x_{2t} on the fixed variable $\frac{1}{2}(x_{2t-1} + x_{2t+1})$ and that an exact test of H_0 can be conducted by the usual Student's t test on b. Hannan (1955) extended Ogawara's test to the regression context and showed that in the neighbourhood of $\varrho = 0$ the test is asymptotically efficient. A disadvantage of Hannan's test is that half the sample is discarded and an OLS regression with $2k$ regressors is run on the remainder of the sample. Hence, one would expect it to have poor power for small n and moderate k.

Further extensions of Ogawara's test to the regression model were made by Krishnaiah and Murthy (1966). A particular case they considered in detail is the trend regression,

$$y_t = \alpha + \beta t + u_t\,, \qquad t = 1, \ldots, n,$$

with u_t generated by (3.1). They discussed simultaneous F tests of the null hypotheses $\alpha = \beta = 0$ and $\alpha = \beta = \varrho = 0$ while Hannan (1969) examined the asymptotic efficiency of these exact tests.

Durbin (1969) considered a frequency-domain approach to the problem of testing for serial correlation in the disturbances of (2.1). He proposed two bounds tests based on the Cumulated Periodogram (CP),

$$s_j = \sum_{r=1}^{j} p_r \Big/ \sum_{r=1}^{m} p_r\,, \qquad j = 1, \ldots, m,$$

where $n = 2m + 1$,

$$p_r = \frac{2}{n}\left[\left\{\sum_{t=1}^{n} e_t \cos(2\pi rt/n)\right\}^2 + \left\{\sum_{t=1}^{n} e_t \sin(2\pi rt/n)\right\}^2\right]$$

and e is the OLS residual vector. His first test, which can be described as a modified Kolmogorov-Smirnov test and which is now known as Durbin's CP test, uses a plot of s_j against j/m, $j = 1, \ldots, m$. When testing against positive serial correlation, two lines are drawn above and parallel to the $s_j = j/m$ diagonal and H_0 is rejected if the plot of the CP crosses the upper line while H_0 is accepted if the plot does not cross the lower line. Otherwise the test is inconclusive. Durbin's second test is based on

$$\bar{s} = \frac{1}{m-1} \sum_{j=1}^{m-1} s_j$$

which is of the form required by the DW Lemma. Hence, bounding random variables, $\bar{s}_L$ and $\bar{s}_U$ exist such that $\bar{s}_L \leqslant \bar{s} \leqslant \bar{s}_U$ and the test can be applied in an analogous manner to the DW bounds test but with H_0 being rejected for large values of $\bar{s}$. Both tests were presented as tests for general serial correlation rather than specifically being designed to test against AR(1) disturbances.

Cleur's (1973) MC study compared the power of Durbin's CP test with that of the DW test with the inconclusive regions of both tests being included in the respective acceptance regions. He concluded that overall, Durbin's CP test seems to be more powerful than the DW test, but he failed to comment on the unfairness of the power comparison. Because of his choice of critical values, the true significance level of the DW test is often much lower than that of Durbin's CP test, at least for the particular design matrices considered by Cleur. Smith (1977) used the MC method to compare the power against H_a^+ of Durbin's CP test, the DW test and Durbin's (1970b) exact test applied to the simple linear trend regression model. For this particular design matrix, Smith found that the power functions of the DW and Durbin's exact tests are almost identical and that these two tests are consistently more powerful than the CP test. Given Smith's choice of the upper significance line as the critical boundary for the CP test[22] and his choice of design matrix, this conclusion is not surprising. The X matrix with a constant and a trend variable as its only regressors has a column space which is approximately spanned by the two eigenvectors associated with the two smallest eigenvalues of A_1. For such design matrices, therefore, the DW and Durbin exact tests almost coincide and both are approximately UMPI.

9 Robustness properties of tests for AR(1) disturbances

Kariya and Eaton (1977), Kariya (1977, 1980) and King (1979, 1980a, 1980c) have studied the robustness of various tests for serial correlation in the disturbances of (2.1) under the assumption that u follows an elliptically symmetric distribution. An $n \times 1$ random vector, w, is spherically symmetric if its distribution laws are invariant to orthogonal transformations. w is elliptically symmetric with characteristic matrix Γ if $\Gamma^{-1/2}w$ is spherically symmetric. $N(0,\tau^2 I_n)$ and $N(0,\tau^2\Gamma)$ are examples of spherically symmetric and elliptically symmetric distributions, respectively. For a recent review of the growing literature on this class of distributions, see Chmielewski (1981).

The most general result concerning the robustness of tests for serial correlation is given by King (1979, 1980c). He showed that any statistic which is invariant to the scale of the disturbances of (2.1) has the same distribution when $u \sim N(0,\tau^2\Gamma)$ as it does when u is assumed to follow any other elliptically symmetric distribution with characteristic matrix Γ. Because all the tests discussed above are invariant to the scale of u, King's result implies that they have the same size, the same power and the same optimal power properties when $\varepsilon = (\varepsilon_1, \ldots, \varepsilon_n)'$ of (3.1) is assumed to be spherically symmetric instead of distributed $N(0,\sigma^2 I_n)$.

In a simple MC experiment, Gastwirth and Selwyn (1980) studied the robustness of the size and power of the SC and DW tests when the ε_t in (3.1) are independent drawings from a double exponential distribution or from a symmetric Pareto distribution. They restricted their attention to the simple case of (2.1) with a constant as the only regressor and found that, generally, the DW test[23] is more robust and powerful than the SC test. Bartels and Goodhew (1981) conducted a MC study of the robustness of the size of the DW test to a variety of non-normal disturbance distributions. They estimated the Type I error for three design matrices at three nominal significance levels and concluded that the size of the DW test is quite robust to different disturbance distributions, especially at the five per cent level.

A technique developed by Davis (1976) was used by Knight (1983) to examine the null distribution of the DW statistic assuming the disturbances come from (i) a non-normal distribution of the Edgeworth type characterized by skewness and kurtosis and (ii) a mixture of two normal distributions with different means and equal variances. Based on calculations for two X matrices, he concluded that the DW test is very robust to departures of the former type while robustness in the latter case depends critically on the X matrix.

Harrison and McCabe (1975) and Epps and Epps (1977) investigated the robustness of the size and power of the DW and SC tests to the occurrence of heteroscedasticity in the ε_t of (3.1). Harrison and McCabe used the MC method to estimate the powers of the tests for two simple regression models. They concluded that the power functions of both tests are largely unaffected by heteroscedasticity in ε_t. Epps and Epps agreed with this finding. Their large sample analysis led them to add that the DW test appears to be less robust when the regressors are autocorrelated than when they are non-autocorrelated.

Blattberg (1973) studied the power function of the DW test against AR(2) and against first-order Moving Average (MA(1)) disturbances in (2.1). As a result of both his large sample and his empirical small sample analyses, he concluded that the DW test is powerful against either alternative, the level of power depending upon, among other things, the first-order autocorrelation coefficient of the process in question.

Smith (1976) estimated the power functions of the DW test, the SC test, Durbin's CP test and Durbin's (1970b) exact test applied to the simple linear trend regression model with AR(2) disturbances and also with MA(1) disturbances using the MC method.[24] The powers of Schmidt's (1972) test for AR(2) disturbances were also calculated when appropriate. Smith found that against AR(2) disturbances, the DW and Durbin's exact tests are often more powerful than Schmidt's test with the latter being more powerful when the absolute values of the first-order and second-order autocorrelation coefficients are moderate or large and almost equal. The SC test was found generally to be less powerful than the other tests. As a rule the power of the CP test was found to be slightly lower than that of the DW test. Against MA(1) disturbances, Smith found the DW and Durbin exact tests to be consistently more powerful than the other two tests while the SC test always has the weakest power.

In a rather poorly designed MC experiment, Weber and Monarchi (1982), among other things, investigated the power of the DW test against a restricted form of AR(2) disturbances and concluded that the test has good power against this alternative.

Recently, Revankar (1980, p. 194) discussed the adequacy of the DW test as a test against disturbances which are the sum of independent white noise and AR(1) components. He concluded that the DW test is inappropriate as it is 'always biased in favour of the null hypothesis'. King (1982) disputed Revankar's finding, arguing that there is no bias under the null hypothesis and that for this problem the DW test is approximately LBI. Obviously, an AR(1) process is much more difficult to detect when combined with an independent white noise component, but this does not make the DW test inappropriate as the small sample powers computed by King (1982, 1986) show.

The DW test has also been shown to be approximately LBI against MA(1) disturbances [King (1983c)], particular forms of spatial autocorrelated disturbances [King and Evans (1985, 1986b)], ARMA(1,1) disturbances, sums of independent ARMA(1,1) disturbances and disturbances from a stochastic cycle model which is a special case of an ARMA(2,1) process [King and Evans (1986b)]. Its usefulness as a test against block autocorrelation effects, resulting from the use of cluster or multi-stage sampling data, has been investigated by King and Evans (1986a).

In summary, the evidence available in the literature suggests that the DW test is reasonably robust against non-normality and against heteroscedasticity. It also appears to have good power against various forms of serial correlation with the level of power generally depending upon, among other things, the magnitude of the first-order autocorrelation coefficient of the disturbances.

10 Testing when a lagged dependent variable is a regressor

In their seminal paper, Durbin and Watson (1950, p. 410) warned that their test procedure is not applicable to regression models in which a lagged dependent variable occurs as a regressor.[25] However, it appears that econometricians are not in total agreement about whether the DW test can usefully be used in such circumstances.

Nerlove and Wallis (1966) investigated the large sample behaviour of the DW test statistic, d, applied to the simple model

$$y_t = \alpha y_{t-1} + u_t , \qquad t = 1, \ldots , n,$$

where the u_t are generated by the AR(1) process (3.1). They found that for $\varrho \neq 0$, the probability limit of d is closer to two than it would be if the true disturbances were used to calculate d. They argued that this implied that the DW test would tend to favour the null hypothesis in such circumstances and hence should not be used uncritically. The main objection to this line of reasoning is that their findings concerning the probability limit of d may purely be a reflection of the fact that the inclusion of a regressor which is a function of the previous disturbance, makes it more difficult to detect AR(1) disturbances. The evidence presented by Nerlove and Wallis does not preclude the DW test from still being a powerful test relative to other tests.

The real problem with the use of the DW test in regressions which include a lagged dependent variable as a regressor, is, as Durbin (1970a) observed, with the null distribution of d. In general the size of the test does not converge to the nominal size as n increases. Durbin noted that this problem can be corrected by an appropriate adjustment to the test statistic.

He first considered a general problem in which maximum likelihood estimation under the null hypothesis is straightforward compared to estimation under the alternative, and derived some asymptotic tests. He then applied these tests to the problem of testing $H_0 : \varrho = 0$ against $H_a^+ : \varrho > 0$ (or $H_a^- : \varrho < 0$, etc.) in the regression model,

$$y_t = \beta_1 y_{t-1} + \ldots + \beta_r y_{t-r} + \beta_{r+1} x_{1t} + \ldots + \beta_{r+s} x_{st} + u_t , \qquad (10.1)$$
$$t = 0, \ldots , n,$$

where the disturbances $u_0, \ldots , u_n$ are generated by the AR(1) process (3.1), the x's are assumed constant and to follow certain regularity conditions and $y_{-1}, \ldots , y_{-r}$ are known constants. Rejecting H_0 against H_a^+ (H_a^-) for large (small) values of

$$h = (1 - \tfrac{1}{2}d) \, [n/\{1 - n\hat{V}(b_1)\}]^{1/2} ,$$

where $\hat{V}(b_1)$ is the usual estimate of the variance of the OLS estimator of β_1 from (10.1), has become known as Durbin's h test. h has a standard normal asymptotic null distribution.

Unfortunately, this test breaks down whenever $\{1 - n\hat{V}(b_1)\}$ is negative. Durbin also presented an alternative and asymptotically equivalent test which doesn't suffer this drawback. Let $e_0, \ldots, e_n$ be the OLS residuals from (10.1). H_0 can be tested by using OLS regression procedures to test the significance of the coefficient of e_{t-1} in the regression of e_t on e_{t-1}, y_{t-1}, $\ldots$, x_{st}. We shall call this Durbin's t test.

Murray (1976) discussed the circumstances in which Durbin's h test breaks down while Godfrey (1978a) derived a version of Durbin's h test for equations that have been estimated by the method of instrumental variables. Breusch (1978) and Aldrich (1978) explored the relationship between Durbin's h test and the LM test and found that the two are asymptotically equivalent. Breusch also showed that Durbin's t test can be derived as a LM test with a particular choice of estimate of the information matrix.[26] An alternative derivation of Durbin's h test that does not assume that the ε_t are independent $N(0,\sigma^2)$ is given by Phillips and Wickens (1978) while Sargan (1975) suggests a modification of the h statistic which always can be computed. [Also see Sargan and Tse (1981) and Tse (1985).]

Wald-type tests of H_0 have been suggested by Dhrymes (1971, ch.11) and McNown and Hunter (1980). Dhrymes proposed a test based on the instrumental variables estimator of (10.1). McNown and Hunter considered (10.1) and (3.1) with $r = 1$ and $s = 1$ which can be combined as

$$\begin{aligned} y_t &= (\beta_1 + \varrho)y_{t-1} - \varrho\beta_1 y_{t-2} + \beta_2 x_{1t} - \varrho\beta_2 x_{1t-1} + \varepsilon_t \\ &= a_1 y_{t-1} + a_2 y_{t-2} + a_3 x_{1t} + a_4 x_{1t-1} + \varepsilon_t , \end{aligned}$$

and suggested testing H_0 by an asymptotic test of the significance of a_4.

A number of authors have conducted MC studies in order to investigate the small sample properties of the various tests. Maddala and Rao (1973) compared the power of Durbin's tests with that of the LR test for the simple model

$$y_t = \alpha y_{t-1} + \beta x_t + u_t , \tag{10.2}$$

where the disturbances, u_t, follow the AR(1) process (3.1). They found that their choice of x_t critically affected their results. For an x series with trend and/or high autocorrelation, Durbin's h test was often found to be inapplicable when α and ϱ are small and σ^2 is not too small. Also, the performance of the LR test was relatively poor for trending x. In terms of power, Maddala and Rao concluded that, overall, there is little to choose between Durbin's h and t tests.

Kenkel (1974) used Maddala and Rao's model, but with a superfluous intercept term fitted at estimation, to compare the size and power of Durbin's h test with that of the DW test when DW lower and upper bounds are used as critical values. In all 24 cases considered, the Kolmogorov-Smirnov test rejected the null hypothesis that h is distributed $N(0,1)$ when $\varrho = 0$. In these cases, Kenkel found that the DW upper bound test almost always has approximately the correct size while the size of Durbin's h test tends to be less than the nominal five per cent. He also found this version of the DW test to be more powerful than Durbin's h test.

In a later paper, Kenkel (1975) reported some further results. This time a nonzero intercept term was included in (10.2) and the DW upper bound was the only critical value used for the DW test. Again he found evidence of the null distribution of h not being N(0,1) in small samples. In this experiment, however, he found a greater incidence of inapplicability of Durbin's h test, especially for small α and ϱ and large σ^2. Also the size of Durbin's h test was generally found to be much greater than the stated size. The 2.5 per cent h test often has greater size and lower power than the five per cent DW test using the upper bound. These findings led Kenkel to suggest that one should perhaps use the DW test with the upper bound as the critical value rather than Durbin's h test when testing a regression with a lagged dependent variable as a regressor.

In a limited MC experiment, Spencer (1975) compared the observed sizes of Durbin's h and t tests. He found that the observed size of the t test is roughly correct while that of the h test appears to be biased. A more comprehensive MC study was conducted by Park[27] (1975) who compared the size and power of Durbin's two tests with those of the DW test when the lower bound is used as the critical value. The DW test was found by Park to be less powerful than each of Durbin's tests, having a Type I error which is less than its stated size while the Type I errors of both of Durbin's tests tend to be greater than their stated sizes. Park also reported that the h test appeared to be slightly more powerful than the t test against H_a^+ with the reverse being the case against H_a^-.

Kenkel (1976) rejected Park's (1975) conclusion concerning the lack of power of the DW test. He criticised Park's use of the lower bound as the DW critical value and pointed out that in any comparison of power, one should employ critical regions that have approximately the same size. This is not the case in Park's study. In reply, Park (1976) observed that in his experiment, the DW test with the upper bound as critical value has a higher Type I error than the h test in 16 out of 23 cases. He therefore disagreed with Kenkel on the usefulness of the DW test for regressions with a lagged dependent variable as a regressor.

McNown and Hunter (1980) compared the size and power of their test with that of Durbin's h test and the DW test with the upper bound as critical value. They found the observed size of their test and the h test to be less than the stated size while that of the DW test generally exceeded the nominated size. For a model with a correlated exogenous series, the power of their test was found to be very inferior to that of the other two tests. When this exogenous series is replaced by a more random artificial series, their test has similar power to the h test. The DW test was found to be the most powerful of the three tests, no doubt partly because of its relatively high Type I error.

Judge *et al.* (1980, p.220) remarked that no one has yet compared the power of Durbin's (1970a) recommended procedure[28] with that of the DW test which makes use of one of the better approximation procedures when the bounds test is inconclusive. They conjectured that such a comparison would show Durbin's procedure to have better small sample properties than the DW test.

The point that a number of authors seem to have overlooked is that the nub of the problem is with finding the appropriate critical value of the DW test. A major obstacle is that in small samples the null distribution of the DW statistic is a function of unknown regression parameters. Durbin's solution is to make an adjustment to the DW test statistic so that it has a N(0,1) asymptotic distribution.

Recently, Inder (1984) used the MC method to find the critical values of the DW and Durbin's h tests conditional on assumed values of the regression parameters. He then compared the powers of the two tests and found that the DW test is generally more powerful than the h test. In some cases the h test has comparatively poor power and, not surprisingly, these tend to be situations in which $\hat{V}(b_1)$ is a poor estimator of the variance of the OLS estimator of β_1. Subsequently, Inder (1985a, 1986) used small disturbance asymptotics to find a practical approximation to the true DW critical value in (10.1) when there is one lagged dependent variable as a regressor; i.e., $r = 1$. The approximation is the exact DW critical value for (10.1) when the lagged dependent variable is omitted as a regressor. Therefore, one may use existing computer algorithms for calculating DW critical values (see Section 4.2), or tables of bounds (see Section 4.4), or further approximations (see Section 4.1) appropriate for the static model. In a MC comparison, Inder found that his DW approximation generally yields sizes closer to the nominal size than do the asymptotic critical values of Durbin's h and t tests.

Inder (1985a, 1985b) also proposed a modified version of King's (1985a) $s(\varrho_1)$ test for use in the dynamic regression model. Using small disturbance asymptotics Inder found that the critical value of his test can be approximated by that of the $s(\varrho_1)$ test in the static model. A MC study showed that this approach typically yields sizes below but slightly closer to the nominal size than do the asymptotic critical values of Durbin's h and t tests. The MC experiment also showed that the power of the new test can be vastly superior to that of existing tests, especially for large values of ϱ.

11 Tests against other forms of serial correlation

Until the late 1960's, the literature on testing for serially correlated disturbances in the linear regression model was preoccupied with the problem of detecting AR(1) errors. Since then the increased understanding of other forms of serial correlation, no doubt helped by the work of Box and Jenkins (1970) and others, has led to the development of tests designed to detect forms of serial correlation other than AR(1). Such test procedures are reviewed in this section.

11.1 LBI tests

The majority of hypothesis testing problems discussed below can be parameterized as problems of testing $H_0 : \theta = 0$ against $H_a : \theta > 0$ (or $H'_a : \theta \neq 0$) in the context of (2.1) where $u \sim N(0,\sigma^2\Omega(\theta))$ and $\Omega(\cdot)$ is a known matrix function such that $\Omega(0) = I_n$ while σ^2 and θ are unknown scalar parameters. King and Hillier (1985) showed that a LBI test against H_a is to reject H_0 for small values of

$$e'A_0e/e'e \ ,$$

where

$$A_0 = -\partial\Omega(\theta)/\partial\theta|_{\theta=0} = \partial\Omega^{-1}(\theta)/\partial\theta|_{\theta=0}$$

and e is the OLS residual vector. The appropriate critical value for this test can be found using methods analogous to those for the DW test discussed in Section 4.2. King and Hillier demonstrated the equivalence of this test to a one-sided version of the LM test. They also presented a locally best unbiased invariant test of H_0 against H'_a.

In some cases the LBI test is also UMPI. For example, consider $\Omega(\theta) = (I_n + \theta A)^{-1}$ where A is a known non-zero matrix such that $A \neq \tau I_n$ and $MA \neq 0$. If the column space of X is spanned by k of the eigenvectors of A then the LBI test which rejects H_0 for small values of $e'Ae/e'e$ is UMPI. Other examples are given by King and Inder (1983).

A satisfactory generalization of these results to situations in which θ is a vector has yet to be found. The following is a possible approach which is probably only suited to cases in which the dimension of θ is small. For the purpose of constructing a test, fix θ up to an unknown scalar, i.e., $\theta = \tau^2\theta^*$. Then King and Hillier's test of $H_0 : \tau^2 = 0$ against $H_a : \tau^2 > 0$ is a LBI test in the direction of θ^*. In other words, this test has the steepest sloping power function in the direction of θ^* for all invariant tests of the same size.

11.2 Tests for higher order autoregressive disturbances

Schmidt (1972) considered the problem of testing H_0: $\varrho_1 = \varrho_2 = 0$ in the AR(2) process

$$u_t = \varrho_1 u_{t-1} + \varrho_2 u_{t-2} + \varepsilon_t , \tag{11.1}$$

where $\varepsilon_t \sim IN(0,\sigma^2)$. He proposed the use of the test statistic

$$d_2 = e'(A_1 + A_2)e/e'e ,$$

where A_1 is the first-differencing matrix defined in Section 3 and

$$A_2 = \begin{bmatrix} 1 & 0 & -1 & 0 & \cdot & \cdot & \cdot & \cdot & \cdot & 0 & 0 \\ 0 & 1 & 0 & -1 & & & & & & 0 & 0 \\ -1 & 0 & 2 & 0 & & & & & & 0 & 0 \\ 0 & -1 & 0 & 2 & & & & & & & \cdot \\ \cdot & & & & & & & & & & \cdot \\ \cdot & & & & & & & & & & \cdot \\ \cdot & & & & & & & & & & \cdot \\ 0 & 0 & & & & & & & 2 & 0 & -1 \\ 0 & 0 & & & & & & & 0 & 1 & 0 \\ 0 & 0 & \cdot & & \cdot & & \cdot & \cdot & -1 & 0 & 1 \end{bmatrix}$$

Against $H_a : \varrho_1 \geqslant 0,\ \varrho_2 \geqslant 0$,[29] H_0 is rejected for small values of d_2. The approach discussed in the preceeding paragraph can be used to show that this test is approximately LBI in the direction of $(1,1)'$ in the $(\varrho_1,\varrho_2)'$ parameter space. Schmidt discussed the problem of finding the α level critical value for d_2 and tabulated bounds for selected 0.01, 0.05 and 0.1 critical values for regressions without an intercept.

The problem of testing against simple fourth-order Autoregressive (AR(4)) disturbances in (2.1), has been considered by many authors. Formally, the problem is one of testing $H_0 : \varrho = 0$ against $H_a^+ : \varrho > 0$ (or $H_a^- : \varrho < 0$ or H_a': $\varrho \neq 0$) when the disturbances of (2.1) follow a stationary simple AR(4) process,

$$u_t = \varrho u_{t-4} + \varepsilon_t, \quad |\varrho| < 1, \quad \varepsilon_t \sim IN(0,\sigma^2). \tag{11.2}$$

Observe that under (11.2), $u \sim N(0,\sigma^2\Sigma_4(\varrho))$, where if n is an integer multiple of 4, i.e., $n = 4m$,

$$\Sigma_4(\varrho) = [(1-\varrho)^2 I_n + \varrho A_4 + \varrho(1-\varrho)C_4]^{-1} ,$$

where $A_4 = A_1 \otimes I_4$, $C_4 = C_1 \otimes I_4$ and A_1 and C_1 are $m \times m$ matrices defined in Section 3.

As a test of H_0, Thomas and Wallis (1971) proposed the fourth-order counterpart to the nonparametric test suggested by Griliches *et al.* (1962) for the AR(1) case. Wallis (1972) and Vinod (1973) separately developed the fourth-order analogue to the DW test. Their test, which has become known as the Wallis test, rejects H_0 against H_a^+ (H_a^-) for small (large) values of

$$d_4 = \sum_{t=5}^{n} (e_t - e_{t-4})^2 / \sum_{t=1}^{n} e_t^2$$

$$= e'A_4e/e'e \ .$$

This test is approximately UMPI when the column space of X is spanned by k eigenvectors of A_4. It is also approximately LBI for any X matrix. Like the DW test statistic, the null distribution of d_4 depends on the X matrix. Bounds for the critical values of d_4 havc bccn tabulated by Wallis (1972), Vinod (1973), King and Giles (1977) and Giles and King (1978).

Using the approach outlined above, one can show that a true LBI test against H_a^+ (H_a^-) is to reject H_0 for small (large) values of

$$d_4' = e'(A_4 + C_4)e/e'e \ .$$

This test is also UMPI when the column space of X is spanned by k eigenvectors of $(A_4 + C_4)$.

Webb (1973) constructed the fourth-order generalization of the Berenblut and Webb (1973) test. Webb's test rejects H_0 against H_a^+ for small values of

$$g_4 = \tilde{u}'B_4\tilde{u}/e'e \ ,$$

where $\tilde{u}$ is the GLS residual vector from (2.1) assuming covariance matrix B_4^{-1} and B_4 is the $n \times n$ matrix A_4 with the first four main diagonal elements taking the value two instead of unity. If the column space of X is spanned by some k eigenvectors of A_4 including those associated with the zero roots,[30] the test is approximately UMPI against H_a^+. The test is also MPI in the neighbourhood of $\varrho = 1$ against H_a^+ for any design matrix which includes a full set of seasonal dummy variables amongst its regressors.

King and Giles (1978) suggested the use of a sign change test based on the number of sign changes occurring between pairs of residuals four observations apart. In a limited MC experiment, they compared the power of this test with that of Thomas and Wallis's test and the Wallis test. They concluded that in terms of power, the latter test is to be preferred.

More recently, King (1984) generalized his proposed solution for the AR(1) testing problem to that of testing H_0 against H_a^+ (or H_a^-) with respect to (2.1) and (11.2). He studied the test which rejects H_0 against H_a^+ (H_a^-) for small values of

$$s_4(\varrho_1) = \hat{u}'\Sigma_4^{-1}(\varrho_1)\hat{u}/e'e \ ,$$

where $\varrho_1 > 0$ ($\varrho_1 < 0$) is fixed and known and $\hat{u}$ is the GLS residual vector assuming covariance matrix $\Sigma_4(\varrho_1)$. By construction, this test is MPI in the neighbourhood of $\varrho = \varrho_1$ for all design matrices. It is also approximately

UMPI when the column space of X is spanned by some k eigenvectors of $\Sigma_4(\varrho_1)$. The null distribution of $s_4(\varrho_1)$ depends on the X matrix and its critical value can be calculated using the methods for finding d_α^* discussed in Section 4.2. King (1984) tabulated attainable bounds for the critical values of $s_4(0.5)$ for testing (i) regressions with an intercept and (ii) regressions with a full set of quarterly seasonal dummy variables against H_a^+. Tables of bounds for the use of $s_4(-0.5)$ as a test against H_a^- are also given.

King's choice of $\varrho_1 = 0.5$ was made as the result of an empirical comparison of the power of the Wallis, LBI, Webb, $s_4(0.25)$, $s_4(0.5)$ and $s_4(0.75)$ tests. He found that the $s_4(0.5)$ test is generally more powerful than the Wallis, LBI and Webb tests with the difference in power being slight for most economic applications. For certain design matrices for which OLS is relatively inefficient and for which a powerful test is most needed, the power advantage of the $s_4(0.5)$ test over the Wallis and LBI tests is very real. Hence a sensible strategy for minimizing the chance of making an incorrect inference in critical circumstances is to routinely use $s_4(0.5)$ rather than d_4 when testing against H_a^+.

As well as considering the simple AR(4) case, Vinod (1973) generalized the DW procedure to test against simple AR(j) disturbances. He published tables of bounds of the tests' critical values for $j = 2, 3, 4$. He also suggested a sequential test for general AR(4) disturbances along the following lines. At each stage a test against simple AR(j) disturbances is performed and if the null hypothesis is accepted then one tests against simple AR(j+1) disturbances. The sequence begins with the DW test against AR(1) disturbances and ends whenever a test rejects its null hypothesis of independent disturbances or after the last component test.

Dhrymes (1978, p. 402) objected to this sequential procedure on two counts. The first is that the significance level of the overall test is unknown because of the interdependence between the various component tests and the second objection is that it is not always clear how one should proceed if a null hypothesis is rejected. He suggested regressing the OLS residuals, e_t on e_{t-1}, e_{t-2}, e_{t-3} and e_{t-4} and applying a joint asymptotic significance test to the estimated coefficients.

Durbin (1980) also considered the problem of sequentially testing for higher-order autoregressive disturbances. He proposed the use of a particular form of the partial autocorrelation coefficient as the test statistic at each stage. Unfortunately, his analysis is based on the somewhat limiting assumption that one is testing the disturbances of a regression on Fourier series. He found that under the null hypothesis of independent disturbances, the partial autocorrelation coefficients follow, approximately, independent beta distributions.

The problem of testing against simple AR(j) disturbances in (2.1) for j = 2,3,8,12 has been studied by Evans (1983). For each j value she considered the LBI test as well as the jth order analogues of the DW, Berenblut and

Webb, and King (1984) tests. Empirical power comparisons led her to recommend the use of the $s_j(0.5)$ test which is the jth order analogue of the $s(0.5)$ and $s_4(0.5)$ tests. Some of these results are reported in Evans and King (1985b).

Mention should also be made of a paper by Pierce (1971) who generalized Box and Pierce's (1970) asymptotic test, in order to test against Autoregressive-Moving Average (ARMA) disturbances in (2.1). Because this is a test which assumes a wide range of models under the alternative hypothesis, its power against a particular alternative model is likely to be comparatively poor. It also relies on the OLS residuals converging to the true disturbances, a process which for some combinations of X matrices and ARMA disturbances, may be slow.

11.3 Tests against moving average disturbances

Until recently, very little attention has been given to the problem of detecting moving average disturbances in the linear regression model (2.1). The main emphasis has been on testing against MA(1) disturbances; i.e., testing $\text{H}_0 : \gamma = 0$ against $\text{H}_\text{a}^+ : \gamma > 0$ (or $\text{H}_\text{a}^- : \gamma < 0$, etc.) when the disturbances of (2.1) are generated by the MA(1) process

$$u_t = \varepsilon_t + \gamma\varepsilon_{t-1}, \quad \varepsilon_t \sim \text{IN}(0,\sigma^2), \quad t = 0, \ldots, n.$$

Observe that u, therefore, is distributed $\text{N}(0,\sigma^2\Sigma(\gamma))$, where

$$\Sigma(\gamma) = (1 + \gamma)^2 I_n - \gamma(A_1 + C_1). \tag{11.3}$$

As noted in Section 9, Blattberg (1973) and Smith (1976) both found the DW test to have good power against MA(1) disturbances. King (1979, 1983c) showed the DW test to be an approximately LBI test against MA(1) disturbances while the d' version of the DW test discussed in Section 4.7 is a true LBI test.

King (1979) also proposed the following simple exact test. The eigenvalues of (11.3) are

$$\lambda_t = \gamma^2 + 2\gamma\cos(\pi t/(n + 1)) + 1, \qquad t = 1, \ldots, n,$$

and the associated orthogonal eigenvectors are

$$\tau_t = (2/(n + 1))^{1/2}[\sin(\pi t/(n + 1)), \ldots, \sin(n\pi t/(n + 1))]'.$$

Transforming (2.1) by premultiplying by $T = (\tau_1, \tau_2, \ldots, \tau_n)$ yields a regression whose disturbances are homoscedastic under H_0 and heteroscedastic with variances

$$\sigma_t^2 = \sigma^2\lambda_t, \qquad t = 1, \ldots, n,$$

under H_a^+ (or H_a^-). Hence H_0 can be tested using Goldfeld and Quandt's

(1965) F test on the transformed regression. A limited empirical power comparison reported by King suggests that this test is less powerful than the exact DW test against H_a^+ but preferable to the use of the DW test with the lower bound as its critical value.

In a later paper, King (1983c) considered the class of tests which are MPI in a given neighbourhood of the alternative hypothesis of MA(1) disturbances. These tests reject H_0 against H_a^+ (H_a^-) for small values of

$$r(\gamma_1) = \hat{u}'\Sigma^{-1}(\gamma_1)\hat{u}/e'e ,$$

where $\gamma_1 > 0$ ($\gamma_1 < 0$) is fixed and known and $\hat{u}$ is the GLS residual vector assuming covariance matrix $\Sigma(\gamma_1)$. By construction, this test is MPI in the neighbourhood of $\gamma = \gamma_1$ for all design matrices. Its critical values can be calculated by methods similar to those discussed in Section 4.2. King tabulated attainable bounds for the critical values of $r(0.5)$ and $r(-0.5)$ applied to regressions with an intercept. In an empirical power comparison he found the $r(0.5)$ test to be more powerful than the DW test against H_a^+ whenever $\gamma \geqslant 0.3$, often by a reasonably large margin. Similar results were found for the $r(-0.5)$ test against H_a^-. An alternative method of calculating γ_1 is given in King (1985b).

11.4 Testing for AR(1) disturbances with missing observations

Savin and White (1978a)[31] investigated the problem of testing $H_0 : \varrho = 0$ against $H_a^+ : \varrho > 0$ in (2.1) when the disturbances follow the AR(1) process (3.1) but with m missing observations after the first n_1 observations. They observed that for this model, $Gu \sim N(0,\sigma^2 I_n)$, where G is the $n \times n$ matrix,

$$G = \begin{bmatrix}
\sqrt{1-\varrho^2} & 0 \;\cdots & 0 & 0 & 0 & 0 & \cdots & 0 \\
-\varrho & 1 & 0 & 0 & 0 & 0 & \cdots & 0 \\
\vdots & & \vdots & \vdots & \vdots & \vdots & & \vdots \\
0 & \cdots & -\varrho & 1 & 0 & 0 & \cdots & 0 \\
0 & \cdots & 0 & -g\varrho^{m+1} & g & 0 & \cdots & 0 \\
0 & \cdots & 0 & 0 & -\varrho & 1 & \cdots & 0 \\
\vdots & & \vdots & \vdots & \vdots & \vdots & & \vdots \\
0 & \cdots & 0 & 0 & 0 & 0 & \cdots -\varrho & 1
\end{bmatrix} \begin{matrix} \\ \\ \\ \leftarrow n_1^{\text{th}} \\ \text{row.} \\ \\ \\ \\ \end{matrix} ,$$

and $g^2 = (1 - \varrho^2)/(1 - \varrho^{2(m+1)})$. Hence $u \sim N(0,\sigma^2(G'G)^{-1})$. Savin and

White considered two DW-type tests.[32] The first is the usual DW test applied as if there are no missing observations and the second is based on the test statistic

$$d_* = e'A_*e/e'e ,$$

where

$$A_* = \begin{bmatrix} A_1(n_1) & 0 \\ 0 & A_1(n_2) \end{bmatrix} ,$$

$n_2 = n - n_1$ and $A_1(n_i)$, $i = 1, 2$, denotes the $n_i \times n_i$ first differencing matrix A_1 defined in Section 3.

Against H_a^+, both tests are approximately LBI. They are also approximately UMPI when the column space of X is spanned by k eigenvectors of the $n \times n$ matrix A_1 in the case of the former test and of A_* for the latter test. The results of Section 11.1 imply that rejecting H_0 for small values of $e'A_{**}e/e'e$ is a true LBI test against H_a^+ where A_{**} is A_* with all elements of the main diagonal taking the value two.

The advantage of the usual DW test for this problem is that one can make use of existing tables of bounds and algorithms for calculating the exact critical value of d. Because $d_* \leqslant d$, one can use tabulated DW upper bounds as upper bounds for the critical value of d_*. Richardson and White (1979) compared the power of the usual DW test with that of the d_* test for three data sets with various observations assumed missing. They concluded that neither test dominates the other, although the d_* test shows a tendency to be more powerful for larger m values and for larger ϱ values.

More recently, Dufour and Dagenais (1985) proposed a further two DW-type tests. The first, which is approximately LBI, is based on the application of the DW test to an expanded regression model with zero-one dummy variables as additional regressors. This allows the use of existing tables of bounds and critical value algorithms and approximations. The second test is the true LBI test discussed above which can be applied as King's (1981b) d' test on the expanded regression model.

11.5 Testing for random walk disturbances

Recently, Sargan and Bhargava (1983) considered the problem of testing the null hypothesis that the disturbances of (2.1) are generated by the Gaussian random walk process,

$$u_t = u_{t-1} + \varepsilon_t , \qquad t = 1, \ldots, n$$

where $\varepsilon_t \sim IN(0,\sigma^2)$, against the alternative that they are generated by the AR(1) process, (3.1). For regression models with an intercept term, three tests are proposed. Each is based on rejecting the null hypothesis for large values of the DW test statistic, the Berenblut and Webb test statistic and

$$R = \hat{e}'\hat{e}/\hat{e}'F\hat{e} ,$$

respectively, where $\hat{e}$ is the OLS residual vector from (2.1) in first-differenced form and F is the $(n-1) \times (n-1)$ matrix,

$$F = \frac{1}{n}\begin{bmatrix} n-1 & n-2 & n-3 & \ldots & 1 \\ n-2 & 2(n-2) & 2(n-3) & & 2 \\ n-3 & 2(n-3) & 3(n-3) & & 3 \\ \cdot & & & & \cdot \\ \cdot & & & & \cdot \\ \cdot & & & & \cdot \\ 1 & 2 & 3 & \ldots & n-1 \end{bmatrix} .$$

Sargan and Bhargava show that all three tests are approximately UMPI when the column space of X is spanned by k eigenvectors of the first-differencing matrix, A_1. For any X matrix which includes an intercept, the Berenblut and Webb based test is also approximately locally MPI in the neighbourhood of $\varrho = 0$ while the R test is locally MPI in the neighbourhood of $\varrho = 1$. A limited empirical power comparison reported by Sargan and Bhargava suggests that of the three tests, the Berenblut and Webb based test has the best power properties in small samples.

The related problem of testing for Gaussian random walk disturbances in the fixed effects linear regression model has been considered by Bhargava, Franzini and Narendranathan (1982). They discussed analogues of the tests suggested by Sargan and Bhargava (1983) and also generalized the DW test in order to test for serial independence in the fixed effects model.

11.6 Testing for spatial autocorrelation

Another problem which has attracted interest in the literature is that of testing for first-order spatial autoregression in (2.1). It is assumed that the disturbances are generated as

$$u = \varrho W u + \varepsilon ,$$

where the elements of the known $n \times n$ matrix W, $\{w_{ij}\}$, are such that $w_{ii} = 0$, $w_{1i} + \ldots + w_{ni} = 1$, $i = 1, \ldots n$, $|\varrho| < 1$ and $\varepsilon \sim \mathrm{N}(0,\sigma^2 I_n)$. Hence

$$u \sim \mathrm{N}(0, \sigma^2\{(I_n - \varrho W')(I_n - \varrho W)\}^{-1}).$$

The problem is one of testing $\mathrm{H}_0 : \varrho = 0$ against $\mathrm{H}_a^+ : \varrho > 0$ (or $\mathrm{H}_a^- : \varrho < 0$, etc.).

Based on the work of Anderson (1948), Moran (1950a, 1950b) and Durbin and Watson (1950), Cliff and Ord (1972) proposed the test which rejects H_0 against H_a^+ (H_a^-) for large (small) values of

$$I = e'We/e'e ,$$

where e is the OLS residual vector.[33] In their book, Cliff and Ord (1973) considered a number of other tests such as nonparametric tests, a test based on a generalization of Geary's (1954) coefficient and the above mentioned tests applied using Theil's (1965) BLUS residuals in place of OLS residuals. They concluded from a limited MC study that the test based on I appears to have the best power properties.

Further power studies by Bartels and Hordijk (1977) and Brandsma and Ketellapper (1979) support Cliff and Ord's conclusion. In the latter study, the LR test for this problem is found to perform comparatively poorly. More recently, Burridge (1980) demonstrated that the test based on I can be derived as a one-sided LM test while King (1981d) showed that it is LBI against H_a^+.

11.7 Testing against other forms of autocorrelation when a lagged dependent variable is a regressor

The tests against non-AR(1) forms of autocorrelation reviewed so far are generally considered not to be applicable when a lagged dependent variable is a regressor. We now review those test procedures that have been developed for such regression models.

Box and Pierce (1970) proposed test procedures for linear autoregressive models without exogenous regressors. A test against MA(1) disturbances in a simple linear autoregressive model was developed by Fitts (1973) using Durbin's (1970a) approach to the corresponding problem for AR(1) disturbances.

With respect to the more general regression model with a lagged dependent variable as a regressor, Kenward (1976) used Durbin's approach to construct a procedure for testing against general ARMA disturbances. Breusch (1978) and Godfrey (1978b) independently derived LM tests against various forms of ARMA disturbances. In particular, when the regression disturbances are assumed to be generated by the stationary AR(m) scheme

$$u_t = \varrho_1 u_{t-1} + \ldots + \varrho_m u_{t-m} + \varepsilon_t ,$$

where $\varepsilon_t \sim IN(0,\sigma^2)$, their test of $H_0 : (\varrho_1, \ldots, \varrho_m)' = 0$ against $H_a : (\varrho_1, \ldots, \varrho_m)' \neq 0$ is based on the statistic

$$l = e'U[U'U - U'X(X'X)^{-1}X'U]^{-1}U'e/\hat{\sigma}^2 ,$$

where e is the vector of OLS residuals, $U = [e_{-1}, \ldots, e_{-m}]$, e_{-i} is the

$n \times 1$ vector, $(0, \ldots, 0, e_1, \ldots, e_{n-i})'$, X is the matrix of observations on the regressors including lagged dependent variable regressors and $\hat{\sigma}^2 = e'e/n$. Under H_0 and suitable regularity conditions, l has an asymptotic $\chi^2(m)$ distribution. l is also the statistic for the LM test of $H_0 : (\gamma_1, \ldots, \gamma_m)' = 0$ against $H_a : (\gamma_1, \ldots, \gamma_m)' \neq 0$ when the disturbances are assumed to be generated by the MA(m) scheme

$$u_t = \varepsilon_t + \gamma_1\varepsilon_{t-1} + \ldots + \gamma_m\varepsilon_{t-m} ,$$

where $\varepsilon_t \sim IN(0,\sigma^2)$. That is the LM tests against AR(m) and MA (m) disturbances are identical and hence the LM test against MA(1) disturbances is asymptotically equivalent to Durbin's h test.

These LM tests are reviewed by Breusch and Pagan (1980)[34] who discussed their relationship to Pierce's (1971) test based on the autocorrelation function. Breusch and Pagan noted that for the regression model with a lagged dependent variable and exogenous variables as regressors, Pierce's test is inappropriate.

12 Concluding remarks

The vast literature concerned with testing for autocorrelation in the linear regression model is particularly rich in empirical comparisons of power functions of various test procedures under differing circumstances. Because power is the name of the game in any hypothesis testing problem, this broadens the interest in the following conclusions drawn from this literature.

It is noticeable that the design matrix has an important effect on both the relative and absolute power of many tests for serial correlation. For example, the relative power of the DW test against AR(1) disturbances is very good for an X matrix comprised of smoothly evolving regressors but for some design matrices, such as Watson's X matrix, both its relative and absolute power are particularly poor. Therefore, in any empirical comparison of powers, it is essential to include a range of X matrices with differing properties rather than design matrices comprised purely of smoothly evolving annual time series which was the case for many of the early studies. Far too many of the empirical studies reviewed above are based solely on the simple linear trend regression model. As noted in Section 8, the DW test is approximately UMPI for this particular X matrix so this choice of design matrix obviously favours the DW test.

It would seem that the LR test is a particularly unreliable test for serial correlation. Dent (1973) found it to have poor power against AR(1) disturbances in (2.1), while Brandsma and Ketellapper (1979) reported a similar finding for the LR test against first-order spatial autoregression. Maddala and Rao (1973) were so puzzled by the poor power of the LR test against AR(1) disturbances in the lagged dependent variable model, they repeated their calculations using a different algorithm for computing the MLE's. This is an especially interesting result in view of the high regard held for the LR test procedure in econometrics.

For the majority of hypothesis testing problems discussed in this paper, the one-sided LM test is a LBI test. This means that it has the steepest sloping power function in the neighbourhood of the null hypothesis amongst all power functions of invariant tests of the same significance level. However, this does not guarantee that the LM test is always the most suitable test. For example, its power against AR(1) disturbances tends to collapse for some design matrices such as Watson's X matrix. Against MA(1) disturbances, King's (1983c) $r(0.5)$ test is clearly preferable given its better power against moderate and large values of the MA(1) parameter.

The LR and LM test procedures have been widely adopted by the econometric profession in recent years because they provide methods of test construction for many testing problems. The above discussion suggests that they cannot always be relied upon to have good power. Hence they should not be recommended as the solution for a given hypothesis testing problem unless their power functions have been investigated empirically. Also most econometric testing problems are potentially one-sided problems because economic theory is usually good at providing information regarding the signs of various parameters. However, the LR and LM test procedures are generally applied as two-sided tests to make use of the familiar chi-squared approximations. Ignoring information about the signs of parameters may lead to a considerable loss of power in small samples.

Our main tool in the search for a powerful test is the Neyman-Pearson lemma which tells us that the LR test is the most powerful test of a simple null hypothesis against a simple alternative. However, most econometric hypothesis testing problems, even after reduction through invariance, involve at least one composite hypothesis. The question then is, how should the Neyman-Pearson lemma be applied in such cases? The conventional LR approach is to estimate the unknown parameters assuming the composite hypothesis to be true and then apply the Neyman-Pearson lemma. It is difficult to see why this should lead to a powerful test, especially if the estimates are biased and have high variance. Also note that the values of the parameters being estimated vary as the true model varies. On the other hand, the alternative approach of choosing fixed values for the unknown parameters under the composite hypothesis, appears to show promise, at least for the problems of testing against AR(1) (King, 1985a), simple AR(j) (King, 1984 and Evans, 1983) and MA(1) (King, 1983c, 1985b) disturbances in (2.1). In these three cases, this approach results in a test which is MPI in a pre-determined neighbourhood of the alternative hypothesis. Therefore, it might be expected to be more powerful than other invariant tests such as the LM and LR tests, at least for part of the alternative hypothesis parameter space. As a general hypothesis testing strategy, it certainly deserves further study.

Notes

1 This paper was largely written while I was a guest of Trinity College, Cambridge and the Department of Statistics at the University of Melbourne. I wish to thank both institutions for their hospitality. I am also grateful to Gene Savin for many long discussions on hypothesis testing in econometrics, to James Durbin for his personal recollections of Cambridge in the late 1940's, and to Bill Farebrother, Andrew Harvey, Alberto Holly and Peter Phillips for helpful comments on earlier drafts.

2 See Scheffé (1942) for the definition of a type B_1 test.

3 Alternatively, X may be stochastic but independent of u.

4 In his paper, Anderson actually considered testing H_0 with respect to $u \sim N(0,\sigma^2[\psi + \lambda\Theta]^{-1})$, where ψ and Θ are known $n \times n$ matrices such that $[\psi + \lambda\Theta]^{-1}$ is positive definite. Note that this can be reduced to (2.2) without loss of generality by an appropriate transformation of (2.1).

5 Also see Cochrane (1948) and Orcutt and Cochrane (1949).

6 Also see Watson and Durbin (1951).

7 See Farebrother (1984b) for a comparison of the performance of Koerts and Abrahamse's, Davies' and Farebrother's algorithms.

8 Because H_0 is rejected for large values of d against H_a^-, the $1 - \alpha$ significance point is used as the critical value.

9 Within the class of orthogonal X matrices, this is the X matrix Watson (1955) found causes the OLS estimator to have minimum efficiency relative to the best linear unbiased estimator under Tillman's approximation.

10 Recall that the DW test is an approximately LBI test.

11 Also see Theil (1971).

12 See Theil (1965, 1968), Koerts (1967), Neudecker (1969) and Grossman and Styan (1972) for results on the efficiency and optimality of BLUS residuals. Also see Chow (1976) for an alternative derivation of BLUS residuals.

13 Also see Styan (1973) and Savin and White (1978a).

14 A useful survey of these tests is given in Dubbelman (1978). In some cases it may be more accurate to call these residual vectors, disturbance estimators, but we shall not make this distinction.

15 For further developments on the AK BLUF residual vector, see Abrahamse and Louter (1971) and Neudecker (1977).

16 For further examples see Conover (1971), Kendall (1976), Dufour (1981) and Bartels (1984). Also an extensive bibliography on non-parametric testing for time series has been compiled by Dufour, Lepage and Zeidan (1982).

17 Robustness properties of the SC test are discussed in Section 9.

18 Also see Berenblut and Webb (1973, p. 49).

19 See Webb (1973) for more detailed proofs.

20 For example, for the 30×5 Watson's X matrix with an intercept, the power at $\varrho = 0.9$ of the five per cent DW test is 0.294 while that of the $s(0.5)$ test is 0.970. In the 15×5 case, the corresponding powers are 0.039 and 0.556, respectively.

21 The application of the LR test to the one-sided problem is much less straightforward since the familiar chi-squared approximation no longer applies.

22 Smith used the DW upper bound as the critical value for the DW test, but his choice of design matrix meant that this was a very good approximation to the true DW critical value (King, 1981c).

23 They report results for both von Neumann's ratio and the DW test but for their particular model these two test statistics coincide. Their results suggest the use of

an incorrect critical value for the test they call the DW test.
24 See the previous section for a discussion of the weaknesses of this experiment. Also, Smith's choice of the upper bounding line for the critical boundary of the CP test appears to be inappropriate.
25 Indeed, this warning is also valid for almost all the tests reviewed so far. It is not clear whether it applies to nonparametric tests.
26 Also see Breusch and Godfrey (1981) for a review of this literature.
27 See Park (1972) for a description of an earlier version of this study.
28 Durbin's h test followed by his t test if the h test is inapplicable.
29 Excluding $\varrho_1 = \varrho_2 = 0$. Schmidt is vague about the exact form of the alternative hypothesis. More strictly, it perhaps should be $H_a^* : \varrho_1 - \varrho_1\varrho_2/2 \geqslant 0, \varrho_2 \geqslant 0$, excluding $\varrho_1 = \varrho_2 = 0$.
30 Note that one set of eigenvectors associated with the zero roots of A_4 is the set of quarterly seasonal dummy variables.
31 Also see Wallis (1972), Dhrymes (1978, pp. 174-5) and Robinson (1985).
32 They also discussed LUS, LR and related tests.
33 The statistic I has been given various names in the literature including the Moran Coefficient, the Generalized Moran Contiguity Coefficient and the Cliff-Ord test statistic.
34 Also see Breusch and Pagan (1980) for a more comprehensive discussion of these particular LM tests.

References

Abrahamse, A.P.J., and Koerts, J. (1969), 'A Comparison Between the Power of the Durbin-Watson Test and the Power of the BLUS Test', *Journal of the American Statistical Association*, 64, 938-48.

Abrahamse, A.P.J., and Koerts, J. (1971), 'New Estimators of Disturbances in Regression Analysis', *Journal of the American Statistical Association*, 66, 71-4.

Abrahamse, A.P.J., and Louter, A.S. (1971), 'On a New Test for Autocorrelation in Least Squares Regression', *Biometrika*, 58, 53-60.

Aldrich, J. (1978), 'An Alternative Derivation of Durbin's *h* Statistic', *Econometrica*, 46, 1493-4.

Ali, M.M. (1983), 'A Note on Approximating the Distribution of the Durbin-Watson Statistic', *Journal of Time Series Analysis*, 4, 217-20.

Ali, M.M. (1984), 'An Approximation to the Null Distribution and Power of the Durbin-Watson Statistic', *Biometrika*, 71, 253-61.

Anderson, R.L. (1942), 'Distribution of the Serial Correlation Coefficient', *Annals of Mathematical Statistics*, 13, 1-13.

Anderson, R.L., and Anderson, T.W. (1950), 'Distribution of the Circular Serial Correlation Coefficient for Residuals from a Fitted Fourier Series', *Annals of Mathematical Statistics*, 21, 59-81.

Anderson, T.W. (1948), 'On the Theory of Testing Serial Correlation', *Skandinavisk Aktuarietidskrift*, 31, 88-116.

Bartels, C.P.A., and Hordijk, L. (1977), 'On the Power of the Generalized Moran Contiguity Coefficient in Testing for Spatial Autocorrelation Among Regression Disturbances', *Regional Science and Urban Economics*, 7, 83-101.

Bartels, R. (1984), 'The Rank Von Neumann Test as a Test for Autocorrelation in Regression Models', *Communications in Statistics—Theory and Methods*, 13, 2495-502.

Bartels, R., Bornholt, G., and Hanslow, K. (1982), 'The Polynomial Trend Model

with Autocorrelated Residuals', *Communications in Statistics – Theory and Methods*, 11, 1393-402.
Bartels, R., and Goodhew, J. (1981), 'The Robustness of the Durbin-Watson Test', *Review of Economics and Statistics*, 63, 136-9.
Belsley, D.A. (1973), 'The Relative Power of the τ-Test: A Furthering Comment', *Review of Economics and Statistics*, 55, 132.
Belsley, D.A. (1974), 'The τ-Test and High Order Serial Correlation: A Reply', *Review of Economics and Statistics*, 56, 417-8.
Bera, A.K., and Jarque, C.M. (1981), 'Efficient Tests for Normality, Homoscedasticity and Serial Independence of Regression Residuals: Monte Carlo Evidence', *Economics Letters*, 7, 313-8.
Bera, A.K., and Jarque, C.M. (1982), 'Model Specification Tests: A Simultaneous Approach', *Journal of Econometrics*, 20, 59-82.
Berenblut, I.I., and Webb, G.I. (1973), 'A New Test for Autocorrelated Errors in the Linear Regression Model', *Journal of the Royal Statistical Society B*, 35, 33-50.
Bhargava, A., Franzini, L., and Narendranathan, W. (1982), 'Serial Correlation and the Fixed Effects Model', *Review of Economic Studies*, 49, 533-49.
Blattberg, R.C. (1973), 'Evaluation of the Power of the Durbin-Watson Statistic for Non-First Order Serial Correlation Alternatives', *Review of Economics and Statistics*, 55, 508-15.
Box, G.E.P., and Jenkins, G.M. (1970), *Time Series Analysis: Forecasting and Control*, San Francisco: Holden-Day.
Box, G.E.P., and Pierce, D.A. (1970), 'Distribution of Residual Autocorrelations in Autoregressive-Integrated Moving Average Time Series Models', *Journal of the American Statistical Association*, 65, 1509-26.
Brandsma, A.S., and Ketellapper, R.H. (1979), 'Further Evidence on Alternative Procedures for Testing of Spatial Autocorrelation Among Regression Disturbances', in *Exploratory and Explanatory Statistical Analysis of Spatial Data*, eds. C.P.A. Bartels and R.H. Ketellapper, Boston: Martinus Nijhoff, 113-36.
Breusch, T.S. (1978), 'Testing for Autocorrelation in Dynamic Linear Models', *Australian Economic Papers*, 17, 334-55.
Breusch, T.S., and Godfrey, L.G. (1981), 'A Review of Recent Work on Testing for Autocorrelation in Dynamic Economic Models', in *Essays in Macroeconomics and Econometrics*, eds. D. Currie, R. Nobay and D. Peel, London: Croom Helm.
Breusch, T.S., and Pagan, A.R. (1980), 'The Lagrange Multiplier Test and Its Applications to Model Specification in Econometrics', *Review of Economic Studies*, 47, 239-53.
Burridge, P. (1980), 'On the Cliff-Ord Test for Spatial Correlation', *Journal of the Royal Statistical Society B*, 42, 107-8.
Cassing, S.A., and White, K.J. (1983), 'An Examination of the Eigenvector Condition in the Durbin-Watson Test', *The Australian Journal of Statistics*, 25, 17-22.
Chmielewski, M.A. (1981), 'Elliptically Symmetric Distributions: A Review and Bibliography', *International Statistical Review*, 49, 67-74.
Chow, G.C. (1976), 'A Note on the Derivation of Theil's BLUS Residuals', *Econometrica*, 44, 609-10.
Cleur, E.M. (1973), 'A Simulation Study on the Powers of Three Tests for Serial Correlation in the Errors from Least Squares Analysis', *Statistica*, 33, 285-300.
Cliff, A.D., and Ord, J.K. (1972), 'Testing for Spatial Autocorrelation Among Regression Residuals', *Geographical Analysis*, 4, 267-84.
Cliff, A.D., and Ord, J.K. (1973), *Spatial Autocorrelation*, London: Pion.

Cochrane, D. (1948), 'A Study in Demand Analysis', unpublished Ph.D. thesis, University of Cambridge.

Cochrane, D., and Orcutt, G.H. (1949), 'Application of Least Squares Regression to Relationships Containing Auto-Correlated Error Terms', *Journal of the American Statistical Association*, 44, 32-61.

Conover, W.J. (1971), *Practical Non-Parametric Statistics*, New York: Wiley.

Davies, R.B. (1980), 'Algorithm AS155. The Distribution of a Linear Combination of χ^2 Random Variables', *Applied Statistics*, 29, 323-33.

Davis, A.W. (1976), 'Statistical Distributions in Univariate and Multivariate Edgeworth Populations', *Biometrika*, 63, 661-70.

Dent, W.T. (1973), 'A Power Study of Several Tests for Autocorrelation', *New Zealand Economic Papers*, 7, 109-20.

Dent, W.T. (1974), 'An Analytic Approximation to the Distribution of the Durbin-Watson Statistic in Certain Alternative Cases', *Sankhyā B*, 36, 163-74.

Dent, W.T., and Cassing, S. (1978), 'On Durbin's and Sims' Residuals in Autocorrelation Tests', *Econometrica*, 46, 1489-92.

Dent, W.T. and Styan, G.P.H. (1978), 'Uncorrelated Residuals from Linear Models', *Journal of Econometrics*, 7, 211-25.

Dhrymes, P.J. (1971), *Distributed Lags: Problems of Estimation and Formulation*, San Francisco: Holden-Day.

Dhrymes, P.J. (1978), *Introductory Econometrics*, New York: Springer-Verlag.

Dixon, W. (1944), 'Further Contributions to the Problem of Serial Correlation', *Annals of Mathematical Statistics*, 15, 119-44.

Dubbelman, C. (1972), 'A Priori Fixed Covariance Matrices of Disturbance Estimators', *European Economic Review*, 3, 413-36.

Dubbelman, C. (1978), *Disturbances in the Linear Model: Estimation and Hypothesis Testing*, The Hague: Martinus Nijhoff.

Dubbelman, C., Abrahamse, A.P.J., and Koerts, J. (1972), 'A New Class of Disturbance Estimators in the General Linear Model', *Statistica Neerlandica*, 26, 127-41.

Dubbelman, C., Louter, A.S., and Abrahamse, A.P.J. (1978), 'On Typical Characteristics of Economic Time Series and the Relative Qualities of Five Autocorrelation Tests', *Journal of Econometrics*, 8, 295-306.

Dufour, J.-M. (1981), 'Rank Tests for Serial Dependence', *Journal of Time Series Analysis*, 2, 117-28.

Dufour, J.-M., and Dagenais, M.G. (1985), 'Durbin-Watson Tests for Serial Correlation in Regressions with Missing Observations', *Journal of Econometrics*, 27, 371-81.

Dufour, J.-M., Lepage, Y., and Zeidan, H. (1982), 'Nonparametric Testing for Time Series: A Bibliography', *The Canadian Journal of Statistics*, 10, 1-38.

Durbin, J. (1957), 'Testing for Serial Correlation in Systems of Simultaneous Regression Equations', *Biometrika*, 44, 370-7.

Durbin, J. (1969), 'Tests for Serial Correlation in Regression Analysis Based on the Periodogram of Least Squares Residuals', *Biometrika*, 56, 1-15.

Durbin, J. (1970a), 'Testing for Serial Correlation in Least Squares Regression When Some of the Regressors Are Lagged Dependent Variables', *Econometrica*, 38, 410-21.

Durbin, J. (1970b), 'An Alternative to the Bounds Test for Testing for Serial Correlation in Least Squares Regression', *Econometrica*, 38, 422-9.

Durbin, J. (1980), 'The Approximate Distribution of Partial Serial Correlation Coefficients Calculated from Residuals from Regression on Fourier Series', *Biometrika*, 67, 335-49.

Durbin, J., and Watson, G.S. (1950), 'Testing for Serial Correlation in Least Squares Regression I', *Biometrika*, 37, 409-28.

Durbin, J., and Watson, G.S. (1951), 'Testing for Serial Correlation in Least Squares Regression II', *Biometrika*, 38, 159-78.

Durbin, J., and Watson, G.S. (1971), 'Testing for Serial Correlation in Least Squares Regression III', *Biometrika*, 58, 1-19.

Epps, T.W., and Epps, M.L. (1977), 'The Robustness of Some Standard Tests for Autocorrelation and Heteroskedasticity When Both Problems Are Present', *Econometrica*, 45, 745-53.

Evans, G., and Patterson, K.D. (1985), 'The Lagrange Multiplier Test for Autocorrelation in the Presence of Linear Restrictions', *Economics Letters*, 17, 237-41.

Evans, M.A. (1983), 'Inference and Non-Ideal Conditions in the Linear Regression Model', unpublished Ph.D. thesis, Monash University.

Evans, M.A. (1986), 'BLUF Disturbance Estimators with Quarterly Seasonal Economic Data', *Journal of Quantitative Economics*, 2, 19-32.

Evans, M.A., and King, M.L. (1985a), 'Critical Value Approximations for Tests of Linear Regression Disturbances', *Australian Journal of Statistics*, 27, 68-83.

Evans, M.A., and King, M.L. (1985b), 'Higher Order Generalisations of First Order Autoregressive Tests', *Communications in Statistics—Theory and Methods*, 14, 2907-18.

Farebrother, R.W. (1980a), 'Algorithm AS153. Pan's Procedure for the Tail Probabilities of the Durbin-Watson Statistic', *Applied Statistics*, 29, 224-7 and 30, 189.

Farebrother, R.W. (1980b), 'The Durbin-Watson Test for Serial Correlation When There Is No Intercept in the Regression', *Econometrica*, 48, 1553-63 and 49, 227.

Farebrother, R.W. (1984a), 'The Distribution of a Linear Combination of Central χ^2 Random Variables. A Remark on AS153: Pan's Procedure for the Tail Probabilities of the Durbin-Watson Statistic', *Applied Statistics*, 33, 363-6.

Farebrother, R.W. (1984b), 'A Remark on Algorithms AS106, AS153 and AS155: The Distribution of a Linear Combination of χ^2 Random Variables', *Applied Statistics*, 33, 366-9.

Fitts, J. (1973), 'Testing for Autocorrelation in the Autoregressive Moving Average Error Model', *Journal of Econometrics*, 1, 363-76.

Fomby, T.B., and Guilkey, D.K. (1978), 'On Choosing the Optimal Level of Significance for the Durbin-Watson Test and the Bayesian Alternative', *Journal of Econometrics*, 8, 203-13.

Fraser, D.A.S., Guttman, I., and Styan, G.P.H. (1976), 'Serial Correlation and Distributions on the Sphere', *Communications in Statistics*, A5, 97-118.

Fuller, W.A. (1976), *Introduction to Statistical Time Series*, New York: Wiley.

Gastwirth, J.L., and Selwyn, M.R. (1980), 'The Robustness Properties of Two Tests for Serial Correlation', *Journal of the American Statistical Association*, 75, 138-41.

Geary, R.C. (1954), 'The Contiguity Ratio and Statistical Mapping', *The Incorporated Statistician*, 5, 115-45.

Geary, R.C. (1970), 'Relative Efficiency of Count of Sign Changes for Assessing Residual Autoregression in Least Squares Regression', *Biometrika*, 57, 123-7.

Giles, D.E.A., and Beattie, M. (1987), 'Autocorrelation Pre-Test Estimation in Models with a Lagged Dependent Variable', Chapter 6 of this volume.

Giles, D.E.A., and King, M.L. (1978), 'Fourth-Order Autocorrelation: Further Significance Points for the Wallis Test', *Journal of Econometrics*, 8, 255-9.

Godfrey, L.G. (1976), 'Testing for Serial Correlation in Dynamic Simultaneous Equation Models', *Econometrica*, 44, 1077-84.

Godfrey, L.G. (1978a), 'A Note on the Use of Durbin's *h* Test When the Equation Is Estimated by Instrumental Variables', *Econometrica*, 46, 225-8.
Godfrey, L.G. (1978b), 'Testing Against General Autoregressive and Moving Average Error Models When the Regressors Include Lagged Dependent Variables', *Econometrica*, 46, 1293-301.
Godfrey, L.G. (1978c), 'Testing for Higher Order Serial Correlation in Regression Equations When the Regressors Include Lagged Dependent Variables', *Econometrica*, 46, 1303-10.
Godolphin, E.J., and De Tullio, M. (1978), 'Invariance Properties of Uncorrelated Residual Transformations', *Journal of the Royal Statistical Society B*, 40, 313-21.
Goldfeld, S.M., and Quandt, R.E. (1965), 'Some Tests for Homoscedasticity', *Journal of the American Statistical Association*, 60, 539-47.
Golub, G.H. (1965), 'Numerical Methods for Solving Linear Least Squares Problems', *Numerische Mathematik*, 7, 206-16.
Golub, G.H., and Styan, G.P.H. (1973), 'Numerical Computations for Univariate Linear Models', *Journal of Statistical Computation and Simulation*, 2, 253-74.
Griffiths, W.E., and Beesley, P.A.A. (1984), 'The Small-Sample Properties of Some Preliminary Test Estimators in a Linear Model with Autocorrelated Errors', *Journal of Econometrics*, 25, 49-61.
Griliches, Z., Maddala, G.S., Lucas, R., and Wallace, N. (1962), 'Notes on Estimated Aggregate Quarterly Consumption Functions', *Econometrica*, 30, 491-500.
Grossman, S.I., and Styan, G.P.H. (1972), 'Optimality Properties of Theil's BLUS Residuals', *Journal of the American Statistical Association*, 67, 672-3.
Guilkey, D.K. (1974), 'Alternative Tests for a First-Order Vector Autoregressive Error Specification', *Journal of Econometrics*, 2, 95-104.
Guilkey, D.K. (1975), 'A Test for the Presence of First-Order Vector Autoregressive Errors When Lagged Endogenous Variables Are Present', *Econometrica*, 43, 711-7.
Habibagahi, H., and Pratschke, J.L. (1972), 'A Comparison of the Power of the von Neumann Ratio, Durbin-Watson and Geary Tests', *Review of Economics and Statistics*, 54, 179-85.
Hannan, E.J. (1955), 'Exact Tests for Serial Correlation', *Biometrika*, 42, 133-42.
Hannan, E.J. (1957), 'Testing for Serial Correlation in Least Squares Regression', *Biometrika*, 44, 57-66.
Hannan, E.J. (1969), 'A Note on an Exact Test for Trend and Serial Correlation', *Econometrica*, 37, 485-9.
Hannan, E.J. (1970), *Multiple Time Series*, New York: Wiley.
Hannan, E.J., and Terrell, R.D. (1968), 'Testing for Serial Correlation after Least Squares Regression', *Econometrica*, 36, 133-50.
Harrison, M.J. (1972), 'On Testing for Serial Correlation in Regression When the Bounds Test Is Inconclusive,' *Economic and Social Review*, 4, 41-57.
Harrison, M.J. (1975), 'The Power of the Durbin-Watson and Geary Tests: Comment and Further Evidence', *Review of Economics and Statistics*, 57, 377-9.
Harrison, M.J., and McCabe, B.P.M. (1975), 'Autocorrelation with Heteroscedasticity: A Note on the Robustness of the Durbin-Watson, Geary and Henshaw Tests', *Biometrika*, 62, 214-5.
Hart, B.I. (1942a), 'Tabulation of the Probabilities for the Ratio of the Mean Square Successive Difference to the Variance', *Annals of Mathematical Statistics*, 13, 207-14.
Hart, B.I. (1942b), 'Significance Levels for the Ratio of the Mean Square Successive Difference to the Variance', *Annals of Mathematical Statistics*, 13, 445-7.

Harvey, A.C., and Phillips, G.D.A. (1980), 'Testing for Serial Correlation in Simultaneous Equation Models', *Econometrica*, 48, 747-59.
Harvey, A.C., and Phillips, G.D.A. (1981), 'Testing for Serial Correlation in Simultaneous Equation Models: Some Further Results', *Journal of Econometrics*, 17, 99-105.
Henshaw, R.C. (1966), 'Testing Single-Equation Least Squares Regression Models for Autocorrelated Disturbances', *Econometrica*, 34, 646-60.
Hsu, P.L. (1946), 'On the Asymptotic Distributions of Certain Statistics Used in Testing the Independence between Successive Observations from a Normal Population', *Annals of Mathematical Statistics*, 17, 350-4.
Imhof, P.J. (1961), 'Computing the Distribution of Quadratic Forms in Normal Variables', *Biometrika*, 48, 419-26.
Inder, B.A. (1984), 'Finite-Sample Power of Tests for Autocorrelation in Models Containing Lagged Dependent Variables', *Economics Letters*, 14, 179-85, and 16, 401-2.
Inder, B.A. (1985a), 'Testing for First Order Autoregressive Disturbances in the Dynamic Linear Regression Model', unpublished Ph.D. thesis, Monash University.
Inder, B.A. (1985b), 'A New Test for Autocorrelation in the Disturbances of the Dynamic Linear Regression Model', paper presented at the Fifth World Congress of the Econometric Society, Boston.
Inder, B.A. (1986), 'An Approximation to the Null Distribution of the Durbin-Watson Statistic in Models Containing Lagged Dependent Variables', *Econometric Theory*, forthcoming.
Jarque, C.M., and Bera, A.K. (1980), 'Efficient Tests for Normality, Homoscedasticity and Serial Independence of Regression Residuals', *Economics Letters*, 6, 255-9.
Jeong, K.J. (1985), 'A New Approximation of the Critical Point of the Durbin-Watson Test for Serial Correlation', *Econometrica*, 53, 477-82.
Johnston, J. (1972), *Econometric Methods*, 2nd ed., New York: McGraw-Hill.
Judge, G.G., and Bock, M.E. (1978), *The Statistical Implications of Pre-Test and Stein-Rule Estimators in Econometrics*, Amsterdam: North-Holland.
Judge, G.G., Griffiths, W.E., Hill, R.C., and Lee, T-C. (1980), *The Theory and Practice of Econometrics*, New York: Wiley.
Kadiyala, K.R. (1970), 'Testing for the Independence of Regression Disturbances', *Econometrica*, 38, 97-117.
Kariya, T. (1977), 'A Robustness Property of the Tests for Serial Correlation', *The Annals of Statistics*, 5, 1212-20.
Kariya, T. (1980), 'Locally Robust Tests for Serial Correlation in Least Squares Regression', *The Annals of Statistics*, 8, 1065-70.
Kariya, T., and Eaton, M.L. (1977), 'Robust Tests for Spherical Symmetry', *The Annals of Statistics*, 5, 206-15.
Kendall, M.G. (1976), *Time-Series*, 2nd ed., London: Griffin.
Kenkel, J.L. (1974), 'Some Small-Sample Properties of Durbin's Tests for Serial Correlation in Regression Models Containing Lagged Dependent Variables', *Econometrica*, 42, 763-9.
Kenkel, J.L. (1975), 'Small-Sample Tests for Serial Correlation in Models Containing Lagged Dependent Variables', *Review of Economics and Statistics*, 57, 383-6.
Kenkel, J.L. (1976), 'Comment on the Small-Sample Power of Durbin's *h*-Test', *Journal of the American Statistical Association*, 71, 96-7.
Kenward, L.R. (1976), 'A New Test for Residual Randomness in a Class of Dynamic

Autocorrelated Econometric Models', *Canadian Journal of Statistics*, 4, 51-64.
King, M.L. (1979), 'Some Aspects of Statistical Inference in the Linear Regression Model', unpublished Ph.D. thesis, University of Canterbury.
King, M.L. (1980a), 'Robust Tests for Spherical Symmetry and Their Application to Least Squares Regression', *The Annals of Statistics*, 8, 1265-71.
King, M.L. (1980b), 'The Durbin-Watson Test for Serial Correlation: Bounds for Regressions with Trend and/or Seasonal Dummy Variables', Department of Econometrics and O.R., Monash University, Working Paper No. 12/80.
King, M.L. (1980c), 'Small Sample Properties of Econometric Estimators and Tests Assuming Elliptically Symmetric Disturbances', paper presented to the Fourth World Congress of the Econometric Society, Aix-en-Provence, France.
King, M.L. (1981a), 'The Durbin-Watson Test and Regressions Without an Intercept', *Australian Economic Papers*, 20, 161-70.
King, M.L. (1981b), 'The Alternative Durbin-Watson Test: An Assessment of Durbin and Watson's Choice of Test Statistic', *Journal of Econometrics*, 17, 51-66.
King, M.L. (1981c), 'The Durbin-Watson Test for Serial Correlation: Bounds for Regressions with Trend and/or Seasonal Dummy Variables', *Econometrica*, 49, 1571-81.
King, M.L. (1981d), 'A Small Sample Property of the Cliff-Ord Test for Spatial Correlation', *Journal of the Royal Statistical Society B*, 43, 263-4.
King, M.L. (1982), 'Testing for a Serially Correlated Component in Regression Disturbances', *International Economic Review*, 23, 577-82.
King, M.L. (1983a), 'Testing for Autoregressive Against Moving Average Errors in the Linear Regression Model', *Journal of Econometrics*, 21, 35-51.
King, M.L. (1983b), 'The Durbin-Watson Test for Serial Correlation: Bounds for Regressions Using Monthly Data', *Journal of Econometrics*, 21, 357-66.
King, M.L. (1983c), 'Testing for Moving Average Regression Disturbances', *Australian Journal of Statistics*, 25, 23-34.
King, M.L. (1984), 'A New Test for Fourth-Order Autoregressive Disturbances', *Journal of Econometrics*, 24, 269-77.
King, M.L. (1985a), 'A Point Optimal Test for Autoregressive Disturbances', *Journal of Econometrics*, 27, 21-37.
King, M.L. (1985b), 'A Point Optimal Test for Moving Average Regression Disturbances', *Econometric Theory*, 1, 211-22.
King, M.L. (1986), 'Efficient Estimation and Testing of Regressions with a Serially Correlated Error Component', *Journal of Quantitative Economics*, 2, 231-47.
King, M.L., and Evans, M.A. (1984), 'A Joint Test for Serial Correlation and Heteroscedasticity', *Economics Letters*, 16, 297-302.
King, M.L., and Evans, M.A. (1985), 'The Durbin-Watson Test and Cross-Sectional Data', *Economics Letters*, 18, 31-4.
King, M.L., and Evans, M.A. (1986a), 'Testing for Block Effects in Regression Models Based on Survey Data', *Journal of the American Statistical Association*, 81, 677-9.
King, M.L., and Evans, M.A. (1986b), 'Locally Optimal Properties of the Durbin-Watson Test', mimeo, Monash University.
King, M.L., and Giles, D.E.A. (1977), 'A Note on Wallis' Bounds Test and Negative Autocorrelation', *Econometrica*, 45, 1023-6.
King, M.L., and Giles, D.E.A. (1978), 'A Comparison of Some Tests for Fourth-Order Autocorrelation', *Australian Economic Papers*, 17, 323-33.
King, M.L., and Giles, D.E.A. (1984), 'Autocorrelation Pre-Testing in the Linear Model: Estimation, Testing and Prediction', *Journal of Econometrics*, 25, 35-48.

King, M.L., and Hillier, G.H. (1985), 'Locally Best Invariant Tests of the Error Covariance Matrix of the Linear Regression Model', *Journal of the Royal Statistical Society B*, 47, 98-102.

King, M.L., and Inder, B.A. (1983), 'Testing the Covariance Matrix of the Linear Regression Model: Some Further Results', mimeo, Monash University.

King, M.L., and McAleer, M. (1984), 'Further Results on Testing AR(1) Against MA(1) Disturbances in the Linear Regression Model', paper presented at the Australasian Meeting of the Econometric Society, Sydney.

King, M.L., and Skeels, C.L. (1984), 'Joint Testing for Serial Correlation and Heteroscedasticity in the Linear Regression Model', paper presented at the Australasian Meeting of the Econometric Society, Sydney.

Klein, L.R. (1947), 'The Use of Econometric Models as a Guide to Economic Policy', *Econometrica*, 15, 111-51.

Knight, J.L. (1983), 'The Sensitivity of the Durbin-Watson Statistic to the Assumption of Normal Disturbances', paper presented at the European Meeting of the Econometric Society, Pisa.

Koerts, J. (1967), 'Some Further Notes on Disturbance Estimates in Regression Analysis', *Journal of the American Statistical Association*, 62, 169-83.

Koerts, J., and Abrahamse, A.P.J. (1968), 'On the Power of the BLUS Procedure', *Journal of the American Statistical Association*, 63, 1227-36.

Koerts, J., and Abrahamse, A.P.J. (1969), *On the Theory and Application of the General Linear Model*, Rotterdam: Rotterdam University Press.

Koopmans, T.C. (1942), 'Serial Correlation and Quadratic Forms in Normal Variables', *Annals of Mathematical Statistics*, 13, 14-33.

Kramer, G. (1971), 'On the Durbin-Watson Bounds Test in the Case of Regression Through the Origin', *Jahrbucher für Nationalökonomie und Satistik*, 185, 345-58.

Krämer, W. (1985), 'The Power of the Durbin-Watson Test for Regressions Without an Intercept', *Journal of Econometrics*, 28, 363-70.

Krishnaiah, P. R., and Murthy, V.K. (1966), 'Simultaneous Tests for Trend and Serial Correlation for Gaussian Markoff Residuals', *Econometrica*, 34, 472-80.

Lee, L.-F. (1984), 'The Likelihood Function and a Test for Serial Correlation in a Disequilibrium Market Model', *Economics Letters*, 14, 195-200.

Lehmann, E.L. (1947), 'On Optimum Tests of Composite Hypotheses with One Constraint', *Annals of Mathematical Statistics*, 18, 473-94.

Lehmann, E.L. (1959), *Testing Statistical Hypotheses*, New York: Wiley.

Lehmann, E.L., and Stein, C. (1948), 'Most Powerful Tests of Composite Hypotheses, I. Normal Distributions', *Annals of Mathematical Statistics*, 19, 495-516.

Leipnik, R.B. (1947), 'Distribution of the Serial Correlation Coefficient in a Circularly Correlated Universe', *Annals of Mathematical Statistics*, 18, 80-7.

L'Esperance, W.L., Chall, D., and Taylor, D. (1976), 'An Algorithm for Determining the Distribution Function of the Durbin-Watson Test', *Econometrica*, 44, 1325-6.

L'Esperance, W.L., and Taylor, D. (1975), 'The Power of Four Tests of Autocorrelation in the Linear Regression Model', *Journal of Econometrics*, 3, 1-21.

Maddala, G.S. (1977), *Econometrics*, Tokyo: McGraw-Hill Kogakusha.

Maddala, G.S., and Rao, A.S. (1973), 'Tests for Serial Correlation in Regression Models with Lagged Dependent Variables and Serially Correlated Errors', *Econometrica*, 41, 761-74.

Madow, W.G. (1945), 'Note on the Distribution of the Serial Correlation Coefficient', *Annals of Mathematical Statistics*, 16, 308-10.

Malinvaud, E. (1966), *Statistical Methods of Econometrics*, Amsterdam: North-Holland.
Maritz, A. (1978), 'A Note of Correction to Guilkey's Test for Serial Independence in Simultaneous Equations Models', *Econometrica*, 46, 471.
Mauchly, J.W. (1940), 'Significance Test for Sphericity of a Normal n-Variate Distribution', *Annals of Mathematical Statistics*, 11, 204-9.
McGregor, J.R. (1960), 'An Approximate Test for Serial Correlation in Polynomial Regression', *Biometrika*, 47, 111-9.
McNown, R.F., and Hunter, K.R. (1980), 'A Test for Autocorrelation in Models with Lagged Dependent Variables', *The Review of Economics and Statistics*, 62, 313-7.
Moran, P.A.P. (1950a), 'Notes on Continuous Stochastic Phenomena', *Biometrika*, 37, 17-23.
Moran, P.A.P. (1950b), 'A Test for the Serial Independence of Residuals', *Biometrika*, 37, 178-81.
Murray, G.L. (1976), 'The Existence of Durbin's *h*-Statistic', *Australian Economic Papers*, 15, 321-2.
Nakamura, A., and Nakamura, M. (1978), 'On the Impact of the Tests for Serial Correlation upon the Test of Significance for the Regression Coefficient', *Journal of Econometrics*, 7, 199-210.
Nerlove, M., and Wallis, K.F. (1966), 'Use of the Durbin-Watson Statistic in Inappropriate Situations', *Econometrica*, 34, 235-8.
Neudecker, H. (1969), 'A Note on BLUS Estimation', *Journal of the American Statistical Association*, 64, 949-52.
Neudecker, H. (1977), 'Abrahamse and Koerts' 'New Estimator' of Disturbances in Regression Analysis', *Journal of Econometrics*, 5, 129-33.
Ogawara, M. (1951), 'A Note on the Test of Serial Correlation Coefficients', *Annals of Mathematical Statistics*, 22, 115-8.
Orcutt, G.H., and Cochrane, D. (1949), 'A Sampling Study of the Merits of Autoregressive and Reduced Form Transformations in Regression Analysis', *Journal of the American Statistical Association*, 44, 356-72.
Owen, A.D. (1981), 'The Power of Alternative Tests for Serial Correlation in Dynamic Models Estimated by Instrumental Variables', *Journal of Statistical Computation and Simulation*, 12, 81-91.
Pagan, A.R., and Hall, A.D. (1983), 'Diagnostic Tests as Residual Analysis', *Econometric Reviews*, 2, 159-218.
Palm, F.C. and Sneek, J.M. (1984), 'Significance Tests and Spurious Correlation in Regression Models with Autocorrelated Errors', *Statistische Hefte*, 25, 87-105.
Pan Jie-Jian (1968), 'Distribution of Noncircular Serial Correlation Coefficients', *Selected Translations in Mathematical Statistics and Probability*, 7, 281-91.
Park, S. (1972), 'Some Small-Sample Properties of Durbin's *h* Statistic', *American Statistical Association 1972 Proceedings of the Business and Economic Statistics Section*, 413-9.
Park, S. (1975), 'On the Small-Sample Power of Durbin's *h* Test', *Journal of the American Statistical Association*, 70, 60-3.
Park, S. (1976), 'Rejoinder to "Comment on the Small-Sample Power of Durbin's *h*-Test" ', *Journal of the American Statistical Association*, 71, 97-8.
Phillips, G.D.A., and Harvey, A.C. (1974), 'A Simple Test for Serial Correlation in Regression Analysis', *Journal of the American Statistical Association*, 69, 935-9.
Phillips, P.C.B., and Wickens, M.R. (1978), *Exercises in Econometrics, Vol. 2*, Oxford: Philip Allan.
Pierce, D.A. (1971), 'Distribution of Residual Autocorrelations in the Regression

Model with Autoregressive-Moving Average Errors', *Journal of the Royal Statistical Society B*, 33, 140-6.

Praetz, P.D. (1987), 'Some Aspects of Mis-Specification in the Linear Model', Chapter 7 of this volume.

Press, S.J. (1969), 'On Serial Correlation', *Annals of Mathematical Statistics*, 40, 188-96.

Press, S.J., and Brooks, R.B. (1969), 'Testing for Serial Correlation in Regression', unpublished manuscript, Report No. 6911, Center for Mathematical Studies in Business and Economics, University of Chicago.

Ramsey, J.B. (1969), 'Tests for Specification Errors in Classical Linear Least-Squares Regression Analysis', *Journal of the Royal Statistical Society B*, 31, 350-71.

Revankar, N.S. (1980), 'Analysis of Regressions Containing Serially Correlated and Serially Uncorrelated Error Components', *International Economic Review*, 21, 185-99.

Richardson, S.M., and White, K.J. (1979), 'The Power of Tests for Autocorrelation with Missing Observations', *Econometrica*, 47, 785-8.

Robinson, P.M. (1985), 'Testing for Serial Correlation in Regression with Missing Observations', *Journal of the Royal Statistical Society*, 47, 429-37.

Robinson, P.M., Bera, A.K., and Jarque, C.M. (1985), 'Tests for Serial Dependence in Limited Dependent Variable Models', *International Economic Review*, 26, 629-38.

Rubin, H. (1945), 'On the Distribution of the Serial Correlation Coefficient', *Annals of Mathematical Statistics*, 16, 211-5.

Sargan, J.D. (1964), 'Wages and Prices in the United Kingdom: A Study in Econometric Methodology', in *Econometric Analysis for National Economic Planning*, eds. P.E. Hart, G. Mills and J.K. Whitaker, London: Butterworths, 25-63.

Sargan, J.D. (1975), 'Testing for Misspecification after Estimating Using Instrumental Variables', mimeo, London School of Economics.

Sargan, J.D., and Bhargava, A. (1983), 'Testing Residuals from Least Squares Regression for Being Generated by the Gaussian Random Walk', *Econometrica*, 51, 153-74.

Sargan, J.D. and Tse, Y.K. (1981), 'Edgeworth Approximations to the Distributions of Various Test Statistics', in *Proceedings of the Econometric Society European Meeting 1979*, ed. E.G. Charatsis, Amsterdam: North-Holland, 281-95.

Savin, N.E., and White, K.J. (1977), 'The Durbin-Watson Test for Serial Correlation with Extreme Sample Sizes or Many Regressors', *Econometrica*, 45, 1989-96.

Savin, N.E., and White, K.J. (1978a), 'Testing for Autocorrelation with Missing Observations', *Econometrica*, 46, 59-67.

Savin, N.E., and White, K.J. (1978b), 'Estimation and Testing for Functional Form and Autocorrelation: A Simultaneous Approach', *Journal of Econometrics*, 8, 1-12.

Scheffé, H. (1942), 'On the Theory of Testing Composite Hypotheses with One Constraint', *Annals of Mathematical Statistics*, 13, 280-93.

Schmidt, P. (1972), 'A Generalization of the Durbin-Watson Test', *Australian Economic Papers*, 11, 203-9.

Schmidt, P., and Guilkey, D.K. (1975), 'Some Further Evidence on the Power of the Durbin-Watson and Geary Tests', *Review of Economics and Statistics*, 57, 379-82.

Schmidt, P., and Guilkey, D.K. (1982), 'An Improved Version of the Geary Test', *Communications in Statistics – Theory and Methods*, 11, 359-74.

Sims, C.A. (1975), 'A Note on Exact Tests for Serial Correlation', *Journal of the American Statistical Association*, 70, 162-5.
Smith, V.K. (1976), 'The Estimated Power of Several Tests for Autocorrelation with Non-First-Order Alternatives', *Journal of the American Statistical Association*, 71, 879-83.
Smith, V.K. (1977), 'A Note on the Power of the Cumulated Periodogram Test for Autocorrelation', *European Economic Review*, 9, 373-7.
Smith, V.K. (1978), 'A Note on the Power of the Durbin-Watson Test with 2SLS (Two-Stage Least Squares)', *Journal of Statistical Computation and Simulation*, 7, 115-22.
Spencer, B.G. (1975), 'The Small Sample Bias of Durbin's Tests for Serial Correlation When One of the Regressors Is the Lagged Dependent Variable and the Null Hypothesis Is True', *Journal of Econometrics*, 3, 249-54.
Styan, G.P.H. (1973), 'LUSH and Other Uncorrelated Residuals from Linear Models', *Canadian Journal of Statistics*, 1, 131-2.
Swed, F.S., and Eisenhart, C. (1943), 'Tables for Testing Randomness of Grouping in a Sequence of Alternatives', *Annals of Mathematical Statistics*, 14, 66-87.
Theil, H. (1965), 'The Analysis of Disturbances in Regression Analysis', *Journal of the American Statistical Association*, 60, 1067-79.
Theil, H. (1968), 'A Simplification of the BLUS Procedure for Analyzing Regression Disturbances', *Journal of the American Statistical Association*, 63, 242-51.
Theil, H. (1971), *Principles of Econometrics*, New York: Wiley.
Theil, H., and Nagar, A.L. (1961), 'Testing the Independence of Regression Disturbances', *Journal of the American Statistical Association*, 56, 793-806.
Theil, H., and Shonkwiler, J.S. (1986), 'Monte Carlo Tests of Autocorrelation', *Economics Letters*, 20, 157-60.
Thomas, J.J., and Wallis, K.F. (1971), 'Seasonal Variation in Regression Analysis', *Journal of the Royal Statistical Society A*, 134, 57-72.
Tiao, G.C., and Guttman, I. (1967), 'Analysis of Outliers with Adjusted Residuals', *Technometrics*, 9, 541-59.
Tillman, J.A. (1974), 'The Relative Power of the τ-Test: A Comment', *Review of Economics and Statistics*, 56, 416-7.
Tillman, J.A. (1975), 'The Power of the Durbin-Watson Test', *Econometrica*, 43, 959-74.
Tse, Y.K. (1985), 'Some Modified Versions of Durbin's h-Statistic', *Review of Economics and Statistics*, 67, 534-8.
Vinod, H.D. (1973), 'Generalization of the Durbin-Watson Statistic for Higher Order Autoregressive Processes', *Communications in Statistics*, 2, 115-44.
Von Neumann, J. (1941), 'Distribution of the Ratio of the Mean Square Successive Difference to the Variance', *Annals of Mathematical Statistics*, 12, 367-95.
Von Neumann, J. (1942), 'A Further Remark Concerning the Distribution of the Ratio of the Mean Square Successive Differences to the Variance', *Annals of Mathematical Statistics*, 13, 86-8.
Von Neumann, J., Kent, R.H., Bellinson, H.R., and Hart, B.I. (1941), 'The Mean Square Successive Difference', *Annals of Mathematical Statistics*, 12, 153-62.
Wallis, K.F. (1972), 'Testing for Fourth Order Autocorrelation in Quarterly Regression Equations', *Econometrica*, 40, 617-36.
Ward, L.L. (1973), 'Is Uncorrelating the Residuals Worth It?', unpublished M.Sc. thesis, McGill University.
Watson, G.S. (1955), 'Serial Correlation in Regression Analysis I', *Biometrika*, 42, 327-41.
Watson, G.S., and Durbin, J. (1951), 'Exact Tests of Serial Correlation Using Non-

Circular Statistics', *Annals of Mathematical Statistics*, 22, 446-51.
Webb, G.I. (1973), 'Autocorrelations and the General Linear Model', unpublished Ph.D. thesis, The City University, London.
Weber, J.E., and Monarchi, D.E. (1982), 'Performance of the Durbin-Watson Test and WLS Estimation When the Disturbance Term Includes Serial Dependence in Additional to First-Order Autocorrelation', *Journal of the American Statistical Association*, 77, 117-28.
Williams, J.D. (1941), 'Moments of the Ratio of the Mean Square Successive Difference to the Mean Square Difference in Samples from a Normal Universe', *Annals of Mathematical Statistics*, 12, 239-41.
Young, L.C. (1941), 'On Randomness in Ordered Sequences', *Annals of Mathematical Statistics*, 12, 293-300.

4 Linear regression with correlated errors: bounds on coefficient estimates and t-values

Grant H. Hillier and Maxwell L. King

1 Introduction

In the classical $n \times k$ linear regression model

$$y = X\beta + u \tag{1}$$

with $E(u) = 0$, $\text{Var}(u) = \sigma^2\Sigma$, the Ordinary Least Squares (OLS) estimator

$$\hat{\beta} = (X'X)^{-1}X'y$$

is Best Linear Unbiased (BLU) if, and only if, $X = \Sigma^*C$, where the columns of the $n \times k$ matrix Σ^* are k linearly independent eigenvectors of Σ and C is a $k \times k$ non-singular matrix (Watson (1967), Anderson (1971)). That is, X must lie in a space spanned by k linearly independent eigenvectors of Σ. If this is so then $\hat{\beta}$ is (almost surely) equal to the BLU estimator

$$b = (X'\Sigma^{-1}X)^{-1}X'\Sigma^{-1}y,$$

and the covariance matrices of these two estimators,

$$\text{Var}(\hat{\beta}) = \sigma^2(X'X)^{-1}X'\Sigma X(X'X)^{-1}$$

and

$$\text{Var}(b) = \sigma^2(X'\Sigma^{-1}X)^{-1},$$

respectively, are identical.

When the condition above does not hold then clearly $\text{Var}(c'b) \leqslant \text{Var}(c'\hat{\beta})$ for any non-null vector of constants c, which implies that the matrix

$$\text{Var}(\hat{\beta}) - \text{Var}(b) = \sigma^2\{(X'X)^{-1}X'\Sigma X(X'X)^{-1} - (X'\Sigma^{-1}X)^{-1}\}$$

is positive semi-definite, and hence that $|\text{Var}(\hat{\beta})| \geqslant |\text{Var}(b)|$. Since, in practice, Σ is usually unknown, it is of interest to know how poor the OLS estimator, $\hat{\beta}$, can be relative to b. Hannan (1970) showed that

$$\text{Var}(c'b)/\text{Var}(c'\hat{\beta}) \geqslant 4\lambda_1\lambda_n/(\lambda_1 + \lambda_n)^2, \tag{2}$$

where $\lambda_1 \leqslant \ldots \leqslant \lambda_n$ are the ordered eigenvalues of Σ. Watson (1967), Bloomfield and Watson (1975), and Knott (1975), have extended this result to the generalized variances $|\text{Var}(\hat{\beta})|$ and $|\text{Var}(b)|$. Defining the efficiency of least squares by

$$\varepsilon = |\text{Var}(b)|/|\text{Var}(\hat{\beta})|, \quad \varepsilon \leqslant 1 ,$$

they have shown that

$$\varepsilon \geqslant \prod_{s=1}^{\min(k,n-k)} 4\lambda_s\lambda_{n-s+1} /(\lambda_s + \lambda_{n-s+1})^2 . \tag{3}$$

In both (2) and (3), the lower bound is attainable for a suitable choice of X (and in (2), of c). Evidently, OLS can provide quite inefficient estimates in certain circumstances.

Further, if $\Sigma \neq I$, then it is well known that the usual t-tests and F-tests of restrictions on regression coefficients may be misleading. In particular, the true size of such a test may differ greatly from the nominal size. This problem is discussed by Watson (1955), Watson and Hannan (1956), Sathe and Vinod (1974), Vinod (1976), and Kiviet (1980) who provide bounds on the true critical values of these tests for certain classes of Σ matrices, hence facilitating the use of the familiar t- and F-tests based on OLS estimates. Unfortunately, these tests are not satisfactory because they may lack power. This is perhaps best illustrated by the results of a Monte Carlo study conducted by King and Giles (1984) which, amongst other things, investigated the size and power of a one-sided t-test of a coefficient of (1) when the disturbances follow the first-order autoregressive (AR(1)) process

$$u_t = \varrho u_{t-1} + \varepsilon_t, \qquad \varepsilon_t \sim \text{IN}(0,\sigma^2). \tag{4}$$

For example, at $\varrho = 0.9$ in the case of a 60×3 matrix comprised of economic time-series data and at a nominal significance level of 0.05, King and Giles estimated the OLS-based and maximum-likelihood-estimator-based t-test sizes to be 0.322 and 0.066, respectively, while corresponding powers were estimated to be 0.589 and 0.836. Clearly, if the critical value of the OLS-based test is adjusted so the two tests have the same size, the difference in power will be even more considerable.

This paper makes two contributions to the literature reviewed above. The following section presents bounds for an arbitrary linear combination, $c'b$, of the elements of b in terms of $c'\hat{\beta}$, the OLS equivalent, and the characteristic roots of Σ. In Section 3 these results are applied to provide bounds on a more appropriate test of restrictions on β. A condition is also given which is sufficient to ensure that $c'b$ and $c'\hat{\beta}$ both have the same sign.

2 Bounds on linear combinations of the elements of *b*

It follows from the definitions of b and $\hat{\beta}$ that

$$\frac{(y-X\hat{\beta})'\Sigma^{-1}(y-X\hat{\beta})}{(y-Xb)'\Sigma^{-1}(y-Xb)} \geqslant 1 \tag{5}$$

and

$$\frac{(y-Xb)'(y-Xb)}{(y-X\hat{\beta})'(y-X\hat{\beta})} \geqslant 1 \ . \tag{6}$$

From Cleveland (1971, p.618), we also have the following theorem:

Theorem (Cleveland): For $z \in \mathrm{R}^n$, let P^*z and Pz be the projections of z onto a subspace of dimension k in R^n through the inner products $[\cdot,\cdot]$, and $(\cdot,\cdot)$, respectively.[1] If the norm of z is defined as $\|z\| = (z,z)^{1/2}$, then

$$\|z - P^*z\|^2/\|z - Pz\|^2 \leqslant (\alpha_1 + \alpha_2)^2/(4\alpha_1\alpha_2),$$

where

$$\alpha_1 = \inf_z \ [z,z]/(z,z)$$

and

$$\alpha_2 = \sup_z \ [z,z]/(z,z).$$

First, taking $[\cdot,\cdot]$ to be the inner product defined by the identity matrix, and $(\cdot,\cdot)$ that defined by Σ^{-1}, we obtain an upper bound corresponding to (5),

$$\frac{(y-X\hat{\beta})'\Sigma^{-1}(y-X\hat{\beta})}{(y-Xb)'\Sigma^{-1}(y-Xb)} \leqslant \frac{(\lambda_1 + \lambda_n)^2}{4\lambda_1\lambda_n} \ , \tag{7}$$

because $\inf z'z/z'\Sigma^{-1}z = \lambda_1$ and $\sup z'z/z'\Sigma^{-1}z = \lambda_n$. Similarly, taking $[\cdot,\cdot]$ to be the inner product defined by Σ^{-1}, and $(\cdot,\cdot)$ that defined by I, we obtain an upper bound corresponding to (6),

$$\frac{(y-Xb)'(y-Xb)}{(y-X\hat{\beta})'(y-X\hat{\beta})} \leqslant \frac{(\lambda_1 + \lambda_n)^2}{4\lambda_1\lambda_n} \ , \tag{8}$$

because $\inf z'\Sigma^{-1}z/z'z = \lambda_n^{-1}$ and $\sup z'\Sigma^{-1}z/z'z = \lambda_1^{-1}$.

Using the facts that

$$(y-Xb)'\Sigma^{-1}(y-Xb) = (y-X\hat{\beta})'\Sigma^{-1}(y-X\hat{\beta}) - (\hat{\beta}-b)'X'\Sigma^{-1}X(\hat{\beta}-b)$$

and

$$(y-X\hat{\beta})'(y-X\hat{\beta}) = (y-Xb)'(y-Xb) - (\hat{\beta}-b)'X'X(\hat{\beta}-b),$$

we obtain from (7) and (8) :

$$(\hat{\beta}-b)'X'\Sigma^{-1}X(\hat{\beta}-b) \leqslant [\ \frac{(\lambda_1 + \lambda_n)^2}{4\lambda_1\lambda_n} - 1]\ (y-Xb)'\Sigma^{-1}(y-Xb) \tag{9}$$

$$= \frac{(\lambda_1 - \lambda_n)^2}{4\lambda_1\lambda_n} (y-Xb)'\Sigma^{-1}(y-Xb)$$

and

$$(\hat{\beta}-b)'X'X(\hat{\beta}-b) \leqslant \frac{(\lambda_1 - \lambda_n)^2}{4\lambda_1\lambda_n} (y-X\hat{\beta})'(y-X\hat{\beta}) \ . \tag{10}$$

But, by a version of the Cauchy-Schwarz inequality,

$$|c'(\hat{\beta}-b)| \leqslant \{c'A^{-1}c(\hat{\beta}-b)'A(\hat{\beta}-b)\}^{1/2} \ ,$$

where A is a $k \times k$ positive definite matrix, so that (9) and (10) imply

$$|c'(\hat{\beta}-b)| \leqslant [\frac{(\lambda_1 - \lambda_n)^2}{4\lambda_1\lambda_n} (y-Xb)'\Sigma^{-1}(y-Xb)c'(X'\Sigma^{-1}X)^{-1}c]^{1/2} \tag{11}$$

and

$$|c'(\hat{\beta}-b)| \leqslant [\frac{(\lambda_1 - \lambda_n)^2}{4\lambda_1\lambda_n} (y-X\hat{\beta})'(y-X\hat{\beta})c'(X'X)^{-1}c]^{1/2} \tag{12}$$

for any $k \times 1$ vector of constants c.

The inequalities (11) and (12) provide bounds on the possible values of any linear combination, $c'b$ of the elements of b:

$$c'b \in (c'\hat{\beta} \pm [\frac{(\lambda_1 - \lambda_n)^2}{4\lambda_1\lambda_n} (n-k)v(c'b)]^{1/2}) \ , \tag{13}$$

$$c'b \in (c'\hat{\beta} \pm [\frac{(\lambda_1 - \lambda_n)^2}{4\lambda_1\lambda_n} (n-k)v(c'\hat{\beta})]^{1/2}) \ , \tag{14}$$

where

$$v(c'b) = \frac{1}{(n-k)} (y-Xb)'\Sigma^{-1}(y-Xb)c'(X'\Sigma^{-1}X)^{-1}c$$

and

$$v(c'\hat{\beta}) = \frac{1}{(n-k)} (y-X\hat{\beta})'(y-X\hat{\beta})c'(X'X)^{-1}c.$$

Whether (13) or (14) provides a shorter interval for $c'b$ depends on the relative magnitudes of $v(c'b)$ and $v(c'\hat{\beta})$, and it appears to be impossible to rank these quantities unambiguously. However, as we shall see, both intervals are useful.

3 Hypothesis tests when Σ is unknown

In this section we will consider the problem of testing $H_0 : c'\beta = 0$ against $H_a : c'\beta \neq 0$ with respect to the linear regression model (1) when $u \sim$

$N(0,\sigma^2\Sigma)$. If Σ is known, the Uniformly Most Powerful Invariant[2] (UMPI) test of H_0 against H_a is the critical region

$$t_c^2(\Sigma) > F_\alpha(1,n-k), \tag{15}$$

where

$$t_c(\Sigma) = c'b/\{v(c'b)\}^{1/2}$$

and $F_\alpha(1,n-k)$ is the usual $100(1-\alpha)$ percentile of the central F-distribution with 1 and $n-k$ degrees of freedom. When Σ is unknown, ideally we would like to know whether the calculated value of $t_c^2(\Sigma)$ would or would not lie in this critical region because this information would enable us to apply a UMPI test of H_0 against H_a. As we shall see, the results of Section 2 at least provide us with a partial answer to this question.

Dividing both sides of (13) by $\{v(c'b)\}^{1/2}$ we have

$$t_c(\Sigma) \in [\{v(c'\hat{\beta})/v(c'b)\}^{1/2}\, t_c(I) \pm \{(n-k)(\lambda_1-\lambda_n)^2/(4\lambda_1\lambda_n)\}^{1/2}]. \tag{16}$$

That is, $t_c(\Sigma)$ lies in an interval centred at $\{v(c'\hat{\beta})/v(c'b)\}^{1/2}\, t_c(I)$ of width $2\{(n-k)(\lambda_1-\lambda_n)^2/(4\lambda_1\lambda_n)\}^{1/2}$. Clearly, if this interval is entirely within the rejection region (15), then so is $t_c(\Sigma)$. It follows that a sufficient condition for rejection of H_0 is

$$|t_c(I)| \geqslant \{v(c'b)/v(c'\hat{\beta})\}^{1/2}[|t_\alpha| + \{(n-k)(\lambda_1-\lambda_n)^2/(4\lambda_1\lambda_n)\}^{1/2}], \tag{17}$$

where $|t_\alpha| = \{F_\alpha(1,n-k)\}^{1/2}$. Applying the same argument to (14) yields the alternative sufficient condition:

$$|t_c(I)| \geqslant \{v(c')/v(c'\hat{\beta})\}^{1/2}|t_\alpha| + \{(n-k)(\lambda_1-\lambda_n)^2/(4\lambda_1\lambda_n)\}^{1/2}. \tag{18}$$

Evidently, (18) is weaker than (17) whenever $v(c'b)/v(c'\hat{\beta}) > 1$, and the opposite is true if $v(c'b)/v(c'\hat{\beta}) < 1$. In practice, this ratio will not be known, but it is easy to see that $v(c'b)/v(c'\hat{\beta}) \leqslant \lambda_n/\lambda_1$, so that (18) is certainly satisfied if

$$|t_c(I)| \geqslant (\lambda_n/\lambda_1)^{1/2}|t_\alpha| + \{(n-k)(\lambda_1-\lambda_n)^2/(4\lambda_1\lambda_n)\}^{1/2}. \tag{19}$$

This appears to be the weakest sufficient condition depending only on the eigenvalues of Σ possible.

As an example, for disturbances generated by the AR(1) process (4) we have $\lambda_n/\lambda_1 \approx (1+|\varrho|)^2/(1-|\varrho|)^2$. Thus for $n-k = 36$ and $|t_\alpha|=2$, i.e. $\alpha \approx 0.05$, the right-hand side of (19) has the following values:

ϱ :	0.0	± 0.1	± 0.2	± 0.3	± 0.4	± 0.5
RHS of (19) :	2	3.65	4.95	6.68	8.77	11.46 .

The interpretation of (19) is that it indicates how sensitive inferences about H_0 may be to any departure from the assumptions upon which the statistic $t_c(I)$ is based. Thus, for example, in the case of AR(1) disturbances, an observation of $|t_c(I)| = 7$ provides an unambiguous basis for the inference that H_0 is false only if there is some assurance that $|\varrho|$ is no greater than about 0.3.

Because $\Pr\{|t_c(\Sigma)| > |t_\alpha| \mid H_0\} = \alpha$, and (19) implies (16), it is clear that

$$\Pr[|t_c(I)| \geqslant (\lambda_n/\lambda_1)^{1/2}\ |t_\alpha| + \{(n-k)(\lambda_1-\lambda_n)^2/(4\lambda_1\lambda_n)\}^{1/2} \mid H_0] \leqslant \alpha.$$

In other words, using the right hand side of (19) as a critical value for H_0 would provide a test of size no larger than α. In this sense, (19) is a conservative adjustment to the critical value $|t_\alpha|$ and when the resultant test does have size less than α, naturally it is no longer UMPI within the class of tests of size α. On the other hand, Vinod's (1976) results suggest that using the unadjusted $|t_\alpha|$ generally implies a test of unknown, but necessarily larger size than α.

Of course the argument above does *not* imply that H_0 should be accepted when (19) does not hold. In fact, it is clear that the sample provides an unambiguous basis for the inference that H_0 is correct, in the absence of knowledge of Σ, only if the interval (16) [or its equivalent derived from (14)] is entirely within the acceptance region $t_c^2(\Sigma) < F_\alpha(1,n-k)$. Only then can we be sure that the inference based on $t_c(I)$ implies the same inference from the UMPI test based on $t_c(\Sigma)$. However, only minor departures from the assumption $\Sigma = I$ can be entertained if an inference that H_0 is correct is to be sustained. This is because for (16) to be within the acceptance region requires

$$\{v(c'\hat{\beta})/v(c'b)\}^{1/2}t_c(I) \text{ to lie between } \pm[|t_\alpha|-\{(n-k)(\lambda_1-\lambda_n)^2/(4\lambda_1\lambda_n)\}^{1/2}]$$

and this interval is empty unless

$$(n-k)(\lambda_1-\lambda_n)^2/(4\lambda_1\lambda_n) < F_\alpha(1,n-k).$$

This apparent 'asymmetry' in the robustness of inferences to the assumption $\Sigma = I$ carries a clear message for the problem of model choice: any doubts about the error structure in the model in turn cast doubts, in particular, on attempts to obtain a more parsimonious model for the data. To put it another way, genuine parsimony can only be achieved through confidence in the assumed properties of the stochastic components in the model.

Finally, it is perhaps worth noting that (14) yields a simple sufficient condition for $c'b$ to have the same sign as $c'\hat{\beta}$, for if

$$t_c^2(I) \geqslant (n-k)(\lambda_1-\lambda_n)^2/(4\lambda_1\lambda_n)\ ,$$

the interval (14) clearly does not contain the origin.

Notes

1 [·,·] may be thought of as the 'wrong', and (·,·) as the 'right' inner product.
2 See Seber (1980) for a description of the transformations on y invariance refers to

here. This form of invariance is not necessarily appropriate for all economic problems involving a test of H_0. The remarks which follow apply only to problems for which it is appropriate.

References

Anderson, T.W. (1971), *The Statistical Analysis of Time Series*, New York: Wiley.

Bloomfield, P., and Watson, G.S. (1975), 'The Inefficiency of Least Squares', *Biometrika*, 62, 121-8.

Cleveland, W.S. (1971), 'Projection with the Wrong Inner Product and Its Application to Regression with Correlated Errors and Linear Filtering of Time Series', *Annals of Mathematical Statistics*, 42, 616-24.

Hannan, E.J. (1970), *Multiple Time Series*, New York: Wiley.

King, M.L., and Giles, D.E.A. (1984), 'Autocorrelation Pre-Testing in the Linear Model: Estimation, Testing and Prediction', *Journal of Econometrics*, 25, 35-48.

Kiviet, J.F. (1980), 'Effects of ARMA Errors on Tests for Regression Coefficients: Comments on Vinod's Article; Improved and Additional Results', *Journal of the American Statistical Association*, 75, 353-8.

Knott, M. (1975), 'On the Minimum Efficiency of Least Squares', *Biometrika*, 62, 129-32.

Sathe, S.T., and Vinod, H.D. (1974), 'Bounds on the Variance of Regression Coefficients Due to Heteroscedastic or Autoregressive Errors', *Econometrica*, 42, 333-40.

Seber, G.A.F. (1980), *The Linear Hypothesis: A General Theory* (2nd ed.), London: Griffin.

Vinod, H.D. (1976), 'Effects of ARMA Errors on the Significance Tests for Regression Coefficients', *Journal of the American Statistical Association*, 71, 929-33.

Watson, G.S. (1955), 'Serial Correlation in Regression Analysis I', *Biometrika*, 42, 327-41.

Watson, G.S. (1967), 'Linear Least Squares Regression', *Annals of Mathematical Statistics*, 38, 1679-99.

Watson, G.S. and Hannan, E.J. (1956), 'Serial Correlation in Regression Analysis II', *Biometrika*, 43, 436-48.

5 Efficiency of estimators in the regression model with first-order autoregressive errors

*L. Magee, A. Ullah and V. K. Srivastava**

1 Introduction

For a linear regression model with first-order autocorrelated disturbances, a variety of estimators for the regression coefficients have been proposed in the literature. One of the most commonly used estimators for this situation has been the Cochrane-Orcutt (1949) estimator (CO) due to its intuitive and computational simplicity. Since its introduction, several alternative estimators have also been proposed and their efficiency properties have been investigated. For example, Kadiyala (1968) showed that ordinary least squares (OLS) is a better estimator than CO for known autocorrelation coefficient ϱ in $0 < \varrho \leq 1$ for the model containing only an intercept.[1,2] Maeshiro (1976), then showed that OLS is better than CO with known ϱ for all $\varrho > 0$ in a similar model where the matrix of explanatory variables contains an intercept and a strongly trended variable, even for sample sizes of $T = 100$. In addition, OLS is vindicated by Harvey and McAvinchey (1978), who suggest that it performs acceptably when the variable is trended; by Spitzer (1979), who recommends its use when the absolute value of the autocorrelation coefficient is ≤ 0.2; and by Krämer (1980), who proves that the efficiency (when measured by the trace of the variance-covariance matrix) of OLS with respect to the generalized least squares (GLS) approaches one as ϱ approaches one when the model includes a constant term. However, recently Taylor (1981) has pointed out that Maeshiro's result only applies to a special case: very strong trends in the explanatory variable, and where this variable is fixed, as opposed to the Monte Carlo studies of Griliches and Rao (1969) and Spitzer (1979) in which the explanatory variable is drawn from a prespecified stochastic process. In this latter case, the first observation no longer remains as important for large T, hence the improved performance of CO.

In addition to the above mentioned work there are studies which compare CO with the Prais-Winsten (1954) estimator (PW). For example, Maeshiro (1979) and Park and Mitchell (1980) found that CO was always worse than PW. Maeshiro considered the known ϱ case analytically, and both Maeshiro and Park and Mitchell used Monte Carlo methods for the ϱ unknown case.

The only mention of CO ever outperforming PW is made by Spitzer (1979) who finds CO slightly better than PW when the absolute value of the autocorrelation coefficient is close to one.

It should be noted that all the previous efficiency studies have either been analytical with the assumption that ϱ is known *a priori*, or have used Monte Carlo methods. No expressions have been obtained specifically in the context of two-step CO and PW estimators which use an estimated autocorrelation coefficient. This paper is an attempt in this direction. We consider classes of two-step CO and PW estimators which arise due to various choices of the estimated autocorrelation coefficient. We have shown that these two-step estimators are unbiased if their mean vectors exist and disturbances are symmetrically distributed. Further, taking the disturbances to be normal, we have presented in Section 2 the expressions for the large sample asymptotic approximations of the variance-covariance matrices. Using these expressions, the efficiencies of the estimators are then analyzed with the help of a numerical experiment in Section 3. Some remarks are also placed in this Section. Finally, in Section 4 we have provided the proofs of results in Section 2.

2 The estimators and their properties

Consider the linear regression model with first-order autocorrelated disturbances:

$$\begin{aligned} y_t &= x_t\beta + u_t \\ u_t &= \varrho u_{t-1} + \varepsilon_t, \qquad (t = 1,2, \ldots, n) \end{aligned} \tag{1}$$

where y_t is the tth observation on the variable to be explained, x_t is a $1 \times k$ vector of observations on k explanatory variables, β is the coefficient vector associated with them, u_t is the disturbance term following a first-order autoregressive scheme with unknown autocorrelation coefficient ϱ ($|\varrho|<1$) and

$$\begin{aligned} \mathrm{E}(\varepsilon_t) &= 0 \quad \text{for all } t , \\ \mathrm{E}(\varepsilon_t\varepsilon_{t+s}) &= \Psi \quad \text{if } s = 0 , \\ &= 0 \quad \text{otherwise.} \end{aligned} \tag{2}$$

Defining

$$\begin{aligned} y' &= (y_1,y_2, \ldots ,y_n) \\ X' &= (x'_1,x'_2, \ldots ,x'_n) \\ u' &= (u_1,u_2, \ldots ,u_n) \end{aligned} \tag{3}$$

we can write

$$y = X\beta + u \tag{4}$$

with

$$\begin{aligned} \mathrm{E}(u) &= 0 \\ \mathrm{E}(uu') &= \sigma^2\Sigma, \end{aligned} \tag{5}$$

where $\sigma^2 = \Psi/(1 - \varrho^2)$ and Σ is a $k \times k$ symmetric matrix with the $(i,j)^{\text{th}}$ element equal to $\varrho^{|i-j|}$.

The OLS estimator of β is

$$b = (X'X)^{-1}X'y \tag{6}$$

which is unbiased with variance-covariance matrix:

$$\mathrm{E}(b-\beta)(b-\beta)' = \sigma^2(X'X)^{-1}X'\Sigma X(X'X)^{-1}. \tag{7}$$

The estimator b ignores the autocorrelated nature of disturbances and is therefore not efficient. This is accounted for in the GLS estimator given by

$$\beta^* = (X'\Sigma^{-1}X)^{-1}X'\Sigma^{-1}y \tag{8}$$

which is unbiased with variance-covariance matrix:

$$\mathrm{E}(\beta^*-\beta)(\beta^*-\beta)' = \sigma^2(X'\Sigma^{-1}X)^{-1} . \tag{9}$$

The estimator β^* can be construed as the OLS estimator in the transformed model

$$Py = PX\beta + Pu \tag{10}$$

where P is an $n \times n$ triangular matrix given by

$$P = \begin{bmatrix} (1-\varrho^2)^{1/2} & 0 & 0 & \dots & 0 & 0 \\ -\varrho & 1 & 0 & \dots & 0 & 0 \\ 0 & -\varrho & 1 & \dots & 0 & 0 \\ \cdot & & & & & \cdot \\ \cdot & \cdot & \cdot & & \cdot & \cdot \\ \cdot & \cdot & \cdot & & \cdot & \cdot \\ 0 & 0 & 0 & \dots & 1 & 0 \\ 0 & 0 & 0 & \dots & -\varrho & 1 \end{bmatrix} . \tag{11}$$

Since ϱ is generally not known, we can replace ϱ by a consistent estimator in order to get the following operational estimator:

$$\hat{\beta} = (X'\hat{P}'\hat{P}X)^{-1}X'\hat{P}'\hat{P}y \tag{12}$$

where $\hat{P}$ is the same as P except that ϱ is replaced by a consistent estimator $\hat{\varrho}$.

If $\hat{u}_t$ is the tth element of the OLS residual vector $\hat{u} = (y - Xb)$, a simple choice of $\hat{\varrho}$ is

$$\hat{\varrho}_1 = \frac{\sum_{t=1}^{n-1} \hat{u}_t \hat{u}_{t+1}}{\sum_{t=1}^{n} \hat{u}_t^2} . \tag{13}$$

Some alternative estimators for ϱ have been suggested in the literature (Judge *et al.* (1980, p. 183)). For example, Theil (1971) modifies $\hat{\varrho}_1$ as

$$\hat{\varrho}_2 = \frac{(n-k)}{(n-1)} \hat{\varrho}_1 . \tag{14}$$

Next, an estimate derived from the Durbin-Watson statistic is given by

$$\hat{\varrho}_3 = 1 - \tfrac{1}{2} d \tag{15}$$

where

$$d = \frac{\sum_{t=2}^{n} (\hat{u}_t - \hat{u}_{t-1})^2}{\sum_{t=1}^{n} \hat{u}_t^2} \tag{16}$$

is the Durbin-Watson statistic. Theil and Nagar (1961) suggested the following estimator

$$\hat{\varrho}_4 = \frac{n^2(1-d/2)+k^2}{n^2-k^2} . \tag{17}$$

Finally, the Durbin (1960) estimator, $\hat{\varrho}_5$, is obtained by estimating ϱ (the coefficient of y_{t-1}) in the following equation using OLS:

$$y_t = \varrho y_{t-1} + \beta_0(1-\varrho) + x_t^0\beta^0 - \varrho x_{t-1}^0\beta^0 + \varepsilon_t, \quad t=2, \ldots ,n , \tag{18}$$

where x_t^0 is the tth row of X with the constant term deleted, i.e., $x_t = [1 \; x_t^0]$ in (1). If $x_t = x_t^0$ then $\beta_0(1 - \varrho)$ gets dropped out in (18).

Now denoting by $\hat{P}_s$ the matrix P in (11) with ϱ replaced by $\hat{\varrho}_s$, $s=1, \ldots ,5$, we can write a class of two-step PW-type estimators from (12) as

$$\hat{\beta}_s = (X'\hat{P}_s'\hat{P}_sX)^{-1}X'\hat{P}_s'\hat{P}_sy , \quad s=1, \ldots ,5 . \tag{19}$$

For $s = 1$, the estimator $\hat{\beta}_1$ is often termed the PW estimator.

The CO-type two-step estimators are analytically similar to the PW-type two-step estimators, and can be constructed as the OLS estimator in the transformed model (corresponding to (10)):

$$CPy = CPX\beta + CPu \tag{20}$$

where

$$C = [0{:}\ I_{n-1}] \tag{21}$$

is an $n-1 \times n$ constant matrix such that $CPu = \varepsilon$ is an $n-1 \times 1$ vector of disturbances and CP is the same as P in (11) except that the first row is deleted; 0 in (21) is an $n-1 \times 1$ vector and I_{n-1} is an $n-1 \times n-1$ identity matrix. With ϱ replaced by $\hat{\varrho}_s$, $s=1, \ldots ,5$, these estimators can be written as

$$\tilde{\beta}_s = (X'\hat{P}_s'C_0\hat{P}_sX)^{-1}X'\hat{P}_s'C_0\hat{P}_sy \ ; \qquad C_0 = C'C \ . \tag{22}$$

For $s = 1$, the estimator $\tilde{\beta}_1$ is a well known CO two-step estimator. We note that the CO-type estimators differ from the PW-type estimators in (19) with respect to the C_0 matrix.

We shall now present the variance-covariance matrices of $\hat{\beta}_s$ and $\tilde{\beta}_s$. However, before doing this we introduce the following matrices for the sake of simplicity in exposition.

Let D be an $n \times n$ diagonal matrix with first and last diagonal elements equal to 1 and the remaining diagonal elements equal to $1 - \varrho^2$, let D_0 be a diagonal matrix with a first element of 1 and the other diagonal elements equal to zero, and let B be an $n \times n$ symmetric matrix with $(i,j)^{\text{th}}$ element equal to $-\varrho$ if $i = j$, $\frac{1}{2}$ if $i = j\pm1$, and 0 otherwise. Further, define

$$\begin{aligned} &C_1 = [I_{n-1}{:}0], && C_\varrho = C - \varrho C_1 \\ &M = I - X(X'X)^{-1}X' \ , && M_Z = I - Z(Z'Z)^{-1}Z' \ , \\ &\Omega = (X'\Sigma^{-1}X)^{-1}, && Q = \Sigma - X\Omega X' \ , \end{aligned} \tag{23}$$

where C_1 and C_ϱ are $n-1 \times n$ matrices, M is an $n \times n$ matrix, and M_Z is an $n-1 \times n-1$ matrix in which $Z' = [z_2', \ldots ,z_n']$; $z_t = [1 : x_{t-1}^0 : x_t^0]$ when $x_t = [1 : x_t^0]$ in (1) and $z_t = [x_{t-1}^0 : x_t^0]$ when there is no constant in x_t.

It is assumed that the matrix $X'X/n$ tends to a finite non-singular matrix as n tends to infinity. This assumption implies the absence of trend as an explanatory variable. We can now state the main results. These are proved in the following section.

Theorem 1: If the disturbances are symmetrically distributed the Prais-Winsten type two-step estimators $\hat{\beta}_s$, $s=1,\ldots,5$, are unbiased provided their mean vectors exist. Further, if the distribution of disturbances is normal, the variance-covariance matrices to order $0(n^{-2})$ of the asymptotic distribution of $\hat{\beta}_s$ are given by

$$\mathrm{V}(\hat{\beta}_s) = \sigma^2\Omega + \sigma^2\,\frac{(1-\varrho^2)}{n\varrho^2}\,\Omega X'QX\Omega \ , \qquad s=1, \ldots ,5 \tag{24}$$

Theorem 2: If the disturbances are symmetrically distributed the Cochrane-Orcutt two-step estimator $\tilde{\beta}_1$ is unbiased provided its mean vector exists.

Further, if the distribution of disturbances is normal, the variance-covariance matrix to order $0(n^{-2})$ of the asymptotic distribution of $\tilde{\beta}_1$ is given by

$$V(\tilde{\beta}_1) = V(\hat{\beta}_1) + \sigma^2 \Omega X' D_0 X \Omega \,. \tag{25}$$

From (9) and (24), we see that the variance-covariance matrix, to order $0(n^{-2})$, of $\hat{\beta}_s$, $s=1, \ldots, 5$, exceeds the corresponding matrix of β^* by

$$\sigma^2 \frac{(1-\varrho^2)}{n\varrho^2} \Omega X' Q X \Omega \tag{26}$$

which can be attributed to replacement of ϱ by $\hat{\varrho}$ in β^*. Note that

$$Q = \Sigma - X\Omega X' = \Sigma^{1/2}[I - \Sigma^{-1/2}X(X'\Sigma^{-1/2}\Sigma^{-1/2}X)^{-1}X'\Sigma^{-1/2}]\Sigma^{1/2}$$

is a positive semidefinite matrix. This implies that

$$V(\hat{\beta}_s) - V(\beta^*) = \text{positive semidefinite}, \tag{27}$$

that is, the variance-covariance matrix of $\hat{\beta}_s$ is greater than that of β^*.

Similarly, the variance-covariance matrix of $\tilde{\beta}_1$ exceeds that of β^* by (26) plus the second term on the right-hand side of (25) which is positive semidefinite. Thus the variance-covariance matrix of $\tilde{\beta}_1$ is greater than those of β^* as well as $\hat{\beta}_s$.

The result in Theorem 2 has been presented for the CO two-step estimator $\tilde{\beta}_1$. For the case of $\tilde{\beta}_s$, $s=2, \ldots, 5$ the results can be developed in a similar manner. These were not found to be the same as for $\tilde{\beta}_1$. However, it should be noted from Theorem 1 that $V(\hat{\beta}_s)$ is the same for $s=1, \ldots, 5$ in the case of PW-type two-step estimators.

3 Numerical experiment

In this section we evaluate the results of Theorems 1 and 2 of Section 2 using a numerical experiment. These results are stated in Tables 1 to 3 for both the trace and determinant of the variance-covariance matrix measures of relative efficiency. In particular we have obtained numerical values for the following measures:

$$e_1 = \det(b)/\det(\beta^*); \quad e_1^* = \mathrm{tr}(b)/\mathrm{tr}(\beta^*) \tag{28}$$

$$e_2 = \det(\hat{\beta}_s)/\det(\beta^*); \quad e_2^* = \mathrm{tr}(\hat{\beta}_s)/\mathrm{tr}(\beta^*), \quad s=1, \ldots, 5 \tag{29}$$

$$e_3 = \det(\tilde{\beta}_s)/\det(\beta^*); \quad e_3^* = \mathrm{tr}(\tilde{\beta}_s)/\mathrm{tr}(\beta^*), \quad s=1\,, \tag{30}$$

where det(b) and tr(b), for example, respectively represent the determinant and trace of the variance-covariance matrix of b.

The following four models are used:[3]

$$y = X\beta + u,$$

where

$$M_1\colon X = [1\colon x_2\colon x_3] \quad (31)$$

$$M_2\colon X = [x_2\colon x_3] \quad (32)$$

$$M_3\colon X = [1\colon x_4] \quad (33)$$

$$M_4\colon X = [x_5\colon x_6\colon x_7], \quad (34)$$

β is the coefficient vector with appropriate dimension, and in the case $n=10$ $x_2' = [1.723, 0.022, 1.157, 0.504, 2.832, 0.902, 0.853, 1.816, 2.898, 1.019]$, $x_3' = [0.432, 1.376, 1.01, 0.005, 1.393, 1.787, 0.105, 1.339, 1.041, 0.279]$, $x_4' = [1.809, 2.309, 2.691, 3.191, 4.0, 5.191, 6.691, 8.309, 9.809, 11.0]$, $x_5 = (\lambda_1 + \lambda_n)/2^{1/2}$, $x_6 = (\lambda_2 + \lambda_{n-1})/2^{1/2}$, $x_7 = (\lambda_3 + \lambda_{n-2})/2^{1/2}$. The λ_i refers to the normalized characteristic vector corresponding to the ith largest characteristic root of a certain approximation to Σ, call it Σ^*, where

$$\Sigma^{*-1} = \Sigma^{-1} - \varrho(1 - \varrho)/(1 - \varrho^2)D_1 \quad (35)$$

and D_1 is a $T \times T$ matrix of zeros with a one in the upper left- and lower right-hand corner (Tillman (1975, p. 960)).

The model M4 is chosen because the X matrix of (34) is known as 'Watson's X' (Watson (1967)) and is known to be a model in which OLS is particularly poor. The characteristic vectors, λ_i, can be easily derived using formulas given in Tillman (1975, p. 965).[4] M1, M2, and M3 are chosen to correspond with the vectors used in a study by Raj, Srivastava and Upadhyaya (1980). Note that x_1 and x_2 are non-trended while x_3 is strongly trended.

For the $T=40$ case in M1, M2 and M3, the models given above were modified by using each observation from the x vectors four consecutive times. For example, when $n=40$,

$$x_2' = [1.723, 1.723, 1.723, 1.723, 0.022, 0.022, \ldots, 1.019, 1.019].$$

This method of increasing sample size preserves the features of the trend variables while being consistent with the assumption of a finite $\lim(X'X)/n$ as n approaches infinity. For M4 the λ_i's corresponding to Σ^* when $n=40$ are used.

The results are invariant with respect to β's. Scale transformations of exogenous column vectors, however, will affect the trace ratios while they have no effect on the determinant ratios.

3.1 Main results and remarks

(i) b(OLS) is better than $\hat{\beta}_s$ (PW using $\hat{\varrho}_s$), $s=1, \ldots, 5$, for small values of ϱ; roughly for ϱ values less than 0.2 or 0.3 while $\hat{\beta}_s$ is better for higher ϱ

values (seen by comparing e_1, e_1^* with e_2, e_2^* in Tables 1 to 4). This agrees with Monte Carlo findings of Griliches and Rao (1969) and Spitzer (1979).

(ii) The performance of OLS for large ϱ values is particularly bad when there is no constant term (M2 and M4) while PW and CO become almost as good as GLS in that case. This OLS result agrees with an analytical finding of Krämer (1980).

(iii) $\tilde{\beta}_1$ (CO using $\hat{\varrho}_1$) performs worse in models where there is a constant than in those where there is not. It is particularly poor in M3 where there is a constant and a trended variable, which supports a result of Maeshiro (1976). Further, $\tilde{\beta}_1$ is worse than $\hat{\beta}_s$. This is consistent with the result in Section 2 that $-\mathrm{V}(\hat{\beta}_s) + \mathrm{V}(\tilde{\beta}_1)$ is a positive semidefinite matrix. It also implies that in our case the dominance of $\hat{\beta}_s$ over $\tilde{\beta}_1$ with respect to three measures, variance-covariance matrix, determinant of variance-covariance matrix and trace of variance-covariance matrix are equivalent (Kale and Chandrasekar (1982)).

(iv) The fact that the approximate variance-covariance matrices of $\hat{\beta}_s$, $s=1, \ldots, 5$, up to order $0(n^{-2})$, are the same implies that these estimators are both first- and second-order efficient in the Fisher (1925) and Rao (1962) sense; also see Efron (1975). Earlier Monte Carlo studies have also reported similar results. The case in which the estimators (especially $\hat{\beta}_1$ and $\hat{\beta}_5$) tend to differ most in those studies is when ϱ becomes close to one (Harvey and McAvinchey (1978)), which is also the case in which the $0(n^{-2})$ approximation method used here is likely to be least effective since as Σ approaches singularity the deleted terms of the expansion become more important. The higher-order asymptotic efficiency becomes relevant in this context (Akahira and Takeuchi (1981)).

(v) A useful extension of this study would be the derivation of large-sample approximations to the MSE matrices of iterative estimators such as iterated PW, maximum likelihood and CO which have been considered in the Monte Carlo studies of Beach and MacKinnon (1978), Harvey and McAvinchey (1978), Spitzer (1979) and Park and Mitchell (1980).[5] Such an extension would give a more complete analytical picture to complement the Monte Carlo results. The results of this paper can also be extended to a model with a higher order autoregressive process, say AR(2), or to a model with a moving average process, as well as more complex models such as dynamic models, seemingly unrelated regression equations, and simultaneous equation models.

4 Proof of Theorems in Section 2

Suppose B is an $n \times n$ symmetric matrix with $(i,j)^{\text{th}}$ element b_{ij} defined in Section 2 as

$$
\begin{aligned}
b_{ij} &= -\varrho \quad \text{if } i=j \\
&= \tfrac{1}{2} \quad \text{if } i = j\pm 1 \\
&= 0 \quad \text{otherwise.}
\end{aligned}
$$

From (13), we can express

$$
\begin{aligned}
\hat{\varrho}_1 &= \frac{\hat{u}'(\varrho I_n + B)\hat{u}}{\hat{u}'\hat{u}} \qquad (36) \\
&= \varrho + \frac{\hat{u}'B\hat{u}}{\hat{u}'\hat{u}} \\
&= \varrho + \frac{\frac{1}{n}|u'MBMu}{\sigma^2 + (\frac{1}{n}u'Mu - \sigma^2)} \\
&= \varrho + \frac{1}{n\sigma^2}u'MBMu[1 + \frac{1}{\sigma^2}(\frac{1}{n}u'Mu - \sigma^2)]^{-1} .
\end{aligned}
$$

Expanding the expression in square brackets and retaining terms to order $0(n^{-1})$ in probability, we find

$$
\hat{\varrho}_1 - \varrho = \theta_{-1/2} + \theta_{-1} \qquad (37)
$$

where

$$
\begin{aligned}
\theta_{-1/2} &= \frac{1}{n\sigma^2}u'MBMu \\
\theta_{-1} &= -\frac{1}{n\sigma^4}u'MBMu(\frac{1}{n}u'Mu - \sigma^2) .
\end{aligned} \qquad (38)
$$

Here the suffixes of θ indicate the order in probability. Using (37) we have

$$
\begin{aligned}
\hat{P}'\hat{P} = (1 - \varrho^2)\Sigma^{-1} - \frac{\theta_{-1/2}}{\varrho}[D - (1 - \varrho^2)\Sigma^{-1}] + \\
[\frac{\theta^2_{-1/2}}{\varrho^2}(I_n - D) - \frac{\theta_{-1}}{\varrho}(D - (1 - \varrho^2)\Sigma^{-1})]
\end{aligned} \qquad (39)
$$

to order $0(n^{-1})$ in probability, where D is an $n \times n$ diagonal matrix (as defined in Section 2) with first and last diagonal elements equal to 1 and the remaining diagonal elements equal to $1 - \varrho^2$.

4.1 Proof of Theorem 1

From (1) and (19), we have

$$(\hat{\beta}_1 - \beta) = (X'\hat{P}_1'\hat{P}_1X)^{-1}X'\hat{P}_1'\hat{P}_1u\,. \tag{40}$$

Since $(\hat{\beta}_1 - \beta)$ is an odd function of u, it follows that $E(\hat{\beta}_1 - \beta) = 0$ when the distribution of u is symmetrical and $E(\hat{\beta}_1)$ exists. This proves the first part of the theorem. For the second part, the distribution of u is assumed to be multivariate normal.

Substituting (39) into (40), we have, to order $0(n^{-3/2})$ in probability, after a little algebraic simplification[6]

$$(\hat{\beta}_1 - \beta) = \xi_{-1/2} + \xi_{-1} + \xi_{-3/2}$$

so that, to order $0(n^{-2})$,

$$\begin{aligned} E(\hat{\beta}_1 - \beta)(\hat{\beta}_1 - \beta)' &= E(\xi_{-1/2}\xi'_{-1/2}) + E(\xi_{-1}\xi'_{-1/2} + \xi_{-1/2}\xi'_{-1}) \\ &\quad + E(\xi_{-3/2}\xi'_{-1/2} + \xi_{-1/2}\xi'_{-3/2} + \xi_{-1}\xi'_{-1}) \end{aligned} \tag{41}$$

where

$$\xi_{-1/2} = \Omega X'\Sigma^{-1}u \qquad \xi_{-1} = -\frac{\theta_{-1/2}}{\varrho(1-\varrho^2)}\,\Omega X'DQ\Sigma^{-1}u \tag{42}$$

$$\xi_{-3/2} = \frac{1}{\varrho^2(1-\varrho^2)}\,\Omega X'[\theta^2_{-1/2}\{I_n - \frac{1}{(1-\varrho^2)}DX\Omega X'D\} - \varrho\theta_{-1}D]Q\Sigma^{-1}u.$$

Utilizing normality of disturbances, it is easy to see that

$$E(\xi_{-1/2}\xi'_{-1/2}) = \sigma^2\Omega \tag{43}$$

while the second, third, fourth and fifth terms on the right-hand side of (41) are equal to a null matrix. For the last term, we employ the following result which can be obtained from Srivastava and Tiwari (1976):

$$E[(u'Cu)^2uu'] = \sigma^6[\{(\mathrm{tr}\; C\Sigma)^2 + 2\mathrm{tr}\; C\Sigma C\Sigma\}\Sigma + 4(\mathrm{tr}\; C\Sigma)\Sigma C\Sigma + 8\Sigma C\Sigma C\Sigma] \tag{44}$$

where C is any symmetric matrix with nonstochastic elements.

Employing the above along with the results

$$QM = \Sigma M \tag{45}$$

$$Q\Sigma^{-1}Q = Q$$

and observing that $(\mathrm{tr}\; MBM\Sigma MBM\Sigma) = n(1-\varrho^2)/2 + o(n)$ is of order $0(n)$, we have

$$E(\xi_{-1}\xi'_{-1}) = \frac{1}{\varrho^2(1-\varrho^2)^2}\,\Omega X'DQ\Sigma^{-1}E[\theta^2_{-1/2}uu']\Sigma^{-1}QDX\Omega \tag{46}$$

$$= \frac{1}{\sigma^4 n^2 \varrho^2 (1-\varrho^2)^2} \Omega X' D Q \Sigma^{-1} [\mathrm{E}(u' MBMu)^2 uu'] \Sigma^{-1} Q D X$$

$$= \frac{\sigma^2}{n\varrho^2(1-\varrho^2)} \Omega X' DQDX\Omega$$

to order $0(n^{-2})$.

Further observing that $\Omega X'DQDX\Omega = (1-\varrho^2)^2 \Omega X'QX\Omega + o(n^{-1})$ and combining (43) and (46), we find the result (24) stated in Theorem 1 for $s = 1$.[7] The result (24) corresponding to the choice of $\hat{\varrho}_s$, $s = 2,3,4$, given in (14), (15) and (17), can be similarly verified to be the same as that for $s = 1$. For $s = 5$ we proceed as below.

The $\hat{\varrho}_5$ estimate (Durbin's $\hat{\varrho}$) is derived from OLS on the equation

$$y_t = \varrho y_{t-1} + \beta_0(1 - \varrho) + x_t^0\beta^0 - \varrho x_{t-1}^0\beta^0 + \varepsilon_t; \quad t = 2, \ldots, T. \tag{47}$$

It is given by

$$\hat{\varrho}_5 = \frac{y'_{-1} M_Z y_0}{y'_{-1} M_Z y_{-1}} \tag{48}$$

where $y_0 = (y_2, \ldots, y_n)'$, $y_{-1} = (y_1, \ldots, y_{n-1})'$,

$$M_Z = I - Z(Z'Z)^{-1}Z' \text{ and } Z = [1\colon X^0 \colon X^0_{-1}].$$

Now from (4) $y_{-1} = [1:X^0_{-1}]\beta + u_{-1}$ and $y_0 = [1:X^0]\beta + u_0$ and noting that $M_Z Z = 0$ it can be verified that

$$\hat{\varrho}_5 = \frac{u'_{-1} M_Z u_0}{u'_{-1} M_Z u_{-1}} = \frac{u' C_1' M_Z C u}{u' C_1' M_Z C_1 u} \tag{49}$$

where C and C_1 are as defined in (21) and (23), respectively. Following the steps similar to those for $\hat{\varrho}_1$ in (36) we can obtain

$$\hat{\varrho}_5 - \varrho = \theta^*_{-1/2} + \theta^*_{-1} \tag{50}$$

where $\theta^*_{-1/2} = u'C_1'M_Z C_\varrho u/n\sigma^2$, $\theta^*_{-1} = -u'C_1'M_Z C_\varrho u\{(u'C_1'M_Z C_1 u)/n - \sigma^2\}/n\sigma^4$ and $C_\varrho = C - \varrho C_1$. Further,

$$\hat{\beta}_5 - \beta = \xi^*_{-1/2} + \xi^*_{-1} + \xi^*_{-3/2} \tag{51}$$

where $\xi^*_{-1/2}$, ξ^*_{-1} and $\xi^*_{-3/2}$ are the same as $\xi_{-1/2}$, ξ_{-1} and $\xi_{-3/2}$, respectively, given in (42) with $\theta_{-1/2}$ and θ_{-1} replaced by $\theta^*_{-1/2}$ and θ^*_{-1}. In fact $\xi^*_{-1/2} = \xi_{-1/2}$.

It is easy to verify that

$$\begin{aligned} \mathrm{E}(\xi^*_{-1/2}\xi^{*\prime}_{-1/2}) &= \sigma^2\Omega \\ \mathrm{E}(\xi^*_{-1}\xi^{*\prime}_{-1/2}) &= \mathrm{E}(\xi^*_{-1/2}\xi^{*\prime}_{-1}) = \mathrm{E}(\xi^*_{-3/2}\xi^{*\prime}_{-1/2}) = \mathrm{E}(\xi^*_{-1/2}\xi^{*\prime}_{-3/2}) = 0 \\ \mathrm{E}(\xi^*_{-1}\xi^{*\prime}_{-1}) &= \frac{1}{\varrho^2(1-\varrho^2)^2} \Omega X' D Q \Sigma^{-1} [\mathrm{E}\theta^{*2}_{-1/2} uu'] \Sigma^{-1} Q D X \Omega \end{aligned} \tag{52}$$

where

$$\mathrm{E}(\theta^{*2}_{-1/2}uu') = \frac{1}{n^2\sigma^4}\mathrm{E}[(u'C_l'M_ZC_\varrho u)^2uu']$$

$$= \frac{1}{n^2\sigma^4}[\{(\mathrm{tr}\ \Sigma C_1'M_ZC_\varrho)^2 + \mathrm{tr}\ \Sigma C_1'M_ZC_\varrho\Sigma C_1'M_ZC_\varrho$$

$$+ \mathrm{tr}\ \Sigma C_\varrho'M_ZC_1\Sigma C_1'M_ZC_\varrho\}\Sigma+2(\mathrm{tr}\ \Sigma C_1'M_ZC_\varrho)(\Sigma C_1'M_ZC_\varrho\Sigma$$

$$+ \Sigma C_\varrho'M_ZC_1\Sigma) + 2\Sigma(C_1'M_ZC_\varrho + C_\varrho'M_ZC_1)\Sigma(C_1'M_ZC_\varrho +$$

$$C_\varrho'M_ZC_1)\Sigma] \qquad (53)$$

has been obtained by modifying the result (44) for the nonsymmetric matrix $C_1'M_ZC_\varrho$. Using (53) in (52), and noting that tr $N = 0 + \mathrm{o}(n)$, tr N^2 + tr $\Sigma N_1'N = n(1-\varrho^2) + \mathrm{o}(n)$, $\Omega X'DQDX\Omega = (1-\varrho^2)^2\Omega X'QX\Omega + \mathrm{o}(n^{-1})$ $(N_1 = C_1'M_ZC_\varrho,\ N = \Sigma N_1)$, we get the result in Theorem 1 for $s = 5$ (Durbin's case) to be the same as those for s=1, . . . ,4.

4.2 *Proof of Theorem 2*

From (1) and (22) we can write the sampling error of the CO estimator as

$$\tilde{\beta}_1 - \beta = (X'\hat{P}_1'C_0\hat{P}_1X)^{-1}X'\hat{P}_1'C_0\hat{P}_1y$$

where $C_0 = C'C$ and

$$\hat{P}_1'C_0\hat{P}_1 = \hat{P}_1'\hat{P}_1 - D_0(1-\hat{\varrho}_1^2);$$

D_0 is a $T \times T$ diagonal matrix of zeros with a one in the upper left corner (defined in Section 2) and $\hat{P}_1$ is as used in Prais-Winsten estimator. Using (39) we can write

$$\hat{P}_1'C_0\hat{P}_1 = (1-\varrho^2)(\Sigma^{-1}-D_0) + \theta_{-1/2}(R+2\varrho D_0) + \theta_{-1}(R+2\varrho D_0) + \theta^2_{-1/2}(D_1+D_0)$$

where $D_1 = (I_n - D)/\varrho^2$ and $R = \dfrac{1-\varrho^2}{\varrho}\Sigma^{-1} - \dfrac{D}{\varrho}$ is an $n \times n$ matrix.

Proceeding as for the PW estimator in (36) we get

$$\tilde{\beta}_1 - \beta = \eta_{-1/2} + \eta_{-1} + \eta_{-3/2}$$

where, using (42)

$$\eta_{-1/2} = \xi_{-1/2}, \qquad \eta_{-1} = \xi_{-1} - \Omega X'D_0u$$

$$\eta_{-3/2} = \xi_{-3/2} + \Omega X'D_0X\Omega X'\Sigma^{-1}u + \left\{\frac{\theta-\frac{1}{2}}{\varrho(1-\varrho^2)}\right\}\Omega X'\{(1+\varrho^2)\mathrm{I}_n -$$

$$DX\Omega X'\}D_0u.$$

Now writing $(\tilde{\beta}_1-\beta)(\tilde{\beta}_1-\beta)'$ and taking expectation we get the result stated in Theorem 2.

Table 1 *Efficiency measures of estimators for M1*

Sample size: 10

ϱ	e_1	e_2	e_3	e_1^*	e_2^*	e_3^*
.05	1.005	1.215	1.431	1.002	1.066	1.112
.10	1.021	1.199	1.419	1.007	1.060	1.106
.20	1.084	1.167	1.397	1.026	1.047	1.097
.30	1.193	1.139	1.384	1.055	1.036	1.095
.40	1.360	1.121	1.386	1.093	1.030	1.105
.50	1.607	1.113	1.408	1.134	1.032	1.138
.60	1.971	1.115	1.455	1.170	1.045	1.204
.70	2.505	1.122	1.528	1.192	1.068	1.315
.80	3.269	1.118	1.628	1.182	1.088	1.477
.90	4.292	1.075	1.756	1.124	1.067	1.684
.95	4.874	1.032	1.845	1.072	1.030	1.811

Sample size: 40

ϱ	e_1	e_2	e_3	e_1^*	e_2^*	e_3^*
.05	1.004	1.052	1.102	1.002	1.022	1.035
.10	1.019	1.060	1.115	1.008	1.026	1.039
.20	1.082	1.077	1.142	1.034	1.032	1.047
.30	1.209	1.093	1.170	1.083	1.037	1.055
.40	1.440	1.104	1.193	1.162	1.039	1.060
.50	1.857	1.105	1.209	1.275	1.036	1.062
.60	2.631	1.094	1.217	1.423	1.028	1.063
.70	4.162	1.078	1.228	1.581	1.022	1.078
.80	7.603	1.075	1.278	1.662	1.031	1.145
.90	17.807	1.116	1.450	1.511	1.091	1.364
.95	31.244	1.132	1.634	1.313	1.122	1.591

Table 2 *Efficiency measures of estimators for M2*

Sample size: 10

ϱ	e_1	e_2	e_3	e_1^*	e_2^*	e_3^*
.05	1.007	1.286	1.448	1.003	1.130	1.185
.10	1.026	1.297	1.462	1.013	1.123	1.175
.20	1.113	1.325	1.492	1.054	1.111	1.156
.30	1.284	1.356	1.522	1.125	1.106	1.146
.40	1.594	1.381	1.539	1.241	1.108	1.144
.50	2.170	1.383	1.528	1.428	1.112	1.143
.60	3.322	1.348	1.472	1.745	1.107	1.135
.70	5.923	1.266	1.363	2.329	1.087	1.110
.80	13.064	1.154	1.219	3.582	1.053	1.069
.90	42.226	1.048	1.080	7.475	1.017	1.026
.95	110.978	1.013	1.029	15.309	1.005	1.009

Sample size: 40

ϱ	e_1	e_2	e_3	e_1^*	e_2^*	e_3^*
.05	1.003	1.033	1.072	1.002	1.023	1.038
.10	1.012	1.039	1.081	1.008	1.026	1.043
.20	1.053	1.054	1.102	1.036	1.034	1.052
.30	1.137	1.072	1.127	1.089	1.042	1.061
.40	1.292	1.093	1.155	1.180	1.048	1.067
.50	1.584	1.117	1.184	1.329	1.052	1.071
.60	2.180	1.144	1.214	1.576	1.054	1.071
.70	3.626	1.168	1.235	2.017	1.056	1.072
.80	8.519	1.162	1.217	2.978	1.054	1.067
.90	42.269	1.091	1.121	6.381	1.032	1.040
.95	181.808	1.035	1.051	14.026	1.012	1.017

Table 3 *Efficiency measures of estimators for M3*

Sample size: 10

ϱ	e_1	e_2	e_3	e_1^*	e_2^*	e_3^*
.05	1.001	1.055	1.323	1.001	1.028	1.277
.10	1.005	1.063	1.354	1.002	1.032	1.301
.20	1.018	1.079	1.423	1.009	1.039	1.354
.30	1.040	1.098	1.504	1.019	1.046	1.413
.40	1.069	1.118	1.595	1.032	1.051	1.479
.50	1.106	1.137	1.697	1.046	1.055	1.552
.60	1.146	1.150	1.806	1.057	1.055	1.633
.70	1.184	1.152	1.910	1.063	1.053	1.722
.80	1.209	1.133	1.988	1.058	1.050	1.821
.90	1.201	1.075	2.007	1.039	1.040	1.918
.95	1.176	1.030	1.994	1.023	1.021	1.956

Sample size: 40

ϱ	e_1	e_2	e_3	e_1^*	e_2^*	e_3^*
.05	1.000	1.006	1.072	1.000	1.004	1.067
.10	1.002	1.007	1.080	1.001	1.004	1.074
.20	1.009	1.011	1.099	1.005	1.006	1.090
.30	1.021	1.016	1.124	1.012	1.010	1.112
.40	1.041	1.025	1.158	1.025	1.015	1.140
.50	1.075	1.039	1.205	1.045	1.023	1.179
.60	1.133	1.062	1.274	1.080	1.037	1.234
.70	1.242	1.102	1.382	1.142	1.059	1.314
.80	1.482	1.166	1.550	1.267	1.090	1.430
.90	2.165	1.216	1.757	1.512	1.110	1.583
.95	3.016	1.169	1.820	1.584	1.105	1.706

Table 4 *Efficiency of estimators for M4*

Sample size: 10

ϱ	e_1	e_2	e_3	e_1^*	e_2^*	e_3^*
.05	1.020	1.980	2.686	1.007	1.258	1.401
.10	1.082	1.950	2.635	1.027	1.252	1.390
.20	1.370	1.839	2.453	1.111	1.228	1.354
.30	2.025	1.681	2.203	1.268	1.191	1.304
.40	3.472	1.509	1.931	1.527	1.149	1.247
.50	6.859	1.349	1.674	1.942	1.106	1.188
.60	15.542	1.215	1.455	2.626	1.067	1.134
.70	40.626	1.115	1.282	3.838	1.037	1.086
.80	126.944	1.048	1.152	6.354	1.015	1.048
.90	552.844	1.011	1.061	14.049	1.004	1.020
.95	–	1.003	1.027	29.526	1.001	1.009

Sample Size: 40

ϱ	e_1	e_2	e_3	e_1^*	e_2^*	e_3^*
.05	1.029	1.309	1.397	1.010	1.094	1.118
.10	1.121	1.300	1.387	1.039	1.092	1.115
.20	1.576	1.270	1.350	1.164	1.083	1.105
.30	2.785	1.228	1.299	1.407	1.071	1.091
.40	6.209	1.181	1.241	1.839	1.057	1.075
.50	17.733	1.135	1.183	2.610	1.043	1.058
.60	67.173	1.093	1.130	4.075	1.030	1.042
.70	362.582	1.057	1.084	7.180	1.019	1.027
.80	–	1.029	1.046	15.105	1.010	1.015
.90	–	1.009	1.016	44.708	1.003	1.005
.95	–	1.002	1.006	109.573	1.001	1.002

Note: the '–' in columns of e_1 indicates that the number was greater than one thousand.

Notes

* The research supports to A. Ullah from the SSHRC and Air Force Office of Scientific Research, grant F49629-82-K-001, at the Center for Multivariate Analysis, University of Pittsburgh, are gratefully acknowledged. This paper was presented at the Sixth International Symposium on Multivariate Analysis at the University of Pittsburgh. The authors are thankful to L. Bauwens, B. Raj, K. Kadiyala, M. L. King and D. E. A. Giles for useful comments and suggestions. A. Ullah is also grateful to T. Kariya for many discussions on the subject matter of this paper.

1 'Better' means smaller mean square error or, equivalently in this paper, smaller variance, since the estimators of β considered here are unbiased.

2 When using CO, the use of the correct ϱ does not necessarily result in the smallest mean square error (MSE). In fact, in the case of Kadiyala's model, the smallest MSE of CO estimators is obtained by using $\hat{\varrho}=-1$ regardless of the true value of ϱ; see Magee (1982).

3 Results are presented here for four models only, although there were many other models considered, as well as results for $n = 20$ and $n = 30$.

4 We are grateful to an anonymous referee for bringing Watson's X matrices to our attention.

5 A result from work in progress suggests that the approximate MSE's for the iterated PW and the ML estimators are both identical to the two-stage PW result.

6 Expansions for the class of estimators $(X'\hat{S}^{-1}X)^{-1}X'\hat{S}^{-1}y$ where $\hat{S}^{-1}$ is such that $X'(\hat{S}^{-1}-S^{-1})X$ has $0(n^{1/2})$ for some fixed S can be shown to be suitable for asymptotic expansion procedures using conditions described by Sargan (1974, p. 172).

7 Note that in Ullah *et al.* (1983) the term tr $MBM\Sigma MBM\Sigma$ and $\Omega X'DQDX\Omega$ are not simplified to proper orders and hence their paper which deals only with the case $s=1$ contains different expressions than presented here.

References

Akahira, M. and Takeuchi, K. (1981), *Asymptotic Efficiency of Statistical Estimators: Concepts and Higher Order Asymptotic Efficiency*, New York: Springer-Verlag.

Beach, C. M. and MacKinnon, J. G. (1978), 'A Maximum Likelihood Procedure for Regression with Autocorrelated Errors,' *Econometrica*, 46, 51-8.

Cochrane, D. and Orcutt, G. H. (1949), 'Application of Least Squares Regressions to Relationships Containing Autocorrelated Error Terms,' *Journal of the American Statistical Association*, 44, 32-61.

Durbin, J. (1960), 'Estimation of Parameters in Time-Series Regression Models,' *Journal of the Royal Statistical Society* B, 22, 139-53.

Efron, B. (1975), 'Defining the Curvature of a Statistical Problem (with Application to Second Order Efficiency),' *Annals of Statistics*, 3, 1189-242.

Fisher, R.A. (1925), 'Theory of Statistical Estimation', *Proceedings of the Cambridge Philosophical Society*, 22, 700-25.

Griliches, Z. and Rao, P. (1969), 'Small Sample Properties of Several Two Stage Regression Methods in the Context of Auto-Correlated Disturbances,' *Journal of the American Statistical Association*, 64, 253-72.

Harvey, A. C. and McAvinchey, D. (1978), 'The Small Sample Efficiency of Two-Step Estimators in Regression Models with Autoregressive Disturbances,' University of British Columbia, Economics Discussion Paper No. 78-10.

Judge, G. G., Griffiths, W. E., Hill, R. C. and Lee, T. C. (1980), *The Theory and Practice of Econometrics*, New York: Wiley.
Kadiyala, K. R. (1968), 'A Transformation used to Circumvent the Problem of Autocorrelation,' *Econometrica*, 36, 93-6.
Kale, B. K. and Chandrasekar, B. K. (1982), 'On the Equivalence of Optimality Criteria for Vector Unbiased Statistics', mimeo, Department of Statistics, University of Poona.
Krämer, W. (1980), 'Finite Sample Efficiency of Ordinary Least Squares in the Linear Regression Model with Autocorrelated Errors,' *Journal of the American Statistical Association*, 75, 1005-9.
Krämer, W. (1982), 'Note on Estimating Linear Trend When Residuals are Autocorrelated,' *Econometrica*, 50, 1065-8.
Maeshiro, A. (1976), 'Autoregressive Transformation, Trended Independent Variables and Autocorrelated Disturbance Terms,' *Review of Economics and Statistics*, 58, 497-500.
Maeshiro, A. (1979), 'On the Retention of the First Observations in Serial Correlation Adjustment of Regression Models,' *International Economic Review*, 20, 259-65.
Magee, L. (1982), 'Efficiency of Estimators in Regression Model with AR(1) Errors: An Analytical Study,' mimeo, Department of Economics, University of Western Ontario.
Park, R. E. and Mitchell, B. M. (1980), 'Estimating the Autocorrelated Error Model with Trended Data,' *Journal of Econometrics*, 13, 185-201.
Prais, S. J. and Winsten, C. B. (1954), 'Trend Estimators and Serial Correlation,' unpublished Cowles Commission Discussion Paper, University of Chicago.
Raj, B., Srivastava, V. K. and Upadhyaya, S. (1980), 'The Efficiency of Estimating a Random Coefficient Model,' *Journal of Econometrics*, 12, 285-99.
Rao, C. R. (1962), 'Efficient Estimates and Optimum Inference Procedures in Large Sample,' *Journal of Royal Statistical Society* B, 24, 46-72.
Sargan, J. D. (1974), 'The Validity of Nagar's Expansion for the Moments of Econometric Estimators,' *Econometrica*, 42, 169-76.
Spitzer, J. J. (1979), 'Small-Sample Properties of Nonlinear Least Squares and Maximum Likelihood Estimators in the Context of Autocorrelated Errors,' *Journal of the American Statistical Association*, 74, 41-7.
Srivastava, V. K. and Tiwari, R. (1976), 'Evaluation of Expectation of Products of Stochastic Matrices,' *Scandinavian Journal of Statistics*, 3, 135-8.
Taylor, W. E. (1981), 'On the Efficiency of the Cochrane-Orcutt Estimator,' *Journal of Econometrics*, 17, 67-82.
Theil, H. (1971), *Principles of Econometrics*, New York: Wiley.
Theil, H. and Nagar, A. L. (1961), 'Testing the Independence of Regression Disturbances,' *Journal of the American Statistical Association*, 56, 793-806.
Tillman, J. A. (1975), 'The Power of the Durbin-Watson Test,' *Econometrica*, 43, 959-74.
Ullah, A., Srivastava, V. K., Magee, L. and Srivastava, A. (1983), 'Estimation of Linear Regression Model with Autocorrelated Disturbances,' *Journal of Time Series Analysis*, 4, 127-35.
Watson, G. S. (1967), 'Linear Least Squares Regression,' *Annals of Mathematical Statistics*, 38, 1679-99.

6 Autocorrelation pre-test estimation in models with a lagged dependent variable

*David E. A. Giles and Murray Beattie**

1 Introduction

This paper considers some of the implications for the finite-sample properties of several regression estimators for models which include a lagged value of the dependent variable as a regressor, when estimation is conditional upon a preliminary test for first-order autocorrelation in the (least squares) residuals.

Various forms of preliminary test strategies are commonly adopted in applied econometric analysis, often unbeknown to the reader of reported work, and sometimes unbeknown to the researcher! However, despite the early recognition that, in general, a preliminary hypothesis test using the same sample of data biases a subsequent least squares estimator (e.g. Bancroft (1944)), it is only relatively recently that econometricians have paid proper attention to the consequences of pre-testing (e.g. Wallace (1977)).

One example of such a strategy is to estimate a regression relationship by (say) ordinary least squares; use the associated residuals to test for the presence of autocorrelation in the model errors, using (say) the Durbin-Watson (1950) test; and then, depending upon the outcome of this test, either retain the least squares estimates or else re-estimate the relationship using an estimator which 'corrects' for the autocorrelation (e.g. the Cochrane-Orcutt (1949) procedure). Thus, the final estimator is a stochastic mixture of ordinary least squares and the Cochrane-Orcutt estimator, the randomisation of the strategy being determined by the distribution of the Durbin-Watson test statistic.

Of course, an implication of pre-testing is that the resultant estimator has sampling properties which differ, in general, from those of either of its component parts, and which depend upon the true values of the parameters, the sample data, and the form and size of the test itself. Autocorrelation pre-testing for regressions involving non-stochastic orthornormal regressors has been discussed[1] by Judge and Bock (1978), King and Giles (1984) and Griffiths and Beesley (1984). The nature of the problem precludes analytical results, and these authors report Monte Carlo investigations of the risks of several autocorrelation pre-test estimators. This paper extends their work by considering a simple dynamic model, typical of the type encountered in econometric analysis with time-series data. This extension is non-trivial, as the form of the model suggests the use of different tests from those considered by these authors, and different estimators if the hypothesis of error serial independence is rejected.

The plan of the rest of the paper is as follows. In Section 2 the pre-test problem in question is formalised. The various tests and estimators to be analysed are described in Section 3, and Section 4 deals with the design of the Monte Carlo experiment. The results of this experiment are reported in Section 5. Here, the main emphasis is on the risks (under quadratic loss) of the various pre-test estimators. However, these are also compared with the risks of the naive strategies of either always ignoring possible autocorrelation, or always allowing for it without any preliminary test. Also reported in each case are the biases of the various estimators of the coefficient of the lagged dependent variable in the model. The final section summarises the conclusions to be drawn from the study, and suggests some directions for further investigation.

2 Autocorrelation pre-testing

We shall be considering the estimation of a simple dynamic relationship of the form:

$$y_t = \gamma + \beta x_t + \delta y_{t-1} + u_t \; ; \quad t = 1, 2, \ldots, T$$

or

$$\mathbf{y} = Z\theta + \mathbf{u} \, , \tag{1}$$

where $\theta' = (\gamma, \beta, \delta)$, $Z = (\mathbf{1}, \boldsymbol{x}, \mathbf{y}_{-1})$, and $\boldsymbol{x}$ is non-stochastic.

It is well known that if $\mathbf{u} \sim (0,\sigma^2 I)$, then the Ordinary Least Squares (OLS) estimator of θ is biased, but it is asymptotically unbiased and consistent. However, if

$$u_t = \varrho u_{t-1} + e_t; \qquad |\varrho| < 1 \; ; \qquad e_t \text{ iid } (0,\sigma^2) \; ; \qquad t = 1, 2, \ldots, T \tag{2}$$

then OLS is inconsistent, and in this case a variety of alternative estimators have been proposed. For the purposes of the discussion in this section, denote the OLS estimator of θ by $\hat{\theta}(\mathbf{y})$ and let $\tilde{\theta}(\mathbf{y})$ be a consistent estimator of θ, chosen to take account of the dual complications of a lagged endogenous regressor and autocorrelated errors.

In practice, the decision as to whether or not to use $\tilde{\theta}(\mathbf{y})$ in place of $\hat{\theta}(\mathbf{y})$ often is based on the prior test of the hypothesis, $H_0 : \varrho = 0$. If H_0 cannot be rejected (at some chosen level of significance, α%) then $\hat{\theta}(\mathbf{y})$ is adopted; but if H_0 is rejected (in favour of $H_1 : \varrho > 0$, or $H_2 : \varrho \neq 0$, say) then $\tilde{\theta}(\mathbf{y})$ is used to estimate θ. The test of H_0 is based on a statistic, $S(\mathbf{y})$, constructed from the same sample of data as is used to construct $\hat{\theta}(\mathbf{y})$ or $\tilde{\theta}(\mathbf{y})$, usually via the OLS residuals for (1). The presence of $\mathbf{y}_{-1}$ in (1) invalidates conventional tests for autocorrelation, such as that of Durbin and Watson (DW), but various alternatives have been suggested.[2]

Thus, for a chosen significance level, the pre-test estimator of θ may be expressed as:

$$\begin{aligned} \theta^*(\mathbf{y}) &= \hat{\theta}(\mathbf{y})\ ; \qquad \text{if } H_0 \text{ is not rejected} \\ &= \tilde{\theta}(\mathbf{y})\ ; \qquad \text{if } H_0 \text{ is rejected.} \end{aligned}$$

That is,

$$\theta^*(\mathbf{y}) = I_R(\alpha)\ .\ \tilde{\theta}(\mathbf{y}) + I_{\bar{R}}(\alpha)\ .\ \hat{\theta}(\mathbf{y})\ ,$$

$$\begin{aligned} \text{where } I_R(\alpha) &= 1\ ; \qquad \text{if } S(\mathbf{y}) \in R \\ &= 0\ ; \qquad \text{otherwise} \\ I_{\bar{R}}(\alpha) &= 1\ ; \qquad \text{if } S(\mathbf{y}) \in \bar{R} \\ &= 0\ ; \qquad \text{otherwise.} \end{aligned}$$

R is the rejection region for the test based on $S(\mathbf{y})$ and the α% significance level, and $\bar{R}$ is the complement of R. Depending upon the choice of $\tilde{\theta}(\mathbf{y})$ and of $S(\mathbf{y})$, a variety of autocorrelation pre-test estimators, $\theta^*(\mathbf{y})$, may be generated for θ in (1).

For the particular pre-test situation under study here, the sampling properties of $\theta^*(\mathbf{y})$ are unknown, and indeed they do not admit of analytical derivation. A similar situation arose in the study[3] by Judge and Bock (1978), where the model concerned contained only fixed regressors, and various autocorrelation pre-test estimators were examined. As in that earlier study, we shall be concerned primarily with the risks of various $\theta^*(\mathbf{y})$ estimators, especially as functions of the degree of autocorrelation in the model errors. For comparative purposes we shall consider the finite-sample risks of $\hat{\theta}(\mathbf{y})$ and various $\tilde{\theta}(\mathbf{y})$ estimators as functions of ϱ, and the finite-sample biases of the various estimators for δ in (1). This parameter is of special interest – among other things, the magnitude of δ determines the stability (or instability) of this dynamic model.

The risk of any of the estimators under study is taken under a simple quadratic loss function, so that the risk of $\theta^*(\mathbf{y})$ is:

$$\begin{aligned} r(\theta^*(\mathbf{y})) &= \mathrm{E}(\theta^*(\mathbf{y}) - \theta)'(\theta^*(\mathbf{y}) - \theta) \\ &= \mathrm{tr}(\mathrm{MSE}(\theta^*(\mathbf{y}))), \end{aligned} \tag{3}$$

where E is the expectation over the sample space; MSE denotes matrix Mean Squared Error; and corresponding definitions apply for the risks of $\hat{\theta}(\mathbf{y})$ and $\tilde{\theta}(\mathbf{y})$. The risk in (3) may be expressed in terms of the sampling variances and squared small-sample biases of the estimators for each of the elements of θ, and in the simulation experiment described in Section 4 these expressions are evaluated numerically. Clearly, (3) depends on the (unknown) values of θ, σ^2 and ϱ; on α and the sample data; and on the particular choice of $\tilde{\theta}(\mathbf{y})$ and $S(\mathbf{y})$.

3 Estimators and Tests

A variety of estimators may be considered for model (1) when the disturbances satisfy (2). These estimators have asymptotic justification, and a good discussion of this literature is given by Dhrymes (1971). We have noted already that for this estimation problem, OLS is not even consistent, and two other points are worth mentioning. First, if the true value of ϱ were known, then exact Generalised Least Squares (GLS) could be used to deal with the error structure and to estimate θ consistently.[4] In this case GLS is *not* best linear unbiased[5], given the presence of $\mathbf{y}_{-1}$ in (1). Secondly, the traditional Cochrane-Orcutt estimator is *not* to be recommended in this case. As is discussed by Betancourt and Kelejian (1981), the usual version of this estimator is *inconsistent* when the regressors include a lagged value of the dependent variable.[6]

Apart from considering OLS as a 'naive' bench-mark, we shall deal only with consistent estimators of θ in this study, and we have limited our attention to some computationally simple and frequently encountered estimators. Clearly, the study could be extended to include additional consistent estimators, but with computational cost in mind we have elected to deal with fewer estimators more thoroughly, rather than more estimators in less detail.

To retain some comparability with the Judge and Bock study, exact GLS is used as a second bench-mark. Two traditional estimators of θ which allow for the correlation between Z and $\mathbf{u}$, but do *not* take explicit account of the structure of (2), also are considered. The first is Liviatan's (1963) Instrumental Variables (IV) estimator, in which $\mathbf{x}_{-1}$ serves as an instrument for $\mathbf{y}_{-1}$, and $\mathbf{x}$ and the intercept dummy act as their own instruments. This estimator was proposed for the model (1) when $\mathbf{u}$ follows a first-order moving average process, but it is equally applicable (and frequently used) when $\mathbf{u}$ satisfies (2). The second of these estimators is the simple Two-Step (TS) procedure whereby $\mathbf{y}_{-1}$ is regressed (by OLS) on lagged values[7] of $\mathbf{x}$, and the resulting prediction, $\hat{\mathbf{y}}_{-1}$, is used in place of $\mathbf{y}_{-1}$ in the OLS estimation of (1).

The final estimator considered is Wallis's (1967) three-step procedure (W). Liviatan's IV estimator is applied to (1), yielding residuals $\tilde{u}_t$; $t = 1, 2, \ldots, T$. Then, with an approximate correction for bias,[8] ϱ is estimated consistently as:

$$\tilde{\varrho} = \left[\sum_{t=2}^{T} (\tilde{u}_t \tilde{u}_{t-1})/(T-1) \right] \Big/ \left[\sum_{t=1}^{T} (\tilde{u}_t^2)/T \right] + (3/T).$$

Finally, feasible GLS (with $\tilde{\varrho}$ replacing ϱ) is applied to (1) to yield a consistent estimate of θ. Given that Wallis's estimator *does* take explicit account of the form of the error process in (2), at least asymptotically it is efficient relative to the above IV and TS procedures. Wallis (1967) provides some Monte Carlo evidence in support of this estimator's finite-sample properties, and additional Monte Carlo evidence on the sampling properties of different estimators of (1) when the errors are serially correlated is given by Dhrymes (1971; pp. 355-401).

Each of the (feasible) consistent estimators, IV, TS and W may be used in conjunction with the OLS estimator to construct a pre-test estimator of θ, as described in Section 2. Thus, for any particular test of H_0, three pre-test estimators are defined. We shall consider three such tests, and so nine pre-test estimators are discussed in the study described in the next section.

The first test of H_0 that we consider is Durbin's (1970) *h*-test, where:

$$h = (1 - \tfrac{1}{2}\text{DW})\{T/(1 - T\hat{V}(\hat{\delta}))\}^{\frac{1}{2}},$$

DW is the usual Durbin-Watson statistic calculated from the OLS residuals for (1), and $\hat{V}(\hat{\delta})$ is the estimated variance of the OLS estimator of δ. Under H_0, the *h* statistic is asymptotically standard normal in distribution. Of course, if $T\hat{V}(\hat{\delta}) > 1$, then the *h*-test is not operational. Partly for this reason, Durbin (1970) proposed a second test of H_0. OLS is applied to (1), yielding the residuals $\hat{\mathbf{u}}$. Regress $\hat{\mathbf{u}}$ on $\hat{\mathbf{u}}_{-1}$, $\mathbf{y}_{-1}$ and $\mathbf{x}$ (including an intercept) by OLS, and test the significance of the coefficient of $\hat{\mathbf{u}}_{-1}$ by the usual *t*-test. Rejection of the null hypothesis that this coefficient is zero is equivalent to rejecting $H_0 : \varrho = 0$.

Some Monte Carlo evidence on the small-sample sizes of these two asymptotic tests is given by Kenkel (1974, 1975), and on their small-sample powers by Maddala and Rao (1973), Park (1975), Spencer (1975), and McNown and Hunter (1980). The latter authors and Kenkel compare these tests with the DW test, and find that although the latter test is, strictly, inappropriate for models which include stochastic regressors, nonetheless it is at least as powerful as Durbin's *h*-test in many finite sample cases.[9] Finally, the evidence on the relative merits of Durbin's *h*-test and his second test (which we shall refer to as the *m*-test) is rather mixed. Maddala and Rao conclude that there is little to choose between the two tests, while Spencer's results suggest that the *m*-test may be preferable to the *h*-test. Of course, this apparent conflict is to be expected in Monte Carlo studies.

As noted above, these three tests are used as the basis for studying the consequences of autocorrelation pre-testing in models of the form (1). As well as extending the number of estimators considered in the study, additional tests and/or strategies also could be examined. For example, the likelihood ratio test of H_0 could be considered, as in the study by Maddala and Rao. Further, a pre-test strategy involving the use of the *m*-test (or DW test, or likelihood ratio test) only if the *h*-test were inapplicable, could be adopted in conjunction with any of the estimators discussed earlier.

4 Experimental Design

The investigation of the finite-sample properties of the various autocorrelation pre-test estimators is based on the following Monte Carlo experiment. The data for $\mathbf{x}$ in (1) are the observations on seasonally adjusted Australian non-farm GNP, at constant 1966-67 prices.[10] Two sample sizes are considered – 1960(1) – 1964(4) ($T = 20$), and 1960(1) – 1974(4) ($T = 60$). Pre-sample values of $\mathbf{x}$ are needed for some parts of the experiment, and these are $x_0 = 3631.0$ and $x_{-1} = 3594.0$.

The random disturbances $\{e_t\}$, are generated to be $N(0,\sigma^2)$ by applying the Box-Muller transformation to [0,1] uniform random deviates produced by the RAN intrinsic[11] on a VAX 11-780 computer. The disturbances were (satisfactorily) subjected to a variety of non-parametric tests for randomness and normality. In the generation of $\mathbf{u}$ from (2), we set $u_0 = 0.0$. It should be noted that this initialization affects the covariance matrix of $\mathbf{u}$, and hence the form of the GLS and W estimators. If GLS is implemented by means of the usual data transformation, then instead of scaling the first sample observations by $(1 - \varrho^2)^{1/2}$, these observations are left at their sample values. For $t = 2, \ldots, T$ the usual transformation applies – y_t becomes $(y_t - \varrho y_{t-1})$, *etc.* We have also experimented with a randomly generated u_0 (and the usual data transformation for GLS) and found that the results are insensitive to this initialization

All values of $\varrho \in [0.0(0.1)0.9]$ are examined, but only a limited number of values are considered for the other parameters. These values are chosen to ensure realistic signal/noise ratios in the model. Some preliminary OLS and IV estimates of (1) were made with $\mathbf{y}$ taken to be real seasonally adjusted Australian private consumption expenditure. The residuals from these regressions were moderately autocorrelated, and $\bar{R}^2$ values of the order 0.98 were obtained. Consequently, the following parameter values are considered:

$$\sigma = 5.0,\ 25.5\ ;\ (\gamma,\beta) = (0.18,\ 0.31),(179.0,\ 0.27);\ \delta = 0.34,\ 0.57,\ 0.80.$$

The initial value of $\mathbf{y}$ is set at $y_0 = 2644.0$, and a five per cent significance level is used for all of the hypothesis tests.[12]

All of the above one hundred and twenty parameter space locations are considered for each of the sample sizes. In each of these two hundred and forty cases the experiment is replicated one thousand times, the same one thousand samples being used across all cases to facilitate direct comparisons.

The moments of the (approximate) sampling distributions for each of the estimators in each of the cases are used to construct empirical risk functions corresponding to (3).

5 Discussion of results

The results of the Monte Carlo experiment are reported in this section in three parts. First, the evidence on the finite-sample properties of the various pre-test estimators is discussed. The risks of these estimators are compared under the various conditions examined in the experiment, and the finite-sample biases of the nine pre-test estimators of δ are also discussed. Secondly, the naive, no pre-testing, strategies are considered, and their sampling properties are discussed in an analogous manner. Together, these two broad sets of results allow some conclusions to be drawn about the relative merits of the pre-test and naive estimation strategies in the third part of this section.

Only a selection of the results of the experiment is reported explicitly in this section, but the commentary is based on the full study, and full details (including a large selection of graphs) are available in Giles and Beattie (1983). The cases for which the various risks and biases are reported have been selected as being representative of the various patterns which emerge in the results. To facilitate a direct examination of the effect of the degree of autocorrelation on the finite-sample properties of the various estimators, these risks and biases are tabulated as functions of ϱ.

(a) The pre-test estimators:

(i) Risk functions

Turning first of all to the risks functions for the pre-test estimators, the following general patterns are apparent. As the sample size (T) increases, the risk of the pre-test Wallis (W) estimator decreases, regardless of any other factor (including the choice of preliminary test for autocorrelation). The same is true for the other two (IV and TS) pre-test estimators if δ = 0.34 or 0.57, but if δ = 0.8 then for some cases the risks of these latter estimators *increase* with T. The W, IV and TS estimators themselves are consistent for θ, and although the corresponding pre-test estimators stochastically incorporate the OLS estimator, which is inconsistent unless ϱ = 0 (or δ = 0), these pre-test strategies may be expected to be consistent in general under the alternative hypothesis because the associated tests are consistent. The rate of convergence of these estimators to the parameter values may be expected to increase as ϱ and/or δ increase, *ceteris paribus*, and this is borne out in the results. The effects of increasing T (and ϱ) may be seen in Table 1.

As the variance (σ^2) of e_t in (2) is increased, the risks of all nine pre-test estimators increase, *ceteris paribus*. This result is independent of the values of the other parameters, and is apparent when the data in parts (a) of Tables 1 and 2 are compared.

The effects of varying the values of γ and β are illustrated in Table 2. For a given case, the values of γ and β have little bearing on the general results. As γ and β are varied, the orders of magnitude of the risks of the pre-test estimators, and the rankings of these estimators (in terms of risk) are essentially unaltered, *ceteris paribus*.

The sensitivity of the results to the value of δ is somewhat mixed, but the following patterns emerge regardless of the values of γ and β, or the choice of the preliminary test for autocorrelation. For $T = 60$ (and any value of σ) the risks of all of the pre-test estimators increase as δ increases. This occurs most markedly for the IV and TS pre-test estimators[13] as δ goes to 0.8. For the smaller sample size, the risks of the W and IV pre-test estimators fall as δ increases towards unity. In this case the same is true for the TS estimator for large ϱ values, but not for values of ϱ close to zero.

Finally, and obviously from all of the results reported so far, the risks of all of the pre-test estimators are increasing (or at least non-decreasing) functions of ϱ, especially as $\varrho \rightarrow 1$.

In attempting to rank the various pre-test estimators in terms of risks, the following conclusions may be drawn. Often there is little to choose numerically between the IV and TS pre-test estimates (for a particular choice of hypothesis test) over quite a large range of values for ϱ. The W pre-test estimator is superior to its IV and TS counterparts, especially for $\varrho > 0.1$. This suggests that the asymptotic superiority of the pure W estimator over the pure IV and TS estimators also holds in smaller samples, and carries over to the pre-test strategy. That this superiority is most marked for large values of ϱ is of no surprise – in these cases the preliminary test tends to reject H_0, so that the OLS component of any of the pre-test estimators is included less frequently than for smaller values of ϱ. Generally, the risk of the W pre-test estimator exceeds that of naive OLS, but often only marginally, even for small ϱ values. For $\varrho > 0.7$, the latter estimator is always dominated by the W pre-test option, regardless of the choice of test.

As noted already, the choice of the preliminary test has little effect on the ordinal rankings of the risks of the various pre-test estimators. However, this choice *does* have some bearing on the *cardinal* rankings of the estimators. Even in this respect, all of the results are very similar whether the DW or *h* tests are used, but in general the use of the *m* test in this context alters the results to some extent. Often, the differences between the magnitudes of the various pre-test risks are less under the *m* test than with either of the other two tests, and frequently the risks themselves are absolutely lower in this case than in the other two cases.

(ii) Biases

As far as the biases of the various pre-test estimators of δ are concerned, all of the general comments above apply in broad terms. The directions of the biases vary according to the choice of estimator and test, and parameter space location. As the sample size increases the absolute biases generally decline, especially when ϱ is close to unity. This is not surprising, for when ϱ is large the (inconsistent) OLS component is likely to have a small weight in the pre-test estimators. This general tendency is less regular for the IV and TS pre-test estimators than for the W pre-test estimator. Several other points emerge. Often the biases of all of the pre-test estimators are close to zero in absolute value, regardless of the value of ϱ. Secondly, in the case of the m test the pre-test biases differ among themselves less than when the DW or h tests are adopted. Thirdly, and as with the risk functions, as $\varrho \to 0$ the pre-test biases converge to the OLS bias, and as $\varrho \to 1$ they converge to the biases of their naive (no pre-test) counterparts, the latter being discussed in Section 5(b) below.

As σ increases, the biases of the various pre-test estimators increase, as may be seen in Table 3. The values of γ and β (and to a lesser extent, δ) have little effect on the rankings of the pre-test estimators on the basis of bias. Of course, as δ changes the absolute biases of its estimators alter, although the changes in relative bias generally are small.

In conclusion, the ranking of the pre-test estimators on the basis of the bias in the estimation of δ is the same as on the basis of risk. The W pre-test estimator is to be preferred to either the IV or TS pre-test estimators, for any given form of the preliminary test. The choice between the DW and h tests again has little bearing on the ranking of the pre-test estimators, and frequently the use of the m test results in substantially less absolute bias in the estimators (other than W) of δ.

(b) The naive estimators

We shall discuss the results for the naive (no pre-test) strategies only briefly. In many cases the tables which follow speak for themselves, and these estimators are considered here primarily for comparison with their pre-test counterparts, rather than for their own interest.

(i) Risk functions

Table 4 illustrates some of the following points. Generally, risk (TS) > risk (IV) > risk (OLS) > risk (W), especially as $\varrho \to 1$. Although this strongly favours the W estimator, for small values of ϱ the risks sometimes 'crossover'. As expected, the W estimator quite clearly dominates the IV and TS estimators overall. In many cases risk (OLS) > risk (IV), risk (TS) for $\varrho \geqslant 0.6$.

The general patterns that emerge in this no pre-testing case are that risk is a non-decreasing function of ϱ, δ and σ, and a decreasing function of T. The last point reflects the consistency of all but the OLS estimator (unless $\delta = 0$). Generally, the results are insensitive to the values of γ or β.

(ii) Biases
The biases of the naive estimators of δ are summarized in Table 5. Generally, the biases of the W, TS and IV estimators of δ are small and fairly constant as ϱ increases, while the OLS biases are also quite small in absolute value, but increase with ϱ. Again, the (absolute) bias generally is a non-decreasing function of δ and σ, and a decreasing function of T.

(c) Comparing the naive and pre-test estimators
The OLS estimator was compared with the pre-test estimators in Section 5(a), where we noted that, in terms of risk, OLS generally is to be preferred to the other estimators for small ϱ, but for $\varrho > 0.7$ the Wallis pre-test estimator has smaller risk than has OLS.

As $\varrho \to 0$, each pre-test estimator gives more weight to OLS (depending on the significance level of the preliminary test). Conversely, as $\varrho \to 1$ each pre-test estimator approaches its no-test counterpart. In terms of risk, one of the broad conclusions which may be drawn from the study is that in general the risk of any of the consistent estimators may be reduced *slightly* by pre-testing, especially if it happens that ϱ is fairly small in value. Some insights into this result may be gained by comparing Tables 2(a) and 4(a); and 2(b) and 4(b).

Whether or not there are risk reductions from pre-testing depends on the choices of estimator and test, and on the various parameter values. It is clear, however, that if attention is confined to the m test and the Wallis estimator, then the recommended strategy is: use naive OLS if any available prior information suggests that ϱ is small (say, less than 0.7); otherwise use the pre-test W estimator based on the m test. Generally this strategy will be at least as good as any of the others considered here.

If the bias in estimating δ is the sole criterion for choosing a preferred strategy, then either the naive W estimator or any of the pre-test W estimators might be used with some confidence.

6 Conclusions

As with all Monte Carlo experiments, the results that we have reported are of a limited nature, and extreme care must be taken in attempting to generalise our conclusions to cases other than those investigated here. We have limited our attention to only a very few of the possible estimators that could be considered in this context, and it would be interesting to broaden the investigation in that direction, especially to include some of the many iterative procedures that have been proposed for estimating models of the type that we have considered. Our study has been limited further in the range of sample sizes, test significance levels and areas of the parameter space that have been investigated. Finally, it would be especially interesting to generalise model (1) to include additional exogenous regressors, and then examine the consequences of varying the degree of multicollinearity in the design matrix.

Despite these limitations, this study offers some interesting insights into a very practical problem, and the consequences of dealing with this problem in a variety of commonly encountered ways. Part of its interest also lies in its generalisation to the case of a dynamic model, of the earlier study by Judge and Bock (1978). Finally, this particular experiment is interesting among investigations of this type as, even under the null hypothesis, *none* of the estimators considered is unbiased (or has any other 'optimal' finite-sample properties).

The principal conclusions to be drawn from the results may be stated quite briefly, and in some cases they reinforce the conclusions of Judge and Bock. First, if one is concerned at all with asymptotic properties then the OLS estimator is ruled out, and of the naive consistent estimators considered, the Wallis estimator performs best in finite samples.

Secondly, if a pre-test strategy is to be adopted (as is frequently the case in practice), then the use of the *m* test is marginally preferred in order to minimize finite-sample risk. If this test is used in a pre-test context, then the choice of the component estimator is of less importance than if the DW or *h* tests are used, as the risks of the various *m* pre-test estimators are very similar in each case. However, the Wallis pre-test estimator has smallest risk among those considered, regardless of the form of the preliminary test. The asymptotic advantages of the Wallis estimator over the instrumental variables and two-step estimators seem to extend to finite samples, at least in the cases considered here. It would be especially interesting to compare the Wallis pre-test estimator with other pre-test strategies based on consistent estimators which also take explicit account of the form of the error process. The finding that the risks of the pre-test estimators vary considerably according to the choice of the component estimators is consistent with the results of Judge and Bock.

Thirdly, and also in keeping with the findings of Judge and Bock, autocorrelation pre-test estimation can lead to significant reductions in risk over large parts of the parameter space, especially (in our case) if the Wallis pre-test estimator is employed.

Finally, unless one has strong prior information that $\varrho < 0.7$, one can do at least as well (in terms of risk) by using the Wallis pre-test estimator based on the *m* test as any of the other strategies considered here. If one is confident, *a priori*, that $\varrho < 0.7$, then the simple least squares estimator performs as well as any of the others, at least for the relatively small sample sizes considered in this study.

Table 1 *Risks of pre-test estimators ($\sigma = 25.5$, $\gamma = 179.0$, $\beta = 0.27$, $\delta = 0.57$)*
(a) $T = 20$*

Test	*DW*			*h*			*m*		
ϱ	*IV*	*TS*	*W*	*IV*	*TS*	*W*	*IV*	*TS*	*W*
0.0	0.1881	0.1848	0.1840	0.1840	0.1826	0.1803	0.1747	0.1747	0.1747
0.1	0.2035	0.2006	0.1931	0.1947	0.1933	0.1890	0.1809	0.1809	0.1809
0.2	0.2366	0.2322	0.2203	0.2195	0.2166	0.2097	0.1940	0.1940	0.1940
0.3	0.2782	0.2786	0.2482	0.2648	0.2621	0.2422	0.2154	0.2151	0.2151
0.4	0.3343	0.3409	0.2835	0.3192	0.3203	0.2760	0.2464	0.2462	0.2462
0.5	0.4205	0.4275	0.3271	0.3960	0.4070	0.3251	0.2926	0.2922	0.2921
0.6	0.5203	0.5368	0.3769	0.4961	0.5113	0.3811	0.3610	0.3614	0.3550
0.7	0.6736	0.6996	0.4509	0.6453	0.6657	0.4501	0.4737	0.4742	0.4513
0.8	0.8881	0.9309	0.5634	0.8588	0.8974	0.5626	0.6086	0.6066	0.5805
0.9	1.2956	1.3762	0.7895	1.2476	1.3264	0.7875	0.8344	0.8333	0.7919

*(b)** $T = 60$*

0.0	0.2058	0.2033	0.1858	0.1964	0.1952	0.1851	0.1906	0.1898	0.1841
0.1	0.3039	0.3006	0.2298	0.2649	0.2640	0.2278	0.2612	0.2607	0.2279
0.2	0.4481	0.4468	0.2900	0.4120	0.4091	0.2906	0.3876	0.3847	0.2886
0.3	0.6343	0.6563	0.3775	0.5910	0.6149	0.3767	0.5711	0.5916	0.3743
0.4	0.8180	0.8569	0.5015	0.8105	0.8511	0.5021	0.7926	0.8329	0.5017
0.5	1.0712	1.1404	0.7035	1.0686	1.1351	0.7036	1.0673	1.1334	0.7032
0.6	1.4939	1.6046	1.0520	1.4884	1.5988	1.0508	1.4864	1.5955	1.0510
0.7	2.3123	2.4501	1.7138	2.3119	2.4500	1.7137	2.3119	2.4500	1.7137
0.8	4.3107	4.3521	3.1914	4.3107	4.3521	3.1914	4.3107	4.3521	3.1914
0.9	11.1790	10.2855	7.4344	11.1790	10.2855	7.4344	11.1790	10.2855	7.4344

* The recorded values should be scaled up by 10^5.
** The recorded values should be scaled up by 10^3.

Table 2 *Risks of pre-test estimators* (T = 20, δ = 0.57, σ = 5.0)*
(a) γ = 179.0, β = 0.27

Test	DW			h			m		
ϱ	IV	TS	W	IV	TS	W	IV	TS	W
0.0	0.6579	0.6345	0.6392	0.6265	0.6239	0.6281	0.6223	0.6223	0.6238
0.1	0.7491	0.7232	0.7175	0.7208	0.7104	0.7102	0.7008	0.7010	0.7030
0.2	0.8734	0.8479	0.8175	0.8436	0.8229	0.8146	0.8098	0.8063	0.8072
0.3	1.0346	1.0078	0.9353	0.9903	0.9724	0.9414	0.9446	0.9422	0.9392
0.4	1.2347	1.2082	1.0803	1.1906	1.1717	1.1069	1.1240	1.1185	1.1113
0.5	1.4867	1.4732	1.2459	1.4537	1.4473	1.3006	1.3556	1.3527	1.3321
0.6	1.8083	1.8307	1.4660	1.8053	1.8140	1.5339	1.6730	1.6670	1.6320
0.7	2.3068	2.3549	1.8062	2.2989	2.3327	1.8561	2.1267	2.1324	2.0764
0.8	3.0445	3.1477	2.3444	3.0506	3.1280	2.3822	2.8150	2.8167	2.7703
0.9	4.2494	4.4367	3.3597	4.2499	4.4028	3.4353	4.0883	4.1172	3.9895

(b) γ = 0.18, β = 0.31

0.0	0.4580	0.4475	0.4536	0.4467	0.4447	0.4464	0.4436	0.4436	0.4441
0.1	0.5308	0.5172	0.5208	0.5205	0.5138	0.5131	0.5133	0.5115	0.5112
0.2	0.6210	0.6091	0.6009	0.6120	0.6021	0.6069	0.6024	0.6001	0.5995
0.3	0.7518	0.7342	0.7136	0.7318	0.7239	0.7201	0.7224	0.7188	0.7189
0.4	0.9034	0.8961	0.8406	0.8917	0.8891	0.8579	0.8828	0.8791	0.8749
0.5	1.1206	1.1212	1.0263	1.1216	1.1177	1.0551	1.1079	1.1053	1.0935
0.6	1.4137	1.4384	1.2688	1.4374	1.4468	1.3082	1.4287	1.4314	1.4084
0.7	1.8792	1.9210	1.6389	1.9081	1.9324	1.6879	1.9074	1.9119	1.8593
0.8	2.5929	2.6608	2.2091	2.6238	2.6742	2.2571	2.6423	2.6520	2.5462
0.9	3.7372	3.8565	3.1928	3.7753	3.8704	3.2341	3.7573	3.7914	3.6298

* The recorded entries should be scaled up by 10^3.

Table 3 *Biases of pre-test estimators of* δ^* *(*$T = 60, \gamma = 179.0, \beta = 0.27, \delta = 0.34$*)*
(a) $\sigma = 5$

Test	*DW*			*h*			*m*		
ϱ	*IV*	*TS*	*W*	*IV*	*TS*	*W*	*IV*	*TS*	*W*
0.0	0.262	0.265	0.220	0.234	0.229	0.221	0.179	0.174	0.230
0.1	0.349	0.324	0.033	0.310	0.275	0.069	0.096	0.072	0.075
0.2	0.519	0.481	0.051	0.403	0.384	0.056	0.359	0.330	0.091
0.3	0.176	0.177	0.036	0.220	0.169	0.071	0.212	0.132	0.123
0.4	0.408	0.398	0.023	0.408	0.426	0.026	0.176	0.211	0.057
0.5	0.275	0.350	0.007	0.215	0.258	0.011	0.164	0.175	0.027
0.6	−0.009	0.070	−0.005	−0.037	0.048	−0.004	−0.083	−0.028	0.001
0.7	−0.357	−0.256	−0.013	−0.353	−0.255	−0.012	−0.359	−0.264	−0.001
0.8	−0.865	−0.758	−0.018	−0.865	−0.758	−0.018	−0.865	−0.758	−0.002
0.9	−1.829	−1.716	0.007	−1.829	−1.716	0.007	−1.829	−1.716	0.007

(b) $\sigma = 25.5$

0.0	0.760	0.655	0.381	0.911	0.809	0.475	0.488	0.417	0.548
0.1	2.049	1.440	−0.221	1.144	0.765	0.117	0.276	−0.086	0.315
0.2	2.651	1.931	−0.116	2.907	2.374	0.210	0.587	0.061	0.998
0.3	0.789	0.183	−0.367	1.149	0.670	0.109	−1.874	−2.985	1.116
0.4	0.658	0.264	−0.427	1.187	1.035	−0.249	−2.354	−2.777	0.807
0.5	−1.306	−0.731	−0.337	−1.297	−0.867	−0.250	−2.798	−2.482	0.366
0.6	−4.192	−2.427	−0.102	−4.345	−2.539	−0.092	−4.676	−3.151	0.152
0.7	−8.394	−4.433	0.266	−8.394	−4.433	0.266	−8.518	−4.715	0.330
0.8	−15.022	−6.609	0.791	−15.022	−6.609	0.790	−15.016	−6.689	0.857
0.9	−28.601	−8.979	1.810	−28.601	−8.979	1.810	−28.515	−8.978	1.962

* The recorded values should be scaled by 10^{-3}

Table 4 *Risks of estimators (no pre-testing)* ($T = 20$, $\sigma = 5$, $\delta = 0.57$)*
(a) $\gamma = 179.0$, $\beta = 0.27$

ϱ	*OLS*	*GLS*	*IV*	*TS*	*W*
0.0	0.0622	0.0622	0.0842	0.0685	0.0665
0.1	0.0701	0.0696	0.0894	0.0769	0.0734
0.2	0.0803	0.0780	0.0969	0.0878	0.0814
0.3	0.0934	0.0878	0.1077	0.1019	0.0912
0.4	0.1105	0.0998	0.1228	0.1205	0.1036
0.5	0.1332	0.1149	0.1445	0.1459	0.1201
0.6	0.1646	0.1348	0.1767	0.1818	0.1429
0.7	0.2105	0.1620	0.2255	0.2347	0.1762
0.8	0.2821	0.2031	0.3009	0.3146	0.2295
0.9	0.4118	0.2886	0.4220	0.4444	0.3319

(b) $\gamma = 0.18$, $\beta = 0.31$

ϱ	*OLS*	*GLS*	*IV*	*TS*	*W*
0.0	0.0443	0.0443	0.0530	0.0461	0.0465
0.1	0.0510	0.0506	0.0580	0.0527	0.0530
0.2	0.0598	0.0582	0.0649	0.0614	0.0601
0.3	0.0716	0.0678	0.0747	0.0730	0.0700
0.4	0.0877	0.0802	0.0884	0.0886	0.0830
0.5	0.1103	0.0966	0.1082	0.1105	0.1002
0.6	0.1431	0.1190	0.1379	0.1424	0.1250
0.7	0.1923	0.1497	0.1835	0.1904	0.1612
0.8	0.2669	0.1943	0.2545	0.2643	0.2180
0.9	0.3829	0.2762	0.3683	0.3838	0.3150

* The recorded values should be scaled up by 10^4.

Table 5 *Biases of estimators of δ (no pre-testing)**
(T = 20, σ = 5, δ = 0.57) (a) γ = 179.0, β = 0.27

ϱ	*OLS*	*GLS*	*IV*	*TS*	*W*
0.0	−0.294	−0.294	−0.135	−0.124	−0.383
0.1	−0.225	−0.310	−0.132	−0.126	−0.374
0.2	−0.152	−0.321	−0.128	−0.127	−0.357
0.3	−0.069	−0.324	−0.124	−0.127	−0.333
0.4	0.026	−0.319	−0.121	−0.128	−0.301
0.5	0.141	−0.306	−0.120	−0.132	−0.261
0.6	0.280	−0.286	−0.123	−0.139	−0.214
0.7	0.454	−0.262	−0.130	−0.151	−0.161
0.8	0.674	−0.241	−0.143	−0.169	−0.105
0.9	0.965	−0.239	−0.162	−0.195	−0.049

(b) γ = 0.18, β = 0.31

ϱ	*OLS*	*GLS*	*IV*	*TS*	*W*
0.0	−0.283	−0.283	−0.130	−0.124	−0.367
0.1	−0.218	−0.301	−0.128	−0.125	−0.358
0.2	−0.148	−0.312	−0.124	−0.125	−0.342
0.3	−0.072	−0.316	−0.120	−0.125	−0.318
0.4	0.016	−0.314	−0.117	−0.126	−0.288
0.5	0.118	−0.304	−0.116	−0.128	−0.250
0.6	0.242	−0.288	−0.118	−0.134	−0.206
0.7	0.395	−0.267	−0.124	−0.146	−0.157
0.8	0.599	−0.245	−0.136	−0.162	−0.104
0.9	0.901	−0.236	−0.154	−0.187	−0.044

* The recorded values should be scaled by 10^{-2}.

Notes

* A preliminary version of this paper was presented at the First Meeting of the Australian Econometrics Study Group, Monash University, August 1982, and at various seminars. We are grateful to Adrian Pagan for bringing to our attention an error in an earlier version of this paper. We are also grateful to Bill Farebrother, Max King, Jan Kmenta and Eric Sowey for their comments, and to Olive Chin and Ali Avsar for their research assistance. This work was supported by a Monash University Special Research Grant.

1 For a discussion of some related issues, see Fomby and Guilkey (1978), and Nakamura and Nakamura (1978).
2 For example, see Judge *et al., op. cit.*, Chapter 5. Typically, these tests have only asymptotic justification, although a certain amount of Monte Carlo evidence is available concerning their small-sample powers.
3 Some earlier results were reported by Judge and Morey (1975).
4 For example, see Judge *et al.* (1980; p. 181).
5 Some evidence about the finite sample properties of exact GLS and of OLS in this context is given by Wallis (1967).
6 A full search for the global minimum of the residual sum of squares results in a consistent estimator, but sometimes such a search is impractical.
7 In our study, $\mathbf{y}_{-1}$ is regressed on $\mathbf{x}$, $\mathbf{x}_{-1}$, $\mathbf{x}_{-2}$ and an intercept, so the TS estimator is an Instrumental Variables estimator, and is consistent. (See McCarthy (1972; pp. 110-15).)
8 See Wallis, *op. cit.*, for a discussion of various bias corrections in this context.
9 Kenkel (1974) recommends the use of the tabulated upper bound for the Durbin-Watson statistic and we have followed this.
10 See Australian Bureau of Statistics (1982). As a limited test of the sensitivity of the results to the choice of data, this **x** series was de-trended, and the experiment was repeated. While the magnitudes of the risks and biases are affected to some degree by the form of **x**, all but one of the results and conclusions discussed in the next two sections still apply for de-trended **x**.
11 This intrinsic is a multiplicative congruential pseudo-random number generator.
12 In all cases the alternative hypothesis is $H_1 : \varrho > 0$. In those cases where the *h*-test cannot be applied because $T\hat{V}(\hat{\delta}) > 1$, additional replications are generated to maintain the total of one thousand.
13 This result does not hold for the IV pre-test estimator, in general, when the detrended data are used.

References

Australian Bureau of Statistics (1982), 'Time Series Data on Magnetic Tape: March Quarter 1982'.

Bancroft, T.A. (1944), 'On Biases in Estimation Due to the Use of Preliminary Tests of Significance', *Annals of Statistics*, 15, 190-204.

Betancourt, R. and Kelejian, H. (1981), 'Lagged Endogenous Variables and the Cochrane-Orcutt Procedure', *Econometrica*, 49, 1073-8.

Cochrane, D. and Orcutt, G.H. (1949), 'Application of Least Squares Regression to Relationships Containing Auto-Correlated Error Terms', *Journal of the American Statistical Association*, 44, 32-61.

Dhrymes, P.J. (1971), *Distributed Lags: Problems of Estimation and Formulation*, San Francisco: Holden-Day.

Durbin, J. (1970), 'Testing for Serial Correlation in Least-Squares Regression When Some of the Regressors are Lagged Dependent Variables,' *Econometrica*, 38, 410-21.

Durbin, J. and Watson, G.S. (1950), 'Testing For Serial Correlation in Least Squares Regression I', *Biometrika*, 37, 409-28.

Fomby, T.B. and Guilkey, D.K. (1978), 'On Choosing the Optimal Level of Significance for the Durbin-Watson Test and the Bayesian Alternative', *Journal of Econometrics*, 8, 203-13.

Giles, D.E.A. and Beattie, M. (1983), 'Autocorrelation Pre-Test Estimation in Models With a Lagged Dependent Variable', Working Paper No. 6/83, Department of Econometrics and Operations Research, Monash University.

Griffiths, W.E. and Beesley, P.A.A. (1984), 'The Small Sample Properties of Some Preliminary Test Estimators in a Linear Model With Autocorrelated Errors', *Journal of Econometrics*, 25, 49-61.

Judge, G.G. and Bock, M.E. (1978), *The Statistical Implications of Pre-Test and Stein-Rule Estimators in Econometrics*, Amsterdam: North-Holland.

Judge, G.G., Griffiths, W.E., Hill, R.C. and Lee, T.-C. (1980), *The Theory and Practice of Econometrics*, New York: Wiley.

Judge, G.G. and Morey, M. (1975), 'The Statistical Consequences of Autocorrelation: Preliminary Test Estimators Under Squared Error Loss', Paper Presented at the Third World Congress of the Econometric Society, Toronto.

Kenkel, J.L. (1974). 'Some Small Sample Properties of Durbin's Tests for Serial Correlation in Regression Models Containing Lagged Dependent Variables', *Econometrica*, 42, 763-9.

Kenkel, J.L. (1975), 'Small Sample Tests For Serial Correlation in Models Containing Lagged Dependent Variables', *Review of Economics and Statistics*, 57, 383-6.

King, M.L. and Giles, D.E.A. (1984), 'Autocorrelation Pre-Testing in the Linear Model: Estimation, Testing and Prediction', *Journal of Econometrics*, 25, 35-48.

Liviatan, N. (1963), 'Consistent Estimation of Distributed Lags', *International Economic Review*, 4, 44-52.

Maddala, G.S. and Rao, A.S. (1973), 'Tests For Serial Correlation in Regression Models With Lagged Dependent Variables and Serially Correlated Errors', *Econometrica*, 41, 761-74.

McCarthy, M.D. (1972), 'The Wharton Quarterly Econometric Forecasting Model, Mark III', Philadelphia: Economics Research Unit, University of Pennsylvania.

McNown, R.F. and Hunter, K.R. (1980), 'A Test for Autocorrelation in Models With Lagged Dependent Variables', *Review of Economics and Statistics*, 62, 313-7.

Nakamura, A. and Nakamura, M. (1978), 'On the Impact of the Tests for Serial Correlation Upon the Test of Significance for the Regression Coefficient', *Journal of Econometrics*, 7, 199-210.

Park, S.-B. (1975), 'On the Small-Sample Power of Durbin's *h* Test', *Journal of the American Statistical Association*, 70, 60-3.

Spencer, B.G. (1975), 'The Small Sample Bias of Durbin's Tests For Serial Correlation When One of the Regressors is the Lagged Dependent Variable and the Null Hypothesis is True', *Journal of Econometrics*, 7, 199-210.

Wallace, T.D. (1977), 'Pretest Estimation in Regression: A Survey', *American Journal of Agricultural Economics*, 59, 431-43.

Wallis, K.F. (1967), 'Lagged Dependent Variables and Serially Correlated Errors: A Reappraisal of Three-Pass Least Squares', *Review of Economics and Statistics*, 49, 555-67.

7 Some aspects of mis-specification in the linear model

Peter Praetz

1 Introduction

This paper is concerned with certain aspects of mis-specification in the multiple linear regression model. It considers the detection by the Durbin-Watson statistic of mis-specification such as the omission of variables or their inclusion in an incorrect functional form. These often generate serially correlated disturbances whose effects on the t, F and R^2 statistics are also studied.

Cochrane and Orcutt (1949) discussed the modification of OLS estimation methods when autocorrelated errors were present and showed that most error terms in economic models were highly positively autocorrelated and that calculated residuals gave a bias to randomness when used to estimate autoregressive parameters. They also discussed loss of efficiency and gave a tentative solution using their transformation.

They discussed the triple problems of simultaneous relationships, autocorrelated errors, and errors-in-variables in building economic models with time series data but were mainly concerned with the second problem and its solution. They argued that most of the then current applied econometric studies had correlated error terms. The simulation method was used to measure this effect as well as to show a bias in residual based estimates of autoregressive parameters and that Cochrane and Orcutt's transformation produce error terms which are almost random. In the real world, with short time series and unknown autoregressive parameters, things are more complex, but the transformation is still used.

Orcutt and Cochrane (1949) is a simulation study of autoregressive and reduced form transformations in regression. It analyses regression with autocorrelated errors and several relationships between the variables and tries autoregressive and reduced form transformations as solutions. With short series and unknown error intercorrelations, precise estimation is not easy.

These two Cochrane-Orcutt papers were a very important contribution to econometric methodology as they documented many cases of autocorrelated residuals and introduced their transformation to remove its deleterious effects.

After the Cochrane-Orcutt papers, Theil (1957) proved the result on mis-specification bias and discussed linear, quadratic and log models. He and Griliches (1957) were simply concerned with the bias and ignored serial correlation in the residuals. However Griliches (1961) felt that it was evidence of mis-specification and that revision of the model was needed. Ramsey (1969) has treated mis-specification thoroughly but seems unaware of the connection between mis-specification and correlated residuals. Several specification error tests are defined in terms of the best linear unbiased scalar covariance matrix residuals for mis-specifications of omitted variables, incorrect functional forms and inadequately accounted for simultaneity, which have similar effects as the coefficient vectors are biased. Heteroscedasticity is also considered but this has quite a different effect. Application of these tests are rare, possibly due to their lack of power.

Durbin and Watson (1950, 1951) considered the problem of testing for first-order autoregressive (AR(1)) disturbances and calculated bounds for their test statistic, d_1. Wallis (1972) investigated the problem of testing for simple fourth-order autoregressive disturbances and tabulated bounds for the fourth-order analogue of the Durbin-Watson statistic, d_4, with and without dummy variables. King and Giles (1977) have shown that Wallis's suggested bounds for negative autocorrelation with no seasonal dummies are inappropriate and have tabulated bounds for this situation. Selected bounds of second, third, and fourth-order analogues of the Durbin-Watson statistic, d_2, d_3 and d_4, are given by Vinod (1973). The case of Durbin-Watson bounds for regressions through the origin is discussed by Kramer (1971). Chaudhuri (1977) studied ordinary least squares (OLS) residuals after omission of variables and found their sampling variance biased upwards, the Durbin-Watson statistic biased towards 2 and the Durbin two-step and Prais-Winsten estimation methods biased as well. King (1982) discusses testing for a serially correlated component in regression disturbances. He proves d_1 is good at detecting disturbances with white noise and AR(1) components. King (1980) has also shown that the assumption of normality upon which the above tests are based can be broadened to one of spherical symmetry.

In the last few years, the methodology for testing for the many possible forms of mis-specification has become much more unified and coherent. Some important examples are Breusch and Pagan (1980) on the Lagrange multiplier test, Davidson and MacKinnon (1981) with several different tests, Godfrey and Wickens (1981) on log-linear regression and Pesaran and Deaton (1978) on testing non-tested nonlinear models.

This paper considers certain aspects of specification analysis in the general linear regression model. In particular, Section 2 derives the probability limits of Durbin-Watson statistics when a set of explanatory variables is omitted. This is such a general result that Section 3 considers the special cases of omitting one variable from a bivariate model and also a quarterly seasonal pattern. Section 4 generalizes the result in Section 2 to include functional form mis-specification. Section 5 looks at how autocorrelated errors, which usually arise from some form of mis-specification, affect the F, t and R^2 statistics as well as regression inferences. Finally, Section 6 concludes by briefly discussing some possible causes and remedies for autocorrelation and mis-specification. It does not attempt the impossible task of giving a complete solution to this difficult problem. The material in Section 4 is new and Section 5 is an improved version of Praetz (1981) but the rest of this paper is mainly based on Praetz (1979).

2 The effect of mis-specification by omission of variables upon Durbin-Watson statistics

Consider the regression model

$$y = X\beta + u \tag{1}$$

where y is an $n \times 1$ vector, X is an $n \times k$ matrix of explanatory variables which is regarded as fixed, β is a $k \times 1$ vector of unknown regression parameters, and u is an $n \times 1$ vector of disturbances. The matrix X is assumed to have rank k. We assume $E(u) = 0$, u has a covariance matrix $\Gamma = \{\gamma_{ij}\}$; $i, j = 1, \ldots, n$; $\Gamma = \{\gamma(|i - j|)\}$ by the stationarity assumption, an autocorrelation matrix $\{\varrho_{ij}\} = \{\varrho(|i - j|)\}$; where $\gamma(i) = \sigma^2\varrho(i)$ and the variance σ^2 is defined by $\sigma^2 = \gamma(0) = E(u_i^2)$. Equation (1) is assumed to be the true relationship.

Let $X = [X_1, X_2]$ and $\beta = [\beta'_1, \beta'_2]'$ where X_1 is $n \times s$, X_2 is $n \times (k - s)$, β_1 is $s \times 1$, and β_2 is $(k - s) \times 1$ so (1) can be expressed as

$$y = X_1\beta_1 + X_2\beta_2 + u. \tag{2}$$

Assume that $X_2\beta_2$ is omitted inadvertently from (2) and that instead

$$y = X_1\beta_1 + w$$

is used, where $w = X_2\beta_2 + u$ is a $(n \times 1)$ error vector. Estimation using OLS gives

$$\begin{aligned}\hat{\beta}_1 &= (X'_1X_1)^{-1}X'_1y \\ &= \beta_1 + (X'_1X_1)^{-1}X'_1X_2\beta_2 + (X'_1X_1)^{-1}X'_1u,\end{aligned}$$

so that

$$E(\hat{\beta}_1) = \beta_1 + P\beta_2$$

where $P = (X'_1X_1)^{-1}X'_1X_2$ and $E(\hat{\beta}_1) = \beta_1$ when $P\beta_2 = 0$.

The vector e of OLS residuals is defined by

$$\begin{aligned}e &= y - X_1\hat{\beta}_1 \\ &= \{I_n - X_1(X'_1X_1)^{-1}X'_1\}y = My\end{aligned}$$

$$= Mu + (X_2 - X_1P)\beta_2 = M(X_2\beta_2 + u)$$

where

$$M = I_n - X_1(X_1'X_1)^{-1}X_1',$$

I_n is the $n \times n$ unit matrix and M is idempotent.

The generalized Durbin-Watson statistics, denoted by d_i, $i = 1, 2, 3, 4, \ldots$, are defined by

$$d_i = e'A_ie/e'e \tag{3}$$

where A_i is a real symmetric matrix and, when n is a multiple of i, is given by

$$A_i = A_1 \otimes I_i \,.$$

Here

$$A_1 = \begin{bmatrix} 1 & -1 & 0 & \cdots & & 0 \\ -1 & 2 & -1 & \cdots & & 0 \\ 0 & -1 & 2 & \cdots & & 0 \\ \cdot & \cdot & \cdot & \cdots & & \cdot \\ \cdot & \cdot & \cdot & \cdots & 2 & -1 \\ 0 & \cdot & \cdot & \cdots & -1 & 1 \end{bmatrix}$$

and has dimensions $v \times v$ where $v = n/i$. When n is not a multiple of i, A_i is defined by rounding n up to the nearest multiple, applying $A_i = A_1 \otimes I_i$ and then deleting the appropriate number of cross diagonals. d_i has the well known form

$$d_i = \sum_{t=i+1}^{n} (e_t - e_{t-i})^2 / \sum_{t=1}^{n} e_t^2 \,. \tag{4}$$

It is assumed that d_i will provide a test of $\varrho = 0$ in the simple i^{th} order autoregression

$$u_t = \varrho u_{t-i} + \varepsilon_t, \qquad |\varrho| < 1$$

where the $\{\varepsilon_t\}$ are independent normal random variables and $\mathrm{E}(u_tu_{t+q}) = 0$ except if q is divisible by i, when it is equal to $\sigma^2\varrho^r$ with $r = q/i$. It is reasonable to start with such a simple linear case even though more complex and even non-stationary models may apply, e.g., serial correlation in the omitted variables and disturbances when the sample was generated.

Substituting $e = M(X_2\beta_2 + u)$ for e in equation (3) gives

$$d_i = \frac{\beta_2'X_2'MA_iMX_2\beta_2 + 2u'MA_iMX_2\beta_2 + u'MA_iMu}{\beta_2'X_2'MX_2\beta_2 + 2u'MX_2\beta_2 + u'Mu} \,. \tag{5}$$

The probability limit (plim) of d_i in (5) as n becomes infinite will be evaluated. Clearly $\beta_2'X_2'MA_iMX_2\beta_2/n$ and $\beta_2'X_2'MX_2\beta_2/n$ are constants and so will remain in plim. Also $u'MA_iMX_2\beta_2$ and $u'MX_2\beta_2$ have an expectation of zero as by assumption $\mathrm{E}(u) = 0$ so they will contribute nothing to plim as

n becomes infinite. This is proved in Praetz (1979).

As n becomes infinite, $E(u'MA_iMu)/n$ tends to $2\sigma^2(1 - \varrho(i))$ and $E(u'Mu)/n$ tends to σ^2, assuming the double sums remain finite. So plim d_i can be expressed as

$$\text{plim } d_i = \frac{(\overline{\beta_2'X_2'MA_iMX_2\beta_2/n}) + 2\sigma^2(1 - \varrho(i))}{(\overline{\beta_2'X_2'MX_2\beta_2/n}) + \sigma^2} \tag{6}$$

where the bar over $\beta_2'X_2'MX_2\beta_2/n$ and $\beta_2'X_2'MA_iMX_2\beta_2/n$ is used to denote the limits of these functions as n becomes infinite, assuming they exist. It seems that these expressions cannot be simplified any further in the general case. We can define them in terms of their contributions to the mis-specification which is denoted m. Let $\gamma_m(0)$ and $\gamma_m(i)$ be defined by

$$\overline{\beta_2'X_2'MA_iMX_2\beta_2/n} = 2\gamma_m(0) - 2\gamma_m(i) \tag{7}$$

and

$$\overline{\beta_2'X_2'MX_2\beta_2/n} = \gamma_m(0) \; . \tag{8}$$

Thus $\gamma_m(i)$ represents the contribution of the variance ($i = 0$) and covariance ($i \neq 0$), and (6) becomes

$$\text{plim } d_i = 2\{1 - \varrho^*(i)\} \tag{9}$$

where

$$\varrho^*(i) = \{\gamma_m(i) + \gamma(i)\}/\{\gamma_m(0) + \gamma(0)\} \; . \tag{10}$$

Denote by $d_i^m = \{2\gamma_m(0) - 2\gamma_m(i)\}/\gamma_m(0)$ the Durbin-Watson statistic for the mis-specification in the limit. It corresponds to the statistic defined on the vector $MX_2\beta_2$ instead of the residual vector e. Let $d_i^s = \{2\gamma(0) - 2\gamma(i)\}/\gamma(0)$ denote the usual Durbin-Watson limit, where s denotes serial correlation, then

$$\text{plim } d_i = \Theta d_i^m + (1 - \Theta)d_i^s \tag{11}$$

where $\Theta = \gamma_m(0)/\{\gamma_m(0) + \gamma(0)\}$, $0 \leqslant \Theta \leqslant 1$, depends on the ratio of the true variances. Thus plim d_i is the weighted average of the effects of mis-specification and serial correlation.

Some useful conclusions are:

(a) min $(d_i^m, d_i^s) \leqslant$ plim $d_i \leqslant$ max (d_i^m, d_i^s) as $0 \leqslant \Theta \leqslant 1$,
(b) if $d_i^m = d_i^s$ for all i, then d_i will still detect serial correlation d_i^s, (i.e. when u and $MX_2\beta_2$ have identical correlation behaviour),
(c) if $\gamma_m(i) + \gamma(i) = 0$, then plim $d_i = 2$ from (9).

The bias of $\hat{\beta}_1$ is $P\beta_2 = (X_1'X_1)^{-1}X_1'X_2\beta_2$ which is zero if $P\beta_2 = 0$ and more importantly if $X_1'X_2 = 0$ (X_1 and X_2 orthogonal), but the bias does not in general disappear from plim d_i even when $X_1'X_2 = 0$ as can be seen from equation (14).

The most likely scenario for (c) is that both parts of it would be positive or negative. If they cancel, then the regression model is probably a reasonable approximation for reality.

3 The omission of one variable and of a seasonal pattern from a two-variable model

3.1 Omission of one variable

As the main result of Section 2 is so general, this example illustrates clearly how the probability limits behave and how the two variables and their parameters contribute to the mis-specification.

A two-variable model in deviation form can be expressed as

$$y_t = \beta_1 x_{1t} + \beta_2 x_{2t} + u_t \tag{12}$$

where β_1 and β_2 are scalars, as $k = 2$ and $s = 1$, where x_{2t} will be omitted from (12). The probability limits of $\beta_2' X_2 M X_2 \beta_2 / n$ and $\beta_2' X_2' M A_i M X_2 \beta_2 / n$ are needed. Here $X_2 = \{x_{2t}\} = x_2$ and $X_1 = \{x_{1t}\} = x_1$ are $n \times 1$ vectors, $X_1'X_1 = \Sigma x_{1t}^2$ is a scalar and $\varrho_{12}(0)$ is the correlation coefficient at lag 0 between x_1 and x_2, treating them as random variables for this example. Now $\varrho_{12}(0)$ is defined as the population correlation coefficient between x_1 and x_2 and plim $[\Sigma x_{2t}^2/n] = \sigma_2^2$ (the variance of x_2).

Define $\varrho_1(i)$, $\varrho_2(i)$ and $\varrho_{12}(i)$ as correlation coefficients at lag i of x_1, x_2, and x_1 and x_2, respectively. Thus plim d_i is given by

$$\text{plim } d_i = \frac{2\beta_2^2\sigma_2^2[1-\varrho_{12}(0)^2-\varrho_2(i)-\varrho_1(i)\varrho_{12}(0)^2+\varrho_{12}(i)\varrho_{12}(0)+\varrho_{12}(-i)\varrho_{12}(0)]+2\sigma^2(1-\varrho(i))}{\beta_2^2\sigma_2^2[1-\varrho_{12}(0)^2]+\sigma^2} \tag{13}$$

Clearly, the effect of mis-specification is present in equation (13) whether or not the residuals are autocorrelated, as it is contained in the square brackets of numerator and denominator.

More importantly, when x_1 and x_2 are uncorrelated ($\varrho_{12}(i) = 0$, for all i) and u_t non-autocorrelated, then (13) becomes

$$\text{plim } d_i = \frac{2\beta_2^2\sigma_2^2[1-\varrho_2(i)]+2\sigma^2}{\beta_2^2\sigma_2^2+\sigma^2}. \tag{14}$$

Equation (14) is interesting because it shows that even when x_1 and x_2 are uncorrelated, the effect of the mis-specification still remains via the autocorrelations of x_2 and only vanishes when they are zero.

3.2 Omission of a seasonal pattern

This case has been considered explicitly for quarterly regression by Praetz (1975), so it will only be summarized briefly. The model is an additive fixed seasonal pattern treated by dummy variables. Initially, there are no other regressors so that the model can be expressed as

$$y_t = s_t + u_t$$

where $s_t = s_j$, $j = 1, 2, 3, 4$ are the four fixed seasonal factors defined by $t = 4(m - 1) + j$, where m denoted years and j quarters, and $\Sigma_j s_j = 0$. The following was proved for the sample serial correlations $r(j)$ of the residuals: when $\gamma(i) = 0$ for $i \neq 0$, then plim $r(1)$ = plim $r(3) \leqslant 0$, plim $r(4) > 0$ and the sign of plim $r(2)$ depends on the s_j values. This result was generalized to include regressors for Durbin-Watson statistics used to detect autocorrelation. When $\gamma(i) = 0$ for $i \neq 0$, then plim d_1 = plim $d_3 \geqslant 2$, plim $d_4 < 2$ and plim d_2 depends as before on the signs of the seasonal factors. This is one of the few cases where it is possible to obtain exact algebraic results on how the omission of variables affects residuals.

4 Functional form mis-specification

The mis-specification of equation (2) by the omission of a set of explanatory variables $X_{s+1}, \ldots, X_k$ can be generalized to include the case of variables which should be included but which appear in an incorrect functional form. This is achieved by approximating any arbitrary functional form by its power-series expansion which is equivalent to using a polynomial to model the variable. Thus the result obtained here on bias from omission of variables applies also to mis-specification of variables from incorrect functional forms. In practice, if the truncation remainder from the polynomial approximation is correlated with the terms in the expansion, the expansion results can be upset. Harvey and Collier (1977) tested for functional mis-specification in regression analysis using the recursive residuals which seemed reasonably powerful compared with the Durbin-Watson and other tests.

Consider a single variable X with a true functional form $g(X_i) = f(x_i)$, where $x_i = X_i - \bar{X}$ is a deviation from mean variable. We expand $f(x)$ as a power series in x with coefficients $\{\Theta_j\}$,

$$f(x) = \sum_{j=0}^{\infty} \Theta_j x^j \approx \sum_{j=0}^{m} \Theta_j x^j$$

if the truncation remainder

$$\left| \sum_{j=m+1}^{\infty} \Theta_j x^j \right|$$

is negligibly small. For example, an interest rate variable I often appears in economic theory in the form I^{-1} from summing a perpetuity of payments discounted at the interest rate I. If $i = I - \bar{I}$, then

$$f(i) = I^{-1} = (\bar{I} + i)^{-1} = (1 - (\frac{i}{\bar{I}}) + (\frac{i}{\bar{I}})^2 - \ldots)/\bar{I}$$

expanding by the binomial theorem, if $|i/\bar{I}| < 1$.

If w variables $\{X_{il}\}$, $l = k - w + 1, \ldots, k$ with forms $f_l(x_{il})$ and coefficients of expansion of $\{\Theta_{lj}\}$ are truncated after m_l terms respectively, we have that

$$f_l(x_{il}) \approx \sum_{j=0}^{m_l} \Theta_{lj} x_{il}^j \ .$$

The regression can be written again as

$$y = X_1\beta_1 + X_2\beta_2 + u$$

where X_1 is $n \times (k - w)$, β_1 is $(k - w) \times 1$, β_2 is $w \times 1$ and X_2 can be written as the $n \times w$ matrix $X_2 = \{f_l(x_{il})\}$. When the polynomial expansion is used to approximate $f_l(x_{il})$, then $X_2\beta_2$ becomes

$$X_2\beta_2 = \{\sum_l \sum_j \beta_l \Theta_{lj} x_{il}^j\} \qquad (15)$$

where

$$X_2 \text{ is } n \times W, \beta_2 \text{ is } W \times 1, \text{ with } W = \sum_l m_l - w \ .$$

The w is subtracted from W as we want to remove the constant terms from X_2 and group them all as a single constant term in X_1 with coefficient β_1, i.e. we have reverted to a deviation from means formulation. So, in terms of the original model of equation (2) for mis-specification,

$$y = X_1\beta_1 + X_2\beta_2 + u,$$

β_1 is now $k \times 1$ as it includes in the estimated equation the linear term for each of the mis-specified variables. Hence β_2 is now $(W - w) \times 1$ as it represents as omitted variables the non-linear effects of the mis-specified variables. The results of Section 2 now apply, with k replacing s and $(k + W - w)$ replacing k. The bias, therefore, will depend on the correlations of the X_1 variables with the X_2 variables, i.e. on the correlations of the k linear variables with the w non-linear variables.

As different polynomial expansions are possible, some improvement could be achieved by positing orthogonal polynomials, for the expansions in equation (15). For the w mis-specified variables, this has the advantage of rendering their linear and higher-order terms uncorrelated. However, there are still many other correlations which may be non-zero. In general, however, we expect bias to be present from this type of mis-specification of the functional form, and to appear in the Durbin-Watson statistics which are used to detect mis-specification of the economic model under test.

The accuracy of the results also depends on the possibility of ignoring the truncation remainder. In some cases, the functional form may have an exact quadratic or cubic form, although this is not thought to be very likely with economic variables. Functional forms likely to need approximation include exponential (growth) and logistic curves, for which polynomial approximation should be adequate over a restricted range. A logarithmic transformation would have rendered the exponential variable linear, although no such simple transformation exists for the logistic curve. Praetz (1973), in a study of estimation models for growth rates in economic time series, has two mis-specification models, log-for-linear and linear-for-log.

5 The effect of autocorrelation on the F and R^2 statistics

This section, which is based on Praetz (1981), is concerned with the effect of autocorrelation in the disturbances of the multiple linear regression model estimated by OLS on the F and R^2 statistics. It gives the bias in F and R^2 and tabulates it for an example with a linear trend and first-order autoregressive disturbances.

5.1 The bias in the F statistic from autocorrelated disturbances

When there is some form of mis-specification in the underlying theoretical model present, it is highly probable that the actual disturbances of the estimated regression are autocorrelated. Assuming the first column of X is the constant regressor represented as $l = (1, 1, \ldots, 1)'$, write

$$X = (l, X_*), \qquad \beta = (\beta_1, \beta_*')',$$

where X_* is $n \times (k-1)$ and β_* is $(k-1) \times 1$. Also let $\hat{\beta}_*$ be the OLS estimator of β_*, $S = I_n - l(l'l)^{-1}l'$, and $M = I_n - X(X'X)^{-1}X'$. The F statistic with $k-1$ and $n-k$ degrees of freedom used to test $H_0 : \beta_* = 0$ against $H_1 : \beta_* \neq 0$ is

$$F = \hat{\beta}_*' X_*' S y(n-k)/\{e'e(k-1)\}.$$

Under $H_0 : \beta_* = 0$

$$F = u'Au(n-k)/\{e'e(k-1)\},$$

where $A = \{a_{ij}\} = SX_*(X_*'SX_*)^{-1}X_*'S$.

When $u \sim N(0, \sigma^2 I_n)$, Cochran's Theorem implies that $u'Au/\sigma^2 \sim \chi^2_{k-1}$, as rank $(A) = k-1$, where χ^2_{k-1} is the chi-squared distribution with $k-1$ degrees of freedom. Similarly, $e'e/\sigma^2 = u'Mu/\sigma^2 \sim \chi^2_{n-k}$. Hence $E(u'Au) = (k-1)\sigma^2$ and $E(u'Mu) = (n-k)\sigma^2$. Furthermore, $AM = 0$ which is required for the two chi-squared distributions to be independent and the ratio to have an F distribution. We now develop an asymptotic expansion for F to see its bias when autocorrelation is present under $H_0 : \beta_* = 0$.

Note that we can write $M = S - A$. Define

$$\Theta = E(u'Au) = \sum_i \sum_j a_{ij}\gamma(i-j),$$

$$\begin{aligned} E(e'e) &= \sum_i \sum_j m_{ij}\gamma(i-j) \\ &= n\gamma(0) - \sum_i \sum_j \gamma(i-j)/n - \Theta, \end{aligned}$$

$$\begin{aligned} F &= F_*(1+\zeta)/(1-\eta) \\ &= F_*(1 + \zeta - \eta + \eta^2 - \zeta\eta + \ldots) \end{aligned}$$

for $|\eta| < 1$, where

$$\begin{aligned} \zeta &= u'Au/\Theta - 1 \\ \eta &= u'Mu/(n\sigma^2 - \sum_i \sum_j \gamma(i-j)/n - \Theta) - 1 \end{aligned}$$

and

$$F_* = \Theta(n-k)/\{(n\sigma^2 - \sum_i \sum_j \gamma(i-j)/n - \Theta)(k-1)\}$$

so

$$E(F) = F_*(1 + \text{var}\,\eta - \text{cov}(\zeta, \eta) + \ldots). \tag{16}$$

The magnitude of (16) depends on n, k and $\phi = \Theta/\gamma(0)$ which depends on the X matrix through $\{a_{ij}\}$ and on the autocorrelation structure of the disturbances. Any tabulation of $E(F)$ needs more explicit assumptions about X and the autocorrelation function. As an example of the result given by (16), assume the residuals follow a first-order autoregressive process with parameter ϱ, so that $\varrho(i-j) = \varrho^{|i-j|}$, and X_* is a linear trend regressor so that $SX_* = (-q, -(q-1), \ldots, q)'$, where $n = 2q+1$. Thus $X_*'SX_* = nq(q+1)/3$ and $SX_*X_*'S = \{(i-q-1)(j-q-1)\}$.

Then, for large n,

$$\begin{aligned} \phi &= 3\sum_i \sum_j (i-q-1)(j-q-1)\varrho^{|i-j|}/\{q(q+1)n\} \\ &\approx 1 + 2\varrho + 2\varrho^2 + \ldots \\ &= \frac{(1+\varrho)}{(1-\varrho)}. \end{aligned}$$

For large n (16) becomes

$$E(F) \approx \frac{(1+\varrho)(n-2)}{(n-\psi)(1-\varrho) - (1+\varrho)}\{1+\text{var}\, u'Mu/(n\sigma^2-\sigma^2\psi-\Theta)^2 \ldots\} \qquad (17)$$

as $k = 2$ and $\text{cov}(\zeta, \eta) = 0$, where

$$\psi = \sum_i\sum_j \varrho^{|i-j|}/n.$$

Table 1 tabulates values of E(F) given by (17) for $n = 20$, 40, 100 and $\varrho = 0, \pm0.2, \pm0.5, \pm0.8$.

The effect of autocorrelation can be very serious when ϱ is not close to zero. Sample size does not seem to matter much, except when ϱ is near ±1.0. When $\varrho > 0(< 0)$, it is possible to commit a type I (II) error and assume the regression does (does not) exist due to the bias in E(F).

The convergence of the expansion for F depends on $|\eta| < 1$, or

$$0 < u'Mu < 2(n\sigma^2 - \sum_i\sum_j \gamma(i - j)/n - \Theta).$$

For the example

$$\eta = [u'u/n - (\Sigma u_i)^2/n^2 - 3\{\sum_i (i - q - 1)u_i\}^2/\{n^2q(q + 1)\}]$$

$$/(\sigma^2 - \sum_i\sum_j \gamma(i - j)/n^2 - \Theta/n) - 1.$$

Since $u'u/n \to \sigma^2$ a.s. and $\Sigma\, u_i/n \to 0$ a.s., by the strong law of large numbers it follows that $(\Sigma\, u_i)^2/n^2 \to 0$ a.s. and

$$\{\sum_i(i - q - 1)u_i\}^2/\{n^2q(q + 1)\} \to 0 \text{ a.s.},$$

hence $\eta \to 0$ a.s.

As the t statistic can be represented as a special case of an F statistic, results analogous to those found in this section can be obtained for the t test.

Table 1 *Expected value of F for selected values of the sample size (n) and correlation coefficient (ϱ)*

n	$\varrho = 0.8$	0.5	0.2	0.0	−0.2	−0.5	−0.8
20	17.92	3.74	1.64	1.05	0.69	0.36	0.15
40	13.45	3.35	1.56	1.02	0.68	0.35	0.14
100	10.58	3.13	1.52	1.01	0.67	0.34	0.12

5.2 *The bias in the R^2 statistic from autocorrelated disturbances*

$$R^2 = \hat{\beta}'_* X'_* Sy / y'Sy$$
$$= u'Au/u'Su,$$

when $\beta_* = 0$.

$$E(u'Su) = n\gamma(0) - \sum_i \sum_j \gamma(i-j)/n$$

so now define

$$\eta = u'Su/(n\sigma^2 - \sum_i \sum_j \gamma(i-j)/n) - 1.$$

Then

$$R^2 = E(u'Au)(1+\zeta)/\{E(u'Su)(1+\eta)\}$$
$$= [\Theta/\{n\sigma^2 - \sum_i \sum_j \gamma(i-j)/n\}]\{1+\zeta\}\{1-\eta+\eta^2-\ldots\},$$

assuming $|\eta| < 1$, so that

$$E(R^2) = \phi/(n-\psi)\{1 + \text{var}\,\eta - \text{cov}(\zeta, \eta) + \ldots\}$$
$$\approx (1+\varrho)/\{(1-\varrho)(n-\psi)\} \qquad (18)$$

for the example in Section 5.1 and large values of n.

Tabulated values of $E(R^2)$ given by (18) may be found in Table 2. The bias is only severe for small sample sizes and large positive values of ϱ. The convergence of the expansion for R^2 depends on $|\eta| < 1$ and as in Section 5.1 one can show that for the example, $\eta \to 0$ a.s. Because $\bar{R}^2 = 1 - (1-R^2)(n-1)/(n-k)$, the bias of $\bar{R}^2$ can also be found.

Table 2 *Expected value of R^2 for the selected values of the sample size (n) and correlation coefficient (ϱ)*

n	$\varrho = 0.8$	0.5	0.2	0.0	−0.2	−0.5	−0.8
20	0.56	0.16	0.08	0.05	0.03	0.02	0.01
40	0.25	0.07	0.04	0.02	0.02	0.01	0.00
100	0.09	0.03	0.02	0.01	0.01	0.00	0.00

6 Conclusion

Autocorrelation may be caused by the omission of important variables from the regression model when they are correlated with the dependent variable, the inclusion of variables in an incorrect functional form or inadequately modelled seasonality. Errors in the independent variables, ignoring a simultaneous equation system, inaccurate modelling of dynamic systems, changing regression parameters, heteroscedasticity, temporal aggregation or other transformations of independent variables, such as their deflation or the use of proportions, may also be causes.

Many tests exist for detecting serial correlation, most of which focus on the residuals in the regression. Often, a Durbin-Watson test is used, a Durbin h if a lagged dependent variable is present, or a fourth-order analogue for seasonality, such as discussed by Wallis (1972).

The consequences of autocorrelated disturbances are so serious that the cause of the autocorrelation should be identified if possible. The specification of the model should be examined carefully to see if it needs to be changed. When the model and data are both felt to be satisfactory, and some autocorrelation still remains, it is then essential to incorporate this in the estimation process to avoid the statistical consequences of mis-specification mentioned above. It may be caused by minor omitted variables and may be modelled by a low-order autoregression or moving average, the parameters of which must be estimated and incorporated into a covariance matrix which can be used in a (possibly iterative) generalized least squares estimation by maximum likelihood or some other method.

After the stimulus from the pioneering Cochrane-Orcutt papers, only in the last ten years has research accelerated. Much further work needs to be done, especially on joint departures from assumptions. It will be years before regression packages, which test for all the departures from assumptions listed above, are readily available.

References

Breusch, T.S., and Pagan, A.R. (1980), 'The Lagrange Multiplier Test and Its Applications to Model Specification in Econometrics', *Review of Economic Studies*, 47, 239-53.

Chaudhuri, M. (1977), 'Autocorrelated Disturbances in the Light of Specification Analysis', *Journal of Econometrics*, 5, 301-13.

Cochrane, D., and Orcutt G.H. (1949), 'Application of Least Squares Regression to Relationships Containing Auto-Correlated Error Terms', *Journal of the American Statistical Association*, 44, 32-61.

Davidson, R., and MacKinnon, J.G. (1981), 'Several Tests for Model Specification in the Presence of Alternative Hypotheses', *Econometrica*, 49, 781-93.

Durbin J., and Watson, G.S. (1950), 'Testing for Serial Correlation in Least Squares Regression I', *Biometrika*, 37, 409-28.
Durbin J., and Watson, G.S. (1951), 'Testing for Serial Correlation in Least Squares Regression II', *Biometrika*, 38, 159-78.
Godfrey, L.G., and Wickens, M. (1981), 'Testing Linear and Log-Linear Regressions for Functional Form', *Review of Economic Studies*, 48, 487-96.
Griliches, Z. (1957), 'Specification Bias in Estimates of Production Functions', *American Journal of Agricultural Economics*, 39, 8-20.
Griliches, Z. (1961), 'A Note on Serial Correlation Bias in Estimates of Distributed Lags', *Econometrica*, 29, 65-73.
Harvey, A.C., and Collier, P. (1977), 'Testing for Functional Mis-Specification in Regression Analysis', *Journal of Econometrics*, 6, 103-20.
King, M.L. (1980), 'Robust Tests for Spherical Symmetry and Their Application to Least Squares Regression', *Annals of Statistics*, 8, 1265-71.
King, M.L. (1982), 'Testing for a Serially Correlated Component in Regression Disturbances', *International Economic Review*, 23, 577-82.
King, M.L., and Giles, D.E.A. (1977), 'A Note on Wallis' Bounds Test and Negative Autocorrelation', *Econometrica*, 45, 1023-6.
Kramer, G. (1971), 'On the Durbin-Watson Bounds Test in the Case of Regression through the Origin', *Jahrbucher für Nationalökonomie und Statistik*, 185, 345-58.
Orcutt, G.H., and Cochrane, D. (1949), 'A Sampling Study of the Merits of Autoregressive and Reduced Form Transformations in Regression Analysis', *Journal of the American Statistical Association*, 44, 356-73.
Pesaran, M.H., and Deaton, A.S. (1978), 'Testing Non-Nested Nonlinear Regression Models', *Econometrica*, 46, 677-94.
Praetz, P.D. (1973), 'The Estimation of Rates of Growth for Economic Time Series', *Australian Journal of Statistics*, 15, 118-27.
Praetz, P.D. (1975), 'Seasonality and Quarterly Regression', *Sankhyā*, C, 37, 173-84.
Praetz, P.D. (1979), 'The Detection of Omitted Variables by Durbin-Watson Statistics in Multiple Regression Models', *Australian Journal of Statistics*, 21, 129-38.
Praetz, P.D. (1981), 'A Note on the Effect of Autocorrelation on Multiple Regression Statistics', *Australian Journal of Statistics*, 23, 309-13.
Ramsey, J.B. (1969), 'Tests for Specification Error in Classical Linear Least Squares Regression Analysis', *Journal of the Royal Statistical Society*, B, 31, 350-71.
Theil, H. (1957), 'Specification Errors and the Estimation of Economic Relationships', *Review of the International Statistical Institute*, 25, 41-51.
Vinod, H.D. (1973), 'Generalization of the Durbin-Watson Statistic for Higher Order Autoregressive Processes', *Communications in Statistics*, 2, 115-44.
Wallis, K.F. (1972), 'Testing for Fourth Order Autocorrelation in Quarterly Regression Equations', *Econometrica*, 40, 617-36.

Part II
General Model Specification Issues

8 Joint conditional probability functions for modeling national economies

Guy H. Orcutt

Preface

Without a doubt, the two years 1946-8, which I spent under the direction of J.R.N. Stone as a Senior Research Worker in the Department of Applied Economics, Cambridge University, were of central importance to my development as a research scientist. Among the many reasons why I am hopelessly in debt to Stone, one in particular stands out in my mind. It was he who brought Donald Cochrane, then a PhD student at Cambridge University, and me together with all that has meant to me personally and intellectually. For this I have always been and remain extremely grateful.

Both Cochrane and I already were converts to Tinbergen's version of developing policy relevant, econometrically estimated, dynamic process models of national economics. However, it had become evident to me that the highly autocorrelated nature of omitted variables, in models by Tinbergen, Klein and others, was a matter requiring careful attention if Tinbergen type models were to be developed to their full potential. It was to this matter that Cochrane and I devoted ourselves in the two articles which we jointly produced (Orcutt and Cochrane (1949); Cochrane and Orcutt (1949)). In this connection our debt to Richard Stone should be noted for he not only provided support, suggestions and encouragement but also ensured my personal interaction with Tinbergen and with Herman Wold, who has done so much over the years to develop the econometrics of Tinbergen type, recursive equation modeling. This paper, written in the hope of honoring Donald Cochrane while he still lived, seeks to embed the Tinbergen and Wold recursive equation modeling in a somewhat broader statistical framework and to extend it so as to permit effective utilization of the enormous bodies of microentity data which can now be brought to bear on hypothesis testing and on estimation relating to the behavior of microentities which I believe should play a central role in modeling national economies.

If, as I hope, this paper does succeed in conveying an adequate understanding of the type of structural modeling which I deem appropriate for microanalytic, process modeling of economic systems, then a considerable amount of credit is due to a number of individuals who have helped me clarify my own thinking, improve my exposition, and avoid a number of misstatements. In particular I wish to thank Harriet Duleep, John Hartigan,

Richard Murnane, Alice and Masao Nakamura, Randy Olsen, and T.N. Srinivasan.

1 Introduction

At the present time there are three quite different approaches to process modeling of economic systems: the macro time series or national accounts approach, the interindustry approach, and the microanalytic approach.

Attempts to quantitatively implement the macro time series approach date back to the pathbreaking work of Tinbergen (1937, 1939, 1951). In this approach, major sectors such as the household and business sectors are used as basic components. Macro-economic relationships for these components are specified, estimated and tested on the basis of annual or quarterly time series data of such variables as aggregate consumption and income of the household sector. The relationships developed have been finite difference equations of a stochastic nature. Both recursive and simultaneous equation systems have been developed.

The second oldest and the second most widely utilized approach to construction of models of the United States stems from Leontief's highly important work (1951, 1953). Industries are used as basic components in these models. Emphasis is placed on the cross-sectional structure of the economy rather than on its dynamic features. Physical outputs of industries are assumed to be strictly proportional to physical inputs classified by industry or origin.

The main features of microanalytic simulation modeling were conceived by me in 1956 (1957) and first implemented by Greenberger, Korbel and Rivlin, working with Orcutt (1961). While being of the same general statistical type as other models of national economies, microanalytic models are the most general in terms of their statistical structure. Each major type of model of a national economy may include stochastic or random elements, use previous values of variables as part of what is treated as given, and be expressed as a system of equations. Microanalytic simulation models are more general than macroeconometric and interindustry models in that they contain one or more populations of microunits, such as individuals, families, enterprises and metropolitan areas, instead of but a single case of each kind of unit, as is true with both the Tinbergen and Leontief type models. Consequently, microanalytic simulation models open up important possibilities for substantially improving the simulation of economies and other large-scale socioeconomic systems in support of social and economic policy. By offering an excellent framework for applying past and future research work of many individuals and by effectively utilizing developments in computers and statistics, microanalytic simulation models provide a fruitful way of mobilizing the understanding and data which are or could be available for policy analysis. Descriptions of a number of policy oriented, microanalytic simulation modeling efforts, as of the second half of the 1970s, may be found in Orcutt, *et al.* (1976), Bergmann, Eliasson and Orcutt (1980), Haveman and Hollenbeck (1980), and in a symposium volume edited by Orcutt, Merz and Quinke (1986).

The hope behind this paper is that it will encourage use of joint determination conditional probability functions in modeling national economies. Representation of a joint determination conditional probability function by a set of recursive equations is pointed out as an ever present possibility and estimation of such recursive sets of regression equation is discussed.

2 Structural modeling

In macro time series modeling, researchers have focussed on establishing individual equations as structural elements. Thus, each of Tinbergen's national economy models is expressed as a system of recursive regression equations, and I believe Tinbergen regarded each equation in such a recursive system of regression equations as an estmate of a structural equation which described a response pattern of an identifiable sector of the economy. Herman Wold more than anyone else explored the statistical properties of least-squares regression estimation methods for unidirectional equations of the type hypothesized by Tinbergen. (See, for example, Wold (1964).) He was able to show that under fairly general assumptions these estimation methods would provide consistent parameter estimates of expected value predictors. However, it must be noted that a serious difficulty cannot be dealt with by any kind of statistical method no matter how clever.

If models are to provide understanding of the functioning of real economies, they must embody more than imaginative hypotheses about behavior, regardless of how clever, suggestive and appealing such hypotheses may be and how fancy the mathematics and statistics used in specifying them or in solving the models which embody them. Effective testing of embodied hypotheses is essential, and this is the crux of the difficulties with models developed in terms of one-of-a-kind entities such as is characteristic of macroeconometric and interindustry models. It is not that achieved testing of embodied substantive hypotheses has been totally absent, but achieved testing has been so woefully weak that resulting models are clearly inadequate for informing policymakers about consequences of contemplated actions.

A primary difficulty in testing hypotheses about one-of-a-kind entities can be seen by considering what could be learned experimentally under otherwise favorable circumstances for experimentation. Thus, suppose it were possible to carry out whatever planned experiments one might devise, but they could only be implemented with a single experimental animal, say a dog. With but one dog, it would be impossible to simultaneously apply different levels of treatment to different dogs thought to be roughly similar and in roughly similar conditions, except for the differential application of the treatment. It would still be possible to apply different levels of treatment of interest at different points in time and seek to relate hypothesized differential responses over time to applied differential treatments. Even so, the prospect for learning would be dim. Many things change over time in ways which cannot be controlled and their effect might easily be inadvertently attributed to the treatment. The experimental animal might learn or in some other way be permanently affected by the treatment so that effective replication of the experiment would be impossible, etc. Thus, even under favorable conditions, it seems evident that the possibilities of effectively testing hypotheses about one-of-a-kind entities are extremely unpromising.

Unfortunately, the prospects for testing critical hypotheses about one-of-a-kind macroeconomic entities, such as the United States household sector, are further compromised by the near impossibility of doing planned experimentation at this level of aggregation. Furthermore, highly aggregative time series simply do not contain enough degrees of freedom to permit extensive testing and estimation. This would be true even if the observations in such series resulted from well-planned experiments. The fact that the available aggregative series are autocorrelated, multicollinear and imbedded in an operating system involving many relatively rapid feedbacks only augments this fundamental difficulty.

For evidence on the ubiquity of highly autocorrelated economic time series and the resulting damage done to the possibility of effective testing, the reader is referred to Orcutt (1948), Orcutt and James (1948), Cochrane and Orcutt (1949), Orcutt and Cochrane (1949) and A. Nakamura, M. Nakamura and Orcutt (1976). These studies, taken in conjunction with what is known about the nature of economic time series, indicate that the evidence available in national accounts data for testing hypotheses is much less than even the fewness of observations per parameter to be estimated suggests. It also is worth noting that while transformations designed to randomize error terms, such as suggested by Cochrane and Orcutt, may be useful in estimation, they cannot undo the basic damage done to the possibility of effective testing by the ubiquity of high auto-correlations among macroeconomic time series. For evidence on the loss of estimation precision with aggregation of micro-unit data before estimation, see Orcutt (1968), Orcutt, Watts and Edwards (1968), and Orcutt and Edwards (1969).

Since much of the hoped-for payoff of policy oriented research is at the highly aggregative level, it is reasonable to exploit whatever testing and estimation possibilities exist at the national accounts level. However, anyone who recommends primary reliance upon estimation and testing based solely on the use of national accounts data is surely one of the world's greatest optimists. Social scientists simply do not possess a body of theory sufficiently developed and tested to permit the confident specification of variables to be included, forms of equations to be used, the appropriate lags for each variable and the stochastic properties of errors. Existing theory offers some guidance, but it is quite fanciful to believe that it offers much in the above respects.

By taking advantage of autocorrelation and inertial properties, observed expectations, intentions and plans, leading indicators and extensive multicollinearity, and by the use of frequently observed and up-to-date measurements, it has proved possible to develop Tinbergen-type national income models which are useful for short-run forecasting. But how useful are the embodied insights about behaviorally induced consequences of policy, even in such worked-over areas as policies thought to bear on inflation, unemployment and income and wealth distribution? And, even if the reader is more generous in attributing success in these matters than are we, how much of the believed success stems from testing and estimation of hypotheses about one-of-a-kind entities and how much stems from some kind of carry-over from what we think we know about microentities such as ourselves or firms?

By now it is abundantly clear that the information available for estimation and testing can be enormously increased by appropriate use of data relating to microcomponents. In addition, the danger of inappropriately treating different actions as equivalent, just because they are associated with variation of a common variable, is reduced. Of course, estimation and testing problems still abound, even if observations on microunits are used, but at least there is an enormous body of unplanned experiments to work with. These unplanned experiments may be observed in great detail at frequent intervals, and they often involve much wider ranges of variation in the variables than is the case with highly aggregated or averaged data. At the microlevel, there frequently are situations in which those variables which an experimenter would have liked to vary do, in fact, vary, and in which other variables which an experimenter would have liked to hold constant do remain constant. Furthermore, at the microlevel it is possible to relate differential responses to differential treatments as a means of eliminating the biasing effect of major feedbacks.

The consequence of considerations such as those mentioned above is rather widespread recognition of the importance of focusing a great deal of research on hypothesizing, data collection and testing, relating to microunits and associated microunit time series data. *However*, while it is evident that much of social science theorizing and research should relate to the behavior of individuals, families, firms, local areas and relatively small aggregates of such entities, it is unfortunately the case that we do not know how to aggregate nonlinear microrelations into macro time series relations. For example, if family saving depends on family income, wealth and life-cycle variables, then aggregate saving will depend on the joint distribution of family incomes, family wealths and family life-cycle attributes. Not only would such a macro saving funtion be difficult or impossible to specify and estimate directly, but it could not be used appropriately in a macro model without the availability of the joint distribution of all of these microvariables.

Microanalytic simulation modeling was originally devised to facilitate effective use of the output of microanalytic research. The central reason it can be helpful in this respect is that, in microanalytic modeling, operating characteristics can be used at their appropriate level of aggregation with needed aggregate values of variables being obtained by aggregating microentity variables generated by microentity operating characteristics.

Other potential advantages of microanalytic simulation modeling arise because (1) available detailed information about the initial state of microunits such as persons and families can be fully used, (2) tax and transfer laws and regulations relating to microunits can be given a literal representation, (3) available understanding about the behavior of entities met in everyday experience can be used and (4) microunit outputs can be aggregated as desired and can be used to generate univariate and multivariate distributions. This is significant since, not only is it important to predict how aggregate unemployment or income would be affected by alternative policies, but it is also important to predict how unemployment and income would be distributed among individuals and families by various characteristics, such as previous unemployment, age, sex, race and family size.

3 Statistical form of operating characteristics

In understanding what follows in this paper, it is essential to recognize that whereas most structural modeling with which the reader is familiar is likely to treat individual equations as structural elements of overall system models, the situation is actually very different for structural modeling within a microanalytic framework. Here, at least in so far as I have sought to conceptualize microanalytic modeling, the structural elements are best thought of as joint conditional probability functions which are intended to be autonomous characterizations of the behavior of identifiable microentities of which there exist many of each kind. Examples of such entities would be persons, families, firms and ensembles of microentities of which there could still be several of each kind. As will be pointed out, these joint conditional probability functions may be, and typically have been, expressed as recursive *sets of equations*. It is especially to be noted that it is equation sets which are to be regarded as structural characteristics of identifiable microentities rather than individual equations.

In microanalytic simulation modeling, a probabilistic approach to modeling microentity behavior is taken, insofar as possible, with there being many of each type of entity. The use of probabilistic modeling of entity behavior seems highly appropriate to me, but is less central to my thinking than is the framing, testing and using of hypotheses about entities so chosen that it is reasonable and useful to think of there being many identifiable entities of each kind of entity modeled.

Probabilistic modeling of behavior of microentities is reasonable because, no matter how many variables are taken into account in predicting the behavior of either major sectors or microcomponents, a variety of actual behavior always occurs, even for identical values of all input variables. What shall be done about the unexplained variation which is bound to occur? A deterministic operating characteristic merely ignores it and yields something like an expected or average value for the output. A probabilistic operating characteristic goes a little further and states what is thought to be known about how, in a large number of trials, observed behavior will be distributed around the predicted average behavior. This provides a fuller prediction and often a much more useful and meaningful one. This is particularly the case when trying to predict distributions of outcomes of microcomponent behavior.

In current macroeconometric modeling, an entire economy is implicitly represented as a single ongoing probabilistic process by a number of, possibly non-linear, simultaneous, stochastic equations. Solution of the jointly determined macro time series variables is then obtained, period-by-period, by solution of the simultaneous equations. In microanalytic simulation modeling, as I conceive of it, an economy is thought of as represented by an extremely large number of recursively interactive, microentity, probabilistic processes which are ongoing in parallel.

In general, it seems appropriate to regard the output variables of each microentity in each time period as having a joint probability distribution which is conditional on variables which are predetermined by the point in time at which they are used. Thus, for, say, entity i of type k, the conditional joint probability distribution of $x_{1,t}, \ldots, x_{U,t}$, could be written as:

$$G(x_{1,t}, \ldots, x_{U,t} | Z_t), \tag{1}$$

where Z_t is a vector of predetermined variables. This joint probability distribution, G, can be written as a product of conditional probability distributions:

$$G = \prod_{u=1}^{U} g_u(x_{u,t} | X^*_{u,t}, Z_t), \tag{2}$$

where $X^*_{u,t} = (x_{1,t}, x_{2,t}, \ldots, x_{u-1,t})$ and the g_u functions appear more explicitly as:

$$g_1(x_{1,t}|Z_t) = F_1(x_{1,t}, Z_t)$$
$$g_2(x_{2,t}|x_{1,t}, Z_t) = F_x(x_{1,t}, x_{2,t}, Z_t)$$
$$\vdots$$
$$g_U(x_{U,t}|x_{1,t}, \ldots, x_{U-1,t}, Z_t) = F_U(x_{1,t}, \ldots, x_{U,t}, Z_t)$$

Each g_u function is thus the conditional probability density function of a single variable and is a function of that variable and of the variables on which the density is conditional.

Starting with the idea of specifying an entity oriented, joint density function as given in (1) as a product of univariate conditional density functions, as given in (2), one is naturally led to express the entity oriented univariate conditional density functions of (2) in regression equation form as given in (3).

$$x_{1,t} = E(x_{1,t}|Z_t) + \varepsilon_{1,t} \quad (3)$$
$$\vdots$$
$$x_{U,t} = E(x_{U,t}|x_{1,t}, \ldots, x_{U-1,t} Z_t) + \varepsilon_{u,t},$$

where each of the ε terms on the right is a stochastic variable with a mean of zero. By construction, each ε is uncorrelated with every variable upon which the expected value of the associated dependent variable is conditioned. Also, by construction, each ε of set (3) is uncorrelated with every other ε variable of that set. The identical set of regression equations is specified for every entity of type k, although the microentity variables will be specific to the individual entity. Similar sets of regression equations are conceived of, as specified for entities of other types.

4 Recursive regression form estimation

This mode is attractive for estimation purposes because it expresses each joint conditional probability function, which is used in specifying structural hypotheses relating to entities of a given type, as a set of recursive regression equations so selected that the stochastic error term in each equation is, in a population sense, uncorrelated with every other right-hand side variable in the equation in which it appears. This mode also has the added attraction for estimation purposes that the stochastic error term in each equation is uncorrelated, also in a population sense, with the contemporary stochastic error term in every other equation of the set.

Thus, it may be seen that the attractiveness of the entity oriented, recursive mode flows from it having a form in which each equation might bear a close resemblance to the classical linear regression model. Of course, if the assumptions of the classical linear regression model held exactly, then the Gauss-Markov theorem would hold and would guarantee that single equation, linear, least squares would yield the best linear unbiased estimators and predictors (see, for example, Goldberger (1964, pp. 161-71)). If, in addition, errors are known to be normally distributed, then the classical approach to interval estimation and tests of hypotheses becomes available.

Because the variables, on which the joint probability of the dependent variables are conditioned, are taken to be predetermined and in fact may consist primarily of lagged endogenous variables, the assumptions of the Gauss-Markov theorem as originally stated do not hold exactly. Nevertheless, Goldberger (1964, pp. 178-281) introduces what he refers to as the contemporaneously uncorrelated linear regression model, which I believe is general enough to include our case if we stick to regressions which are linear in terms of the parameters. In a development based on Chernoff and Rubin (1953), Goldberger shows that if the assumptions of this model are satisfied, the classical least-squares estimators are consistent.

The importance of these findings is obvious for estimation of joint conditional probability functions which either already are or may conveniently be put in a recursive form. In addition, it should be noted that the attractiveness of carrying out estimation in a recursive form is improved by the fact that Wold and Jureen (1953, pp. 209-15) have shown that the classical least-squares estimators remain consistent under fairly general assumptions, even if successive disturbances are correlated with each other. Also see Wold (1961, 1964) and Lyttkens (1964).

In addition, Goldberger (1964, pp. 272-4), basing his presentation on the work of Mann and Wald (1943), shows that in the autoregressive linear regression model the classical least-squares estimators are consistent. Also, there exists some limited evidence on the basis of Monte Carlo experiments, that the associated predictors are unbiased even for small samples (see, for example, Orcutt & Winokur (1969)).

As previously indicated, the same statistical model may be represented in any one of a number of alternative forms. These forms differ from each other in several significant respects including the specification of stochastic terms. Because of this, estimation of the parameters of the same model in different forms will call for the use of different estimation procedures. Of all the possible forms in which a model might be put, those which leave as little information as possible concentrated in the stochastic part of the model specification have an obvious attraction. Thus, there is some point in trying to specify a model in a form such that errors of individual equations may be conceived of as approximately random in time and as uncorrelated with variables used as predictor variables in the same equation. There is also some point in trying to formulate an equation set such that errors in different equations may be conceived of as essentially uncorrelated with each other. The use of an entity oriented, recursive form, along with provisions for autoregressive transformations, if needed, makes it possible to leave as little information as possible in the stochastic specification of a model. If such an approach to model specification does not result in unmanageable problems due to non-linearities or unduly inhibit a reasonable use of prior information, it would seem to be the obvious choice and would permit the use of single equation least-squares methods. Furthermore, with such an approach, it would be reasonable to give some credence to standard tests of significance.

5 Use of recursive regression estimates

The motivating belief behind this paper has been the idea that the most suitable statistical form, for representing microentity behavior in a microanalytic process model, is the microentity oriented, joint conditional probability form. Of the various modes in which this statistical form could be expressed, this paper has presented the recursive regression equation mode as highly attractive for purposes of specification, estimation, and subsequent use.

In using the joint conditional probability form expressed in a recursive regression equation mode, it is important to bear in mind that it is an entire set of recursive regression equations which is put forth as a structural hypothesis and not the individual equations of such a set. Indeed, it is evident, as has been pointed out, that there exist many alternative recursive regression sets for expressing the same joint conditional probability function considered as a structural hypothesis.

Given the appropriateness of a structural, joint conditional probability hypothesis presented as a set of recursive regression equations, each equation will include an estimated expected value function for the selected dependent variable plus a stochastic error term. However, each equation except the first equation of each such set will likely include as predictor variables one or more current period values of variables determined by the entity being modeled. Thus, to trace out the hypothesized influence of predetermined variables, one must also use the preceding equations in the appropriate set of recursive regression equations. This is essential even if all that is wanted is the expected value of each of the jointly dependent variables given only the required values of predetermined variables. Of course, in this case obtaining the desired solutions is greatly simplified by the fact that the stochastic error terms are supposed to have expected values of zero, to be uncorrelated with each other and to be uncorrelated with all variables appearing on the right-hand side of the regression equation in which they appear.

For, predicting joint outcome features of joint conditional probability functions using a recursive regression mode of representation, it will be essential to take account of estimated properties of stochastic error terms as well as of expected value components of such equations. Here, too, it will be useful to bear in mind the attractive properties of stochastic error components in the recursive equation mode for representation of structural, joint conditional probability hypotheses.

Microanalytic, process models of economic systems of the type I have been associated with make heavy use of structural joint conditional probability hypotheses expressed as sets of recursive equations. In this setting the Monte Carlo simulation approach to model solution and use has proved attractive given the availability of modern computers. In using this approach, a joint output realization is computed each time period for each microentity of sample representations of each population of microentities which is involved. In doing this, a recursive regression set is sequentially evaluated for each microentity with a generated error term drawn from a distribution of appropriate form being fed in for use in evaluating each regression equation. Output from each equation is then used in evaluating subsequent equations in the recursive set of equations.

6 Concluding statement

This paper has presented joint conditional probability functions as attractive for use in structural process modeling of microentity behavior. It would, however, be inappropriate to hope that any statistical form, or any mode of representing such a form, could be of more than modest help in successful structural modeling of behavior of persons, families, firms or other microentities.

At best, a useful loom is available which could facilitate weaving of useful structural representations of microentity patterns of behavior and response. But there is nothing about any statistical form which gives valid guidance concerning choice of dependent variables, choice of predetermined variables, choice of functional forms or choice of lag structures. Nor does choice of any statistical form specify any hypothesis, make any measurements, carry out any estimations, or conduct any testing of hypotheses which are made. And, unfortunately, despite the choice of statistical form used in specifying structural hypotheses for a causal process modeling, omitted variables which are correlated in unknown ways with included variables can always be a source of error in interpreting the estimated role of included variables.

Microentity oriented, joint conditional probability modeling is helpful in structural modeling primarily because it focusses modeling attention on microentities of which there may be very large numbers of each kind. Also, by focussing attention on process modeling rather than on equilibrium modeling, it is helpful in encouraging use of lagged, and thus predetermined, endogenous variables as input variables rather than as output variables. And, finally, microentity oriented, joint conditional probability modeling may be useful in bringing about recognition that just because variables are jointly and simultaneously determined by a person, family, or firm doesn't necessarily mean that simultaneous equation modeling is appropriate.

References

Bergmann, B., Eliasson, G., and Orcutt, G., editors (1980), *Micro Simulation Models, Methods and Applications*, The Industrial Institute for Economic and Social Research, distributed by Almquist and Wiksell International, Stockholm.

Chernoff, H., and Rubin, H. (1953), 'Asympototic Properties of Limited-Information Estimates Under Generalized Conditions', in *Studies in Econometric Method, Cowles Commission Monograph, 14, ed.* W.C. Hood and T.C. Koopmans, New York: John Wiley and Sons.

Cochrane, D., and Orcutt, G.H. (1949), 'Application of Least Squares Regression to Relationships Containing Auto-Correlated Error Terms', *Journal of the American Statistical Association*, 44, 312-61.

Goldberger, A.S. (1964), *Econometric Theory*, New York: John Wiley and Sons.

Haveman, R. and Hollenbeck, K., editors (1980), *Microeconomic Simulation Models for Public Policy Analysis* (vols. 1 & 2), New York, London, Toronto, Sydney: Academic Press.

Leontief, W. *et al.* (1951), *The Structure of the American Economy*, New York: Oxford University Press.

Leontief, W. (1953), 'Static and Dynamic Theory', in *Studies in the Structure of the American Economy*, New York: Oxford University Press.

Lyttkens, E. (1964), 'Standard Error of Regression Coefficients by Autocorrelated Residuals', in *Econometric Model Building, ed. H. Wold, Amsterdam: North-Holland* Publishing Company, Chapter 4, 169-228.

Mann, H.B., and Wald, A. (1943), 'On the Statistical Treatment of Linear Stochastic Difference Equations', *Econometrica*, 11, 173-220.

Nakamura, A., Nakamura, M., and Orcutt, G. (1976), 'Testing for Relationships Between Time Series', *Journal of the American Statistical Association*, 11, 214-22.

Orcutt, G. (1948), 'A Study of the Autoregressive Nature of the Time Series Used for Tinbergen's Model of the Economic System of The United States, 1919-1932, *Journal of the Royal Statistical Society*, Series B, 10, 1-53.

Orcutt, G. (1957), 'A New Type of Socio-Economic System', *Review of Economics and Statistics*, XXXIX, 773-97.

Orcutt, G. (1968), 'Research Strategy in Modeling Economic Systems', in *The Future of Statistics*, ed. D. Watts, New York: Academic Press.

Orcutt, G., Caldwell, S., Wertheimer II, R., Franklin, S., Hendricks, G., Peabody, G., Smith, J., and Zedlewski, S. (1976), *Policy Exploration Through Microanalytic Simulation*, Washington, DC: Urban Institute.

Orcutt, G., and Cochrane, D. (1949), 'A Sampling Study of the Merits of Autoregressive and Reduced Form Transformations in Regression Analysis', *Journal of the American Statistical Association*, 44, 356-72.

Orcutt, G., and Edwards, J. (1969), 'Should Aggregation Prior to Estimation Be The Rule', *The Review of Economics and Statistics*, LI, 409-20.

Orcutt, G., Greenberger, M., Korbel, J., and Rivlin, A. (1961), *Microanalysis of Socio-Economic Systems: A Simulation Study*, New York: Harper & Row.

Orcutt, G., and James, S. (1948), 'Testing the Significance of Correlation Between Time Series', *Biometrika*, 35, 397-413.

Orcutt, G., Merz, J., and Quinke, H., editors (1986), *Microanalytic Simulation Models to Support Social and Financial Policy*. The symposium giving rise to this volume was held June 20-22, 1983 in Bonn. It was sponsored by Gesselschaft Fur Mathematik und Datenverarbeitung of Schloss Birlinghoven and Sonderforschungsvereich 3 'Mikroanalytische Grundlagen Der Gesellschaftspolitik' of Universitaten Frankfurt und Mannheim.

Orcutt, G., and Winokur, H. (1969), 'First Order Autoregression: Inference, Estimation and Prediction', *Econometrica*, 37, 1-14.

Orcutt, G., Watts, H., and Edwards, J. (1968), 'Data Aggregation and Information Loss', *The American Economic Review*, 58, 773-87.

Tinbergen, J. (1937), *An Econometric Approach to Business Cycle Problems*, Paris: Hermann et Cie.

Tinbergen, J. (1939), *Statistical Testing of Business Cycle Theories. II. Business Cycles in the United States of America, 1912-1932*, Geneva: League of Nations.

Tinbergen, J. (1951), *Business Cycles in the United Kingdom, 1870-1914* (2nd ed.), Amsterdam: North-Holland Publishing Co.

Wold, H., and Jureen, L. (1953), *Demand Analysis*, New York: John Wiley and Sons.

Wold, H. (1961), 'Unbiased Predictors', *Proceedings of the Fourth Berkeley Symposium on Mathematical Statistics and Probability* (vol. 1), ed. J. Neyman, Berkeley and Los Angeles: University of California.

Wold, H. (1964), 'Forecasting by the Chain Principle', in *Econometric Model Building. Essay on the Causal Chain Approach*, ed. H. Wold, Amsterdam: North Holland Publishing Co.

9 Specification tests for separate models: a survey

Michael McAleer[1]

1 Introduction

The estimation of econometric relationships and specification testing are two integral parts of applied econometric research. Sophisticated estimation procedures are now available to estimate highly non-linear regression models. Nevertheless, much applied research still concentrates on linear regression models. Consider the standard full rank linear model

$$y = X\beta + \varepsilon. \tag{1}$$

A useful test of the specification given in (1) is Ramsey's (1969) specification error test (see also Anscombe (1961)), namely a test of the hypothesis $\mathrm{H} : \delta = 0$ in the augmented (or artificial) regression equation

$$y = X\beta + X^*\delta + \varepsilon, \tag{2}$$

in which the columns of X^* may be formed by taking powers of the columns of X or some function of the predicted values of y from (1) (see e.g. Ramsey and Schmidt (1976), Thursby and Schmidt (1977)). If X is a matrix of observations on fixed regressors, the standard F test of H has the central F distribution with dimension (δ) (dim(δ)) and dim(y) − dim(β) − dim(δ) degrees of freedom when $\delta = 0$. Note that the test of $\mathrm{H} : \delta = 0$ in (2) is purely a test of the specification given in (1), and the construction of X^* is invariably not predicated by economic theory. In this sense the test of H may lack power because precise information regarding the alternative is not incorporated into the augmented regression (2), that is, X^* is not based on a specific alternative hypothesis.

There are several ways of testing the hypothesis $\mathrm{H} : \delta = 0$ in (2). First, H may be tested by comparing Ordinary Least Squares (OLS) estimates of β from (1) and (2); for more on this, see Durbin (1954), Hausman (1978), Holly (1982) and Hausman and Taylor (1980). Second, (2) may be interpreted as a classical specification error problem (see Theil (1957); for a geometric treatment, see Fisher and McAleer (1984)) in that it is an approximation to the true model (Pagan (1984)). However the tests are performed, there are two outcomes, namely a rejection of H or an acceptance (i.e. non-rejection) of H. Since a specific alternative is not being entertained, an outcome whereby H is rejected may be unable to suggest where next to proceed in the modelling exercise.

In economics, however, there are invariably numerous competing theories to explain a given phenomenon. These may result in different definitions of variables to be used in a specification, or possibly in different functional forms. Specific examples of the former case are the use of average weekly earnings or award wages in labour demand studies, and the determination of a specific interest rate variable in studies of money demand. In such circumstances it is not always sensible to include both sets of competing variables in the same equation because of high collinearity. In addition, it is typically the case that only one of the competing variables should be present at any one time. Specifications such as these, which arise frequently in econometric practice, are termed separate (or non-nested) models.

It will be useful at this point to define what is meant by a separate model. Cox (1961, p. 106; 1962, p. 406) states, in the context of separate families of *distributions*, that two hypotheses are separate if an arbitrary simple hypothesis in one cannot be obtained as a limit of simple hypotheses in the other. In the context of separate (or non-nested) non-linear *regression models*, Fisher and McAleer (1981, p. 104) state that two models are separate if neither may be obtained from the other by the imposition of appropriate parametric restrictions. For a more rigorous definition in terms of global and partial separateness, see Pesaran (1984b). In essence, tests of separate models, also termed separate (or non-nested) tests, are simply specification tests using information about a specific alternative.

Until recently, a common practice among applied econometricians when faced with separate models was to rely on discrimination criteria such as maximizing some modification of R^2 (for example, Theil's (1957) $\bar{R}^2$, Akaike's (1973, 1974) information criterion or Schwarz's (1978) Bayesian information criterion). These criteria measure how well different models fit the data, with some adjustment being made for parsimony. The philosophy behind these criteria is that the best predicting model is the closest approximation to the true specification, an assertion which holds 'on average'. A difficulty with such discrimination criteria is that one model will always be chosen, regardless of whether or not it can predict the consequences of separate alternatives (see Pagan (1981)). The latter requirement is somewhat different from examining whether the model can predict the data. In the use of discrimination criteria, a model is evaluated on the basis of its own performance, whereas in the presence of a separate alternative, the philosophy is to test whether the null can predict the performance of the alternative 'significantly well'. Another way of looking at the problem is to compare the *actual* performance of the alternative with the performance that could be *expected* if the null were true. If the null is true, as presumed, then it should not distort the actual performance of the alternative. In effect, the actual performance should be similar to what is expected under a true null.

An alternative approach to the problem of comparing non-nested models is to nest the separate models in a comprehensive (composite, artificial or general) model and use the standard F test to test the competing separate models as special cases. In the context of equation (2), X and X^* might be matrices of observations on the explanatory variables of two separate models, with X and X^* being linearly independent of each other (i.e. the columns of X^* are *not* formed from those of X). There are, however, several well-known problems with this approach. As mentioned earlier, there may be high collinearity between competing regressors from the separate models and this may lead to difficulties in estimation (for more on this, see e.g. Valentine (1969)). In addition, if there are many regressors in the competing models, there may be few degrees of freedom. If the separate models are non-linear, the estimation problem is likely to be exacerbated. Moreover, it may not be possible to derive a testable artificial model for non-linear models. Perhaps a more important argument against the use of a comprehensive model is that it does not use information regarding the competing separate models in an optimal way, in a sense to be discussed later.

Partially in response to some of these difficulties, several different procedures have been developed to test separate regression models. In this paper, emphasis will be placed on separate linear regression models. Two linear models are separate if neither may be obtained from the other by the imposition of linear parametric restrictions. Extensions to non-linear models are straightforward, but the bulk of research has concentrated upon the selection of regressors. This is not, of course, useful in general for examining functional forms; for empirical considerations of non-linear separate regression models, see Pesaran and Deaton (1978) and Gregory and McAleer (1983).

The purpose of this survey paper is to analyse critically the most recent theoretical developments in the rapidly developing field of testing separate regression models. It attempts to unify, review and extend the recent research in the area by relating various tests based upon Cox's centred likelihood ratio to those generated by artificial regressions. The approach does not attempt to concentrate on the most computationally convenient methods for testing alternative specifications since, on statistical grounds, computational convenience should not rank highly. The interested reader who wishes to compute the test statistics is referred to the useful paper by MacKinnon (1983), and the discussions following his paper.

Although the relations between some separate tests and existing specification error tests are made explicit in the paper, attention is directed towards specification tests for *separate* models. The related issue of modelling is not addressed in detail; useful references in this regard are the papers by Hendry and Richard (1982) and McAleer, Pagan and Volker (1985). While the more general question of testing model adequacy through diagnostic checks is gaining in popularity, it should be emphasized that the testing of separate models is but one in a long list of checks that the careful applied econometrician should undertake. For useful insights into diagnostic checking, the reader is referred to the valuable papers by Pagan and Hall (1983) and Pagan (1984); the first paper places testing procedures within the context of residual analysis while the second considers specification error tests through the addition of variables to a linear regression model.

The plan of the paper is as follows. In Section 2 the separate models are presented and testing procedures are described. In addition, a common misconception regarding the interpretation of separate tests is clarified, the role of the alternative model is addressed, and some concepts are discussed. In Section 3 Cox's centred likelihood ratio principle is presented along with various tests based upon artificial regressions, and some separate tests are related to specification error tests. A general procedure which contains several existing tests as special cases is also examined. The roles of the alternative for asymptotic local power comparisons, as well as test consistency, are analysed in Section 4. The effects of testing a model against multiple separate alternatives, thereby leading to joint separate tests, are compared with a paired (or binary) test against a single separate alternative. In Section 5 the small-sample distributions of several tests are compared. Several procedures for testing linear and log-linear regression models are examined in Section 6, and a novel method is suggested for testing a null model against a one-sided alternative. The finite sample size and power properties of the tests from Monte Carlo experiments are examined in Section 7. In Section 8 published empirical research incorporating separate models is reviewed, with a clear understanding of the outcomes of the tests. Finally, several directions for future work are suggested in Section 9.

2 Separate regression models

Although attention throughout the paper will be focused on testing pairs of separate regression models, for future reference the notation will be developed for $(m + 1)$ separate linear regression models. The specifications take the form

$$\mathrm{H}_0 : y = X\beta + \varepsilon_0, \qquad \varepsilon_0 \sim \mathrm{N}(0, \sigma_0^2 I)$$

$$\mathrm{H}_i : y = Z_i\gamma_i + \varepsilon_i, \qquad \varepsilon_i \sim \mathrm{N}(0, \sigma_i^2 I), \qquad i = 1, 2, \ldots, m$$

where y is an $n \times 1$ vector of observations on the dependent variable, X and Z_i are $n \times k_0$ and $n \times k_i$ matrices of non-stochastic regressors, and β and γ_i are $k_0 \times 1$ and $k_i \times 1$ vectors of unknown parameters, respectively. The $n \times 1$ vectors ε_0 and ε_i contain normally, independently and identically distributed random disturbances, and the index i represents the i'th alternative model. The assumptions on the nature of the regressors can be relaxed in a straightforward manner, as in MacKinnon, White and Davidson (1983).

It should be stressed at the outset that in testing separate models against each other, one model is taken to be the null only temporarily. Since any one of the $(m + 1)$ models given above may be treated as the null, without loss of generality H_0 will be designated as the null and $H_1, \ldots, H_m$ as the alternative models. In this context, it is useful to distinguish between *paired* and *joint* separate tests. A paired comparison is taken to be between H_0 and H_1. The distinction is encapsulated in the following remark:

Remark: A test of H_0 against a single alternative, which may be represented by H_1, is a paired separate test, and a test of H_0 against the multiple alternatives $H_1, \ldots, H_m$ is a joint separate test.

For purposes of discussing the tests, it is customary to assume that the matrices $n^{-1}X'X$ and $n^{-1}Z_i'Z_i$ converge to well-defined finite positive definite limits, and $n^{-1}X'Z_i$ and $n^{-1}Z_i'Z_j$ $(i \neq j;\ i,\ j = 1, 2, \ldots, m)$ converge to non-zero finite limits. Any two models are assumed to be separate in the sense that at least one column of each regressor matrix cannot be expressed as a linear combination of the columns of the others. In analysing the asymptotic distributions of some tests, it will also be necessary to assume that X, Z_i and Z_j are not orthogonal to each other.

Having set up the framework for separate models, it will prove useful to clarify a common misconception as to the purpose of a separate test. When Cox first developed a procedure for testing separate (distributional) families of hypotheses, the test of the null was 'required to have high power for the alternative hypothesis' (Cox (1962, p. 406)). In this sense, the alternative was clearly intended to be meaningful in its own right. Indeed, Cox (1962, p. 411) also stated: 'The most interesting applications are likely to be to situations where two alternative *rather specific theories* are available' (our emphasis). It is precisely for this reason that Fisher and McAleer (1979a) have interpreted a paired comparison of separate models as a test of H_0 against H_1, followed by a test of H_1 against H_0. Dastoor (1981) has also taken up this issue and has demonstrated that a valid inference regarding the alternative cannot be made on the basis of a test of the null model alone. This point simply cannot be overemphasized, especially as it has long been taken for granted that a null model may be rejected in *favour* of the alternative. Such an inference is incorrect since it presumes the alternative is not rejected when it is tested. Of course, in general such an outcome cannot be predicted in advance. Thus, claims by Pesaran (1974, p. 158), Ramsey (1974, p. 37), Harvey (1977, p. 465), Aneuryn-Evans and Deaton (1980, pp. 289-90, Judge *et al.* (1980, p. 438), Harvey (1981, p. 179), Green, Pope and Phipps (1981, p. 402), Gourieroux, Monfort and Trognon (1983, p. 91) Aguirre-Torres and Gallant (1983, p. 6), Hall (1985, p. 150), Anselin (1984, p. 5), Thornton (1985, p. 736), and Brissimis and Leventakis (1985, p. 487) are highly misleading, if not in error, in asserting that an inference can be drawn regarding the alternative on the basis of a test of the null alone.

It is also instructive to examine the role of the specific alternative in a paired comparison. Two test statistics must be calculated to test a pair of separate models. When the roles of the null and the alternative are reversed, it is well known that four outcomes are possible: (i) acceptance of both H_0 and H_1; (ii) rejection of both H_0 and H_1; (iii) acceptance of H_0 only; and (iv) acceptance of H_1 only. Thus, it is possible to accept both models or to reject both, but it is only in cases (iii) and (iv) that it is possible to discriminate between the two models. In the paired situation just considered, it would not be possible to have four outcomes if only one of the models were to be taken seriously. If the intention is to test only H_0 with one or more alternatives serving only as a *guide* to the performance of the null, we have a *uni-directional* test as compared to a paired or joint separate test. In the event that H_1 (say) is not a serious alternative, it will not be tested, and hence the only two possible outcomes are acceptance of H_0 or rejection of H_0. A uni-directional test is precisely what Pesaran and Deaton (1978, p. 678) and Davidson and MacKinnon (1981, p. 781) have in mind when they suggest that a specific alternative need not be a serious alternative model. While a test of the null against *any* alternative may be performed by means of a specification error test, it will be recalled that the purpose of a separate test is to achieve high power against the specified alternative. Thus, a uni-directional test of H_0 against one or more separate alternatives is simply a specification error test of the type given in equation (2), with X^* being formed from the non-overlapping variables appearing in the competing alternative. It follows that a uni-directional test of the null is not, strictly speaking, a separate test.

In this paper we are concerned with paired and joint separate tests, and not uni-directional tests. With m alternatives for a given null, there are $m(m + 1)$ paired test statistics with (possibly) conflicting outcomes. Since there are just $(m + 1)$ statistics for the joint tests of the $(m + 1)$ models taken to be the null in turn, it would seem more straightforward to rank the models on the basis of joint rather than paired tests. As will be seen later, there may also be a difference between paired and joint tests in terms of their power properties.

Although separate models which arise through rigorous specification searches should, in general, be taken seriously, this does not mean that one of the models is true. For this reason, we are primarily concerned with model testing rather than model discrimination, as the title of the paper suggests. When one model is accepted over the other through testing, as in cases (iii) and (iv) above, this allows a probabilistic statement to be made regarding discrimination. Thus, the essential difference between discriminating on the basis of information criteria and on the basis of testing is that the latter enables the classical inferential procedures to be applied (see e.g.

Amemiya (1980, p. 351)). The distinction between the terms *testing* and *discrimination* used here accords with that of Fisher and McAleer (1979a), while Ramsey (1974) uses the terms *absolute* and *relative* discrimination, respectively. While the variety of discrimination procedures in use is enormous, some of the criteria available in the literature are reviewed in Gaver and Geisel (1974), Pereira (1977b), Amemiya (1980), Judge *et al.* (1980, Chapter 11), Sawyer (1980), Harvey (1981, Chapter 5), McAleer (1981a, Chapter 4) and Efron (1984). For the interested reader, two very useful special issues on model selection and non-nested models, respectively, have recently been edited by Maddala (1981) and White (1983). Several doctoral dissertations have also been written, in whole or in part, on separate models; see Sawyer (1980), McAleer (1981a), Ericsson (1982), Dastoor (1983a) and Gill (1983).

3 The centred likelihood ratio and artificial regressions

The first application of the ideas of Cox (1961, 1962) to econometrics in the context of a pair of separate linear Gaussian regression models was made by Pesaran (1972, 1974); see also Dhrymes *et al.* (1972) and Goldfeld and Quandt (1972, p. 139) for early discussions of separate models in econometrics. Various extensions have since been made by several authors. For example, a large body of research has arisen in extending Pesaran's Cox test to non-linear (systems of) equations (Pesaran and Deaton (1978), Fisher and McAleer (1981), Davidson and MacKinnon (1981)), and to situations in which instrumental variable estimation is appropriate (Godfrey (1983), Dastoor and McAleer (1985)). In this section we will use the methods suggested by Pesaran (1982b) and Bera and McAleer (1982) to relate several of these procedures, including the Cox and Atkinson (1970) tests as applied in econometrics.

Denoting $\theta_0' = (\beta', \sigma_0^2)$ and $\theta_1' = (\gamma_1', \sigma_1^2)$, the maximized log-likelihood function under H_i is given by

$$\hat{l}_i = -\tfrac{1}{2}n \log 2\pi - \tfrac{1}{2}n \log \hat{\sigma}_i^2 - \tfrac{1}{2}n, \qquad (i = 0, 1)$$

where $\hat{\sigma}_i^2 = n^{-1}y'(I - P_i)y$ is the maximum likelihood estimate of σ_i^2 ($i = 0$, 1) with $P_0 = X(X'X)^{-1}X'$ and $P_1 = Z_1(Z_1'Z_1)^{-1}Z_1'$. Under H_0, $\hat{\beta} = (X'X)^{-1}X'y$ is the maximum likelihood estimate of β, $X\hat{\beta} = P_0y$, $\hat{\varepsilon}_0 = (I - P_0)y$ and $\hat{\sigma}_0^2$ reflects the *actual* performance of H_0; similarly, under H_1, $\hat{\gamma}_1 = (Z_1'Z_1)^{-1}Z_1'y$ is the maximum likelihood estimate of γ_1, $Z_1\hat{\gamma}_1 = P_1y$, $\hat{\varepsilon}_1 = (I - P_1)y$ and $\hat{\sigma}_1^2$ reflects the *actual* performance of H_1. The difference in maximized log-likelihoods is $\hat{l}_0 - \hat{l}_1$. If H_0 were to be nested within H_1, the asymptotic expectation of $\hat{l}_0 - \hat{l}_1$, evaluated at the (restricted) maximum likelihood estimates $\theta_0 = \hat{\theta}_0$, would be zero. Since the two models are separate, Cox suggested that, to test H_0, the mean of $\hat{l}_0 - \hat{l}_1$ evaluated under H_0 (i.e. at $\theta_0 = \hat{\theta}_0$) should be subtracted from $\hat{l}_0 - \hat{l}_1$. Thus, the Cox test of H_0 is based upon the statistic

$$T_0 = (\hat{l}_0 - \hat{l}_1) - n[\text{plim}_0\, n^{-1}(\hat{l}_0 - \hat{l}_1)]_{\theta_0=\hat{\theta}_0}, \tag{3}$$

where plim_0 denotes probability limit under H_0. Cox demonstrates under general conditions that T_0 will be asymptotic normal with mean zero and variance V_0 under H_0. If a consistent estimate of V_0 under H_0 is given by $\hat{V}_0$, the statistic $N_0 = T_0/(\hat{V}_0)^{\frac{1}{2}}$ will be approximately distributed as a standard normal variate under H_0; see White (1982) for a formal derivation of the regularity conditions. McAleer and Pesaran (1986) have labelled the procedure of centring a test statistic under the null and then deriving its asymptotic null distribution as the Cox Principle of hypothesis testing.

The numerator and denominator of the Cox test for separate linear regression models are given by Pesaran (1974) as

$$T_0 = \tfrac{1}{2}n \log(\hat{\sigma}_1^2/\hat{\sigma}_{10}^2) \tag{4}$$

and

$$\hat{V}_0 = (\hat{\sigma}_0^2/\hat{\sigma}_{10}^4)(y'P_0P_1(I - P_0)P_1P_0y), \tag{5}$$

in which $\hat{\sigma}_{10}^2 = \hat{\sigma}_0^2 + n^{-1}y'P_0(I - P_1)P_0y$ is a consistent estimate of the probability limit of $\hat{\sigma}_1^2$ under H_0. Since $\hat{\sigma}_{10}^2$ may be viewed as the predicted value of σ_1^2 under H_0, it is the expected performance of H_1 under H_0. It is revealing to note that if H_0 is true, then it may be written variously as $y = X\beta + \varepsilon_0 = X\hat{\beta} + \hat{\varepsilon}_0 = Z_1\hat{\gamma}_1 + (X\hat{\beta} - Z_1\hat{\gamma}_1) + \hat{\varepsilon}_0 = Z_1\hat{\gamma}_1 + \hat{\varepsilon}_1$, in which $\hat{\varepsilon}_1 = (X\hat{\beta} - Z_1\hat{\gamma}_1) + \hat{\varepsilon}_0$. Therefore, instead of writing $\hat{\varepsilon}_1'\hat{\varepsilon}_1$ as $y'(I - P_1)y$, we may express it as

$$\hat{\varepsilon}_1'\hat{\varepsilon}_1 = \hat{\varepsilon}_0'\hat{\varepsilon}_0 + 2\hat{\varepsilon}_0'(X\hat{\beta} - Z_1\hat{\gamma}_1) + (X\hat{\beta} - Z_1\hat{\gamma}_1)'(X\hat{\beta} - Z_1\hat{\gamma}_1).$$

Since $\text{plim}_0\, n^{-1}\hat{\varepsilon}_1'\hat{\varepsilon}_1 = \text{plim}_0\, \hat{\sigma}_1^2 = \sigma_{10}^2$, $\text{plim}_0\, n^{-1}\hat{\varepsilon}_0'\hat{\varepsilon}_0 = \text{plim}_0\, \hat{\sigma}_0^2 = \sigma_0^2$ and $\text{plim}_0\, n^{-1}\hat{\varepsilon}_0'(X\hat{\beta} - Z_1\hat{\gamma}_1) = 0$, it follows that

$$\sigma_{10}^2 = \sigma_0^2 + \beta'(\lim n^{-1}X'(I - P_1)X)\beta.$$

Replacing the elements of σ_{10}^2 with their consistent estimates under H_0 yields the relations

$$\hat{\sigma}_{10}^2 = \hat{\sigma}_0^2 + n^{-1}\hat{\beta}'X'(I - P_1)X\hat{\beta} = \hat{\sigma}_0^2 + n^{-1}y'P_0(I - P_1)P_0y.$$

It is in this sense that $\hat{\sigma}_{10}^2$ is the residual variance of H_1 predicted by H_0. A significance test of H_0 may therefore be based upon a comparison of the quantities $\hat{\sigma}_1^2$ and $\hat{\sigma}_{10}^2$. If the difference is significantly different from zero, H_0 is rejected; otherwise, H_0 is not rejected.

As the form of T_0 given in (4) is cumbersome to manipulate, it is convenient to use the upper-bound linearization of T_0 given by Fisher and McAleer (1981) as

$$TL_0 = \tfrac{1}{2}n(\hat{\sigma}_1^2 - \hat{\sigma}_{10}^2)/\hat{\sigma}_{10}^2. \tag{6}$$

Since TL_0 and T_0 are asymptotically equivalent under H_0, they have the same asymptotic variance. Denoting $NL_0 = TL_0/(\hat{V}_0)^{\frac{1}{2}}$, the linearized Cox test is

$$NL_0 = \frac{\tfrac{1}{2}n(\hat{\sigma}_1^2 - \hat{\sigma}_{10}^2)}{\hat{\sigma}_0(y'P_0P_1(I - P_0)P_1P_0y)^{\frac{1}{2}}}\,. \tag{7}$$

Note that the sign of NL_0 depends on the sign of $(\hat{\sigma}_1^2 - \hat{\sigma}_{10}^2)$. Clearly, we have the relations

$$\hat{\sigma}_1^2\{\lesseqqgtr\}\hat{\sigma}_{10}^2 <=> NL_0\{\lesseqqgtr\}0.$$

Thus, if $\hat{\sigma}_1^2 < \hat{\sigma}_{10}^2$, a negative Cox statistic indicates the actual performance of H_1 is better than expected. A significantly negative NL_0 therefore leads to rejection of H_0 because H_1 is performing too well for H_0 to be regarded as true. Note that this result says nothing about H_1 itself since we are testing H_0. Similarly, a significantly positive NL_0 with $\hat{\sigma}_1^2 > \hat{\sigma}_{10}^2$ also leads to rejection of H_0 because H_1 is performing worse than expected under H_0. Only if $\hat{\sigma}_1^2 \simeq \hat{\sigma}_{10}^2$, whence NL_0 is not significantly different from zero, would we not reject H_0 because H_1 is performing as expected under H_0.

An unbiased estimate of $P_1y = Z_1\hat{\gamma}_1$ under H_0 is $P_1P_0y = Z_1\hat{\gamma}_{10}$, where $\hat{\gamma}_{10}$ is a consistent estimate under H_0 of $\text{plim}_0\ \hat{\gamma}_1$. The Atkinson (1970) variation of the Cox test is then based upon the statistic

$$TA_0 = (\hat{l}_0 - \hat{l}_{10}) - n[\text{plim}_0\ n^{-1}(\hat{l}_0 - \hat{l}_{10})]_{\theta_0=\hat{\theta}_0}, \tag{8}$$

in which

$$\hat{l}_{10} = -\tfrac{1}{2}n\log 2\pi - \tfrac{1}{2}n\log\hat{\sigma}_{10}^2 - \tfrac{1}{2}n(n^{-1}y'(I - P_1P_0)'(I - P_1P_0)y)/\hat{\sigma}_{10}^2.$$

In (8), the entire statistic is evaluated under the null hypothesis. Since the second terms on the right-hand sides of (3) and (8) are asymptotically equivalent under H_0, and because $\text{plim}_0\ \hat{\sigma}_1^2 = \text{plim}_0\ \hat{\sigma}_{10}^2 = \text{plim}_0\ n^{-1}y'(I - P_1P_0)'(I - P_1P_0)y = \sigma_{10}^2$, it follows that T_0 and TA_0 are asymptotically equivalent under H_0. In addition, since $\hat{l}_1$ is the maximized log-likelihood under H_1 whereas $\hat{l}_{10}$ is not evaluated at $\theta_1 = \hat{\theta}_1$, we have the inequality relation

$$TA_0 = T_0 + (\hat{l}_1 - \hat{l}_{10}) \geqslant T_0. \tag{9}$$

Since TA_0 and T_0 are asymptotically equivalent under H_0, a consistent estimate of the asymptotic variance of TA_0 is given by $\hat{V}_0$ in (5). Thus, the test statistic $NA_0 = TA_0/(\hat{V}_0)^{\frac{1}{2}}$ is also approximately distributed as a standard normal deviate in large samples. Fisher and McAleer (1981) show that NA_0 may be written as

$$NA_0 = NL_0 + \frac{\tfrac{1}{2}y'(I - P_0)P_1(I - P_0)y}{\hat{\sigma}_0(y'P_0P_1(I - P_0)P_1P_0y)^{\frac{1}{2}}}\,, \tag{10}$$

which is an adjusted linearized Cox statistic. We will return to (10) in Section 5 where we examine alternative small sample adjustments to NL_0.

There are obvious similarities between the Atkinson approach and the Lagrange Multiplier (LM) principle of (nested) hypothesis testing. Breusch and Pagan (1980, pp. 248-9) have, in fact, suggested that the Atkinson approach should be adopted from an LM viewpoint. When both NA_0 and N_0 are negative, the inequality $0 > NA_0 \geqslant N_0$ suggests the Atkinson variation of the Cox test is less likely to reject the null than is the Cox test itself. In this respect, the inequality is reminiscent of the well-known inequality relations between the Wald, Likelihood Ratio and LM principles for testing nested models (see Savin (1976), Berndt and Savin (1977), Breusch (1979)). Pesaran (1981) followed up Breusch and Pagan's argument and showed that a direct application of the LM approach is not entirely valid when an exponential combination of the likelihood functions of the competing models is entertained. The gist of this argument is that when the combined likelihood is evaluated under the null, the parameters of the alternative model disappear (see also Breusch and Pagan (1978, p. 22)). The basic point, therefore, is that the analysis of Breusch and Pagan holds only when H_1 is a simple alternative hypothesis. Dastoor (1985) has recently helped to clarify the issue by demonstrating that with an appropriate weighting scheme for the likelihood functions of the competing models, *both* the Cox and Atkinson test statistics may be interpreted as being based upon the LM principle.

Returning now to equation (10), NA_0 may be rewritten after some algebraic manipulation as

$$NA_0 = \frac{-y'P_0P_1(I - P_0)y}{\hat{\sigma}_0(y'P_0P_1(I - P_0)P_1P_0y)^{\frac{1}{2}}} . \tag{11}$$

Apart from the estimated standard error $\hat{\sigma}_0$, NA_0 may be calculated straightforwardly from the artificial regression

$$y = X\beta + \alpha P_1P_0y + \varepsilon, \tag{12}$$

where $P_1P_0y = Z_1\hat{\gamma}_{10}$ is the predicted value obtained by regressing P_0y on the columns of Z_1. Note that a test of the hypothesis $H_0' : \alpha = 0$ is equivalent to a test of H_0. The t ratio for the OLS estimate of α in (12), given by

$$t(\hat{\alpha}) = \frac{y'P_0P_1(I - P_0)y}{\hat{\sigma}(y'P_0P_1(I - P_0)P_1P_0y)^{\frac{1}{2}}} , \tag{13}$$

is asymptotically equivalent to NA_0 under H_0 because $\hat{\sigma}^2$, the estimated error variance from (12), is consistent for σ_0^2 under H_0. Notice that the artificial equation (12) is in the form of (2) with X^* as a column vector given by P_1P_0y. The distinguishing feature between the two artificial equations is that, in testing H_0, P_1P_0y in (12) uses precise information about the separate alternative H_1 through P_1, whereas a specification error test might use some function of $P_0 y$ alone to construct X^*. It is this factor, combined with an intention also to test H_1 against H_0, which differentiates a separate test from a pure specification error test as in (2). In respect of actually implementing the test, however, the test can also be viewed as testing alternative estimates of β from H_0 and also from (12), as in the Hausman (1978) procedure.

An important point to note in the preceding discussion is that while both T_0 and TA_0 modify a log-likelihood ratio by subtracting its asymptotic expectation under the null model, the log-likelihood ratios differ in that only the Cox statistic uses the maximized log-likelihood of the specific alternative. Another possibility in place of $\hat{l}_1$ or $\hat{l}_{10}$ is to use $\hat{l}_1^*$, the calculated value of the log-likelihood function under H_1, evaluated at $\hat{\theta}_1^{*\prime} = (\hat{\gamma}_1^{*\prime}, \hat{\sigma}_{10}^2)$, where $\hat{\gamma}_1^*$ is an alternative estimate of γ_1. Since $\hat{l}_1$ is the maximized value of l_1, it follows that if T_0^* is given by

$$T_0^* = (\hat{l}_0 - \hat{l}_1^*) - n[\text{plim}_0\, n^{-1}(\hat{l}_0 - \hat{l}_1^*)]_{\theta_0 = \hat{\theta}_0}, \tag{14}$$

then $T_0^* = T_0 + (\hat{l}_1 - \hat{l}_1^*) \geqslant T_0$. We will restrict our attention to a class of estimates of γ_1 which are linear in y. Following Pesaran (1982b) and Bera and McAleer (1982), we substitute Ry for $\hat{\gamma}_1^*$ in the artificial regression

$$y = X\beta + \alpha Z_1 \hat{\gamma}_1^* + \varepsilon, \tag{15}$$

which is a specification error test of H_0 using explicit information about the separate alternative H_1. The $k_1 \times n$ matrix R is also assumed, for our purposes, to be non-stochastic, or at least uncorrelated with the error in large samples. If R is a function of X and/or Z_1, the assumption of R follows from that of X and Z_1. If prior information on the parameters of at least one of the models were available, we would have a test based on the work of Hoel (1947); see also Goldfeld and Quandt (1972, p. 138) and Fisher and McAleer (1979a).

It is straightforward to relate several tests based upon different modified likelihood ratios through $\hat{l}_1^*$ and the test of $H_0' : \alpha = 0$ in the artificial regression (15). If the tests are related to the Cox test through artificial regressions of the form given in (15), we can restrict the possibilities for R to two sets of matrices. The likelihood function for H_1 evaluated at $(\hat{\gamma}_1^{*\prime}, \hat{\sigma}_{10}^2) = (y'R', \hat{\sigma}_{10}^2)$ is

$$\hat{l}_1^* = -\tfrac{1}{2}n \log 2\pi - \tfrac{1}{2}n \log \hat{\sigma}_{10}^2 - \tfrac{1}{2}n(n^{-1}y'(I - Z_1R)'(I - Z_1R)y)/\hat{\sigma}_{10}^2,$$

so that T_0^* may be written as

$$T_0^* = \tfrac{1}{2}n[n^{-1}y'(I - Z_1R)'(I - Z_1R)y - \hat{\sigma}_{10}^2]/\hat{\sigma}_{10}^2. \tag{16}$$

In large samples, T_0^* has mean zero under H_0. Since $y'(I - Z_1R)'(I - Z_1R)y - n\hat{\sigma}_{10}^2 = y'(-2Z_1R + R'Z_1'Z_1R + P_0P_1P_0)y$, upon substituting $X\beta + \varepsilon_0$ for y in (16), the following condition must hold for T_0^* to have zero mean under H_0 :

$$X'(2Z_1R - R'Z_1'Z_1R)X = X'P_1X. \qquad (17)$$

The condition in (17) indicates that Z_1R must be of the form P_1 or P_1P_0. If $Z_1R = P_1P_0$, then T_0^* is equivalent to TA_0. An asymptotically equivalent test to TA_0 is the t ratio for the OLS estimate of α in the artificial regression (12), which is obtained by replacing $Z_1\hat{\gamma}_1^*$ in (15) by P_1P_0y. The test of $\alpha = 0$ in (12) is the *JA* test of Fisher and McAleer (1981). For an LM interpretation of the *JA* test, see Godfrey (1984). Alternatively, if $Z_1R = P_1$, then T_0^* is equivalent to TL_0 in (6). An asymptotically equivalent test statistic is obtained as the t ratio of the OLS estimate of α in (15) when $Z_1\hat{\gamma}_1^*$ is replaced by P_1y, thereby leading to

$$y = X\beta + \alpha P_1y + \varepsilon. \qquad (18)$$

The test of $\alpha = 0$ in (18) is the J test of Davidson and MacKinnon (1981), which is asymptotically distributed under H_0 as a standard normal deviate. The J test is a specification error test of H_0 using the predicted value of y from the separate alternative H_1, rather than a function of the predicted value of y from H_0 itself; for an alternative interpretation of the J test, see Hausman and Pesaran (1983). On the basis of (17), therefore, requiring tests calculated from artificial regressions such as (15) to be asymptotically equivalent to tests derived from the centred likelihood ratio (14) reduces the possibilities for R to only two matrices.

The tests discussed above are 'one-degree-of-freedom' tests since they are distributed as $\chi^2(1)$ under H_0 when they are calculated from artificial regressions such as (12) and (18). A different approach has been advocated by means of the standard F test based upon a comprehensive model formed from the columns of X and Z_1. If X and Z_1 have p linearly dependent columns, then a test of H_0 may be obtained by testing $\bar{\gamma}_1 = 0$ in the artificial regression equation

$$y = X\beta + \bar{Z}_1\bar{\gamma}_1 + \varepsilon, \qquad (19)$$

where $\bar{Z}_1$ is $n \times (k_1 - p)$. In the case where the columns of X and Z_1 are linearly independent, then $p = 0$ and (19) becomes

$$y = X\beta + Z_1\gamma_1 + \varepsilon, \qquad (20)$$

so that a standard F test of H_0 (H_1) in (20) is equivalent to testing $\gamma_1 = 0$ ($\beta = 0$). This approach has been considered by Atkinson (1970) and Quandt (1974), among others. The question of the relative powers of the F test versus the one-degree-of-freedom tests is addressed in the following section. It should, however, be noted at the outset that the assumption of non-orthogonality is unnecessary when the standard F test is used. Moreover, the test of H_0 has the exact F distribution, whereas the J and Cox-type tests only have asymptotic validity, in general.

The test of $\bar{\gamma}_1 = 0$ in (19) may be derived in different ways. Dastoor

(1983b) has developed the R procedure based upon the difference $\hat{\eta}_0 = \hat{\phi}_1 - \hat{\phi}_{10}$, where $\phi_{10} = \text{plim}_0\ \phi_1$ and ϕ_1 is a subset of $\theta_1' = (\gamma_1', \sigma_1^2)$ containing the 'parameters of interest'; see Deaton (1982) and Gourieroux, Monfort and Trognon (1983) for related developments. The R procedure is designed to test whether $\hat{\eta}_0$ is significantly different from zero. If all the parameters under H_1 are of interest, then $\hat{\eta}_0 = \hat{\theta}_1 - \hat{\theta}_{10}$. Dastoor has shown that if γ_1 contains the parameters of interest, then an R test based upon $\hat{\eta}_0 = \hat{\gamma}_1 - \hat{\gamma}_{10}$ is precisely the test of $\bar{\gamma}_1 = 0$ in (19), thereby tying together F-type and Cox-type tests. Mizon and Richard (1986) have recently reviewed tests based upon selected 'parameters of interest'. If the parameters of interest are the elements of γ_1, their encompassing test of H_0 reduces to the test of $\bar{\gamma}_1 = 0$ in (19). The other tests presented above may also be interpreted as being based upon the R and encompassing procedures. For example, if σ_1^2 is the parameter of interest, an R test based upon $\hat{\eta}_0 = \hat{\sigma}_1^2 - \hat{\sigma}_{10}^2$ is equivalent to Fisher and McAleer's (1981) NL_0 in (7). The Cox, Atkinson, J and JA tests may also be viewed as R tests based upon a particular set of parameters of interest; for more on this, see Dastoor (1983b).

Using the nomenclature of Mizon and Richard (1986), the R procedure may be viewed as an encompassing test; for some interesting discussions of the encompassing framework in econometrics, see Hendry (1983b) and Hendry and Richard (1982). Some advocates of encompassing have stated that a model which is fitting poorly (i.e. a model with an estimated error variance that is larger than that for a rival model) cannot explain the findings of a model with a better fit to the data. Indeed, Hendry (1983b) suggests that it is sensible only to test the better-fitting model as the null against the worse-fitting model as the alternative. It should be noted, however, that a model which is fitting poorly in finite samples may, in fact, variance-encompass a better-fitting model asymptotically. The reason for this is that variance-encompassing refers to an asymptotic relationship between a true model and a false alternative, namely the error variance of the true model not exceeding the error variance of the false model that is expected when the true model holds. The superiority of the true model over the false in terms of error variances may not, however, hold in finite samples; for more on this, see McAleer (1980).

As a final comment in this section, it is useful to note that the conditions regarding $\text{plim}_0\ n^{-1}X'\varepsilon_0 = 0$ and $\text{plim}_1\ n^{-1}Z_1'\varepsilon_1 = 0$ ensure that OLS estimation provides consistent estimates of β and γ_1 under H_0 and H_1, respectively. When these assumptions are violated, a set of instruments is typically used in place of X and/or Z_1. For the situation in which a common set of instruments is available for X and Z_1, Godfrey (1983) has derived a G test by minimizing the functions

$$g(Q_w) = (y - X\beta)'Q_w(y - X\beta) \tag{21}$$

and

$$h(Q_w) = (y - Z_1\gamma_1)'Q_w(y - Z_1\gamma_1), \tag{22}$$

in which $Q_w = W(W'W)^{-1}W'$ and W is the matrix of observations on the instruments for both X and Z_1. Since Godfrey's approach assumes that the specified instrumental variable estimators are valid under the relevant models, it is clear from (21) and (22) that X and Z_1 cannot each be used as its own instrument; indeed, the G procedure is not defined for OLS estimation. Nevertheless, the G test formula for H_0 collapses precisely to the NL_0 test statistic given in (7) when OLS estimates are substituted for their instrumental variable counterparts. For further work on instrumental variable approaches to the testing of separate regression models, see Bera and McAleer (1982), Ericsson (1983), MacKinnon, White and Davidson (1983), and Dastoor and McAleer (1985). While the general approach has been to presume that the set of instruments is valid under both separate models, procedures which use specific information as to which subset of regressors is not independent of the disturbances may be developed along the lines of Gregory and McAleer (1981) and Wu (1983).

4 Power comparisons and the role of the alternative model

The purpose of a separate test of H_0 against H_1 was stated explicitly by Cox (1962, p. 406) as follows: 'High power is desired against a composite alternative hypothesis that is not in the same parametric family as the null hypothesis.' It is for this reason that most of the econometric research concerning test consistency, namely the probability of rejecting a false null with probability one in large samples, has dealt with fixed alternatives. However, local alternatives for separate models have been analysed by Pesaran (1982a), Ericsson (1983), Davidson and MacKinnon (1982), and Dastoor and McAleer (1983). The first two papers consider the local powers of a test of H_0 against H_1 in which the alternative H_1 approaches the null H_0 as the sample size increases without limit. Pesaran (1982a) also compared the local powers of the Cox, J and F tests and demonstrated, for the case $k_0 \geqslant k_1$, that the local power of the one-degree-of-freedom tests is not exceeded by that of the standard F test. Of course, if the result is to apply to the paired situation in which the roles of null and alternative are reversed, the analysis holds only when $k_0 = k_1$. Davidson and MacKinnon (1982) consider the case where H_1 is fixed and the process generating the data approaches H_0 for large samples; this extends the previous case in that neither model needs to be true. Dastoor and McAleer (1983) extend the results of Davidson and MacKinnon to the case of joint tests of multiple alternatives, and demonstrate that Pesaran's results on the relative powers of the Cox-type and F tests depend crucially on the type of local alternative specified. They show that, in general, it is not possible to rank the tests in terms of asymptotic local power.

Before continuing on to fixed alternatives, however, it is worth noting that Pesaran (1982b) has provided a set of conditions which ensures that a separate test of H_0 based on an artificial regression such as (15) is asymptotically distributed as a standard normal variate under H_0, is consistent against H_1 and has maximum power against local alternatives for $k_0 \geqslant k_1$. Bera and McAleer (1982) have extended the analysis by providing the necessary and sufficient conditions for exact tests to be asymptotically N(0, 1), to be consistent and to maximize local power. If we are interested in a uni-directional test, therefore, we only need one test to be consistent; otherwise, both paired tests of H_0 and H_1 will be consistent for $k_0 = k_1$. In this context, it is worth mentioning that Godfrey and Pesaran (1983a) and Davidson and MacKinnon (1982) present evidence indicating that the *JA* test has poor power in finite samples in cases where it does not maximize power against local alternatives.

Test consistency has, however, generally been examined within the context of fixed alternatives. A recent potentially important contribution to separate testing has been made by Epps *et al.* (1982), who base their test of separate families of hypotheses on the difference between the sample and theoretical moment generating functions. These authors recognize explicitly the need for a fixed alternative by choosing the argument of the moment generating function to maximize the large sample power of the test of the null. Unfortunately, it has not yet been demonstrated that an analytical solution exists for the argument to maximize the power of the test. This is clearly a useful area for future research, especially in respect of separate regression models.

An alternative investigation of asymptotic power comparisons of separate tests has been made by Gourieroux (1982) and Pesaran (1984a). In these papers, Bahadur's (1960, 1967) method of comparing the approximate slopes of separate tests, and hence the rates at which the sizes of the tests approach zero as the sample size tends to infinity, is applied to several examples. This approach would seem to be particularly useful in situations where the hypotheses under consideration are globally separate in the sense defined by Pesaran (1984b). Pesaran proposed a formal way of classifying the hypotheses into nested and separate categories by means of a measure of 'closeness' of the hypotheses to each other. The local-alternatives approach is not applicable if the hypotheses are globally separate, as it is not then possible to define a limiting process by which one model can be made to approach the other. Thus, when two hypotheses are globally separate, the only method currently available for asymptotic power comparisons of separate tests would seem to be Bahadur's asymptotic relative efficiency criterion.

In considering the consistency of a test of separate distributions, namely H_f that the distribution is log-normal against H_g that it is exponential, Cox (1961, p. 116) stated that since the mean of the test of H_f evaluated under

H_g 'is different from zero, the consistency of the test based on T_f is proved'. However, Cox (1962, p. 407) also stated in general terms that while the mean of a test of H_0 was zero under H_0, it was negative under H_1. It is tempting, therefore, to interpret test consistency as requiring a negative mean under the alternative. On the basis of Cox's general statement, Pereira (1977a) examined the consistency of the Cox and Atkinson tests and demonstrated, for separate distributional families of hypotheses, that the Cox test is consistent for all parameter values whereas the Atkinson test may be inconsistent for some parameter values. Since the Cox test of H_0 against H_1 is *always* consistent, it is clearly unnecessary to 'demonstrate' the consistency of the Cox test for separate regression models (c.f. Davidson and MacKinnon (1981, p. 790)).

Although Pereira's demonstration is correct, its interpretation may be somewhat suspect. A negative mean for N_0 under H_1 does not imply a negative mean for NA_0 under the same H_1. Pereira interpreted the potential positive mean for NA_0 for some parameter values under H_1 in testing separate distributions as indicating inconsistency. In fact, the possible inconsistency arises because NA_0 may have a zero mean under H_1 which is, of course, indistinguishable from its mean under H_0. Fisher and McAleer (1981) have demonstrated that NA_0 is always consistent for separate non-linear regression models. Therefore, Pereira's caveat is unnecessary for many econometric applications and the Atkinson test of H_0 will achieve maximum power against the fixed alternative H_1. The necessary and sufficient condition for NA_0 to be consistent against H_1, namely that NA_0 should have non-zero mean under H_1, has recently been provided by Dastoor (1983b).

The previous tests may readily be extended to handle testing of H_0 against the multiple alternatives $H_1, \ldots, H_m$ jointly. Important contributions to testing multiple models have been made by Williams (1959, pp. 81-9) and Atkinson (1969), although they did not consider the power functions of their tests. More recently, both Sawyer (1984) and Dastoor (1983c) have extended the Cox and Atkinson procedures to test H_0 against multiple separate alternatives, and Sawyer (1982) has proposed a multiple divergence criterion for multiple comparisons of separate hypotheses. These tests are valid in large samples but their small sample properties are as yet unknown. McAleer (1981c, 1983a) has derived a *JA*-type test for H_0 against multiple separate non-linear alternatives, including situations in which the dependent variable is subjected to different data transformations. Finally, Dastoor and McAleer (1983) have applied the *R* procedure to test H_0 jointly against $H_1, \ldots, H_m$ based upon the stacked vector difference

$$\hat{\eta}_0^* = \begin{bmatrix} \hat{\gamma}_1 & - \hat{\gamma}_{10} \\ & \cdot \\ & \cdot \\ & \cdot \\ \hat{\gamma}_m & - \hat{\gamma}_{m0} \end{bmatrix},$$

and have shown that it is equivalent to the standard F test of $H_0' : \gamma = 0$ in the comprehensive regression model

$$y = X\beta + \bar{Z}\gamma + \varepsilon, \qquad (23)$$

in which $\bar{Z}$ contains the linearly independent columns of $Z = [Z_1: \ldots : Z_m]$ that are linearly independent of the columns of X. Of course, if $m = 1$, then $\hat{\eta}_0^* = \hat{\eta}_0$ and (23) collapses to (19).

It has long been held that considerations of power against a specific paired alternative should be balanced with the need for robustness against multiple alternatives. Dastoor and McAleer (1983) have, firstly, demonstrated that even when all possible paired comparisons are made, the paired tests may be inconsistent unless the true alternative is used. Secondly, a joint test can be consistent when the paired Wald test based on the comprehensive model may be inconsistent, thereby formalizing the notion that a joint test may be more widely consistent than a paired test. They also examine the properties of joint and paired tests against *local* alternatives and find that, in general, it is not possible to rank the asymptotic local powers of the F and Cox-type tests. As a special case, they show that when Pesaran-type local alternatives are used, the paired F test will never have greater asymptotic local power than a paired Cox-test. Finally, they compare the finite sample powers of the joint and paired F tests to show that when the *fixed* alternative for the paired test is true, the power of the joint test can never exceed that of the paired test. While the finite sample power gains or losses of a joint test relative to paired tests cannot be shown analytically, the results of Dastoor and McAleer are indicative of the potential usefulness of joint tests.

When a test is evaluated under a specific alternative such as H_1, it is presumed that H_1 is the alternative against which high power is desired. If the alternative is mis-specified, then an attempt is being made to maximize power against a false model. McAleer and Fisher (1982) and McAleer, Fisher and Volker (1982) have examined the case when H_0 is tested against an alternative which is mis-specified by the incorrect inclusion or exclusion of relevant explanatory variables. These authors demonstrated that it is possible for a test of a null against a separate underspecified alternative to be inconsistent. For an alternative approach to test consistency, see Gourieroux, Monfort and Trognon (1983).

On an issue closely related to separate model mis-specification, Mizon and Richard (1986) have discussed the concept of an *implicit null hypothesis*. An implicit null contains the null hypothesis as well as any other hypothesis which yields a probability limit of zero for the relevant test statistic. Since a test must have a non-zero value under an alternative hypothesis if it is to be consistent, the implicit null thereby considers models which may be mis-specified. Hall (1983) uses the concept of an implicit null hypothesis to examine the relationship between the *F* test and Cox test of two separate linear regression models.

Since all models are false in that they are merely approximations to the data generating process, it would seem more sensible to consider testing separate models where both null and alternative are mis-specified. Bierens (1981) has shown that if both H_0 and H_1 are false, the test of H_0 against H_1 may be inconsistent. For this reason, Bierens (1981, 1982) has developed consistent tests of H_0 without a specific (separate) alternative hypothesis in mind, that is, tests of H_0 in the *absence* of alternative hypotheses. It is clear from the discussion in Section 2 that such uni-directional tests are not separate tests, but rather specification error tests. Aguirre-Torres and Gallant (1983) derive the asymptotic distribution of the generalized Cox test for choosing between implicit simultaneous non-linear regression models. Since they study the distribution of their Cox test under both null and non-null distributions, it is not required that either the null or the alternative be correctly specified. Dastoor and McAleer (1983) have provided a thorough examination of test consistency when one or more of *m* multiple alternatives is false, and considered the asymptotic distributions against local alternatives which did not necessarily coincide with any of the specified alternatives.

5 Relations between some exact and asymptotic tests

The tests discussed in the previous sections were based on large-sample theory, and their properties in finite samples are generally unknown. There are, however, occasions in which the tests are *exact* in that their finite sample null distribution is known. This is useful for two reasons. First, a large number of observations is usually not available in applied econometric research. Since the small sample probability of a type 1 error may differ from the nominal size of the test given by asymptotic theory, it is useful to have exact tests for which the size is known. Second, it is sometimes possible to obtain exact test statistics from computed asymptotic test statistics, and the relationship between the two can provide insight into the small sample properties of asymptotic tests. While a test may be termed 'exact' as long as it is possible to find its true critical values either by numerical calculations (however involved) or by the use of tables, in what follows we will be restricting the use of the term to *known null* distributions.

For the reasons given above, it is useful to examine a general method for generating exact separate tests based on the results of Milliken and Graybill (1970). The derivation of exact tests relies on the following straightforward results: (i) $X\hat{\beta} = P_0 y$ and $\hat{\varepsilon}_0 = (I - P_0)y$ are independent of each other; (ii) a function of $X\hat{\beta}$ is independent of a function of $\hat{\varepsilon}_0$. On the basis of these two well-known results, it is possible to derive exact tests simply by adding additional regressors to the null model as long as they are statistically independent of the residuals under the null and the disturbances are normally, independently and identically distributed under the null, as is presumed.

Returning to equation (12), the additional regressor for the *JA* test, namely $P_1 P_0 y$, is obtained by regressing $P_0 y$ on the columns of Z_1, whence $P_1 P_0 y$ is a function of $P_0 y$ and is independent of $\hat{\varepsilon}_0$. Therefore, the *JA* test has the exact *t* distribution with $(n - k_0 - 1)$ degrees of freedom under H_0. The Milliken and Graybill idea was introduced to separate testing by Godfrey (1983) who derived the small sample null distribution of a test of a linear model against a separate linear alternative; see McAleer (1981b) for a different derivation. Godfrey's *T* test is the *t* ratio for the OLS estimate of α in the artificial regression

$$y = X\beta + \alpha(I - P_1)P_0 y + \varepsilon, \tag{24}$$

in which the artificial regressor $(I - P_1)P_0 y$ is a function of $P_0 y$. The *T* test in (24) is simply the negative of the *JA* test in (12). Since the tests are two-sided (see Fisher and McAleer (1979a)), there can be no conflict between them. In testing H_1 rather than H_0, the *JA* test is given as the *t* ratio for the OLS estimate of λ in

$$y = Z_1\gamma_1 + \lambda P_0 P_1 y + \varepsilon. \tag{25}$$

Since $P_0 P_1 y$ is independent of $\hat{\varepsilon}_1 = (I - P_1)y$, the *JA* test of H_1 has the exact *t* distribution with $(n - k_1 - 1)$ degrees of freedom under H_1.

The *J* test of H_0 in (18), however, does not have the *t* distribution because $P_1 y$ is not independent of $\hat{\varepsilon}_0$ under H_0. Similarly, the *J* test of H_1, namely the test of $\lambda = 0$ in

$$y = Z_1\gamma_1 + \lambda P_0 y + \varepsilon, \tag{26}$$

does not have the *t* distribution under H_1. In respect of one-degree-of-freedom tests, Bera and McAleer (1982) have observed that, while the *J* test in (26) is not exact for H_1, it can be made exact for H_0 by suitable variance adjustments (i.e. variance formula and estimated error variance adjustments). The OLS estimate of λ from the test of H_1 in (26), denoted $\hat{\lambda}_J(H_1)$, is given by

$$\hat{\lambda}_J(H_1) = y'P_0(I - P_1)y/(y'P_0(I - P_1)P_0 y). \tag{27}$$

The *J* test of H_1 is not exact because $P_0 y$ is not independent of $\hat{\varepsilon}_1$ under H_1. If $\hat{\lambda}_J(H_1)$ is tested for a significant difference from unity, however, we have from (27) that

$$1 - \hat{\lambda}_J(\mathrm{H}_1) = y'P_0P_1(I - P_0)y/(y'P_0(I - P_1)P_0y). \tag{28}$$

The numerator of $1 - \hat{\lambda}_J(\mathrm{H}_1)$ in (28) is the inner product of P_1P_0y and $(I - P_0)y$, which are independent under H_0. Therefore, if λ in (26) is tested against unity rather than against zero, it is possible to construct an exact test of H_0 from the J test for H_1. It is, of course, more straightforward to obtain an exact JA test for H_0 directly from (12). Nevertheless, while the J test in (26) is not exact for H_1, it can be made exact for H_0, a model which was originally designated as the alternative. A similar result holds for the J test of H_0 in (18).

On the other hand, the JA test in (25), which is exact for H_1, cannot be made exact for H_0 by straightforward variance adjustments. The JA test for H_1 has numerator

$$\hat{\lambda}_{JA}(\mathrm{H}_1) = y'P_1P_0(I - P_1)y/(y'P_1P_0(I - P_1)P_0P_1y),$$

in which P_0P_1y is independent of $(I - P_1)y$ under H_1. Note that a test of λ against unity is based on the statistic

$$1 - \hat{\lambda}_{JA}(\mathrm{H}_1) = -y'P_1P_0(I - P_1)(I - P_0P_1)y/(y'P_1P_0(I - P_1)P_0P_1y),$$

for which the numerator is not equivalent to the numerator of $t(\hat{\alpha})$ in (13) (i.e. it does not have independence between P_1P_0y and $(I - P_0)y$). Thus, the JA test for H_1 cannot be made exact for H_0 through straightforward variance adjustments. A similar result holds for the JA test of H_0 in (12).

A test which is not exact for the null may be made exact for the alternative through suitable variance adjustments. Since exactness of a separate test based on an artificial regression arises through independence of the stochastic regressor and the residuals under the tested model, a one-degree-of-freedom test which is exact for the null cannot, in general, be made exact for the alternative. The exception occurs when Z_1 contains only one column that is linearly independent of the columns of X (e.g. when there is only one regressor in H_1 that is not in H_0). Thus, if $P_1y = Z_1\hat{\gamma}_1$ in (18) and $P_1P_0y = Z_1\hat{\gamma}_{10}$ in (12) are such that Z_1 is an $n \times 1$ column vector and both $\hat{\gamma}_1$ and $\hat{\gamma}_{10}$ are scalars, the J and JA tests are equivalent to a test of $\bar{\gamma}_1 = 0$ in (19). The reason for this is that $\bar{Z}_1$ in (19) is also an $n \times 1$ column vector. In this case, the t ratios for the OLS estimates of α in (12) and (18), and of $\bar{\gamma}_1$ in (19), will be distributed exactly as $t(n - k_0 - 1)$, so that the J, JA and F tests will each reject a true null with the correct probability. If, in addition, there is only one column in X that is linearly independent of the columns of Z_1, the J, JA and F tests of H_1 will have the exact $t(n - k_1 - 1)$ distribution. These results point to the fact that the only separate test which is exact for both models in a paired comparison is the standard F test based on a comprehensive model such as (19) or (20); for an alternative treatment, one could use the procedures discussed in Holly (1982) and Hausman and

Taylor (1980). Of course, if there is only one non-overlapping variable in each model, all three tests will be equivalent.

Some additional aspects regarding exact separate tests should be noted. Bera and McAleer (1982) show that the only test based on an artificial regression such as (15) which is exact, asymptotically distributed as N(0, 1) under H_0, consistent under H_1 and maximizes local power is the *JA* test. Examples are given to show that an exact test does not necessarily maximize power against local alternatives, and that a separate test may be exact and achieve maximum local power regardless of whether OLS or instrumental variable estimation is used. The *JA* test has been adapted by McAleer (1983a) to test H_0 jointly against multiple separate non-linear alternatives with *known* transformations of the dependent variable. The joint test has the central $F(m, n - k_0 - m)$ distribution under H_0. Some particular transformations of the dependent variable will be examined in Section 6. Dastoor and McAleer (1983) compare the finite sample powers of the joint and paired *F* tests to show that when the fixed alternative for the paired test is true, the power of the joint test can never exceed that of the paired test.

With regard to exact joint tests, it is instructive to consider a special case for which the dependent variables are identical in the multiple separate linear models. The extended *JA* test of H_0 against $H_1, \ldots, H_m$ jointly is based on the artificial equation

$$y = X\beta + \sum_{i=1}^{m} \alpha_i P_i P_0 y + \varepsilon, \tag{29}$$

in which $P_i = Z_i(Z_i'Z_i)^{-1}Z_i'$ and P_iP_0y is the predicted value obtained by regressing P_0y on the columns of Z_i ($i = 1, 2, \ldots, m$). The *JA* test of H_0 against H_1 in (12) is a special case of (29) with $m = 1$. Since P_iP_0y is independent of $(I - P_0)y$ for each $i = 1, \ldots, m$, the test of $H_0' : \alpha_1 = \alpha_2 = \ldots = \alpha_m = 0$ is distributed as $F(m, n - k_0 - m)$ under H_0. Thus, if G is the $n \times m$ matrix with typical column P_iP_0y and V is the $n \times (k_0 + m)$ matrix $[X: G]$, the test of H_0 is given by

$$\mathbb{F} = \frac{y'(P_v - P_0)y(n - k_0 - m)}{y'(I - P_v)ym}, \tag{30}$$

in which $P_v = V(V'V)^{-1}V'$.

Notice that $y'(I - P_v)y/(n - k_0 - m)$ is the unrestricted estimate of the error variance from (29). If we follow Atkinson's (1970) suggestion and evaluate the entire statistic under H_0, this would be equivalent to using the restricted estimate of the error variance, namely $y'(I - P_0)y/(n - k_0)$. McAleer (1981c, pp. 6-7) shows that the appropriate statistic for testing H_0, when the restricted estimate of the error variance from (29) replace the unrestricted estimate in (30), is given by

$$M = \frac{y'(P_v - P_0)y}{y'(I - P_0)y} = \frac{y'(P_v - P_0)y}{y'(P_v - P_0)y + y'(I - P_v)y}, \qquad (31)$$

which is the small-sample test of H_0 based upon the LM *principle* of using the restricted estimates only (see e.g. Fisher and McAleer (1980)). Equation (31) is equivalent to equation (2) of McAleer and Fisher (1982, p. 128). Since the two components in the denominator of (31), each divided by the true error variance from (29), are independently distributed as $\chi^2(m)$ and $\chi^2(n - k_0 - m)$, respectively, it follows that M is distributed as $\beta_1(\frac{1}{2}m, \frac{1}{2}(n - k_0 - m))$ exactly under H_0.

An interesting special case of this result may be obtained by setting $m = 1$ in (29) and (30) (c.f. Fisher (1983a)). Recall that the only difference between NA_0 in (11) and $t(\hat{\alpha})$ in (13), which is the JA statistic, is that NA_0 uses a restricted estimate of the error variance from (12) whereas the JA statistic in (13) uses the corresponding unrestricted estimate. It follows immediately that NA_0, the Atkinson variation of the Cox paired test, is exactly distributed as $\beta_1(\frac{1}{2}, \frac{1}{2}(n - k_0 - 1))$ under H_0. Convenience and familiarity will undoubtedly lead to the use of F rather than M, although there can be no conflict between the two statistics based on the corresponding distributions.

In spite of the plethora of asymptotic tests that are available, there is still a debate in the literature as to whether Cox-type one-degree-of-freedom tests are superior to the standard F test based on the comprehensive model. For example, the Monte Carlo simulations based on local alternatives by Pesaran (1982a) in respect of single-equation linear models suggest that while the F test has smaller power than the Cox and J tests, the size of the asymptotic tests is frequently so much greater than the nominal size as to invalidate the use of asymptotic critical values in finite samples; for further details, see Section 7 below. With a view to overcoming the problem of incorrect size, Godfrey and Pesaran (1983a) recently considered a modification to the Cox test incorporating both mean- and variance-adjustments. The mean-adjustment arises from examining the numerator of NL_0 in (7), namely $z_0 = n(\hat{\sigma}_1^2 - \hat{\sigma}_{10}^2) = y'(I - P_1)y - y'(I - P_0)y - y'P_0(I - P_1)P_0y$. Godfrey and Pesaran show that

$$E_0(z_0) = \sigma_0^2\{\text{tr}(P_0P_1) - k_1\},$$

where E_0 denotes expectation under H_0 and $\text{tr}(P_0P_1)$ is the trace of P_0P_1. The mean-adjusted linearized Cox test of H_0 is based on the statistic $\tilde{z}_0 = z_0 - E_0(\tilde{z}_0)$, with estimated variance given by $\tilde{V}_0(\tilde{z}_0)$ which provides a small sample upward adjustment to the asymptotic variance. The statistic $W_0 = \tilde{z}_0/(\tilde{V}_0(\tilde{z}_0))^{\frac{1}{2}}$ incorporates mean- and variance-adjustments and is asymptotically equivalent to NL_0 under H_0. It should be noted that while $\tilde{z}_0$ has zero expectation under H_0, it does not have the property of exactness possessed by the F and JA tests. Moreover, it cannot be readily calculated from standard computer packages.

The simulations reported by Godfrey and Pesaran (1983a) indicate that the statistic W_0 exhibits the correct size and has high power against separate fixed alternatives. However, the mean-adjusted J test derived by the same authors (Godfrey and Pesaran (1983b)) was not as successful in that, while the estimated significance levels were lower than for the (unadjusted) J test, they were still higher than the nominal significance levels. In addition, the estimated probabilities of making the 'correct decision', namely rejecting a false model and accepting the true model, were less than those for Godfrey and Pesaran's mean- and variance-adjusted Cox test. Thus, while the mean-adjusted J test is computationally attractive in that it can be calculated from a simple artificial regression, it is inferior to W on the basis of the reported simulations.

An interesting property of the Atkinson variation of the Cox test is that NA_0 in (10) is written in terms of NL_0 plus a term which essentially adjusts for a non-zero mean. In this sense, NA_0 might be interpreted as a mean-adjusted linearized Cox test, in a similar manner to that of the statistic $\tilde{z}_0$. Indeed, given P_1P_0y, the mean of the numerator of NA_0 in (11) is precisely zero. When Atkinson (1970) modified the Cox test for separate families of distributions, he obtained a statistic which had less bias under the null hypotheses than the Cox test. On the basis of finite sample comparisons, Pereira (1977a) conjectured that the Cox test is preferable to the Atkinson test because it is easier, in general, to correct for lower-order moments of the Cox test than the higher-order moments required for the Atkinson test. Since NA_0 is already mean-adjusted, it is worth examining the variance component of the statistic. The numerator of NA_0 from (11) is

$$v_0 = -y'P_0P_1(I - P_0)y.$$

Under $\mathrm{H}_0 : y = X\beta + \varepsilon_0$, v_0 may be rewritten as

$$v_0 = -\beta'X'P_1(I - P_0)\varepsilon_0 - \varepsilon_0'P_0P_1(I - P_0)\varepsilon_0,$$

from which it is clear that $\mathrm{E}_0(v_0) = 0$. It follows from the normality of ε_0 that the variance of v_0 is

$$\mathrm{V}_0(v_0) = \sigma_0^2\beta'X'P_1(I - P_0)P_1X\beta.$$

A consistent estimate of $\mathrm{V}_0(v_0)$ under H_0 is

$$\hat{\mathrm{V}}_0(v_0) = \hat{\sigma}_0^2y'P_0P_1(I - P_0)P_1P_0y. \tag{32}$$

Since the expression in (32) is the square of the denominator of NA_0 in (11), it follows that $NA_0 = v_0/(\hat{\mathrm{V}}_0(v_0))^{\frac{1}{2}}$ requires no variance-adjustment, unlike the Cox statistic. This would seem to be both an advantage and a disadvantage of the Atkinson test. On the one hand, it is not necessary to adjust NA_0 to improve its small sample size characteristics; on the other, NA_0 cannot be adjusted so as to improve its small sample power properties.

6 Testing linear and log-linear models

The presumption that has been maintained above, namely that the dependent variables should be subjected to the same transformation for all models, is not very realistic. In practice, a common alternative to a linear specification is a model in which the dependent variable and some of the explanatory variables are transformed by natural logarithms, thereby leading to a log-linear (or double logarithmic) specification. Let us, therefore, consider two common alternative models

$$H_0 : \log y_t = \beta_0 + \sum_{j=1}^{J} \beta_j \log x_{jt} + \varepsilon_{0t}, \tag{33}$$

$$H_1 : y_t = \gamma_0 + \sum_{j=1}^{J} \gamma_j x_{jt} + \varepsilon_{1t}, \tag{34}$$

where $t = 1, 2, \ldots, n$. The problem of discriminating between H_0 and H_1 is referred to as the 'pure' log-linear versus linear choice, since the two models differ only in the data transformations on the variables. When the explanatory variables include dummies and other variables that are not transformed, these may be accommodated by the appropriate inclusion of additional regressors in (33) and (34). If the problem is simply one of choosing the model that fits better, the likelihood ratio and LM criteria suggested by Sargan (1964) and Bera and McAleer (1983b), respectively, could be used.

It is straightforward to generate specification error tests of H_0 and H_1 without recourse to explicit information regarding the alternative. Denoting the OLS estimates of β_j and γ_j by $\hat{\beta}_j$ and $\hat{\gamma}_j$, respectively, the predicted values of the dependent variables for H_0 and H_1 are given, respectively, as

$$\widehat{\log y_t} = \hat{\beta}_0 + \sum_j \hat{\beta}_j \log x_{jt} \tag{35}$$

and

$$\hat{y}_t = \hat{\gamma}_0 + \sum_j \hat{\gamma}_j x_{jt}. \tag{36}$$

Inclusion of functions of (35) and (36) in (33) and (34), respectively, leads to

$$\log y_t = \beta_0 + \sum_j \beta_j \log x_{jt} + \delta_0 f(\widehat{\log y_t}) + \varepsilon_{0t} \tag{37}$$

and

$$y_t = \gamma_0 + \Sigma \gamma_j x_{jt} + \delta_1 g(\tilde{y}_t) + \varepsilon_{1t}, \tag{38}$$

where $f(.)$ and $g(.)$ are known invertible transformations. A test of $\delta_0 = 0$ ($\delta_1 = 0$) is equivalent to a test of H_0 (H_1). Before we can discuss the finite sample null distributions of these tests, however, it is necessary to specify the properties of the disturbances ε_{0t} and ε_{1t} under their respective hypotheses.

The log-linear model is not defined when y_t is permitted to be negative. Thus, if y_t is positive for all t, then log y_t is defined and it is reasonable to assume that $\varepsilon_{0t} \sim \text{NID}(0, \sigma_0^2)$ for all t. The logarithmic transformation on y_t requires y_t to be positive, so that ε_{1t} cannot be $\text{NID}(0, \sigma_1^2)$; that is, with y_t always positive, H_1 cannot be true unless the density for ε_{1t} is truncated. Aneuryn-Evans and Deaton (1980, pp. 276-7), for example, consider a symmetric truncation for ε_{1t}. More importantly, they develop tests of H_0 and H_1 against each other based on Cox's centred likelihood ratio principle. Unfortunately, the tests they propose are rather complicated and cannot be calculated using standard computer packages. This has, therefore, prevented their use in both empirical and simulation studies.

When the mean of y_t is several standard deviations above zero, the effects of truncation can be ignored and ε_{1t} will be approximately $\text{NID}(0, \sigma_1^2)$ for all t. In situations where truncation is negligible, perhaps the most straightforward procedures for testing the pure linear and log-linear specifications are those based on the seminal contribution of Box and Cox (1964). The Box-Cox data transformation for a (positive) variable z_t takes the form

$$z_t(\lambda) = \begin{cases} (z_t^\lambda - 1)/\lambda, & \lambda \neq 0 \\ \log z_t, & \lambda = 0 . \end{cases}$$

In this way, both H_0 and H_1 may be nested within the artificial model

$$y_t(\lambda) = \beta_0 + \sum_{j=1}^{J} \beta_j x_{jt}(\lambda) + \varepsilon_t, \tag{39}$$

in which $\varepsilon_t \sim \text{NID}(0, \sigma^2)$ for all t. When $\lambda = 0$, (39) reduces to H_0 and hence a test of $\lambda = 0$ is equivalent to a test of H_0. In the case $\lambda = 1$, (39) reduces to H_1 with $\beta_j = \gamma_j$ ($j = 1, 2, \ldots, J$) and

$$\gamma_0 = 1 + \beta_0 - \sum_j \beta_j,$$

so that a test of $\lambda = 1$ is equivalent to a test of H_1. It is, of course, possible to test λ against values other than 0 or 1; for example, Gregory (1981) considers $\lambda = -1$. Note that in testing λ against zero or unity, H_0 is not being tested against H_1, or H_1 against H_0. The alternative specification in each case is, strictly speaking, the artificial model (39) although, as Godfrey and Wickens (1981, p. 491) duly emphasize, there is no need to believe that

(39) is true since 'a test may reject false null hypotheses even when the selected alternative is incorrect'.

Godfrey and Wickens (1981) develop LM tests of H_0 and H_1 by evaluating the log-likelihood function for the artificial model (39) at $\lambda = 0$ and $\lambda = 1$, respectively. These LM tests are asymptotically distributed as $\chi^2(1)$ and are asymptotically equivalent under the null hypothesis to the likelihood ratio tests suggested by Box and Cox (1964). Bera and McAleer (1983b) have provided an extension of the LM tests of Godfrey and Wickens by considering both symmetric and asymmetric truncation of the density function for the disturbance in the linear model. In both cases, truncation has no effect on the LM statistics for the log-linear model. Truncation does, however, affect the LM statistics for the linear model, although the effect is small if the truncation itself is small. Poirier (1978) has considered a more complicated truncation of the Box-Cox model for the case when the regressors are fixed. Poirier and Ruud (1979) used Poirier's truncated model to derive an LM test of the log-linear model against the class of truncated Box-Cox distributions defined over the positive reals. While the test of the log-linear model is straightforward to compute, it does not yet seem to have been used. The corresponding test of the linear model is not, however, computationally uncomplicated and hence has not been recommended for use by the authors.

Andrews (1971) proposed an alternative to the likelihood ratio test of Box and Cox which has the advantage of being easier to calculate in that the estimate of λ from (39) is not required. By taking a Taylor expansion of (39) around pre-assigned values (namely, $\lambda = 0$ and $\lambda = 1$ for the log-linear and linear models, respectively), (39) can be rewritten in terms of $\log y_t$ and y_t with functions of $\log y_t$ and y_t, respectively, appearing on the right-hand sides of the equations. Upon replacing the dependent variable on the right-hand side by a function of its predicted value under the appropriate null model, Andrews suggested how to construct tests based on the artificial model (39) which have the exact t distribution under the null (recall the discussion of the Milliken and Graybill (1970) results in the previous section).

The Andrews procedure has been applied to test linear and log-linear models by Godfrey and Wickens (1981), who also emphasize that only the test of the log-linear model can have the exact t distribution. This assertion is based on the fact that, from a statistical point of view, a log-linear specification under H_0 requires truncation of the density function of ε_{1t} so that y_t is strictly positive. Therefore, ε_{1t} is not, strictly speaking, normally distributed. However, if the truncation is negligible, ε_{1t} is 'approximately' normally distributed and hence the test of the linear model has the 'approximate' t distribution under H_1. There is, of course, no difficulty with the assumption of normality for ε_{0t} so that an exact test of H_0 is possible. Returning now to the specification error tests in (37) and (38), it is clear from the discussion above that the test of $\delta_0 = 0$ in (37) has the $t(n - J - 2)$ distribution exactly under H_0, while the test of $\delta_1 = 0$ in (38) has the 'approximate' $t(n - J - 2)$ distribution under H_1.

For the more general case in which the dependent variables have different data transformations, and when more than the pure linear versus log-linear choice is being entertained, the procedures suggested by Bera and McAleer (1983b) are worth considering. In order to test (33) and (34), an artificial model is constructed by weighting the errors of H_0 and H_1 as follows

$$(1 - \alpha)(\log y_t - \beta_0 - \sum_j \beta_j \log x_{jt}) + \alpha(y_t - \gamma_0 - \sum_j \gamma_j x_{jt}) = \varepsilon_t, \tag{40}$$

in which ε_t is normally, independently and identically distributed under $H'_0 : \alpha = 0$ and $H'_1 : \alpha = 1$. After appropriate rearrangement of (40), we have the two artificial models

$$\log y_t = \beta_0 + \sum_j \beta_j \log x_{jt} + \theta_0\, \varepsilon_{1t} + \varepsilon_t \tag{41}$$

and

$$y_t = \gamma_0 + \sum_j \gamma_j x_{jt} + \theta_1 \varepsilon_{0t} + \varepsilon_t, \tag{42}$$

in which $\theta_0 = -\alpha/(1 - \alpha)$ and $\theta_1 = -(1 - \alpha)/\alpha$. Tests of $H'_0 : \theta_0 = 0$ in (41) and $H'_1 : \theta_1 = 0$ in (42) are equivalent to tests of $\alpha = 0$ and $\alpha = 1$, respectively. Since ε_{1t} and ε_{0t} are unobservable in (41) and (42), respectively, the tests of H_0 and H_1 can be made tractable by replacing ε_{1t} and ε_{0t} by some function of the residuals obtained from H_0 and H_1, respectively. Consider then the artificial regressions

$$\exp(\log\hat{}\, y_t) = \gamma_0 + \sum_j \gamma_j x_{jt} + \eta_{1t} \tag{43}$$

and

$$\log(\tilde{y}_t) = \beta_0 + \sum_j \beta_j \log x_{jt} + \eta_{0t}, \tag{44}$$

where $\log\hat{}\, y_t$ and $\tilde{y}_t$ are given in (35) and (36). The residuals from (43) and (44) are denoted $\hat{\eta}_{1t}$ and $\tilde{\eta}_{0t}$, respectively, and it is clear that $\hat{\eta}_{1t}$ is a function of $\log y_t$ while $\tilde{\eta}_{0t}$ is a function of $\tilde{y}_t$. Therefore, replacing ε_{1t} in (41) with $\hat{\eta}_{1t}$ and ε_{0t} in (42) with $\tilde{\eta}_{0t}$ will enable H_0 and H_1 to be tested. The test of $\theta_0 = 0$ in (41) will then have the exact $t(n - J - 2)$ distribution under H_0, and the test of $\theta_1 = 0$ in (42) will have the 'approximate' $t(n - J - 2)$ distribution under H_1 if the truncation of the density function of ε_{1t} is negligible.

The tests of Bera and McAleer (1983b) may be extended as follows. In testing H_0, for example, it is possible to replace ε_{1t} in (41) with a function of $\hat{\eta}_{1t}$ or, indeed, with a function of $\log\hat{}\, y_t$ itself, as in (37). For the case of $\hat{\eta}_{1t}$, ε_{1t} might be replaced with $f(\hat{\eta}_{1t})$, where $f(.)$ is the transformation in (37), thereby leading to the artificial equation

$$\log y_t = \beta_0 + \sum_j \beta_j \log x_{jt} + \theta_0 f(\hat{\eta}_{1t}) + \varepsilon_t. \tag{45}$$

The previous discussion was concerned with the identity function $f(\hat{\eta}_{1t}) = \hat{\eta}_{1t}$. If ε_{1t} is replaced with $g(\log\hat{\ } y_t)$, where $g(.)$ is the transformation in (38), this leads to the artificial equation

$$\log y_t = \beta_0 + \sum_j \beta_j \log x_{jt} + \theta_0 g(\log\hat{\ } y_t) + \varepsilon_t. \tag{46}$$

For example, $g(\log\hat{\ } y_t)$ might be $\exp(\log\hat{\ } y_t)$, thereby introducing specific information regarding the alternative model. In addition, the artificial regressor would be of a similar order of magnitude to $\tilde{y}_t$, the predicted value of y_t from the linear model. Similar arguments could be made for a test of H_1 against H_0. The functions $f(.)$ and $g(.)$ in (45) and (46) would be chosen to maximize the power of the test of the null model. Analytical solutions do not seem to be available, so simulations should be very useful in these cases.

Some further remarks should be made in connection with testing linear and log-linear models. The tests just described have the same asymptotic $\chi^2(1)$ distribution under the null, but their finite sample power characteristics may differ from the LM and likelihood ratio tests based on the Box-Cox transformation. Atkinson (1973) shows, for a numerical example, that the Andrews test is uniformly less powerful than two tests derived from the likelihood function. Atkinson (1973, p. 478) argues that, because the Andrews test is not obtained from the likelihood function, it omits the Jacobian of the transformation and hence ignores valuable information on the scaling of the transformed observations. Davidson and MacKinnon (1985) stress the importance of the Jacobian term in their derivation of tests for linear and log-linear models, but the disturbances in both models are required to be normal. Since the tests of Bera and McAleer (1983b) also ignore the Jacobian, the power of their test may be of a similar order of magnitude to that of the Andrews test. There is clearly a trade-off between exactness and computational advantages for these tests.

As an extension of the above analysis, Bera and McAleer (1983a) have proposed several tests for the case where the dependent variable and some of the explanatory variables have the double Box-Cox transformation (see also Blaylock (1980)), which is given as

$$[z_t(\lambda)](\psi) = \begin{cases} \{[z_t(\lambda)]^{\psi} - 1\}/\psi, & \psi \neq 0 \\ \log[z_t(\lambda)], & \psi = 0 \end{cases}$$

where $z_t(\lambda)$ has been given previously. The tests are more general than the LM tests of Godfrey and Wickens (1981) and the 'exact' tests of Andrews (1971). The authors also provide a useful interpretation of the test of the null as either an exact test for homoscedasticity given normality, or as an exact test for normality given homoscedasticity.

A better understanding can be gained of the relationships between the tests described above by considering them in greater detail below. It is clear that the RESET tests of the log-linear and linear models are based on the artificial regressions

$$\log y_t = \beta_0 + \sum_j \beta_j \log x_{jt} + \alpha_0 (\log\hat{\ } y_t)^2 + \theta_0 (\log\hat{\ } y_t)^3 + \delta_0(\log\hat{\ } y_t)^4 + \varepsilon_t \quad (47)$$

and

$$y_t = \gamma_0 + \sum_j \gamma_j x_{jt} + \alpha_1(\tilde{y}_t)^2 + \theta_1(\tilde{y}_t)^3 + \delta_1(\tilde{y}_t)^4 + \varepsilon_t \quad (48)$$

in which $(\log\hat{\ } y_t)^c$ and $(\tilde{y}_t)^c$ are the predicted values of H_0 and H_1, respectively, raised to the power c. The test of H_0 given in (47), which will be denoted RESET (4), is the test of $H_0' : \alpha_0 = \theta_0 = \delta_0 = 0$ against the two-sided alternative $H_{0A}' : \alpha_0 \neq \theta_0 \neq \delta_0 \neq 0$, and is distributed as $F(3, n - J - 4)$ under H_0 (or as $\chi^2(3)$ under H_0 asymptotically). Similarly, the RESET (4) test of H_1 in (48) is the test of $H_1' : \alpha_1 = \theta_1 = \delta_1 = 0$ against $H_{1A}' : \alpha_1 \neq \theta_1 \neq \delta_1 \neq 0$, and is distributed as $F(3, n - J - 4)$ under H_1 (or as $\chi^2(3)$ asymptotically under H_1).

Ramsey and Gilbert (1972) have found RESET (4) to work quite well on the basis of Monte Carlo experiments. For a given size of test, however, adding higher powers of predicted values might be expected to increase the power of the test in finite samples. It is useful, therefore, to consider RESET (3), namely the tests of $H_0' : \alpha_0 = \theta_0 = 0$ and $H_1' : \alpha_1 = \theta_1 = 0$ against two-sided alternatives in

$$\log y_t = \beta_0 + \sum_j \beta_j \log x_{jt} + \alpha_0(\log\hat{\ } y_t)^2 + \theta_0(\log\hat{\ } y_t)^3 + \varepsilon_t \quad (49)$$

and

$$y_t = \gamma_0 + \sum_j \gamma_j x_{jt} + \alpha_1(\tilde{y}_t)^2 + \theta_1(\tilde{y}_t)^3 + \varepsilon_t \quad (50)$$

respectively. The test of H_0' in (49) is distributed as $F(2, n - J - 3)$ under H_0, and that of H_1' in (50) as $F(2, n - J - 3)$ under H_1, while each is asymptotically distributed as $\chi^2(2)$ under their respective null hypotheses. Since both RESET (4) and RESET (3) are based on two-sided alternatives, it may be worth testing H_0' and H_1' against one-sided alternatives to examine the effects on power of the test. Finally, the RESET (2) tests of H_0 and H_1 are the tests of $H_0' : \alpha_0 = 0$ and $H_1' : \alpha_1 = 0$ in

$$\log y_t = \beta_0 + \sum_j \beta_j \log x_{jt} + \alpha_0(\log\hat{\ } y_t)^2 + \varepsilon_t \quad (51)$$

and

$$y_t = \gamma_0 + \sum_j \gamma_j x_{jt} + \alpha_1(\tilde{y}_t)^2 + \varepsilon_t \tag{52}$$

respectively. Each is distributed as $t(n - J - 2)$ under the null hypothesis in small samples, or as N(0, 1) asymptotically. The one-sided alternative for H'_0 is $H'_{0A} : \alpha_0 > 0$ and similarly for $H'_{1A} : \alpha_1 > 0$, while the two-sided alternatives are $H'_{0A} : \alpha_0 \neq 0$ and $H'_{1A} : \alpha_1 \neq 0$, respectively. Denoting RESET (2:1) as the one-sided RESET (2) test, we might expect the former to have higher power than the latter in the direction of the specific alternative given.

The Andrews test involves expanding (39) around $\lambda = 0$ (log-linear) and $\lambda = 1$ (linear) and then evaluating the expansions around estimates obtained under $\lambda = 0$ and $\lambda = 1$, as in (35) and (36), respectively. A first-order expansion of (39) around $\lambda = 0$ leads, after evaluation under H_0, to the Andrews (1) test of $H'_0 : \lambda = 0$ in

$$\log y_t = \beta_0 + \sum_j \beta_j \log x_{jt} + \lambda[-\tfrac{1}{2}(\log\hat{\ } y_t)^2 + \tfrac{1}{2} \sum_j \hat{\beta}_j(\log x_{jt})^2] + \varepsilon_t \tag{53}$$

which is distributed as $t(n - J - 2)$ under H_0, or as N(0, 1) asymptotically. The similarity between the test in (53) and the RESET (2) of H_0 in (51) is worth noting. The hypothesis $H'_0 : \lambda = 0$ is typically tested against the two-sided alternative $H'_{0A} : \lambda \neq 0$ when no information regarding the alternative is used (see Godfrey and Wickens (1981, p. 488 and footnote 8, p. 495)). However, if the linear model is designated as the alternative against which high power is desired, $H'_0 : \lambda = 0$ should be tested against the one-sided alternative $H'_{0A} : \lambda > 0$ (that is, in the direction of $\lambda = 1$). Denoting the one-sided Andrews (1) test by Andrews (1:1), we would expect the latter to be more powerful against the specified alternative than the two-sided test.

The Andrews (1) test of $H'_1 : \lambda = 1$ involves a first-order expansion of (39) around $\lambda = 1$ and evaluation of the expansion under H_1, namely

$$y_t = \gamma_0 + \sum_j \gamma_j x_{jt} + (1 - \lambda)(\tilde{y}_t \log \tilde{y}_t - \tilde{y}_t + 1) - \sum_j \tilde{\gamma}_j(x_{jt} \log x_{jt} - x_{jt} + 1)] + \varepsilon_t. \tag{54}$$

The Andrews (1) test of $H'_1 : \lambda = 1$ (or $1 - \lambda = 0$) is typically tested against the two-sided alternative $H'_{1A} : \lambda \neq 1$, and is distributed as $t(n - J - 2)$ under H_1, or as N(0, 1) asymptotically. If high power is required in the direction of H_0, however, the one-sided alternative is $H'_{1A} : 1 - \lambda > 0$ (or $\lambda < 1$ in the direction of $\lambda = 0$). The one-sided Andrews (1 : 1) test of H'_1 would be expected to be more powerful than Andrews (1). If $\log \tilde{y}_t$ were to be linearized, (54) is seen to be similar to RESET (2) in (52).

It has been conjectured by Andrews (1971, p. 250) and Godfrey and Wickens (1981, p. 492) that higher-order expansions of (39) may lead to increased power, the outcome being ambiguous because power decreases with the degrees of freedom for a fixed non-centrality parameter (see Das Gupta and Perlman (1974)). A similar caveat also holds for the relative powers of RESET (2), RESET (3) and RESET (4). The Andrews (2) test based upon second-order expansions of (39) are calculated from the artificial regressions

$$\log y_t = \beta_0 + \sum_j \beta_j \log x_{jt} + \lambda[-\tfrac{1}{2}(\log\hat{\ } y_t)^2 + \tfrac{1}{2}\sum_j \hat{\beta}_j(\log x_{jt})^2]$$

$$+ \lambda^2[-\tfrac{1}{6}(\log\hat{\ } y_t)^3 + \tfrac{1}{6}\sum_j \hat{\beta}_j(\log x_{jt})^3] + \varepsilon_t \qquad (55)$$

and

$$y_t = \gamma_0 + \sum_j \gamma_j x_{jt} + (1-\lambda)[(\tilde{y}_t \log \tilde{y}_t - \tilde{y}_t + 1)$$

$$- \sum_j \tilde{\gamma}_j(x_{jt} \log x_{jt} - x_{jt} + 1)]$$

$$+ (1-\lambda)^2[-\tfrac{1}{2}(y_t(\log \tilde{y}_t)^2 - 2\tilde{y}_t \log \tilde{y}_t + 2\tilde{y}_t - 2)$$

$$+ \tfrac{1}{2}\sum_j \tilde{\gamma}_j(x_{\mathrm{jt}}(\log x_{jt})^2 - 2x_{jt}\log x_{jt} + 2x_{jt} - 2)] + \varepsilon_t. \qquad (56)$$

In practical applications, the dependent variable would be regressed on all the explanatory variables under the null model, as well as two artificially added variables. Thus, the Andrews (2) test of $H_0' : \lambda = \lambda^2 = 0$ in (55) would be tested against the two-sided alternative $H_{0A}' : \lambda \neq \lambda^2 \neq 0$, and the test of $H_1' : (1-\lambda) = (1-\lambda)^2 = 0$ in (56) against $H_{1A}' : (1-\lambda) \neq (1-\lambda)^2 \neq 0$. These tests are distributed as $F(2, n-J-3)$ under the respective null hypotheses in small samples, or as $\chi^2(2)$ asymptotically.

In testing linear versus log-linear models, two obvious deficiencies in the Andrews (2) tests are that they ignore information concerning the direction of the alternative against which high power is sought, and they also fail to impose the restriction that λ^2 and $(1-\lambda)^2$ cannot be negative under the alternative. If H_0 is tested in the direction of H_1, and vice-versa, the respective alternatives for H_0 and H_1 should be $H_{0A}' : \lambda > 0, \lambda^2 > 0$ and $H_{1A} : (1-\lambda) > 0, (1-\lambda)^2 > 0$. There would seem to be two ways of tackling this problem. The first approach imposes the non-linear restriction between the two added variables, namely that one is the square of the other. Using the Gauss-Newton algorithm for illustrative purposes, one component of the sum of squares to be minimized at any given iteration is $(\lambda - \lambda^*)\cdot(\partial\varepsilon_t/\partial\lambda)_{\lambda=\lambda^*}$, where λ^* is the estimate of λ obtained from the previous iteration. Rewriting (55), for example, as

$$\log y_t = \beta_0 + \sum_j \beta_j \log x_{jt} + \lambda f_1 + \lambda^2 f_2 + \varepsilon_t$$

in which f_1 and f_2 are the first- and second-order expansions of (39) evaluated under H_0, the contribution of λ to the sum of squares is given by

$$(\lambda - \lambda^*)\cdot(\partial\varepsilon_t/\partial\lambda)_{\lambda=\lambda^*} = (\lambda - \lambda^*)(-f_1 - 2\lambda^* f_2).$$

At the first iteration λ^* is set to zero, its value under the null. The contribution of λ, therefore, is seen to be $-\lambda f_1$, which is precisely what is obtained as the contribution of λ to the sum of squares in the Andrews (1) test. If the Gauss-Newton algorithm is terminated after one iteration, there is clearly no sense in using Andrews (2) with a non-linear restriction as this is equivalent to Andrews (1). If second-order efficiency were to be of concern, further iterations might be needed. Note, however, that imposition of the non-linear restriction results in a large sample test, whereas unrestricted estimation of (55) and (56) leads to exact tests (that is, tests with known null distributions). Thus, the non-linear constraint eliminates a desirable small sample property of the Andrews test.

A second approach is to note that the null in joint tests is typically tested against two-sided alternatives, not one-sided. Thus, a straightforward method for implementing one-sided alternatives is to see that setting $\lambda = \lambda^2$ is a valid test of H_0 in the direction of $H_1' : \lambda = 1$, and similarly for setting $(1 - \lambda) = (1 - \lambda)^2$ in order to test H_1 in the direction of $H_0' : \lambda = 0$. Thus (55) and (56) may be simplified to

$$\log y_t = \beta_0 + \sum_j \beta_j \log x_{jt} + \lambda[-\tfrac{1}{2}(\log \hat{} y_t)^2 - \tfrac{1}{6}(\log \hat{} y_t)^3$$
$$+ \tfrac{1}{2}\sum_j \hat{\beta}_j(\log x_{jt})^2 + \tfrac{1}{6}\sum_j \hat{\beta}_j(\log x_{jt})^3] + \varepsilon_t \qquad (57)$$

and

$$y_t = \gamma_0 + \sum_j \gamma_j x_{jt} + (1 - \lambda)[-\tfrac{1}{2}\tilde{y}_t(\log \tilde{y}_t)^2 + (2\tilde{y}_t \log \tilde{y}_t - 2\tilde{y}_t + 2)$$
$$- \sum_j \tilde{\gamma}_j(-\tfrac{1}{2}x_{jt}(\log x_{jt})^2 + 2x_{jt} \log x_{jt} - 2x_{jt} + 2)] + \varepsilon_t. \qquad (58)$$

The one-sided Andrews (2) tests, which will be denoted Andrews (2: 1), are the tests of $H_0' : \lambda = 0$ against $H_{0A}' : \lambda > 0$ in (57) and $H_1' : 1 - \lambda = 0$ against $H_{1A}' : 1 - \lambda > 0$ in (58). Each of these is distributed as $t(n - J - 2)$ under their respective nulls, or N(0, 1) asymptotically. A reasonable conjecture would be that Andrews (2: 1) is more powerful than both Andrews (2) and Andrews (1: 1), although the rankings of the latter two would be uncertain. Finally, it is worth noting the similarity of Andrews (2: 1) in (57) to RESET (3) in (49), and (58) after expansion of $\log \tilde{y}_t$ to (50).

An alternative method for obtaining RESET-type tests of H_0 and H_1 is as follows. Consider testing the null hypothesis $H_0' : \lambda = 0$ in the artificial regression

$$y_t(\lambda) = \beta_0 + \sum_j \beta_j \log x_{jt} + \varepsilon_t. \tag{59}$$

A first-order expansion of $y_t(\lambda)$ around $\lambda = 0$ gives

$$\log y_t = \beta_0 + \sum_j \beta_j \log x_{jt} + \lambda[-\tfrac{1}{2}(\log y_t)^2] + \varepsilon_t. \tag{60}$$

Evaluation of $(\log y_t)^2$ under H_0 gives $(\log\hat{\ } y_t)^2$, substitution of which in (60) yields precisely RESET (2), as in (51). Similarly, a second-order linearization of $y_t(\lambda)$ around $\lambda = 0$ in (59) will lead to a RESET (3) test of H_0 after substitution of $(\log\hat{\ } y_t)^3$ for $(\log y_t)^3$. With a view to testing the linear model, now consider the artificial regression

$$y_t(\lambda) = \gamma_0 + \sum_j \gamma_j x_{jt} + \varepsilon_t \tag{61}$$

for which a first-order linearization is

$$y_t = \gamma_0 + \sum_j \gamma_j x_{jt} + (1 - \lambda)[y_t \log y_t - y_t + 1] + \varepsilon_t. \tag{62}$$

Under $H_1' : \lambda = 1$, we can substitute $\tilde{y}_t$ and $\log \tilde{y}_t$ for y_t and $\log y_t$, respectively, in (62) to obtain

$$y_t = \gamma_0 + \sum_j \gamma_j x_{jt} + (1 - \lambda)(\tilde{y}_t \log \tilde{y}_t) + \varepsilon_t, \tag{63}$$

since $(-\tilde{y}_t + 1)$ is perfectly linearly correlated with the regressors under H_1. The RESET (2)-type test given in (63) is distributed exactly as $t(n - J - 2)$ under H_1. The extension to a second-order linearization is immediate.

An interesting feature of the tests based on the Box-Cox framework is that they can accommodate higher-order expansions. While this has no effect on power under a sequence of local alternatives, power may be increased against a sequence of fixed alternatives in finite samples; for more on this, see McAleer (1983c). Since it is presumed, in general, that tests of linear and log-linear models against each other are more powerful than standard diagnostic checks of the linear and log-linear models individually, Godfrey, McAleer and McKenzie (1986) consider the finite sample sizes and powers of various tests, including those recently developed by White (1980) and Utts (1982). Since the assumption of normality is important when considering linear and log-linear models, Godfrey *et al.* also examine the robustness of separate tests, tests based on the Box-Cox transformation, and diagnostic tests of functional form mis-specification to non-normality of the disturbances.

7 Monte Carlo evidence

Apart from the *F* and *JA* tests in the presence of exogenous regressors, the remaining separate tests are valid only asymptotically. In this section we consider the small-sample evidence that is available from Monte Carlo simulations, and attempt to provide a clear picture of the relative sizes and powers of the various tests. Monte Carlo experiments for testing separate linear regression models have been conducted in the following four published papers, and they will be referenced by the corresponding numbers in this section:

[1] Pesaran (1974);
[2] Pesaran (1982a);
[3] Davidson and MacKinnon (1982);
[4] Godfrey and Pesaran (1983a).

The scope of each paper may be summarized with reference to the way in which the following issues are tackled:

(i) the processes generating the data, and the number of data matrices used;
(ii) the relationship of the models to each other, and also to the data generating process (DGP) if both models are false;
(iii) the use of fixed or local alternatives;
(iv) the sizes of the samples used;
(v) the use of asymptotic or empirical (i.e. size-adjusted) critical values;
(vi) the use of two-sided and one-sided tests;
(vii) the importance of using symmetric and asymmetric empirical critical values when two-sided tests are considered;
(viii) the presence and effect of lagged dependent variables;
(ix) the robustness of the test statistics to non-normality in the disturbances;
(x) the variety of tests examined.

In [1,2,3,4], all the models generating the data are taken to be linear. In [1,2,4], one of the two separate models considered generates the data, whereas [3] considers three linear models, one of which is the DGP. There is only one, and hence only one non-overlapping, variable in each model in [1], whereas [2,3,4] have up to four non-overlapping regressors in the separate models. The regressors in both models in [1,2,4] are drawn from normal populations, and they are correlated across models; in [3], real-life economic data (but for an artificial model) are used and the regressors are correlated both within and across models. The two models in [2] always have the same number of regressors, while in [3] the model with the fewest regressors is the DGP. The alternatives considered in the experiments of [1,3,4] are fixed, although [3] presents the formal analysis in terms of local alternatives; both the formal analysis and Monte Carlo simulations in [2] are presented in terms of local alternatives. The sample sizes used are (20, 40, 80) for [1], (20, 60, 100) for [2], (25, 100) for [3], and (20, 40, 60) for [4]. Asymptotic critical values are used in [1,2,3,4], and [3] also considers empirical critical values. All four papers concentrate upon two-sided tests, although [1, p. 161] suggests a one-sided separate test as being 'advisable'. Only [4] considers the effects of introducing lagged dependent variables into the analysis. The robustness of some tests to non-normality in the disturbances is considered in [4]. However, since Box and Watson (1962) stress that it is the extent of non-normality in the regressors which determines any sensitivity to non-normality in the observations, it would be very useful to consider non-normal errors in the context of separate models with non-normal regressors.

Since the hypotheses considered are separate, a null is taken to be so only temporarily. Thus, the definition of the power of a test in the nested case as the probability of rejecting a false null hypothesis is not directly applicable in the case of separate hypotheses. The 'power' of a separate test is interpreted in [1, p. 163] as the probability of rejecting the false model and not rejecting the true model. This definition of power has also been used by [4], while in [2] the power of the test is calculated directly using the small-sample value of the (asymptotic) non-centrality parameter of the test under the local alternative. In [3], the conventional definition of power as the probability of rejecting a false null hypothesis is used.

As the separate models are linear, it is possible to use the *F* test based on the comprehensive model as a valid separate test. The Cox and *F* tests are compared in [1,2,3,4], while [3] also examines the *J* and *JA* tests. As mentioned in Section 5, [4] presents two modifications of the Cox test that are expected to have better finite sample size (i.e. the probability of rejecting the true null) than the Cox test itself. The results of these experiments may be summarized briefly as follows. The *F* test has empirical size that is very similar to the nominal size in [1,2,4], while the Cox test displays a tendency for over-rejecting the true null so that its size is excessively high. In general, in [1] the Cox test has a higher probability than the *F* test of making a correct decision, and in [2] the Cox test has higher power than *F* based upon the non-centrality parameters. Given the disparities in the sizes of the tests, it is sensible to compare powers of the tests by using either empirical critical values or, as [2, p. 1301] suggests, a weighted sum of the type one and type two errors as a choice criterion. Alternatively, it may be possible to modify the test statistics to adjust for the tendency to over-reject the null, as in [4].

The experiments in [3] are useful because the issue of omitting a regressor that is correlated with the included variables is considered. The true model has three regressors, while the two false separate models have four and five regressors, respectively. Since the *F* test is ignored in comparisons of size, only the *JA* test is found to have good size in relation to the Cox and *J* tests.

In testing a false null against a true alternative, the false null always has more parameters. In such cases, the J and JA tests have similar probabilities of rejecting the false null model. However, when a false null is tested against a false alternative, the JA test has a lower probability than the Cox and J tests of rejecting a false null. No results are available for the probability of rejecting both false models, a desirable outcome in such cases. Somewhat curiously, size/power trade-offs are given for the situation in which both models are false. It would clearly be useful to examine results for the case where the true model has more parameters than the false alternative, since this may have some effect on the sizes and powers of the tests in finite samples.

The Monte Carlo experiments in [4] are thorough and consider several problems that have not previously been analysed. First, mean- and variance-corrected Cox-type tests are developed in an attempt to eliminate the size deficiency of the Cox test. Second, the consequences of having a different number of regressors in both the null and alternative models are considered. Apart from the effect of non-normality in the errors, the effect of including lagged dependent variables is examined. The results presented in [4] are for the F test and two Cox-type tests, namely $\tilde{N}$ and W. The corresponding results for the J and JA tests were not included in [4] but they have been made available to the author by Godfrey and Pesaran. The following discussion of [4] is based on both the published and unpublished results.

The nominal critical value is set at five per cent throughout the experiments. Since $\tilde{N}^2$ and W^2 are squared standard normal variates, the critical values are obtained from the $\chi^2(1)$ distribution; those for J^2 and JA^2 are taken from the F distribution, as is the critical value for the F test. Since the J test is, in general, valid only asymptotically, the use of critical values from the F distribution will lead to a smaller empirical size than would be the case if $\chi^2(1)$ were used. The DGP is set as H_0 throughout, k_0 (= 2, 4) is the number of regressors in H_0, k_1 (= 2, 4) is the number of regressors in the false H_1, n (= 20, 40, 60) is the sample size, R^2 (= 0.3, 0.5, 0.8, 0.85, 0.9) is the population multiple correlation coefficient for H_0, ϱ (= 0.25, 0.3, 0.5, 0.8, 0.85, 0.9, 0.95) is the canonical correlation coefficient between the regressors of the separate models (which is set to a constant value for all regressors), and β (= 0, 0.3, 0.5, 0.7) is the coefficient of the lagged dependent variable.

For $k_0 = 4$, $k_1 = 2$, $R^2 = \varrho^2$ and three different sample sizes, apart from two high sizes for J and two low sizes for W, all tests have estimated significance levels that are very similar to the nominal level of five per cent. The JA test has poor power for this case, and the seemingly slight superiority in power of the J test is purchased at the expense of a slightly higher size. When $n = 20$, $R^2 = 0.5$, $(k_0, k_1) = (2, 4)$ and $(4, 2)$, and different values of ϱ, the J test has an unacceptably high size, especially for $k_0 < k_1$, and W has size that is too low for both $k_0 < k_1$ and $k_0 > k_1$. For tests with acceptable size, $\tilde{N}$ has the highest power. The results for the case of an equal number of regressors, namely $(k_0, k_1) = (2, 2)$ and $(4, 4)$, and where $n = 20$ and $R^2 = 0.5$, are interesting in that the size of the J test is acceptable for $k_0 = k_1 = 2$, but not for $k_0 = k_1 = 4$. For the latter case, the W test has size which is too low on two occasions. When size is acceptable, the $\tilde{N}$ and J tests have similar powers, with a slight preference for the former; however, $\tilde{N}$ dominates when the size of J is too high. The W test has lower power than $\tilde{N}$, but this could be due to its lower size. The JA test has higher power, in general, than the F test, but lower power than $\tilde{N}$ and W. The presence of a lagged dependent variable alters the relative rankings slightly. Both the $\tilde{N}$ and J tests have sizes that are too high, while the F, JA and W tests have acceptable sizes. For different values of $(R^2, \beta, \varrho, k_0, k_1)$, the W test has the highest power, while the JA and F tests cannot be ranked. However, for different values of (β, k_0, k_1), the W test again has highest power, but is then followed by the JA and F tests.

What are we to make of these results? The true model was constructed so that it could have a different number of parameters from the false model. The J test has poor size when the false model has more parameters than the true model (i.e. $k_1 > k_0$), while the JA test has poor power for $k_0 > k_1$. As for the JA test, it can have higher power than the F test and (sometimes) the W test. All tests are dominated by the $\tilde{N}$ test, except for W when a lagged dependent variable is present. Nevertheless, two unresolved issues remain. First, in [4, p. 144], the JA test is found to have poor power when the true model has more parameters than the false model. According to [3], however, the JA test has low power when a false null is tested against a false alternative, regardless of whether the null has more or fewer parameters than the alternative. Since the results in [3] hold only for the case where the true model always has fewer parameters than the false model, it would be useful to investigate whether it is the testing against a false alternative, or the difference in the number of parameters in the true and false models, which explains the poor power of the JA test. Second, which test or tests should be used in practice? As a rule of thumb, it would seem sensible to use more than one test wherever possible. Gregory and McAleer (1983, p. 597) advocate using several test statistics and to examine whether there are any conflicts in their outcomes as a guide to accepting to rejecting the null model.

The Monte Carlo simulations reported above are for separate linear regression models in which the dependent variables are identical across models. The simulations reported in King and McAleer (1984) indicate that the Cox test also has an unacceptably high size when a linear model with a first-order autoregressive error process is tested against a linear model with a first-order moving-average error process. Since both models are intrinsically non-linear, and the separateness arises through the covariance structure, this study reveals some interesting areas for future research.

In the context of testing linear and log-linear models against each other, Aneuryn-Evans and Deaton (1980) find that the Cox test has an acceptable size. This is especially interesting, and perhaps somewhat surprising, in view of all the other results in the literature concerning the penchant of the Cox test for over-rejecting the null. However, as reported in Bera and McAleer (1983b), the Cox test has higher power than several other tests when the linear model is true, but can have relatively low power when the log-linear model is true. For a review and extension of the theoretical literature, and further Monte Carlo work related to testing linear and log-linear models against each other, see Godfrey, McAleer and McKenzie (1986).

8 Some empirical applications

It took more than a decade for the seminal ideas of Cox (1961, 1962) to be discussed in econometrics by Dhrymes *et al.* (1972) and Goldfeld and Quandt (1972, p. 139), and for the derivation of Cox tests for separate linear regression models by Pesaran (1972, 1974) and for non-linear systems of equations by Pesaran and Deaton (1978). In more recent years there have been numerous theoretical developments, yet the effect on empirical applications has been slow in coming. The reason for this may stem in part from the lack of familiarity by econometricians with the nature of separate tests. While the usefulness of separate tests lies in attempting to improve the quality of applied econometric research and, in so doing, to resolve or reconcile some of the ongoing debates in economic theory, the practical merits of separate tests do not yet seem to have been fully appreciated by the profession. On the other hand, the use of separate tests in econometric modelling should not be overemphasized. McAleer, Pagan and Volker (1985) suggest a check-list of five major categories, adherence to which is expected to improve the quality of applied research. While the ability to explain the performance of separate alternatives is an important consideration in econometric modelling, the set of standards includes diagnostic checks such as tests for serial correlation, heteroscedasticity, omission of regressors, functional form mis-specification, and so on. In the empirical examples that follow, therefore, we will be interested in analysing the role played by separate tests in reaching an adequate econometric model.

Some early illustrative economic examples are given in Quandt (1974) and Pesaran and Deaton (1978). The application of the Cox test by Quandt led to neither model being rejected, but no diagnostic checks are given at all. Pesaran and Deaton apply the paired Cox test to five simple aggregate consumption functions, and find that each model is rejected against at least one of the four separate alternatives. Davidson and MacKinnon (1981) use the same set of data and calculate the J test statistic and an asymptotically equivalent test. Fisher and McAleer (1981) also use the same data to calculate the *N*, *NL*, *NA*, *J* and Hoel (1947) tests. While these are intended simply for illustrative purposes, calculation of the Durbin-Watson statistic would have indicated a fundamental inadequacy in each of the models considered. Since the role of separate tests is to test separate models that are *adequate*, standard diagnostic checks should always be used in conjunction with separate tests.

Deaton (1978) was the first to apply the Cox test of Pesaran and Deaton (1978) to test two separate systems of demand equations against each other, and obtained a double rejection. Fisher and McAleer (1979a) examine some of the interesting issues in connection with testing a single-equation model against a separate single equation that is part of a system of equations. However, the theoretical properties of the tests in such circumstances have yet to be established formally. Murray (1984) tests three separate systems of demand equations against each other using paired Cox tests, and rejects all three models. There is as yet no Monte Carlo evidence available on whether the Cox test has a tendency to over-reject the null model in systems of equations, and this is clearly an area for future research.

Two interesting economic examples are provided by Beath (1979) and Bean (1981). Beath considers the issue of the shifting of the corporate income tax in the manufacturing industry, and examines in detail several hypotheses regarding the formation of expectations. After examining standard diagnostic checks for serial correlation, he considers three hypotheses regarding expectations-formations as being adequate. Since he is unable to reject any of the three hypotheses on the basis of paired Cox tests, Beath selects the model with the highest maximized log-likelihood value. Bean is concerned with developing and estimating a simple model of manufacturing investment behaviour in the United Kingdom. After an examination of several diagnostic checks, Bean tests his preferred model against some separate alternatives available in the literature. All four representative alternative specifications are strongly rejected by Bean's preferred model, and the latter is rejected against two of the four alternatives. Bean therefore suggests that information from at least one of the alternatives should be incorporated into his preferred specification.

Each of the above authors has relied on the Cox statistic to test separate models. The majority of paired comparisons has resulted in both models being rejected, with Quandt (1974) and Beath (1979) being the exceptions in that at least one of the models they consider is not rejected. As discussed in Section 7, the Cox test for separate linear regression models has a tendency to reject a true null too frequently. For this reason, it is useful to examine empirical applications in which more than one test is used, with the attendant possibilities for conflict. McAleer and Fisher (1982) examine two separate formulations of structural change in a model of trade union growth for Canada. They do not reject either of the separate hypotheses of smooth or discrete structural change on the basis of the *N*, *NL*, *NA*, *J* and *JA* tests.

McAleer, Fisher and Volker (1982) argue that an alternative should be well specified if it is to provide high power for a test of the null. They illustrate, within the context of the US long-run demand for money function, that by progressively underspecifying a well-specified alternative, a test based on an underspecified alternative could fail to reject a null model that has previously been rejected. A corollary is that as an alternative model becomes progressively more well-specified, the possibilities for rejecting a false null are increased.

An interpretation that is similar to that of McAleer, Fisher and Volker (1982) can be applied to the empirical example of Green, Pope and Phipps (1981) concerning habit formation in single-equation demand models. These authors consider a partial adjustment (PA) model which is nested within a state adjustment (SA) model, as well as a separate time trend (TT) model. In pairwise comparisons of SA and TT for four commodities using the Cox test, the SA model rejects TT in all four cases while TT rejects SA in two cases. When the (relatively) underspecified PA model is tested pairwise against TT, PA is rejected in all four cases while TT is rejected in only two cases. This demonstrates that while TT dominates PA on the basis of single-equation comparisons, TT in turn is dominated by a more well-specified SA model.

Further applications are available in the literature, and the following list illustrates some of the more interesting examples that have been considered. Harvey (1977) applies the Cox and F tests to discriminate between a CES and a Taylor-series approximation to the VES production function. Volker (1980) uses the Cox test to examine separate models relating nominal interest rates to observable inflationary expectations series and to a distributed lag of past inflation rates. Deaton (1982) uses the F test to evaluate separate savings and consumption functions. The Cox and F tests are used by Pesaran (1982c) to test the new classical and Keynesian models of the US employment rate against each other; see also Dadkhah and Valbuena (1985). Pagan, Hall and Trivedi (1983) test a first-order autoregressive error process against a third-order moving-average error process for Australian quarterly unanticipated inflation series using the Cox test; see also McAleer, McKenzie and Hall (1986), who develop several tests for this time series problem. A J-type test is used by Smith and Maddala (1983) to investigate multiple model selection criteria in censored regression models with heteroscedasticity, and to conduct an empirical study of demand deposits. Gregory and McAleer (1983) test the functional form of the demand for money function for Canada using various tests of non-linear separate models as well as linear versus log-linear functional forms. Backus (1984) uses the J test to compare several competing empirical models of the exchange rate for Canada and the US during the seventies.

More recently, various separate test procedures have been used for evaluating money demand functions by Brissimis and Leventakis (1985),

Johannes and Nasseh (1985), Milbourne (1985) and Thornton (1985); for consumption functions by Davis (1984) and Patterson (1986); for aggregate spatial interaction by Anselin (1984); for balance of trade models by Ahumada (1985); for examining the effects of dividend taxes on corporate investment decisions by Poterba and Summers (1983); for alternative investment functions by Wisley and Johnson (1985); for alternative functional forms in production by Rossi (1985); and for testing specifications of intertemporal optimum problems by Singleton (1985).

9 Future research

This paper has attempted to survey the most recent theoretical advances in testing separate models. The treatment given to some of the topics has been far from exhaustive. While some areas of potentially fruitful research have already been mentioned in the paper, some other areas for future research are discussed briefly below.

(i) Although both exact and asymptotic tests are available in certain cases, it is not entirely clear which have greater power in finite samples. The simulation results of Atkinson (1973) are indicative, but a broader study to examine the small-sample properties of the tests of Andrews (1971) and Bera and McAleer (1983a), and the specification error tests suggested in Section 6, would be very useful.

(ii) Since several joint tests have now been developed, simulation studies would provide insight into the finite-sample properties of joint as compared with paired tests.

(iii) As there are indications that the *JA* test can lack power and the *J* test has excessive size in finite samples, it might be worthwhile considering modifications of the two tests of H_0 by adding the artificial variable $P_1y + P_1P_0y = P_1(I + P_0)y$ to H_0 rather than P_1y and P_1P_0y individually. This may lead to a test of H_0 which has better size than *J* while simultaneously having greater power than the *JA* test. It may also be useful to consider modifying the *J* and *JA* tests by including power functions of both P_1y and P_1P_0y in H_0, along the lines of RESET-type tests discussed in the paper.

(iv) The robustness of separate tests should be examined in the presence of non-standard error structures and specification errors of various types. There is clearly a need to develop simple test procedures for separate models under a general error specification such as non-normal and serially dependent errors (McAleer and Bera (1982)), and to examine their small-sample properties. The censored models considered by Smith and Maddala (1983) would also seem to deserve further attention.

(v) Numerical simulations are not yet available for complicated non-linear functions or for systems of equations. Since much of the empirical literature in demand systems, for example, revolves around the presence of competing separate systems of equations, the finite-sample size and power properties of separate tests need to be investigated.

(vi) Several papers have recently considered tests of separate time series models along the lines of Whittle (1951) and Walker (1967). The tests developed by King (1983), King and McAleer (1984), McAleer, McKenzie and Hall (1986) and Gill, McAleer and McKenzie (1986) now permit a wide range of separate time series models with separate error structures to be tested against each other. Since time series models arise frequently in practice, it would be interesting to see these tests applied to economic time series data.

References

Aguirre-Torres, V., and Gallant, A.R. (1983), 'The Null and Non-Null Asymptotic Distribution of the Cox Test for Multivariate Nonlinear Regression: Alternatives and a New Distribution-Free Cox Test', *Journal of Econometrics*, 21, 5-33.

Ahumada, H.A. (1985), 'An Encompassing Test of Two Models of the Balance of Trade for Argentina', *Oxford Bulletin of Economics and Statistics*, 47, 51-70.

Akaike, H. (1973), 'Information Theory and an Extension of the Maximum Likelihood Principle', in *Proceedings of the Second International Symposium on Information Theory*, eds. B.N. Petrov and F. Csaki, Budapest: Akademiai Kiado, 267-81.

Akaike, H. (1974), 'A New Look at the Statistical Model Identification', *IEEE Transactions on Automatic Control, AC-19*, 716-23.

Amemiya, T. (1980), 'Selection of Regressors', *International Economic Review*, 21, 331-54.

Andrews, D.F. (1971), 'A Note on the Selection of Data Transformations', *Biometrika*, 58, 249-54.

Aneuryn-Evans, G., and Deaton, A.S. (1980), 'Testing Linear Versus Logarithmic Regression Models', *Review of Economic Studies*, 47, 275-91.

Anscombe, F.J. (1961), 'Examination of Residuals', *Proceedings of the Fourth Berkeley Symposium on Mathematical Statistics and Probability*, 4, Berkeley: University of California Press, 1-36.

Anselin, L. (1984), 'Specification Tests and Model Selection for Aggregate Spatial Interaction: An Empirical Comparison', *Journal of Regional Science*, 24, 1-15.

Atkinson, A.C. (1969), 'A Test for Discriminating Between Models', *Biometrika*, 56, 337-47.

Atkinson, A.C. (1970), 'A Method for Discriminating Between Models', *Journal of the Royal Statistical Society* B, 32, 323-53.

Atkinson, A.C. (1973), 'Testing Transformations to Normality', *Journal of the Royal Statistical Society* B, 35, 473-9.

Backus, D. (1984), 'Empirical Models of the Exchange Rate: Separating the Wheat from the Chaff', *Canadian Journal of Economics*, 17, 824-46.

Bahadur, R.R. (1960), 'Stochastic Comparison of Tests', *Annals of Mathematical Statistics*, 31, 276-95.

Bahadur, R.R. (1967), 'Rates of Convergence of Estimates and Test Statistics', *Annals of Mathematical Statistics*, 38, 303-24.

Bean, C.R. (1981), 'An Econometric Model of Manufacturing Investment in the UK', *Economic Journal*, 91, 106-21.
Beath, J. (1979), 'Target Profits, Cost Expectations and the Incidence of the Corporate Income Tax', *Review of Economic Studies*, 46, 513-25.
Bera, A., and McAleer, M. (1982), 'On Exact and Asymptotic Tests of Non-Nested Models', unpublished paper, Department of Statistics, Australian National University (*Statistics and Probability Letters*, forthcoming).
Bera, A., and McAleer, M. (1983a), 'Some Exact Tests for Model Specification', *Review of Economics and Statistics*, 65, 351-4.
Bera, A., and McAleer, M. (1983b), 'Further Results on Testing Linear and Log-Linear Regression Models', paper presented to the SSRC Econometric Study Group Conference on Model Specification and Testing, Warwick, 1982.
Berndt, E.R., and Savin, N.E. (1977), 'Conflict Among Criteria for Testing Hypotheses in the Multivariate Linear Regression Model', *Econometrica*, 45, 1263-78.
Bierens, H.J. (1981), 'A Test for Model Specification in the Absence of Alternative Hypotheses', Discussion Paper No. 81-154, Department of Economics, University of Minnesota.
Bierens, H.J. (1982), 'Consistent Model Specification Tests', *Journal of Econometrics*, 20, 105-34.
Blaylock, J.R. (1980), 'The Application of Transformations to Non-Linear Models', *Economics Letters*, 5, 161-4.
Box, G.E.P., and Cox, D.R. (1964), 'An Analysis of Transformations', *Journal of the Royal Statistical Society* B, 26, 211-52.
Box, G.E.P., and Watson, G.S. (1962), 'Robustness to Non-Normality of Regression Tests', *Biometrika*, 49, 93-106.
Breusch, T.S. (1979), 'Conflict Among Criteria for Testing Hypotheses: Extensions and Comments', *Econometrica*, 47, 203-7.
Breusch, T.S., and Pagan, A.R. (1978), 'The Lagrange Multiplier Test and Its Applications to Model Specification in Econometrics', Discussion Paper 7820, C.O.R.E., Universite Catholique de Louvain, Belgium.
Breusch, T.S., and Pagan, A.R. (1980), 'The Lagrange Multiplier Test and Its Applications to Model Specification in Econometrics', *Review of Economic Studies*, 47, 239-53.
Brissimis, S.N., and Leventakis, J.A. (1985), 'Specification Tests of the Money Demand Function in an Open Economy', *Review of Economics and Statistics*, 67, 482-89.
Cox, D.R. (1961), 'Tests of Separate Families of Hypotheses', *Proceedings of the Fourth Berkeley Symposium on Mathematical Statistics and Probability*, 1, Berkeley: University of California Press, 105-23.
Cox, D.R. (1962), 'Further Results on Tests of Separate Families of Hypotheses', *Journal of the Royal Statistical Society* B, 24, 406-24.
Dadkhah, K.M., and Valbuena, S. (1985), 'Non-Nested Test of New Classical vs Keynesian Models: Evidence from European Economies', *Applied Economics*, 17, 1083-98.
Das Gupta, S., and Perlman, M.D. (1974), 'Power of the Noncentral F-Test: Effect of Additional Variates on Hotelling's T^2-Test', *Journal of the American Statistical Association*, 69, 174-80.
Dastoor, N.K. (1980), 'Heteroscedasticity – A Non-Nested Approach', unpublished paper, Department of Economic and Business Studies, University of Liverpool.
Dastoor, N.K. (1981), 'A Note on the Interpretation of the Cox Procedure for Non-Nested Hypotheses', *Economics Letters*, 8, 113-19.

Dastoor, N.K. (1983a), *Some Aspects of Testing Non-Nested Hypotheses in Econometrics*, unpublished Ph.D. thesis, University of Essex.
Dastoor, N.K. (1983b), 'Some Aspects of Testing Non-Nested Hypotheses', *Journal of Econometrics*, 21, 213-28.
Dastoor, N.K. (1983c), 'Testing for Multiple Separate Hypotheses', unpublished paper, Department of Economic and Business Studies, University of Liverpool.
Dastoor, N.K. (1985), 'A Classical Approach to Cox's Test for Non-Nested Hypotheses', *Journal of Econometrics*, 27, 363-70.
Dastoor, N.K., and McAleer, M. (1983), 'Some Comparisons of Joint and Paired Tests of Non-Nested Hypotheses', paper presented to the North American Meeting of the Econometric Society, San Francisco, 1983.
Dastoor, N.K., and McAleer, M. (1985), 'Testing Separate Models with Stochastic Regressors', *Economic Modelling*, 2, 331-8.
Davidson, R., and MacKinnon, J.G. (1980), 'On a Simple Procedure for Testing Non-Nested Regression Models', *Economics Letters*, 5, 45-8.
Davidson, R., and MacKinnon, J.G. (1981), 'Several Tests for Model Specification in the Presence of Alternative Hypotheses', *Econometrica*, 49, 781-93.
Davidson, R., and MacKinnon, J.G. (1982), 'Some Non-Nested Hypothesis Tests and the Relations Among Them', *Review of Economic Studies*, 49, 551-65.
Davidson, R., and MacKinnon, J.G. (1983a), 'Small Sample Properties of Alternative Forms of the Lagrange Multiplier Test', *Economics Letters*, 12, 269-75.
Davidson, R., and MacKinnon, J.G. (1983b), 'Testing the Specification of Multivariate Models in the Presence of Alternative Hypotheses', *Journal of Econometrics*, 23, 301-13.
Davidson, R., and MacKinnon, J.G. (1984), 'Model Specification Tests Based on Artificial Linear Regressions', *International Economic Review*, 25, 485-502.
Davidson, R., and MacKinnon, J.G. (1985), 'Testing Linear and Loglinear Regressions Against Box-Cox Alternatives', *Canadian Journal of Economics*, 18, 499-517.
Davis, E.P. (1984), 'The Consumption Funtion in Macroeconomic Models: A Comparative Study', *Applied Economics*, 16, 799-838.
Deaton, A.S. (1978), 'Specification and Testing in Applied Demand Analysis', *Economic Journal*, 88, 524-36.
Deaton, A.S. (1982), 'Model Selection Procedures, or, Does the Consumption Function Exist?', in *Evaluating the Reliability of Macroeconomic Models*, eds. G.C. Chow and P. Corsi, New York: Wiley, 43-65.
den Butter, F.A.G., and Verbon, H.A.A. (1982), 'The Specification Problem in Regression Analysis', *International Statistical Review*, 50, 267-83.
Dhrymes, P.J., Howrey, E.P., Hymans, S.H., Kmenta, J., Leamer, E.E., Quandt, R.E., Ramsey, J.B., Shapiro, H.T., and Zarnowitz, V. (1972), 'Criteria for Evaluation of Econometric Models', *Annals of Economic and Social Measurement*, 1, 291-324.
Durbin, J. (1954), 'Errors in Variables', *Review of the International Statistical Institute*, 22, 23-32.
Durbin, J. (1970), 'Testing for Serial Correlation in Least Squares Regression When Some of the Regressors are Lagged Dependent Variables', *Econometrica*, 38, 410-21.
Efron, B. (1984), 'Comparing Non-Nested Linear Models', *Journal of the American Statistical Association*, 79, 791-803.
Engle, R.F., Hendry, D.F., and Richard, J.-F. (1983), 'Exogeneity', *Econometrica*, 51, 277-304.
Epps, T.W., Singleton, K.J., and Pulley, L.B. (1982), 'A Test of Separate Families

of Distributions Based on the Empirical Moment Generating Function', *Biometrika*, 69, 391-9.
Ericsson, N.R. (1982), *Testing Non-Nested Hypotheses in Systems of Linear Dynamic Economic Relationships*, unpublished Ph.D. thesis, London School of Economics.
Ericsson, N.R. (1983), 'Asymptotic Properties of Instrumental Variables Statistics for Testing Non-Nested Hypotheses', *Review of Economic Studies*, 50, 287-304.
Evans, G.B.A., and Savin, N.E. (1982), 'Conflict Among the Criteria Revisited: The W, LR and LM Tests', *Econometrica*, 50, 737-48.
Fisher, G.R. (1983a), 'Tests for Two Separate Regressions', *Journal of Econometrics*, 21, 117-32.
Fisher, G.R. (1983b), 'A Guide to Testing Separate Regressions', paper presented to the Canadian Economics Association Meeting, Vancouver, 1983.
Fisher, G.R., and McAleer, M. (1979a), 'On the Interpretation of the Cox Test in Econometrics', *Economics Letters*, 4, 145-50.
Fisher, G.R., and McAleer, M. (1979b), 'Theory and Econometric Evaluation of a Systems Approach to the Demand for Money: The Canadian Case', paper presented to the Fourth World Congress of the Econometric Society, Aix-en-Provence, 1980.
Fisher, G.R., and McAleer, M. (1980), 'Principles and Methods in the Testing of Alternative Models', paper presented to the North American Meeting of the Econometric Society, Denver, 1980.
Fisher, G.R., and McAleer, M. (1981), 'Alternative Procedures and Associated Tests of Significance for Non-Nested Hypotheses', *Journal of Econometrics*, 16, 103-19.
Fisher, G.R., and McAleer, M. (1984), 'The Geometry of Specification Error', *Australian Journal of Statistics*, 26, 310-22.
Gaver, K.M., and Geisel, M.S. (1974), 'Discriminating Among Alternative Models: Bayesian and Non-Bayesian Methods', in *Frontiers in Econometrics*, ed., P. Zarembka, New York: Academic Press, 49-77.
Gill, L. (1982), 'Some Non-Nested Tests in Certain Exponential Families of Distributions', paper presented to the European Meeting of the Econometric Society, Dublin, 1982.
Gill, L. (1983), *Large Sample Tests of Identification and Specification in the Linear Simultaneous Equations Model*, unpublished Ph.D. thesis, University of Edinburgh.
Gill, L., McAleer, M., and McKenzie, C.R. (1986), 'Simple Procedures for Testing Autoregressive Versus Moving Average Errors in Regression Models', paper presented to the Time Series Conference, Canberra, 1986.
Godfrey, L.G. (1983), 'Testing Non-Nested Models After Estimation by Instrumental Variables or Least Squares', *Econometrica*, 51, 355-65.
Godfrey, L.G. (1984), 'On the Uses of Misspecification Checks and Tests of Non-Nested Hypotheses in Empirical Econometrics', *Economic Journal (Supplement)*, 94, 69-81.
Godfrey, L.G., McAleer, M., and McKenzie, C.R. (1986), 'Variable Addition and Lagrange Multiplier Tests for Linear and Logarithmic Regression Models: Theory and Monte Carlo Evidence', paper presented to the European Meeting of the Econometric Society, Budapest, 1986.
Godfrey, L.G., and Pesaran, M.H. (1983a), 'Tests of Non-Nested Regression Models: Small Sample Adjustments and Monte Carlo Evidence', *Journal of Econometrics*, 21, 133-54.
Godfrey, L.G., and Pesaran, M.H. (1983b), 'Small Sample Adjustments for the J-Test', Working Paper in Economics and Econometrics No. 084, Australian National University.

Godfrey, L.G., and Wickens, M.R. (1981), 'Testing Linear and Log-Linear Regressions for Functional Form', *Review of Economic Studies*, 48, 487-96.
Godfrey, L.G., and Wickens, M.R. (1982), 'Tests of Misspecification Using Locally Equivalent Alternative Models', in *Evaluating the Reliability of Macroeconomic Models*, eds. G.C. Chow and P. Corsi, New York: Wiley, 71-99.
Goldfeld, S.M., and Quandt, R.E. (1972), *Nonlinear Methods in Econometrics*, Amsterdam: North Holland.
Gourieroux, C. (1982), 'Asymptotic Comparison of Tests for Non-Nested Hypotheses by Bahadur's A.R.E.', Discussion Paper 8215, CEPREMAP, Paris.
Gourieroux, C., Monfort, A., and Trognon, A. (1983), 'Testing Nested or Non-Nested Hypotheses', *Journal of Econometrics*, 21, 83-115.
Green, R.D., Pope, R.D., and Phipps, T.T. (1981), 'Discriminating Among Alternative Habit Formation Schemes in Single-Equation Demand Models', *Applied Economics*, 13, 399-409.
Gregory, A.W. (1981), *The Demand for Money in Canada: An Econometric Evaluation of the Conventional Specification*, unpublished Ph.D. thesis, Queen's University, Canada.
Gregory, A.W., and McAleer, M. (1981), 'Simultaneity and the Demand for Money in Canada: Comments and Extensions', *Canadian Journal of Economics*, 14, 488-96.
Gregory, A.W., and McAleer, M. (1983), 'Testing Non-Nested Specifications of Money Demand for Canada', *Canadian Journal of Economics*, 16, 593-602.
Hall, A. (1985), 'A Simplified Method of Calculating the Distribution Free Cox Test', *Economics Letters*, 18, 149-51.
Hall, A.D. (1983), 'Confidence Contours for Two Test Statistics for Non-Nested Regression Models', *Journal of Econometrics*, 21, 155-60.
Harvey, A.C. (1977), 'Discrimination Between CES and VES Production Functions', *Annals of Economic and Social Measurement*, 6, 463-71.
Harvey, A.C. (1981), *The Econometric Analysis of Time Series*, Oxford: Philip Allan.
Hausman, J.A. (1978), 'Specification Tests in Econometrics', *Econometrica*, 46, 1251-71.
Hausman, J.A., and Pesaran, M.H. (1983), 'The *J*-Test as a Hausman Specification Test', *Economics Letters*, 12, 277-81.
Hausman, J.A., and Taylor, W.E. (1980), 'Comparing Specification Tests and Classical Tests', unpublished manuscript, Department of Economics, Harvard University.
Hendry, D.F. (1983a), 'Model Specification Tests Against Non-Nested Alternatives: Comment', *Econometric Reviews*, 2, 111-14.
Hendry, D.F. (1983b), 'Econometric Modelling: The Consumption Function in Retrospect', *Scottish Journal of Political Economy*, 30, 193-220.
Hendry, D.F., and Richard, J.-F. (1982), 'On the Formulation of Empirical Models in Dynamic Econometrics', *Journal of Econometrics*, 20, 3-33.
Hillier, G.H., and Inder, B.A. (1983), 'On the Properties of Some Test Procedures for Separate Regressions', unpublished paper, Department of Econometrics and Operations Research, Monash University.
Hoel, P.G. (1947), 'On the Choice of Forecasting Formulas', *Journal of the American Statistical Association*, 42, 605-11.
Holly, A. (1982), 'A Remark on Hausman's Specification Test', *Econometrica*, 50, 749-59.
Jackson, O.A.Y. (1968), 'Some Results on Tests of Separate Families of Hypotheses', *Biometrika*, 55, 355-63.

Johannes, J.M., and Nasseh, A.R. (1985), 'Income or Wealth in Money Demand: An Application of Non-Nested Hypothesis Tests', *Southern Economic Journal*, 51, 1099-106.

Judge, G.G., Griffiths, W.E., Hill, R.C., and Lee, T.-C. (1980), *The Theory and Practice of Econometrics*, New York: Wiley.

Kendall, M., and Stuart, A. (1979), *The Advanced Theory of Statistics, Vol. 2, Inference and Relationship*, Fourth Edition, London: Griffin.

King, M.L. (1983), 'Testing for Autoregressive Against Moving Average Errors in the Linear Regression Model', *Journal of Econometrics*, 21, 35-51.

King, M.L., and McAleer, M. (1984), 'Further Results on Testing AR(1) Against MA(1) Disturbances in the Linear Regression Model', paper presented to the Australasian Meeting of the Econometric Society, Sydney, 1984.

Klein, R.W. (1983), 'Model Specification Tests Against Non-Nested Alternatives: Comment', *Econometric Reviews*, 2, 115-19.

MacKinnon, J.G. (1983), 'Model Specification Tests Against Non-Nested Alternatives', *Econometric Reviews*, 2, 85-110.

MacKinnon, J.G., White, H., and Davidson, R. (1983), 'Tests for Model Specification in the Presence of Alternative Hypotheses: Some Further Results', *Journal of Econometrics*, 21, 53-70.

Maddala, G.S. (ed.) (1981), *Model Selection*, special issue of *Journal of Econometrics*, 16(1).

McAleer, M. (1980), 'The Minimum Error Variance Rule for Non-Linear Regression Models', *Economics Letters*, 6, 17-21.

McAleer, M. (1981a), *Testing Economic Hypotheses*, unpublished Ph.D. thesis, Queen's University, Canada.

McAleer, M. (1981b), 'A Small Sample Test for Non-Nested Regression Models', *Economics Letters*, 7, 335-8.

McAleer, M. (1981c), 'Exact Tests of a Model Against Non-Nested Alternatives', Discussion Paper 431, Institute for Economic Research, Queen's University, Canada.

McAleer, M. (1983a), 'Exact Tests of a Model Against Nonnested Alternatives', *Biometrika*, 70, 285-8.

McAleer, M. (1983b), 'On Specification Error and Separate Tests', forthcoming in *Topics in Applied Statistics*, ed. T.D. Dwivedi, New York: Marcel Dekker.

McAleer, M. (1983c), 'Variable Addition Tests for Linear Versus Log-Linear Regressions', unpublished paper, Department of Statistics, Australian National University.

McAleer, M., and Bera, A. (1982), 'Testing General Forms of Non-Nested Models', paper presented to the European Meeting of the Econometric Society, Dublin, 1982.

McAleer, M., and Bera, A. (1983), 'Model Specification Tests Against Non-Nested Alternatives: Comment', *Econometric Reviews*, 2, 121-30.

McAleer, M., and Fisher, G.R. (1982), 'Testing Separate Regression Models Subject to Specification Error', *Journal of Econometrics*, 19, 125-45.

McAleer, M., Fisher, G.R., and Volker, P. (1982), 'Separate Misspecified Regressions and the U.S. Long Run Demand for Money Function', *Review of Economics and Statistics*, 64, 572-83.

McAleer, M., McKenzie, C.R., and Hall, A.D. (1986), 'Testing Separate Time Series Models', paper presented to the European Meeting of the Econometric Society, Budapest, 1986.

McAleer, M., Pagan, A.R., and Volker, P.A. (1985), 'What Will Take the Con Out of Econometrics?', *American Economic Review*, 75, 293-307.

McAleer, M., and Pesaran, M.H. (1986), 'Statistical Inference in Non-Nested Econometric Models', *Applied Mathematics and Computation*, forthcoming.

Milbourne, R. (1985), 'Distinguishing Between Australian Demand for Money Models', *Australian Economic Papers*, 24, 154-68.

Milliken, G.A., and Graybill, F.A. (1970), 'Extensions of the General Linear Hypothesis Model', *Journal of the American Statistical Association*, 65, 797-807.

Mizon, G.E. (1984), 'The Encompassing Approach in Econometrics', in *Econometrics and Quantitative Economics*, eds. D.F. Hendry and K.F. Wallis, Oxford: Blackwell, 135-72.

Mizon, G.E., and Richard, J.-F. (1983), 'Model Specification Tests Against Non-Nested Alternatives: Comment', *Econometric Reviews*, 2, 131-6.

Mizon, G.E., and Richard, J.-F. (1986), 'The Encompassing Principle and Its Application to Non-Nested Hypotheses', *Econometrica*, 54, 657-78

Morimune, K. (1983), 'Model Specification Tests Against Non-Nested Alternatives: Comment', *Econometric Reviews*, 2, 137-43.

Murray, J. (1984), 'Retail Demand for Meat in Australia: A Utility Theory Approach', *Economic Record*, 60, 45-56.

Pagan, A.R. (1974), 'A Generalized Approach to the Treatment of Autocorrelation', *Australian Economic Papers*, 13, 267-80.

Pagan, A.R. (1981), 'Reflections on Australian Macro-Modelling', Working Paper in Economics and Econometrics No. 048, Australian National University.

Pagan, A.R. (1984), 'Model Evaluation by Variable Addition', in *Econometrics and Quantitative Economics*, eds. D.F. Hendry and K.F. Wallis, Oxford: Blackwell, 103-33.

Pagan, A.R., and Hall, A.D. (1983), 'Diagnostic Tests as Residual Analysis', *Econometric Reviews*, 2, 159-218.

Pagan, A.R., Hall, A.D., and Trivedi, P.K. (1983), 'Assessing the Variability of Inflation', *Review of Economic Studies*, 50, 585-96.

Patterson, K.D. (1986), 'The Stability of Some Annual Consumption Functions', *Oxford Economic Papers*, 38, 1-30.

Pereira, B. de B. (1977a), 'A Note on the Consistency and on the Finite Sample Comparison of Some Tests of Separate Families of Hypotheses', *Biometrika*, 64, 109-13.

Pereira, B. de B. (1977b), 'Discriminating Among Separate Models: A Bibliography', *International Statistical Review*, 45, 163-72.

Pereira, B. de B. (1978), 'Tests and Efficiencies of Separate Regression Models', *Biometrika*, 65, 619-27.

Pesaran, M.H. (1972), *Small Sample Estimation of Dynamic Economic Models*, unpublished Ph.D. thesis, University of Cambridge.

Pesaran, M.H. (1974), 'On the General Problem of Model Selection', *Review of Economic Studies*, 41, 153-71.

Pesaran, M.H. (1981), 'Pitfalls of Testing Non-Nested Hypotheses by the Lagrange Multiplier Method', *Journal of Econometrics*, 17, 323-31.

Pesaran, M.H. (1982a), 'Comparison of Local Power of Alternative Tests of Non-Nested Regression Models', *Econometrica*, 50, 1287-1305.

Pesaran, M.H. (1982b), 'On the Comprehensive Method of Testing Non-Nested Regression Models', *Journal of Econometrics*, 18, 263-74.

Pesaran, M.H. (1982c), 'A Critique of the Proposed Tests of the Natural Rate-Rational Expectations Hypothesis', *Economic Journal*, 92, 529-54.

Pesaran, M.H. (1983), 'Model Specification Tests Against Non-Nested Alternatives: Comment', *Econometric Reviews*, 2, 145-9.

Pesaran, M.H. (1984a), 'Asymptotic Power Comparisons of Tests of Separate

Parametric Families by Bahadur's Approach', *Biometrika*, 71, 245-52.
Pesaran, M.H. (1984b), 'Global and Partial Non-Nested Hypotheses and Asymptotic Local Power', Working Paper in Economics and Econometrics No. 109, Australian National University. (*Econometric Theory*, forthcoming).
Pesaran, M.H., and Deaton, A.S. (1978), 'Testing Non-Nested Nonlinear Regression Models', *Econometrica*, 46, 677-94.
Pesaran, M.H., and Smith, R.P. (1985), 'Evaluation of Macroeconomic Models', *Economic Modelling*, 2, 125-34.
Plosser, C.I., Schwert, G.W., and White, H. (1982), 'Differencing as a Test of Specification', *International Economic Review*, 23, 535-52.
Poirier, D.J. (1978), 'The Use of the Box-Cox Transformation in Limited Dependent Variable Models', *Journal of the American Statistical Association*, 73, 284-7.
Poirier, D.J., and Ruud, P.A. (1979), 'A Simple Lagrange Multiplier Test for Lognormal Regression', *Economics Letters*, 4, 251-5.
Poterba, J.M., and Summers, L.H. (1983), 'Dividend Taxes, Corporate Investment, and "Q"', *Journal of Public Economics*, 22, 135-67.
Quandt, R.E. (1974), 'A Comparison of Methods for Testing Non-Nested Hypotheses', *Review of Economics and Statistics*, 56, 92-9.
Ramsey, J.B. (1969), 'Tests for Specification Errors in Classical Linear Least Squares Regression Analysis', *Journal of the Royal Statistical Society* B, 31, 350-71.
Ramsey, J.B. (1974), 'Classical Model Selection Through Specification Error Tests', in *Frontiers in Econometrics*, ed. P. Zarembka, New York: Academic Press, 13-47.
Ramsey, J.B., and Chesher, A. (1976), 'Some Measures of the "Difference" Between Regression Models', *Journal of the American Statistical Association*, 71, 972-6.
Ramsey, J.B., and Gilbert, R. (1972), 'A Monte Carlo Study of Some Small Sample Properties of Tests for Specification Error', *Journal of the American Statistical Association*, 67, 180-6.
Ramsey, J.B., and Schmidt, P. (1976), 'Some Further Results on the Use of OLS and BLUS Residuals in Specification Error Tests', *Journal of the American Statistical Association*, 71, 389-90.
Rossi, P.E. (1985), 'Comparison of Alternative Functional Forms in Production', *Journal of Econometrics*, 30, 345-61.
Sargan, J.D. (1964), 'Wages and Prices in the United Kingdom: A Study in Econometric Methodology', in *Econometric Analysis for National Economic Planning*, eds. P.E. Hart, G. Mills and J.K. Whitaker, London: Butterworths, 25-63.
Savin, N.E. (1976), 'Conflict Among Testing Procedures in a Linear Regression Model with Autoregressive Disturbances', *Econometrica*, 44, 1303-15.
Sawyer, K.R. (1980), *The Theory of Econometric Model Selection*, unpublished Ph.D. thesis, Australian National University.
Sawyer, K.R. (1982), 'A Multiple Divergence Criterion for Testing Between Separate Hypotheses', *Statistics and Probability Letters*, 1, 26-30.
Sawyer, K.R. (1983a), 'Testing Separate Families of Hypotheses: An Information Criterion', *Journal of the Royal Statistical Society* B, 45, 89-99.
Sawyer, K.R. (1983b), 'The General Problem of Separate Hypothesis Testing', Working Paper 83-7, Department of Economics, University of Iowa.
Sawyer, K.R. (1984), 'Multiple Hypothesis Testing', *Journal of the Royal Statistical Society* B, 46, 419-24.

Schwarz, G. (1978), 'Estimating the Dimension of a Model', *Annals of Statistics*, 6, 461-4.
Singleton, K.J. (1985), 'Testing Specifications of Economic Agents' Intertemporal Optimum Problems in the Presence of Alternative Models', *Journal of Econometrics*, 30, 391-413.
Smith, M.A. (1983), 'Tests of Separate Families of Hypotheses for Limited Dependent Variable Models', unpublished paper, Department of Economics, Wayne State University.
Smith, M.A., and Maddala, G.S. (1983), 'Multiple Model Testing for Non-Nested Heteroskedastic Censored Regression Models', *Journal of Econometrics*, 21, 71-81.
Theil, H. (1957), 'Specification Errors and the Estimation of Economic Relations', *Review of the International Statistical Institute*, 25, 41-51.
Thornton, D.L. (1985), 'The Appropriate Interest Rate and Scale Variable in Money Demand: Results from Non-Nested Tests', *Applied Economics*, 17, 735-44.
Thursby, J.G., and Schmidt, P. (1977), 'Some Properties of Tests for Specification Error in a Linear Regression Model', *Journal of the American Statistical Association*, 72, 635-41.
Tse, Y.K. (1983), 'Testing Linear and Log-Linear Regressions', unpublished paper, Department of Economics and Statistics, National University of Singapore.
Tse, Y.K. (1984a), 'Testing Linear and Log-Linear Regressions with Autocorrelated Errors', *Economics Letters*, 14, 333-7.
Tse, Y.K. (1984b), 'Testing for Linear and Log-Linear Regressions with Heteroscedasticity', *Economics Letters*, 16, 63-9.
Utts, J.M. (1982), 'The Rainbow Test for Lack of Fit in Regression', *Communications in Statistics – Theory and Method*, 11, 2801-15.
Valentine, T.J. (1969), 'A Note on Multicollinearity', *Australian Economic Papers*, 8, 99-105.
Volker, P.A. (1980), 'Expectations of Inflation and Nominal Interest Rates in Australia 1968(1)-1979(2)', in *Interest Rates*, ed. D.J. Juttner, Longman Cheshire, 235-56.
Walker, A.M. (1967), 'Some Tests of Separate Families of Hypotheses in Time Series Analysis', *Biometrika*, 54, 39-68.
White, H. (1980), 'Using Least Squares to Approximate Unknown Regression Functions', *International Economic Review*, 21, 149-70.
White, H. (1982), 'Regularity Conditions for Cox's Test of Non-Nested Hypotheses', *Journal of Econometrics*, 19, 301-18.
White, H. (ed.) (1983), *Non-Nested Models*, special issue of *Journal of Econometrics*, 21(1).
Whittle, P. (1951), *Hypothesis Testing in Time Series Analysis*, Uppsala: Almquist and Wicksell.
Williams, E.J. (1959), *Regression Analysis*, New York: Wiley.
Wisley, T.O., and Johnson, S.R. (1985), 'An Evaluation of Alternative Investment Hypotheses Using Non-Nested Tests', *Southern Economic Journal*, 52, 422-30.
Wu, D.-M. (1983), 'A Remark on a Generalized Specification Test', *Economics Letters*, 11, 365-70.

Notes

1 I would like to thank the following for very helpful discussions and comments: Anthony Atkinson, Anil Bera, Herman Bierens, Noxy Dastoor, Gordon Fisher, Len Gill, Les Godfrey, Grant Hillier, Max King, Colin McKenzie, Grayham Mizon, Adrian Pagan and Hashem Pesaran. I am especially grateful to Les Godfrey and Hashem Pesaran for permission to refer to unpublished results from their numerical simulations.

10 Functional forms in intertemporal duality

Keith R. McLaren and Russel J. Cooper

1 Introduction

Major advantages of duality theory concern the simple derivation of tightly constrained estimating forms and the ease with which testable restrictions implied by the optimization may be derived. While these advantages would appear to be even more useful in intertemporal than in static problems, it is the latter which have so far received the great bulk of attention. One reason for this may be the difficulty in generating functional forms consistent with all the implications of the intertemporal theory. This paper reports some approaches to this problem with particular application to intertemporal consumer theory and to the theory of the firm.

Background developments are surveyed briefly in Section 2. These include relevant concepts and results from static duality theory, as well as background developments in the adjustment cost theory of investment and intertemporal consumer demand theory.

Section 3 begins with a brief coverage of intertemporal duality in the case of the theory of the consumer, for which reasonably complete results are known. (See Cooper and McLaren (1980)). One approach to generating more general functional forms, by deriving the value function for a known model and then embedding this function within a wider class of functions subject to the conditions provided by intertemporal duality, is discussed. An approach to the relaxation of the static price expectations assumption is then considered.

Sections 4 and 5 deal with intertemporal duality in the theory of the firm. In Section 4, existing results are surveyed and the issues involved in characterising a complete duality are canvassed. The relationship between the Optimal Value Function and the Intertemporal Distance Function is examined, and the derivation of optimal investment and variable input and output functions from either of these is demonstrated. Section 5 outlines some approaches to the practical application of the results reported in Section 4.

2 The background developments

2.1 Static duality theory

In this section we provide a brief survey of the results of static or atemporal duality theory. As well as being used in later sections in simplifying the setting up of certain intertemporal problems, these results also provide a motivation for the idea of intertemporal duality of Sections 3 and 4. More details of static duality theory may be found in Diewert (1974, 1982a, 1982b), Blackorby, Primont and Russell (1978) and Fuss and McFadden (1978).

Consider the aggregator (i.e. utility or production) function $f(q)$, where $q \in \Omega^m$ represents commodities or inputs (Ω^m is the non-negative Euclidean m-orthant). Associated with the vector q is the vector $p \in \Omega^m_+$ of prices, and the scalar $e \in \Omega^1_+$, representing total expenditure. f may be assumed to be continuous, non-decreasing and quasi-concave in q. Associated with f are the following dual functions, defined by the appropriate optimization problems.

(a) The indirect aggregator (utility or production) function, defined by

$$g(e, p) = \max_q\{f(q) : q \in \Omega^m, p'q \leq e\} = f(\hat{q}(e, p)).$$

The function $g(e, p)$ will be continuous, non-decreasing in e, non-increasing and quasi-convex in p, and homogeneous of degree zero in e and p. The Marshallian demand functions $\hat{q}(e, p)$ may be derived from $g(e, p)$ by:

$$\text{Roy's Theorem.} \qquad \hat{q}(e, p) = -g_p/g_e.$$

(b) The cost (or expenditure) function, defined by

$$h(u, p) = \min_q\{p'q : q \in \Omega^m, f(q) \geq u\} = p'\tilde{q}(u, p).$$

The function $h(u, p)$ will be continuous and non-negative, non-decreasing in u, and non-decreasing, concave and homogeneous of degree one in p. The Hicksian demand functions $\tilde{q}(u, p)$ may be derived from $h(u, p)$ by:

$$\text{Shephard's Lemma:} \qquad \tilde{q}(u, p) = h_p(u, p).$$

(c) The distance (or transformation) function, defined by

$$d(u, q) = \max_\lambda\{\lambda : \lambda \in \Omega^1, f(q/\lambda) \geq u\}.$$

The function $d(u, q)$ will be continuous, non-increasing in u and non-decreasing, concave and homogeneous of degree one in q.

The functions $f(q)$, $g(e, p)$, $h(u, p)$ and $d(u, q)$ are said to be dual to each other, i.e. each function is an equivalent representation of the underlying preference ordering or technology. In fact, each function can be derived from any of the other functions by an appropriate optimization problem.

(See Blackorby, Primont and Russell (1978, Chapter 2).)

In the context of the theory of the firm, the idea of a cost function may be extended to allow q to represent both inputs and outputs, so that if inputs are represented as negative quantities, $p'q$ represents net profits. The resulting function is then referred to as a profit function. Further, if the vector of inputs and outputs is decomposed as (q, x), where q represents variable inputs and outputs, and x represents fixed inputs, the resulting function is called a variable profit function, i.e.

$$Q(x, p) = \max_q\{p'q : (q, x) \in T\} = p'\bar{q}(x, p).$$

T represents the set of technically feasible combinations of q and x. In this context, the analogy of Shephard's Lemma is Hotelling's Theorem:

$$\bar{q}(x, p) = Q_p(x, p).$$

At least three major areas of application of duality theory may be mentioned:

(i) As a means of specification of functional forms for demand and supply functions. For example, in order to specify a demand equation consistent with constrained utility maximization, one approach would be to specify a functional form for f and explicitly solve the maximization problem to derive q. If, however, a dual function, say g, is initially specified, the corresponding demand equations can be obtained by simple differentiation. The need to obtain an analytic solution of a set of (probably non-linear) simultaneous equations is thus avoided.

(ii) To derive microeconomic results. For example, proof of Slutsky symmetry, reasonably difficult using a direct approach, is virtually immediate when the cost function is used.

(iii) To construct various indices: for example, a constant utility cost of living index.

2.2 The adjustment cost model

Let $x \in \Omega^n$ represent an n-vector of quasi-fixed inputs, and let $\dot{x} \in R^n$ represent the vector of net investments in these goods. Let $c \in \Omega^n_+$ represent the price of new investment goods, and $p \in \Omega^m_+$ be a vector of the prices of outputs and variable inputs. Then at any time t, for any stocks of the fixed factor $x(t)$ and rates of investment $\dot{x}(t)$, the firm's technology is specified by the functional form of the variable profit function $Q(x(t), \dot{x}(t), p)$, which gives the maximum gross revenue conditional on x, $\dot{x}$ and p.

Consider now the following intertemporal optimization problem. At time $t = 0$ the firm has available an endowment of quasi-fixed factors x^0, and holds with certainty static expectations on the price vectors p and c and the discount rate r. The firm's problem is to choose a time path of investment levels $\dot{x}(t)$, $0 < t < \infty$, in order to maximize (subject to $x(0) = x^0$)

$$\int_0^\infty \exp(-rt)[Q(x(t), \dot{x}(t), p) - c'\dot{x}(t)]\mathrm{d}\, t. \tag{1}$$

The problem with this essential nature was first proposed by Eisner and Strotz (1963) for the scalar case, and with the constraint that $Q(x, \dot{x}, p) = P(x, p) - C(\dot{x})$.

Although Eisner and Strotz pre-dated much of the recent work popularizing duality theory, it is clear from the following quotation that they interpreted P as a profit function: 'The rate of profit earned by the firm may therefore be regarded as a function of the size of plant, since we may assume that the amounts of the perfectly variable factors used with a plant of given size are always optimally adjusted' (Eisner and Strotz (1963, p. 69)). Thus Eisner and Strotz were careful not to complicate unnecessarily an intertemporal optimization problem with an essentially irrelevant atemporal optimization problem, a suggestion that many later writers failed to follow.

Eisner and Strotz derived an explicit analytical solution for the case

$$P = \alpha x - (1/2)\beta x^2, \qquad C = \gamma \dot{x}^2, \qquad \alpha, \beta, \gamma > 0.$$

With this specification the closed loop solution is

$$\dot{x} = m(r)(x(t) - x^*)$$

where

$$x^* = (\alpha - rc)/\beta$$

and

$$m(r) = r/2 - [(r/2)^2 + \beta/2\gamma]^{1/2}.$$

The Eisner-Strotz model was generalized to n dimensions by Lucas (1967), whose model is also of the form $Q(x, \dot{x}, p) = P(x, p) - C(\dot{x})$ with the restriction that $\nabla^2 C/\nabla \dot{x}_i \nabla \dot{x}_j = 0$, $i \neq j$. For the quadratic case, Lucas obtains the solution

$$\dot{x}(t) = M(r)(x(t) - x^*)$$

where $M = T\Lambda T^{-1}$, T is a matrix which diagonalises $Q_{\dot{x}\dot{x}'}{}^{-1}Q_{xx'}$, and Λ is a diagonal matrix satisfying

$$\Lambda = (r/2)I - [(r/2)^2 I + (1/2)T^{-1}Q_{\dot{x}\dot{x}'}{}^{-1}Q_{xx'}T]^{1/2}.$$

Lucas also obtains the restrictions that $\nabla x^*/\nabla c'$ and $\nabla \dot{x}/\nabla c'$ are symmetric negative definite matrices, and hence can be viewed as analogous to static profit maximizing input combinations.

Treadway (1971, 1974) demonstrated that the full set of restrictions derived by Lucas held only under the particular separability restrictions imposed on the function Q, for which no a priori justifications exist. Thus Treadway views the firm as being involved in a generalized production process, in which inputs are used to produce both output and the level of new investment $\dot{x}$. For this unrestricted specification of the variable profit function $Q(x, \dot{x}, p)$, Treadway shows that, locally around the neighbourhood $x = x^*$, $\dot{x} = 0$, the optimal investment demand equations can be approximated by the flexible accelerator specification

$$\dot{x}(t) = M(x(t) - x^*)$$

where M satisfies the matrix quadratic equation

$$Q^*_{\dot{x}\dot{x}'}M^2 + (Q^*_{\dot{x}x'} - Q^*_{x\dot{x}'} - rQ^*_{\dot{x}\dot{x}'})M = Q^*_{xx'} + rQ^*_{\dot{x}x'}$$

where the superscript * indicates evaluation at $x = x^*$, $\dot{x} = 0$. (The above formulation of the restriction on M is due to Mortensen (1973).)

This direct approach yields closed form solutions only for the case of $n = 1$ (or possibly $n = 2$; see Epstein (1981, footnote 5)) and Q quadratic in $x, \dot{x}$. Some attempts at empirical implementation are Schramm (1970), Brechling (1975), Berndt, Fuss and Waverman (1979) and Morrison and Berndt (1981), but in general this literature has had little effect on applied investment demand studies. To quote Treadway (1974, pp. 17-8):

> Two of the more serious criticisms of adjustment cost rationalizations of the flexible accelerator had to do with: (1) the local character of the basic result and (2) the fact that the adjustment coefficient generated by these adjustment cost models was generally dependent on exogenous variables. Rationalizations of the flexible accelerator with such glaring weaknesses were cold comfort to those interested in econometric applications. It is not particularly informative to the econometrician to show that a linear approximation is linear, especially when the coefficient in the approximation can be expected to vary over a sample in unknown ways.

The extent of approximation involved in the imposition of the above mentioned restrictions on M away from the stationary state may be illustrated by the following result:

Proposition 1 Let $\phi(x, c, r, p)$ be the synthesized optimal policy function for problem (1) and let $M = \phi_{x'}(x, c, r, p)$. Then at all points of the optimal path M must satisfy

$$Q_{\dot{x}\dot{x}'}\dot{M} + Q_{\dot{x}\dot{x}'}M^2 + (Q_{\dot{x}x'} - Q_{x\dot{x}'} - rQ_{\dot{x}\dot{x}'} + \dot{Q}_{\dot{x}\dot{x}'})M = Q_{xx'} + rQ_{\dot{x}x'} - \dot{Q}_{\dot{x}x'}.$$

Proof In the following, we make use of the result that $(\nabla/\nabla u' \otimes A_{yz'})(b \otimes I) = (\nabla/\nabla z' \otimes A_{yu'})(I \otimes b)$ where A is a scalar function of the $n \times 1$ vectors y, z and u, where b is an $n \times 1$ vector and where $(\nabla/\nabla u' \otimes B) = [\nabla B/\nabla u_1, \ldots, \nabla B/\nabla u_n]$. Using this result we note that, for $Q(x, \phi(x, c, r, p), p)$ and for $M = \phi_{x'}(x, c, r, p)$:

$$\dot{Q}_{\dot{x}x'} = (\nabla/\nabla x' \otimes Q_{\dot{x}x'})(I \otimes \phi) + (\nabla/\nabla \dot{x}' \otimes Q_{\dot{x}x'})(\dot{\phi} \otimes I)$$
$$= (\nabla/\nabla x' \otimes Q_{\dot{x}x'})(I \otimes \phi) + (\nabla/\nabla x' \otimes Q_{\dot{x}\dot{x}'})(I \otimes \dot{\phi}),$$

$$\dot{Q}_{x\dot{x}'} = (\nabla/\nabla x' \otimes Q_{\dot{x}\dot{x}'})(\phi \otimes I) + (\nabla/\nabla \dot{x}' \otimes Q_{\dot{x}\dot{x}'})(\dot{\phi} \otimes I)$$

$$= (\nabla/\nabla\dot{x}' \otimes Q_{\dot{x}x'})(I \otimes \phi) + (\nabla/\nabla\dot{x}' \otimes Q_{\dot{x}x'})(I \otimes \dot{\phi}),$$

$$\dot{M} = (\dot{\phi_{x'}}) = (\nabla/\nabla x' \otimes \phi_{x'})(\phi \otimes I) = (\nabla/\nabla x' \otimes \phi_{x'})(I \otimes \phi).$$

Inserting the optimal policy function into the Euler equation yields the identity

$$Q_x(x, \phi(x, c, r, p), p)$$
$$= rc - rQ_{\dot{x}}(x, \phi(x, c, r, p), p) + \mathrm{d}[Q_{\dot{x}}(x, \phi(x, c, r, p), p)]/\mathrm{d}t.$$

Differentiating with respect to x' and making use of the above results yields

$$\begin{aligned}
&Q_{xx'} + Q_{x\dot{x}'}\phi_{x'} + r(Q_{\dot{x}x'} + Q_{\dot{x}\dot{x}'}\phi_{x'}) \\
&\quad = \nabla[Q_{\dot{x}x'}\phi + Q_{\dot{x}\dot{x}'}\phi_{x'}\phi]/\nabla x' \\
&\quad = (\nabla/\nabla x' \otimes Q_{\dot{x}x'})(I \otimes \phi) + (\nabla/\nabla\dot{x}' \otimes Q_{\dot{x}x'})(I \otimes \phi)\phi_{x'} + Q_{\dot{x}x'}\phi_{x'} \\
&\qquad + (\nabla/\nabla x' \otimes Q_{\dot{x}\dot{x}'})(I \otimes \dot{\phi}) + (\nabla/\nabla\dot{x}' \otimes Q_{\dot{x}\dot{x}'})(I \otimes \dot{\phi})\phi_{x'} \\
&\qquad + Q_{\dot{x}\dot{x}'}(\nabla/\nabla x' \otimes \phi_{x'})(I \otimes \phi) + Q_{\dot{x}\dot{x}'}\phi_{x'}\phi_{x'} \\
&\quad = (\nabla/\nabla x' \otimes Q_{\dot{x}x'})(\phi \otimes I) + (\nabla/\nabla x' \otimes Q_{\dot{x}\dot{x}'})(\phi \otimes I)\phi_{x'} + Q_{\dot{x}x'}\phi_{x'} \\
&\qquad + (\nabla/\nabla\dot{x}' \otimes Q_{\dot{x}x'})(\dot{\phi} \otimes I) + (\nabla/\nabla\dot{x}' \otimes Q_{\dot{x}\dot{x}'})(\dot{\phi} \otimes I)\phi_{x'} \\
&\qquad + Q_{\dot{x}\dot{x}'}(\nabla/\nabla x' \otimes \phi_{x'})(\phi \otimes I) + Q_{\dot{x}\dot{x}'}(\phi_{x'})^2 \\
&\quad = \dot{Q}_{\dot{x}x'} + \dot{Q}_{\dot{x}\dot{x}'}\phi_{x'} + Q_{\dot{x}x'}\phi_{x'} + Q_{\dot{x}\dot{x}'}((\dot{\phi_{x'}}) + (\phi_{x'})^2).
\end{aligned}$$

On rearrangement, the proposition is immediate.

In view of the implications of Proposition 1 for the general structure of $M = \phi_{x'}(x, c, r, p)$, let us return to the two criticisms of adjustment cost rationalizations of the flexible accelerator in the Treadway quotation. Dependence of M on exogeneous variables is only a problem if the functional form of this dependence cannot be specified. But the local nature of the flexible accelerator formulation of the structure of M is a damning criticism. In this case, the variability of the sample required for econometric efficiency is in direct conflict with the accuracy of the approximation. Treadway (1974) addressed the problem of restrictions on Q which generate a globally optimal flexible accelerator specification, but the resulting functional forms were so specialized as to be of little use.

The failure of a direct approach to the solution of the adjustment cost model to generate empirically useful investment demand equations suggests that a dual approach, analogous to that for the atemporal problem, may be fruitful. This avenue is explored in Section 4.

2.3 Intertemporal consumer theory

The consumer's intertemporal optimization problem can be specified as: choose a time path for expenditure $e(t)$, $0 \leq t \leq \infty$, in order to maximize

$$\int_0^\infty \exp(-\delta t) g(e(t), p) \, dt \qquad (2)$$

subject to $\quad \int_0^\infty \exp(-rt) e(t) \, dt \leq w,$

where w is the consumer's given initial net worth, δ is the consumer's rate of time preference, and r is the rate of interest in a perfect capital market. As in the case of the model of the firm, atemporal duality theory has been used in order to simplify the structure of the intertemporal optimization problem.

The first empirically useful solution of this problem was presented by Lluch (1973), who considered problem (2) with the specialization (in our terminology)

$$g(e, p) = \Sigma \beta_i \log[\beta_i(e - p'\gamma)/p_i]$$

where the $\beta_i > 0$, $\gamma_i > 0$ are parameters with $\Sigma \beta_i = 1$. (In fact Lluch specified the problem in terms of the corresponding direct utility function.) Solution of this problem yields the consumption function:

$$\hat{e}(t) = p'\gamma + \delta(w(t) - p'\gamma/r)$$

and application of Roy's Theorem yields the Extended Linear Expenditure System:

$$p_i\hat{q}_i = p_i\gamma_i + \beta_i\delta(w(t) - p'\gamma/r).$$

3 Intertemporal duality in consumer theory

3.1 The value function, intertemporal duality and the intertemporal analogue of Roy's Theorem

In Section 2.1, four related (dual) atemporal optimization problems and their related functions were presented. The advantage was that demand equations, solutions to a potentially difficult optimization problem, could be simply derived from one of the dual functions. Explicit solution of intertemporal optimization problems is even more difficult, usually requiring solutions of non-linear second-order differential equations. It is thus natural to enquire whether these solutions could be obtained more easily from an alternative (dual) functional specification.

By analogy with the duality of Section 2.1 between the direct and indirect aggregator functions, the consumer's optimal value function is defined by

$$V(w, p, r, \delta) = \int_0^\infty \exp(-\delta t) g(\hat{e}(t), p) \, dt.$$

Then the analogue of atemporal duality theory would be a duality between the functions $V(w, p, r, \delta)$ and $g(e, p)$. This type of duality was termed intertemporal duality by Cooper and McLaren (1980) who provide dualities between:

(i) the instantaneous indirect utility function $g(e, p)$ and the total indirect utility function (optimal value function) $V(w, p, r, \delta)$;

(ii) the instantaneous cost function $h(u, p)$ and the total cost function (wealth function) defined by

$$W(v, p, r, \delta) = \min_{\{u(t)\}}\{ \int_0^\infty \exp(-rt)h(u(t), p)\,dt : \int_0^\infty \exp(-\delta t)u(t)\,dt \geq v\};$$

(iii) the optimal value and wealth functions.

An exhaustive set of conditions on $V(w, p, r, \delta)$ are provided in Cooper and McLaren (1980). These include non-decreasingness and concavity of V in w, non-increasingness and quasi-convexity in p, homogeneity of degree zero in w and p, as well as a set of differential-equation conditions on V_w, V_r and V_δ. The latter, in particular, render difficult the generation of appropriately constrained functional forms.

Given an optimal value function, an intertemporal analogue of Roy's Theorem gives the optimal expenditure function

$$\hat{e}(w, p, r, \delta) = rw - (\delta - r){V_{ww}}^{-1}V_w$$

and the Marshallian demand functions

$$\hat{q}(w, p, r, \delta) = -\delta {V_w}^{-1}V_p + (\delta - r){V_{ww}}^{-1}V_{wp}.$$

Dually, Hicksian demand functions are derivable from the wealth function as

$$\tilde{q}(v, p, r, \delta) = rW_p + (\delta - r){W_{vv}}^{-1}W_v W_{vp}.$$

3.2 Generation of functional forms

For the instantaneous indirect utility function specified in Section 2.3, the corresponding optimal value function can be evaluated directly as

$$V(w, p, r, \delta) = (1/\delta)\{\Sigma\, \beta_i \log[\beta_i\delta(w - p'\gamma/r)/p_i] + (r - \delta)/\delta\}$$

which can be written as

$$V = (1/\delta)\{\log[\delta(w - p'\gamma/r)/\pi(p)] + (r - \delta)/\delta\}$$

where $\pi(p)$ is the Cobb-Douglas price index

$$\pi(p) = \Pi\ (p_i/\beta_i)^{\beta_i}.$$

One way in which intertemporal duality theory may be used to generate wider classes of functional forms which provide demand systems consistent with intertemporal utility maximization is to choose a particular functional form for V based on explicit optimization such as that given above, and then generalize it in such a way that it still complies with the conditions provided by intertemporal duality. Thus, in the above case, the log [ ] function could be replaced by an increasing, concave function: for example, by a Box-Cox function. The price index, $\pi(p)$, could be replaced by any linearly homogeneous, quasi-concave function: for example, CES or various generalizations. The 'subsistence term', $p'\gamma$, could be replaced by a linearly homogeneous quasi-concave function.

3.3 Relaxing the static expectations assumption

One problem that always arises in moving from static optimization problems to intertemporal optimization problems is the specification of the time paths of the exogenous variables. In the consumer problem, strictly speaking, the optimal value function should in general be a functional of the entire time paths into the future of the prices and the rate of interest. The usual approach in such models, which is followed in the other sections of this paper, is to rely on the assumption of static expectations and continual replanning. Under this assumption, the complete time paths of the exogenous variables collapse to the observation at the beginning of the planning horizon.

In principle, specification of a complete time path for the exogenous variables causes no real problems. As an illustration, consider the problem of choosing $e(t)$, $0 \leq t < \infty$, in order to maximize

$$\int_0^\infty \exp(-\delta t) g(\mathbf{e}(t), \mathbf{p}(t))\, dt$$

subject to $$\int_0^\infty \exp(-\mathbf{r}t)\mathbf{e}(t)\, dt \leq \mathbf{w},$$

where the boldface characters represent **real** variables, as defined below. This specification generalizes problem (2) by allowing a perfectly variable price function $p(t)$ (assumed known with certainty). For simplicity of exposition, the time preference rate δ and the market **real** rate of interest $\mathbf{r} = r(t) - \dot{\pi}(t)/\pi(t)$ are treated as constants. $\pi(t) = \pi(p(t))$ is a linearly homogeneous quasi-concave price index function, $\mathbf{p}(t) = p(t)/\pi(t)$ is a vector of relative prices, and $\mathbf{e}(t) = e(t)/\pi(t)$, $\mathbf{w}(t) = w(t)/\pi(t)$ are **real** expenditure and wealth respectively.

Let the optimal value function be defined as

$$V(\mathbf{w}, \mathbf{z}, \mathbf{r}, \delta) = \int_0^\infty \exp(-\delta t) g(\hat{\mathbf{e}}(t), \mathbf{p}(t))\, dt$$

where $\hat{\mathbf{e}}(t)$ represents optimal **real** expenditure at time t, and where $\mathbf{z}$ is a functional of all future relative prices: $\mathbf{z} = \psi(\{\mathbf{p}(t)\}_0^\infty)$. This class of variable-price intertemporal problems can be handled by noting that the appropriate generalization of the Hamilton-Jacobi equation is (expressed as an identity for optimal $\dot{\mathbf{w}}$)

$$V_{\mathbf{w}}\dot{\mathbf{w}} + V_{\mathbf{z}}\dot{\mathbf{z}} = \delta V - g(\mathbf{r}\mathbf{w} - \dot{\mathbf{w}}, \mathbf{p}).$$

By differentiating further with respect to $\mathbf{w}$ and noting that $V_{\mathbf{w}} = g_{\mathbf{e}}$ along the optimal path, the intertemporal analogue of Roy's Theorem for the variable price case is obtained. Thus

$$\dot{\mathbf{w}} = (\delta - r)V_{\mathbf{ww}}{}^{-1}V_{\mathbf{w}} - V_{\mathbf{ww}}{}^{-1}V_{\mathbf{zw}}\dot{\mathbf{z}}$$

defines the synthesized optimal saving function.

As an illustration, consider a modification of the optimal value function presented in Section 3.2 to the variable price format

$$V(\mathbf{w}, \mathbf{z}, \mathbf{r}, \delta) = (1/\delta)\{\log[\delta(\mathbf{w} - \mathbf{z})] + (\mathbf{r} - \delta)/\delta\}$$

where
$$\mathbf{z} = \textstyle\int_0^\infty \exp(-\mathbf{r}t)s(\mathbf{p}(t))\,\mathrm{d}t$$

and where $s(\mathbf{p})$ is any linearly homogeneous quasi-concave function of $\mathbf{p}$. The optimal saving function becomes

$$\dot{\mathbf{w}} = (\mathbf{r} - \delta)\mathbf{w} + \delta\mathbf{z} - s(\mathbf{p}),$$

while the corresponding optimal expenditure function is (in nominal terms)

$$\hat{e} = \delta[w - \textstyle\int_0^\infty \exp(-\int_0^t r(\tau)\,\mathrm{d}\tau)s(p(t))\,\mathrm{d}t] + s(p).$$

The instantaneous indirect utility function (recoverable from the generalized Hamilton-Jacobi equation) is

$$g(e, p) = \log[(e - s(p))/\pi],$$

which specializes to the Klein-Rubin indirect utility function when $\pi = \Pi(p_j/\beta_j)^{\beta_j}$ and $s(p) = p'\gamma$. Thus the $\hat{e}$ function given above is an appropriate generalization of the ELES total expenditure function to allow for variable prices.

4 Intertemporal duality in the theory of the firm

4.1 The value function and intertemporal analogue of Hotelling's Theorem

For the case of the firm, the optimal value function is defined by

$$V(x, c, r, p) = \max_{\{\dot{x}(t)\}} \textstyle\int_0^\infty \exp(-rt)[Q(x(t), \dot{x}(t), p) - c'\dot{x}(t)]\,\mathrm{d}t$$

subject to $x(0) = x$. Let $Q(x, \dot{x}, p)$ satisfy the following regularity conditions:

Q1. Q is a proper twice continuously differentiable function of $(x, \dot{x}, p)$.
Q2. Q is non-decreasing in x.
Q3. Q is concave in x and $\dot{x}$.
Q4. Q is non-increasing in $\dot{x}$.
Q5. Q is linearly homogeneous in p.

Q6. Q is convex in p.
Q7. $Q(x, 0, p) \geq 0$.

Then it can be shown (see McLaren and Cooper (1980)) that the optimal policy function $\phi(x, c, r, p)$ (i.e. the function which gives the synthesized form of the optimal value of $\dot{x}$, see Arrow and Kurz (1970)), and the optimal value function satisfy the Hamilton-Jacobi equation:

$$rV(x, c, r, p) = \max_{\dot{x}}\{Q(x, \dot{x}, p) - c'\dot{x} + V_{x'}(x, c, r, p)\dot{x}\}$$

thus implying that for optimal $\dot{x}$, $V_x(x, c, r, p) = c - Q_{\dot{x}}(x, \dot{x}, p)$ and hence

$$V_{x'}(x, c, r, p)\phi(x, c, r, p) = rV(x, c, r, p) - [Q(x, \phi(x, c, r, p), p) - c'\phi(x, c, r, p)].$$

These relationships, the definition of V, and the conditions Q1-Q7 on the function Q then imply that the optimal value function $V(x, c, r, p)$ satisfies the regularity conditions:

V1. V is a proper function differentiable almost everywhere, and $V \geq 0$.
V2. V is non-decreasing in x.
V3. V is concave in x.
V4. V is linearly homogeneous in (p, c).
V5. V is convex in (p, c).
V6. V is non-decreasing (non-increasing) in p_i wherever Q is.
V7. V, Q and ϕ satisfy
 (i) $rV_c = (V_{cx'} - I)\phi$;
 (ii) $rV_p = Q_p + V_{px'}\phi$;
 (iii) $rV_x = Q_x + V_{xx'}\phi$;
 (iv) $rV_r + V = V_{rx'}\phi$.

Note that properties V7(i) and (ii) provide the intertemporal analogue of Hotelling's Theorem:

$$\phi(x, c, r, p) = r(V_{cx'} - I)^{-1}V_c \tag{3}$$

and hence $$q = Q_p(x, \phi, p) = rV_p - V_{px'}\phi.$$

4.2 Intertemporal duality

Section 4.1 has specified a set of necessary conditions which the optimal value function $V(x, c, r, p)$ inherits from the optimization process and the conditions on the profit function $Q(x, \dot{x}, p)$. An intertemporal duality between Q and V would be achieved if a set of necessary and sufficient conditions could be specified; in this case specification of a value function and application of the analogue of Hotelling's Theorem would generate demand equations for investment and demand and supply equations for variable inputs and outputs consistent with the maximization of present value subject to the specification of an appropriate variable profit function. Such a duality was first suggested in McLaren and Cooper (1980), and further developed in Epstein (1981).

Duality between Q and V can be established after defining a way in which an optimal value function can be used to specify a variable profit function. Rewriting the Hamilton-Jacobi equation gives the identity:

$$Q(x, \phi(x, c, r, p), p) = rV(x, c, r, p) - [V_{x'}(x, c, r, p) - c']\phi(x, c, r, p). \quad (4)$$

This identity can be used to define a variable profit function as follows: Given a functional form for V satisfying V1-V7, define ϕ by (3). Then for any feasible values of x, c, r, p, define $\dot{x} = \phi(x, c, r, p)$, and hence define $Q(x, \dot{x}, p)$ by the RHS of (4). Conditions V7 ensure that Q so constructed is well-defined. Clearly a complete duality between Q and V could be established if, to conditions V1 to V7, were appended:

V8′. The function V is such that, if $Q(x, \dot{x}, p)$ is defined by (4), Q so defined satisfies Q1-Q7.

While any V defined by explicit optimization must have this property, since the Q so defined is the original Q (except possibly defined over a smaller domain), condition V8′ is hardly operational as verification of V8′ for any given V could prove extremely difficult.

There are at least two ways to proceed. One would be to attempt to derive an alternative, more easily checked, set of conditions than V8′. For example, conditions V1-V7 may imply that some of the conditions in V8′ are redundant. Such an approach is outside the scope of the present paper. An alternative approach would be to derive a set of sufficient, but perhaps not necessary, conditions on V. Empirically, of course, this is all that is really required. Such optimal value functions would generate demand equations which could have been generated by maximization problem (1) where Q satisfies Q1-Q7, but not all such demand equations could be so generated.

By analogy with Epstein (1981), consider the following (stronger) definition of Q:

$$\bar{Q}(x, \dot{x}, p) = \min_{c,r}\{S(x, \dot{x}, p, c, r) : c \in \Omega^n_+, \quad r > 0\} \quad (5)$$

where $S(x, \dot{x}, p, c, r) = rV(x, c, r, p) - [V_{x'}(x, c, r, p) - c']\dot{x}$.

Consider now the following supplementary conditions on V:

VS1. S is twice continuously differentiable a.e.
VS2. S is non-decreasing in x.
VS3. S is concave in x.
VS4. S is non-increasing in $\dot{x}$.
VS5. S is linearly homogeneous in p.

VS6. S is convex in p.
VS7. $S(x, 0, p, c, r) \geq 0$.
VS8. S is convex in c and r.

Clearly, these conditions are not all independent of conditions V1-V7. For example, VS1 and VS7 imply V1; VS4 implies V2; VS8 and the definition of $\bar{Q}$ imply V7(i) and (iv), etc. Now if S has the above properties in x and p, $\bar{Q}$ being a minimized value has the same properties in x and p. By V2, S and hence $\bar{Q}$ will be non-increasing in $\dot{x}$. Concavity of $\bar{Q}$ in $\dot{x}$ is proved in the following:

Proposition 2 If S satisfies VS1-VS7, then $\bar{Q}$ defined by (5) is concave in $\dot{x}$.
Proof $\bar{Q}(x, \dot{x}^{\xi}, p) = S(x, \dot{x}^{\xi}, p, c^{\xi}, r^{\xi})$ for $\xi = \alpha, \beta, \lambda$, where c^{ξ}, r^{ξ} are the minimizing values corresponding to $\dot{x}^{\xi}$, and where $\dot{x}^{\lambda}$ is defined by $\dot{x}^{\lambda} = \lambda\dot{x}^{\alpha} + (1 - \lambda)\dot{x}^{\beta}$, $0 < \lambda < 1$. Hence

$$\begin{aligned}\bar{Q}(x, \dot{x}^{\lambda}, p) &- \min S(x, \dot{x}^{\lambda}, p, c, r)\\ &= \min \{\lambda S(x, \dot{x}^{\alpha}, p, c, r) + (1 - \lambda)S(x, \dot{x}^{\beta}, p, c, r)\}\\ &\geq \lambda \min S(x, \dot{x}^{\alpha}, p, c, r) + (1 - \lambda) \min S(x, \dot{x}^{\beta}, p, c, r)\\ &= \lambda\bar{Q}(x, \dot{x}^{\alpha}, p) + (1 - \lambda)\bar{Q}(x, \dot{x}^{\beta}, p).\end{aligned}$$

Conditions V1 to V7 and VS1 to VS8 are, with the possible exception of V7(iv), relatively easy to verify in practice. Conditions VS1 to VS8 are probably stronger than necessary, since they only really need to hold for those values of x, c, r, p at which $\dot{x}$ is optimal. One could by analogy with conditions V8′, state conditions on $\bar{Q}(x, \dot{x}, p)$ such that V1-V7 and VS1-VS8 would be necessary and sufficient, and hence derive a more narrow, but complete, duality. This is essentially the approach of Epstein (1981). But just as conditions V8′ were difficult to verify, so would these added conditions on $\bar{Q}$ be. (Consider, for example, the possibility of verifying Epstein's conditions T5 and T6; see Epstein (1981, p. 84).) Epstein's approach is further developed in Epstein and Denny (1983), where a quadratic value function is utilized.

4.3 *Applications of the optimal value function in theory*

One application of the optimal value function V is to derive more general (global) specifications of the price response matrices considered by Lucas, Treadway and Mortensen. The following relationships are easily derived:

$$\begin{aligned}\nabla\dot{x}/\nabla x' &= \phi_{x'} = -(Q_{\dot{x}\dot{x}'})^{-1}[V_{xx'} + Q_{\dot{x}x'}]\\ \nabla\dot{x}/\nabla c' &= \phi_{c'} = (Q_{\dot{x}\dot{x}'})^{-1}[I - V_{xc'}]\\ \nabla\dot{x}/\nabla r &= \phi_r = -(Q_{\dot{x}\dot{x}'})^{-1}V_{xr}.\end{aligned}$$

Thus, for example, if Q is separable in x, $\dot{x}$, then $\phi_{x'}$ can be written as (minus) the product of a negative definite and a negative semi-definite matrix; and a sufficient condition for the short-run price response matrix to be symmetric negative definite is that V be separable in x and c. Of course, separability of V in x and c is a rather strong condition since it implies that $\dot{x} = -rV_c$ (independent of x; however, $\phi_{x'} = 0$ if and only if $Q_{\dot{x}x'} = -V_{xx'}$).

In general, it would be useful to have a collection of results relating structure on the variable profit function to structure on the optimal value function. The following may be useful.

Proposition 3 $Q(x, \dot{x}, p)$ is linearly homogeneous in $(x, \dot{x})$ iff $V(x, c, r, p)$ is linearly homogeneous in x. In this case ϕ is linearly homogeneous in x.

Proof Let the path $x(t)$, $\dot{x}(t)$ be optimal for $x(0) = x^0$. Then $\lambda x(t)$, $\lambda\dot{x}(t)$ is feasible for the initial condition λx^0, and

$$\begin{aligned}&\textstyle\int_0^\infty \exp(-rt)[Q(\lambda x(t), \lambda\dot{x}(t), p) - c'(\lambda\dot{x}(t))]\,dt\\ &= \lambda \textstyle\int_0^\infty \exp(-rt)[Q(x(t), \dot{x}(t), p) - c'\dot{x}(t)]\,dt.\end{aligned}$$

Since the second integral is maximized, so is the first, and hence $V(\lambda x^0, c, r, p) = \lambda V(x^0, c, r, p)$. The linear homogeneity of ϕ follows from (3). The converse follows from (4). Some related results are provided by Hayashi (1982) and Mino (1983).

4.4 The intertemporal distance function

For given x, and arbitrary valuation v, the distance function

$$D(v, x, c, r, p) = \max_\lambda\{\lambda : V(x/\lambda, c, r, p) \geq v\}$$

defines the maximum deflation of initially available resources x consistent with achievement of at least the valuation v. Since V is concave and non-decreasing in x then, for $x \geq \bar{x}$ where $\bar{x} = \inf_x\{x : V(x, c, r, p) \geq V(y, c, r, p)\ \forall\ y \in \Omega^n\}$, V is increasing in x. Hence, for $x \geq \bar{x}$,

$$D(V(x, c, r, p), x, c, r, p) = 1. \tag{6}$$

Duality between $D(v, x, c, r, p)$ and $V(x, c, r, p)$ is obviously a straightforward analogue of the duality between $d(u, q)$ and $f(q)$ in static theory (see Blackorby, Primont and Russell (1978, Chapter 2)). The D Function satisfies the same properties in x, c, r, p as does the V Function (viz. properties V1-V6). Additionally D is non-increasing in v and is linearly homogeneous in x. For $x \geq \bar{x}$, D is decreasing in v and, by virtue of the identity (6), conditions V7(i)-(iv) can be re-expressed as equivalent partial differential equation conditions on D.

A useful feature of the D function approach is that it allows the derivation of optimal investment demand functions in cases where the optimal value function may not be capable of straightforward explicit specification but may merely be implicitly defined by $D(v, x, c, r, p) = 1$. Using (6) the following relationships are seen to exist between the first and second partial derivatives of V and D.

$$D_v V_y + D_y = 0,$$
$$V_y(D_{vv}V_{z'} + D_{vz'}) + D_v V_{yz'} + D_{yv}V_{z'} + D_{yz'} = 0,$$

where $y, z = x, c, r, p$. Thus

$$V_y = -D_y/D_v,$$
$$V_{yz'} = -(D_{vv}D_yD_{z'}/D_v^2 - D_yD_{vz'}/D_v - D_{yv}D_{z'}/D_v + D_{yz'})/D_v.$$

The optimal investment functions may now be expressed in terms of the D function by rewriting (3) as

$$\phi(x, c, r, p) \qquad (7)$$
$$= r(D_{vv}D_cD_{x'}/D_v^2 - D_cD_{cx'}/D_v - D_{cv}D_{x'}/D_v + D_{cx'} + D_vI)^{-1}D_c$$

where the right-hand side by definition is not a function of v.

5 The generation of functional forms

5.1 An aggregator approach

Let $V(x, c, r, p)$ be a given functional form for an optimal value function of an $n \times 1$ quasi-fixed capital stock vector x with associated $n \times 1$ vector of investment prices c. Thus V is the maximized value of problem (1) for a given variable profit function $Q(x, \dot{x}, p)$. Let the elements of the vectors x, c be viewed as aggregator functions of a **disaggregated** set $\mathbf{x}$, $\mathbf{c}$ where $\mathbf{x}$ and $\mathbf{c}$ are $\mathbf{n} \times 1$ vectors, $\mathbf{n} > n$. Without loss of generality we may write the aggregator functions as $x(\mathbf{x}, \mathbf{c})$, $c(\mathbf{x}, \mathbf{c})$. In principle this allows x to use the elements of $\mathbf{c}$ as variable weights in the aggregation of $\mathbf{x}$ and c to use the elements of $\mathbf{x}$ as variable weights in the aggregation of $\mathbf{c}$. We shall show below, however, that simpler fixed weight functions suffice. It is clear that in principle there exists a **disaggregated** optimal value function $\mathbf{V}(\mathbf{x}, \mathbf{c}, r, p)$ such that $\mathbf{V}(\mathbf{x}, \mathbf{c}, r, p) = V(x, c, r, p)$. We seek to generate the corresponding **disaggregated** optimal investment functions $\boldsymbol{\phi}$ from knowledge of the aggregated optimal value function $V(x, c, r, p)$ and the aggregator functions $x(\mathbf{x}, \mathbf{c})$, $c(\mathbf{x}, \mathbf{c})$. The following result on the form of the aggregator functions is useful:

Proposition 4 Let there exist both aggregated and disaggregated optimal value functions $V(x, c, r, p)$ and $\mathbf{V}(\mathbf{x}, \mathbf{c}, r, p)$ respectively, corresponding to problem (1) in the context of associated variable profit functions $Q(x, \dot{x}, p)$ and $\mathbf{Q}(\mathbf{x}, \dot{\mathbf{x}}, p)$. Then there exist linear aggregator functions $x = Z\mathbf{x}$ and $c = (Z^{-})'\mathbf{c}$, where $ZZ^{-} = I$.

Proof Since the disaggregated model solves the same problem as the aggregate model, $\mathbf{Q}(\mathbf{x}, \dot{\mathbf{x}}, p) = Q(x, \dot{x}, p)$ and $\mathbf{V}(\mathbf{x}, \mathbf{c}, r, p) = V(x, c, r, p)$ for all $\mathbf{x}$, $\mathbf{c}$, x, c, r, p. The aggregator functions may be expressed generally as $x = x(\mathbf{x}, \mathbf{c})$, $c = c(\mathbf{x}, \mathbf{c})$. Both V and $\mathbf{V}$ satisfy conditions V1-V7 in x, c, r, p and in $\mathbf{x}$, $\mathbf{c}$, r, p respectively. Applying V7(i) to $\mathbf{V}$, $r\mathbf{V_c} = \mathbf{V_{cx'}}\boldsymbol{\phi} - \boldsymbol{\phi}$ implies $r(x'_{\mathbf{c}}V_x + c'_{\mathbf{c}}V_c) = [(\nabla/\nabla\mathbf{x}' \otimes x'_{\mathbf{c}})(I \otimes V_x) + x'_{\mathbf{c}}(V_{xx'}x_{\mathbf{x}'} + V_{xc'}c_{\mathbf{x}'}) + (\nabla/\nabla\mathbf{x}' \otimes c'_{\mathbf{c}})(I \otimes V_c) + c'_{\mathbf{c}}(V_{cx'}x_{\mathbf{x}'} + V_{cc'}c_{\mathbf{x}'})]\boldsymbol{\phi} - \boldsymbol{\phi}$. Premultiplying this expression by $x_{\mathbf{x}'}$ and recognizing that $\phi = x_{\mathbf{x}'}\boldsymbol{\phi}$ yields $(x_{\mathbf{x}'}c'_{\mathbf{c}})rV_c = (x_{\mathbf{x}'}c'_{\mathbf{c}})\, V_{cx'}\phi - \phi - x_{\mathbf{x}'}[rx'_{\mathbf{c}}V_x - (\nabla/\nabla\mathbf{x}' \otimes x'_{\mathbf{c}}))(I \otimes V_x)\boldsymbol{\phi} - x'_{\mathbf{c}}(V_{xx'}x_{\mathbf{x}'} + V_{xc'}c_{\mathbf{x}'})\boldsymbol{\phi} - (\nabla/\nabla\mathbf{x}' \otimes c'_{\mathbf{c}})(I \otimes V_c)\boldsymbol{\phi} - c'_{\mathbf{c}}V_{cc'}c_{\mathbf{x}'}\boldsymbol{\phi}] = 0$. Now applying V7(i) to V, since the above expression must hold for all x, c, r, p this necessarily implies that $x_{\mathbf{x}'}c'_{\mathbf{c}} = I$ and that the entire term within the brackets [] must be identically zero. The latter requires that $x'_{\mathbf{c}} = 0$ and that $c'_{\mathbf{x}} = 0$. Thus $x = x(\mathbf{x})$, $c = c(\mathbf{c})$. Let $x_{\mathbf{x}'} = Z$. Then $c'_{\mathbf{c}} = Z^{-}$. Since c is not a function of $\mathbf{x}$, Z^{-} and hence Z is not a function of $\mathbf{x}$. Hence x is linear in $\mathbf{x}$. Similarly, c is linear in $\mathbf{c}$.

The usefulness of Proposition 4 is that it extends the range of operational applicability of a given optimal value function. The following result follows immediately from (3).

Proposition 5 Given an aggregated optimal value function $V(x, c, r, p)$, the optimal **disaggregated** investment functions are derivable in terms of the aggregate variables as:

$$\boldsymbol{\phi} = r(Z^{-}V_{cx'}Z - I)^{-1}Z^{-}V_c. \tag{8}$$

It may be noted that, by construction, $\phi = Z\boldsymbol{\phi}$, since $Z(Z^{-}V_{cx'}Z - I)^{-1}Z^{-} = (V_{cx'} - I)^{-1}$. However, since Z does not have full column rank, $\boldsymbol{\phi}$ cannot **in general** be written as a linear function of ϕ, hence the value of a result such as Proposition 5.

5.2 Example: the multivariate flexible accelerator

Consider the variable profit function

$$Q(x, \dot{x}, p) = \gamma(p)'x + (x'\ \dot{x}') \begin{bmatrix} A & C' \\ C & B \end{bmatrix} \begin{bmatrix} x \\ \dot{x} \end{bmatrix}$$

where $\gamma > 0$ and $\begin{bmatrix} A & C' \\ C & B \end{bmatrix}$ is negative definite.

Explicit solution of the primal problem (1) gives the multivariate flexible accelerator

$$\phi\,(x, c, r, p) = M[x - (A + rC)^{-1}(rc - \gamma(p))/2]$$

where M satisfies

$$BM^2 + (C - C' - rB)M = A + rC.$$

Analytical solution of this matrix quadratic expression in M is possible in general only for $n \leqslant 2$. (See Treadway (1971) and Epstein (1981, footnote 5).) In practice, empirical implementation has resorted to $n = 1$. (See Berndt, Fuss and Waverman (1979)).

Suppose now that data exists on stocks $\mathbf{x}$ and investment prices $\mathbf{c}$, where $\mathbf{x}$, $\mathbf{c}$ are $\mathbf{n} \times 1$ vectors, $\mathbf{n} > 2$. If aggregators $x = Z\mathbf{x}$ and $c = (Z^{-})'\mathbf{c}$ (with x, c either scalars or 2×1 vectors) are chosen, then the scalar (or 2×2 matrix) quadratic expression can be explicitly solved for M. The aggregate optimal value function can be derived from the Hamilton-Jacobi equation as:

$$V(x, c, r, p) = [\gamma(p)'x + x'Ax - \phi(x, c, r, p)'B\phi(x, c, r, p)]/r$$

whence
$$V_c = [A + rC']^{-1}M'B\phi$$

and
$$V_{cx'} = [A + rC']^{-1}M'BM.$$

Using result (8), the disaggregated investment functions are

$$\phi = r[Z^{-}(A + rC')^{-1}M'BMZ - I]^{-1}Z^{-}(A + rC')^{-1}M'B\phi.$$

5.3 The optimal value as an implicit function

While the above approach is a useful procedure for handling the problem of dimensionality, it suffers the limitation of requiring an explicit functional form for $V(x, c, r, p)$, albeit for x, c of low dimension. While the flexible accelerator functional form offers one possibility, the difficulty is to formulate other appropriately constrained functions V. The distance function offers a possible solution. For x in the economically relevant range $(< \bar{x})$, $V_x > 0$ and hence the constraint in the definition of the distance function is binding at the optimum. Therefore, given a V function, D may be obtained by inversion of $V(x/\lambda, c, r, p) = v$ in λ.

Specifically, consider the multivariate flexible accelerator. Setting $V(x/\lambda, c, r, p) = v$, the distance function is found to be the positive root of

$$\lambda^2 - [a'x/(rv + s)]\lambda = x'(A - M'BM)x/(rv + s)$$

where
$$a = \gamma + M'BM(A + rC)^{-1}(rc - \gamma)$$

and
$$s = (rc - \gamma)'(A + rC')^{-1}M'BM(A + rC)^{-1}(rc - \gamma)/4.$$

The distance function may be written

$$D(v, x, c, r, p) = (1/2)(a'x/v)/(r + s/v)$$
$$+ [\{(1/2)(a'x/v)/(r + s/v)\}^2 + (x/v)'(A - M'BM)(x/v)/(r/v + s/v^2)]^{1/2}.$$

In this form it is a comparatively simple matter to speculate upon generalizations which implicitly define v but which do not admit of an explicit functional form for v as a function of x, c, r, p and which nevertheless maintain the appropriate constraints on D. We note that, by construction, D is positively linearly homogeneous, increasing and concave in x and is decreasing in v. Consider therefore the generalization

$$D(v, x, c, r, p) = (1/2)(\Sigma_i a_i x_i/v^{\alpha_i})/(r + s/v)$$
$$+ [\{(1/2)(\Sigma_i a_i x_i/v^{\alpha_i})/(r + s/v)\}^2 + (x/v)'(A - M'BM)(x/v)/(r/v + s/v^2)]^{1/2}.$$

If $\alpha_i = 1$ for all i, this reduces to the distance function corresponding to the multivariate flexible accelerator. Clearly all properties of a distance function in x, c, r, p are preserved and, by continuity, properties in v are preserved for α_i sufficiently close to unity. However, the use of (7) generates an expanded class of appropriately constrained optimal investment and variable input demand functions. This class contains the multivariate flexible accelerator model as a special case. For this class, the optimal value function is not (in general) explicitly recoverable.

6 Conclusion

This paper has overviewed existing static and intertemporal duality theory results both in consumer theory and the theory of the firm. The orientation has been toward solving the practical problem of the generation of appropriately constrained functional forms for the Optimal Value Function. In the consumer theory context, an approach which allows relaxation of the static price expectations assumption has been demonstrated. In the context of the theory of the firm, two practical approaches to the solution of the functional form problem have been demonstrated. The first of these involves a theory of aggregation. The aim of this approach is to take an existing optimal value functional form of low dimension and, by application of a theory of aggregation, enable it to handle the derivation of higher dimensional optimal investment functions. The second approach involves the specification of an implicit function for the optimal value of the firm via the Intertemporal Distance Function.

References

Arrow, K. and Kurz, M. (1970), *Public Investment, The Rate of Return, and Optimal Fiscal Policy*, Baltimore: Johns Hopkins Press.

Berndt, E., Fuss, M. and Waverman, L. (1979), 'A Dynamic Model of Cost of Adjustment and Interrelated Factor Demands', Institute For Policy Analysis Working Paper 7925, University of Toronto.

Blackorby, C., Primont, D. and Russell, R.R. (1978), *Duality, Separability and Functional Structure: Theory and Economic Applications*, Amsterdam: North-Holland.

Blackorby, C. and Diewert, W.E. (1979), 'Expenditure Functions, Local Duality and Second Order Approximations', *Econometrica*, 47, 579-601.

Brechling, F. (1975), *Investment and Employment Decisions*, Manchester: Manchester University Press.

Cooper, R.J. and McLaren, K.R. (1980), 'Atemporal, Temporal and Intertemporal Duality in Consumer Theory', *International Economic Review*, 21, 599-609.

Diewert, W.E. (1974), 'Applications of Duality Theory' in M.D. Intriligator and D.A. Kendrick eds., *Frontiers of Quantitative Economics*, Vol. II. Amsterdam: North Holland.

Diewert, W.E. (1982a), 'Duality Approaches to Microeconomic Theory' in K.J. Arrow and M.D. Intriligator eds., *Handbook of Mathematical Economics*, Vol. II. Amsterdam: North-Holland. 535-99

Diewert, W.E. (1982b), *Duality Theory in Economics*, Amsterdam: North-Holland (forthcoming).

Eisner, R.E. and Strotz, R.H. (1963), 'Determinants of Business Investment', in *Impacts of Monetary Policy*, a series of research studies prepared for the Commission on Money and Credit, Englewood Cliffs: Prentice Hall, 59-236.

Epstein, L.G. (1981), 'Duality Theory and Functional Forms for Dynamic Factor Demands', *Review of Economic Studies*, 48, 81-95.

Epstein, L. and Denny, M. (1983), 'The Multivariate Flexible Accelerator Model; Its Empirical Restrictions and an Application to U.S. Manufacturing', *Econometrica*, 51, 647-74.

Fuss, M.A. and McFadden, D. eds. (1978), *Production Economics: A Dual Approach to Theory and Applications*, Amsterdam: North-Holland.

Hayashi, F. (1982), 'Tobin's Marginal q and Average q: A Neoclassical Interpretation', *Econometrica*, 50, 213-27.

Lluch, C. (1973), 'The Extended Linear Expenditure System', *European Economic Review*, 4, 21-32.

Lucas, R.E. (1967), 'Optimal Investment and the Flexible Accelerator', *International Economic Review*, 8, 78-85.

McLaren, K.R. and Cooper, R.J. (1980), 'Intertemporal Duality: Application to the Theory of the Firm', *Econometrica*, 48, 1755-62.

Mino, K. (1983), 'On the Homogeneity of Value Function of the Optimal Control Problem', *Economic Letters*, 11, 149-54.

Morrison, C.J. and Berndt, E.R. (1981), 'Short-Run Labor Productivity in a Dynamic Model', *Journal of Econometrics*, 16, 339-65.

Mortensen, D. (1973), 'Generalized Costs of Adjustment and Dynamic Factor Demand Theory', *Econometrica*, 41, 657-65.

Schramm, R. (1970), 'The Influence of Relative Prices, Production Conditions and Adjustment Costs on Investment Behaviour', *Review of Economic Studies*, 37, 361-75.

Treadway, A.B. (1971), 'The Rational Multivariate Flexible Accelerator', *Econometrica*, 39, 845-55.
Treadway, A.B. (1974), 'The Globally Optimal Flexible Accelerator', *Journal of Economic Theory*, 7, 17-39.

Part III
Some Statistical Issues

11 Asymptotic Spectral Analysis of Cross-Product Matrices

*G.S. Watson**

1 Introduction

T.W. Anderson (1963) derived the asymptotic distribution of the eigenvalues and vectors of the covariance matrix of a sample from a Gaussian distribution. Davis (1977) took his basic method and used it to get some results for the non-Gaussian case. The non-Gaussian case is of interest either because one wants to study the sensitivity of methods to deviations from Gaussianity – e.g. Muirhead (1982) – or because one has to deal with other distributions. For example, the distribution of the random vector might be entirely restricted to some manifold embedded in $\mathbb{R}^q$ like the surface of the unit sphere or an hyperboloid of rotation; the case of special interest to this writer is the sphere (see Watson (1983c)).

Kim (1978) at the suggestion of R.J.W. Beran, used results from the book by Kato (1976, 1980) on the perturbation theory of linear operators to find the asymptotic distribution of the eigenvalues of the matrix

$$M_n = n^{-1} \sum_{1}^{n} x_i x_i'$$

where the x_i's are independently drawn from a certain distribution on the surface Ω of the unit sphere in $\mathbb{R}^q$. Tyler (1979, 1981) also used Kato's method to get results in classical multivariate analysis. But the technique is not well-known, nor immediately evident from Kato's book.

Kato is primarily concerned with linear operators

$$T(x) = T_0 + xT_1 + x^2T_2 + \ldots \tag{1}$$

acting on Banach and Hilbert spaces but begins with the case of interest to us – finite dimensional spaces where the T_i may be thought of as fixed matrices and x is real and small. In our motivating problem,

$$M_n = n^{-1} \sum_{1}^{n} x_i x_i'$$

* This work was partially supported by Grant No. 00014-79-C-0322 from the Office of Naval Research.

(prime denotes transpose) and $x_1, \ldots, x_n$ are independent random vectors in $\mathbb{R}^q$ with a distribution such that $EM_n = M$ and $n^{-1/2}(M_n - M) = G_n$ is asymptotically a $q \times q$ matrix with jointly Gaussian entries. Thus G_n tends in distribution to a Gaussian matrix G. We may write then

$$\begin{aligned} M_n &= M + n^{-1/2}G + n^{-1/2}(G_n - G), \\ &= M + n^{-1/2}G + A_n, \end{aligned} \tag{2}$$

where $n^{1/2}A_n$ a symmetric matrix tends to zero in probability. (1) and (2) are analogous if we identify x with $n^{-1/2}$, T_0 and M, T_1 and G but the remainders are different in form. We will show that A_n is asymptotically negligible.

Thus we really only need Kato's method for finding the eigenvalues and eigen projectors of $T(x)$, as functions of small real x in the simplest of (1),

$$T(x) = T_0 + xT_1, \tag{3}$$

where T_0 and T_1 are $q \times q$ real symmetric matrices. His method calls upon Cauchy's Theorem in complex variable theory. Specifically consider the integral of $(z - z_0)^p$ around (in an anti-clockwise direction) a simple closed curve C in the complex plane which does not go through z_0 (e.g. a circle)

$$\int_C (z - z_0)^p \, dz \tag{4}$$

where p is an integer. Unless $p = -1$, the value of (4) is always zero. When $p = -1$, the value is zero if z_0 is outside C and $2\pi i (i = \sqrt{-1})$ if z_0 is inside C.

Section 2 gives a simple account of Kato's method for (3). Section 3 applies them to (2). These results have of course been obtained before by direct matrix methods. Section 4 gives a quick sketch of these, which convinces this writer that Kato's treatment is much more satisfying to anyone knowing elementary complex variable theory. Section 5 suggests just some of the many other problems that might also be discussed this way with profit.

This paper is of course expository and so rigour and generality are sacrificed for vividness and simplicity. The interested reader should go on to read at least the first two chapters of Kato's book.

2 The key to Kato

If T_0 and T_1 are real symmetric $q \times q$ non-random matrices and x is a small real number,

$$T(x) = T_0 + xT_1 \tag{5}$$

can be thought of as a linear perturbation of T_0. Let the spectral representation of the matrix T_0 be

$$T_0 = \sum_1^r \lambda_j P_j, \qquad r \leq q, \tag{6}$$

where

$$\lambda_1, \ldots, \lambda_r \text{ are distinct real numbers,}$$

$$P_j' = P_j, \qquad P_j P_k = \delta_{jk} P_j, \tag{7}$$

$$\text{rank } P_j = \text{trace } P_j = q_j, \qquad \sum_1^r q_j = q \,.$$

Thus λ_j is an eigenvalue of T_0 that is repeated q_j times. The invariant subspace V_j associated with λ_j has dimension q_j and P_j projects orthogonally on to V_j whose direct sum is $\mathbb{R}^q$.

The matrix $T(x)$ may have q distinct eigenvalues but we would expect these to fall into r clusters about $\lambda_1, \ldots, \lambda_r$ and to condense on $\lambda_1, \ldots, \lambda_r$ as $x \to 0$. Equally the eigenvectors of $T(x)$ should lead us to the eigen subspaces V_j as $x \to 0$. To show how this happens define the resolvent of T_0, $R_0(\zeta)$, as

$$R_0(\zeta) = (T_0 - \zeta I_q)^{-1}, \tag{8}$$

where ζ is a complex number. By (6) we may write

$$R_0(\zeta) = \sum_1^r (\lambda_j - \zeta)^{-1} P_j. \tag{9}$$

Observe that T_0 and $R_0(\zeta)$ commute.

If C is any contour in the complex plane which does not go through any λ_j, which are points on the real axis, Cauchy's Theorem and (9) imply that

$$\frac{1}{2\pi i} \int_C R_0(\zeta)\, d\zeta = \Sigma P_j, \qquad \lambda_j \in C \tag{10}$$

where the sum is over the projectors P_j associated with eigenvalues λ_j inside C. The integral of a matrix is the matrix of integrals. Similarly

$$\frac{1}{2\pi i} \int_C T_0 R_0(\zeta)\, d\zeta = \Sigma \lambda_j P_j, \qquad \lambda_j \in C \,. \tag{11}$$

We observe that the trace of (10) gives the sum of the dimensions of the eigen subspaces associated with λ_j within C. Similarly the trace of (11) gives the sum of the eigenvalues (times their multiplicities) within C.

We now consider the resolvent of $T(x)$,

$$R(x, \zeta) = (T(x) - \zeta I_q)^{-1} = R_0(\zeta)(I_q + xT_1 R_0(\zeta))^{-1}. \tag{12}$$

If we apply the results of the previous paragraph to $R(x, \zeta)$, we will get information about the eigenvalues $\lambda(T(x))$ and projectors $P(T(x))$, of $T(x)$. As $x \to 0$, we would expect the values of $\lambda(T(x))$ to condense on the eigenvalues λ_j of T_0.

To obtain the required formulae, we need to expand (12) as a power series. For a $q \times q$ matrix A,

$$(I_q + xA)^{-1} = I_q - xA + x^2A^2 - \ldots \tag{13}$$

where the series is absolutely convergent provided $|x|\ ||A|| < 1$, where $||A||$ is here the norm of A defined as the absolute value of the largest eigenvalue of A. It is clear that $(I + xA)^{-1}$ exists for all such x. Thus we can say that for x sufficiently small,

$$(I_q + xA)^{-1} = I_q - xA + 0(x^2). \tag{14}$$

Instead of (14) we could use the identity, when $(I + xA)^{-1}$ exists,

$$(I + xA)^{-1} = I - xA + x^2A^2(I + xA)^{-1}, \tag{15}$$

which gives explicitly the error of using $I - xA$ as the inverse of $I + xA$. A discussion of the $0(x^2)$ term in the following formulae is given in the Appendix. Applying (14) to (12), we have, as $|x| \to 0$,

$$R(x, \zeta) = R_0(\zeta) - xR_0(\zeta)T_1R_0(\zeta) + 0(x^2). \tag{16}$$

Consider now the analogue of (10) when C_j is a contour which encloses *only* the eigenvalue λ_j. Then

$$\frac{1}{2\pi i}\int_{C_j} R(x, \zeta)d\zeta = \frac{1}{2\pi i}\int_{C_j} R_0(\zeta)d\zeta - \frac{x}{2\pi i}\int_{C_j} R_0(\zeta)T_1R_0(\zeta)\, d\zeta + 0(x^2). \tag{17}$$

The first term on the right-hand side (RHS) of (17) is P_j. To find the second term, we observe that, if we use (9) twice,

$$R_0(\zeta)T_1R_0(\zeta) = \sum_{k=1}^{r}\sum_{\ell=1}^{r}\frac{P_kT_1P}{(\lambda_k - \zeta)(\lambda_\ell - \zeta)}$$

$$= \sum_{k=1}^{r}\frac{P_kT_1P_k}{(\lambda_k - \zeta)^2} + \sum_{k<\ell}\frac{(P_kT_1P_1 + P_1T_1P_k)}{\lambda_\ell - \lambda_k}\left(\frac{1}{\lambda_k - \zeta} - \frac{1}{\lambda_\ell - \zeta}\right). \tag{18}$$

The contour integral of the first term on the RHS of (18) is zero. We get contributions from the second term when k or ℓ equal j and they add to the symmetric matrix

$$\sum_{k\neq j}\frac{P_kT_1P_j + P_jT_1P_k}{\lambda_k - \lambda_j} \tag{19}$$

Observe, for later use, that this matrix has a zero trace because P_jP_k is null. Thus

$$\frac{1}{2\pi i}\int_{C_j} R(x,\zeta)\,d\zeta = P_j - x\sum_{k\neq j}\frac{P_kT_1P_j + P_jT_1P_k}{\lambda_j - \lambda_k} + 0(x^2) \tag{20}$$

is the analogue of (10).

The analogue of (11) is obtained by integrating $T(x)R(x, \zeta)$ which may, using (5) and (16), be written as

$$T(x)R(x,\zeta) = T_0R_0(\zeta) + x(T_1R_0(\zeta) - T_0R_0(\zeta)T_1R_0(\zeta)T_1R_0(\zeta)) + 0(x^2). \tag{21}$$

The integral of the first term on the RHS of (21) is that in (11). To find the second and third terms we note that

$$T_1R_0(\zeta) = \sum_{k=1}^{r}(\lambda_k - \zeta)^{-1}T_1P_k, \tag{22}$$

$$T_0R_0(\zeta)T_1R_0(\zeta) = \sum_{k=1}^{r}\frac{\lambda_kP_kT_1P_k}{(\lambda_k - \zeta)^2}$$

$$+ \sum_{k<\ell}\frac{\lambda_kP_kT_1P_\ell + \lambda_\ell P_\ell T_1P_k}{(\lambda_\ell - \lambda_k)}\left(\frac{1}{\lambda_k - \zeta} - \frac{1}{\lambda_\ell - \zeta}\right), \tag{23}$$

where we have used (6) and (18). Thus we find that

$$\frac{1}{2\pi i}\int_{C_j} T(x)R(x,\zeta)\,d\zeta = \lambda_jP_j + x\Big(T_1P_j - \sum_{k\neq j}\frac{\lambda_kP_kT_1P_j + \lambda_jP_jT_1P_k}{\lambda_j - \lambda_k}\Big) + 0(x^2). \tag{24}$$

Observe that the trace of the second term in the coefficient of x is zero. (24) is the analogue of (11).

In the applications we have in mind $T(x)$ will have q distinct eigenvalues $\lambda_1(x), \ldots, \lambda_q(x)$ and (orthonormal) eigenvectors $v_1(x), \ldots, v_q(x)$ so that

$$T(x) = \sum_{1}^{q}\lambda_i(x)v_i(x)v_i(x)' \tag{25}$$

is the spectral form for $T(x)$. By using the reasoning that led to (10) and (11) we may then evaluate the LHS's of (20) and (24). Thus

$$\frac{1}{2\pi i}\int_{C_j} R(x,\zeta)\,d\zeta = \Sigma\, v_i(x)v_i(x)', \tag{26}$$

$$\frac{1}{2\pi i}\int_{C_j} T(x)R(x,\zeta)\,d\zeta = \Sigma\, \lambda_i(x)v_i(x)v_i(x)', \tag{27}$$

where both sums are over i such that $\lambda_i(x)$ are points inside the contour C_j.

Since trace $v_i(x)v_i(x)' = v_i'(x)v_i(x) = 1$, taking the trace of both sides of (20) and using (26) yields

$$\# \lambda_i(x) \text{ inside } C_j = q_j + 0(x^2), \tag{28}$$

for any contour C_j enclosing λ_j. As $x \to 0$, one could use smaller and smaller contours. Hence as $x \to 0$, the eigenvalues of $T(x)$ form *clusters* of q_j roots about λ_j ($j = 1, \ldots, r$) which condense upon λ_j. If we do not take the trace of (20) and write

$$\hat{P}_j = \sum_{\lambda_i(x) \subseteq C_j} v_i(x) v_i(x)', \tag{29}$$

then (20) may be written as

$$\hat{P}_j = P_j - x \sum_{k \neq j} \frac{P_k T_1 P_j + P_j T_1 P_k}{\lambda_j - \lambda_k} + 0(x^2). \tag{30}$$

Taking the trace of (24) yields

$$\Sigma\, \lambda_i(x) \text{ within } C_j = q_j \lambda_j + x \text{ trace } T_1 P_j + 0(x^2), \tag{31}$$

so dividing through by q_j and calling the LHS $\bar{\lambda}_j$, the arithmetic mean of the jth cluster, we have

$$\bar{\lambda}_j = \lambda_j + \frac{x}{q_j} \text{ trace } T_1 P_j + 0(x^2) \tag{32}$$

The formulae (30) and (32) are ideal for statistical applications, as will be seen in the next section. We close this section by observing that there is no problem except complexity in getting higher order approximations – one merely takes higher order terms in (14). For example, the coefficient of x^2 in $R(x, \zeta)$ is $R_0 T_1 R_0 T_1 R_0$, so using (9) and partial fraction expansions the contour integral may be evaluated to give a lengthy formula. One then finds that (28) may be improved to

$$\# \lambda_i(x) \text{ inside } C_j = q_j + 0(x^3). \tag{33}$$

3 Large sample theory of symmetric cross-product matrices

Let x be a random vector in $\mathbb{R}^q$ with components $x^1, x^2, \ldots, x^q$ and suppose that $\mathrm{E}x^i x^j x^k x^\ell$ exists for all $i, j, k, \ell = 1, \ldots, q$. Let x' denote the transpose of x. Call $\mathrm{E}xx' = \mathrm{E}[x^i x^j] = M$, a symmetric $q \times q$ matrix with spectral form

$$M = \sum_1^r \lambda_j P_j. \tag{34}$$

If $x_1, \ldots, x_n$ are independent copies of x, define

$$M_n = n^{-1} \sum_1^n x_i x_i'. \tag{35}$$

Then $M_n \to M$ by the law of large numbers and by the multivariate central limit theorem

$$n^{1/2}(M_n - M) \xrightarrow{d} G. \tag{36}$$

The $q(q + 1)/2$ functionally independent elements of the symmetric matrix G are jointly Gaussian with zero means and a covariance matrix V whose elements are

$$\mathrm{E}x^i x^j x^k x^\ell - \mathrm{E}(x^i x^j)\mathrm{E}(x^k x^\ell), \qquad i \leqslant j, \qquad k \leqslant \ell. \tag{37}$$

To use the results of Section 2, we may write

$$M_n = M + n^{-1/2} G_n, \tag{38}$$

instead of

$$T(x) = T_0 + xT_1.$$

From (36), T_1 corresponds to G_n, x to $n^{-1/2}$, and M to T_0. Provided no λ_j in (34) is zero, the matrix M_n will, with probability one, have distinct eigenvalues – Okamoto (1973). If say $\lambda_1 = 0$, $\mathrm{E}(P_1 x)(P_1 x)'$ is a matrix of zeros so that, taking the trace, $\mathrm{E}\|P_1 x\|^2 = 0$. Thus $P_1 x$ is a null vector and M_n will have q_1 zero roots and the data will determine the eigen subspace V_1 exactly. This case has little interest so we assume that all the $\lambda_j > 0$.

The matrix M_n will be used to estimate the λ_j and P_j, $j = 1, \ldots, r$. Combining (38) with (29), (30) and (32), we have for $j = 1, \ldots, r$,

$$n^{1/2}(P_j - \hat{P}_j) = \sum_{k \neq j} \frac{P_k G_n P_j + P_j G_n P_k}{\lambda_j - \lambda_k} + 0(n^{-1/2}), \tag{39}$$

$$n^{1/2}(\bar{\lambda}_j - \lambda_j) = \frac{1}{q_j} \text{trace } G_n P_j + 0(n^{-1/2}), \tag{40}$$

where $0(n^{-1/2})$ stands, respectively, for a random matrix and a random scalar which tend to zero in probability as $n \to \infty$. As G_n tends to G in distribution as $n \to \infty$, (39) and (40) become our key results:

$$n^{1/2}(\hat{P}_j - P_j) \xrightarrow{d} \sum_{k \neq j} \frac{P_k G P_j + P_j G P_k}{\lambda_j - \lambda_k} \tag{41}$$

$$n^{1/2}(\bar{\lambda}_j - \lambda_i) \xrightarrow{d} \frac{1}{q_j} \text{trace } G P_j. \tag{42}$$

In (41) we have used the fact that G and $-G$ have the same distribution. The RHS's of (41) and (42) are linear in the Gaussian matrix G so that the LHS's have asymptotically Gaussian distributions with zero means and variances and covariances that depend upon the covariance matrix V of G.

(42) is univariate and so easy to understand, e.g. it leads to a Gaussian confidence interval for λ_j, although we will see that one will do better with a transformation. (41) describes the difference between estimated and true projectors and needs further simplification. Using the Euclidean matrix norm ($\|A\|^2$ = trace AA'),

$$n\|\hat{P}_j - P_j\|^2 \xrightarrow{d} 2 \sum_{k \neq j} \frac{\text{trace } P_j G P_k G}{(\lambda_j - \lambda_k)^2}. \tag{43}$$

Again, one might examine the different effects of $\hat{P}_j$ and P_j on vectors. For example, if $v \in V_j$,

$$n^{1/2}(\hat{P}_j v - P_j v) \xrightarrow{d} \sum_{k \neq j} \frac{P_k G v}{\lambda_j - \lambda_k}, \tag{44}$$

so

$$n\|\hat{P}_j v - P_j v\|^2 \xrightarrow{d} \sum_{k \neq j} \frac{v' G P_k G v}{\lambda_j - \lambda_k}. \tag{45}$$

More fundamentally if $\hat{V}_j$ is the subspace on to which $\hat{P}_j$ projects, $\hat{V}_j$ will be 'close' to V_j if cos $\theta = v'\hat{v}$ is always large when $v \in V_j$ and $\hat{v} \in \hat{V}_j$, $\|v\| = 1$, $\|\hat{v}\| = 1$. Thus we should seek the stationary values of $(P_j u)'(\hat{P}_j w)$, given $\|P_j u\| = \|\hat{P}_j w\| = 1$, i.e., we should consider

$$2u' P_j \hat{P}_j w - \theta u' P_j u - \phi w' \hat{P}_j w,$$

where θ and ϕ are Lagrangian multipliers. Hence

$$\begin{cases} P_j \hat{P}_j w - \theta P_j u = 0, \\ \hat{P}_j P_j u - \phi \hat{P}_j w = 0, \end{cases} \tag{46}$$

so that

$$\begin{aligned} \theta = \phi &= \text{stationary value of } (P_j u)'(\hat{P}_j w), \\ &= C, \text{ say.} \end{aligned}$$

Then the equations (46) will only have a solution if

$$\begin{vmatrix} -CP_j & P_j \hat{P}_j \\ \hat{P}_j P_j & -C\hat{P}_j \end{vmatrix} = 0. \tag{47}$$

This equation for C may be reduced to

$$\left| P_j \hat{P}_j P_j - C^2 P_j \right| = 0, \tag{48}$$

which has q_j non-zero roots C_ℓ^2. If, however, (41) is used, one finds eventually that all the C_ℓ^2 are unity. Watson (1983a) deals with the case where $r = 2$ and characterizes, by taking the next term in the expansions in Section 2, the asymptotic distributions of $n(1 - C_\ell^2)$. It is conjectured that for any r the asymptotic joint distribution of $n(1 - C_1), \ldots, n(1 - C_{q_j})$ is the joint distribution of the non-zero eigenvalues of

$$\sum_{k \neq j} \frac{P_j G P_k G P_j}{(\lambda_j - \lambda_k)^2}. \tag{49}$$

Some of the above results become easier to understand if we write, since $I_q = P_1 + \ldots + P_r$,

$$y_j = P_j x, \qquad x = y_1 + \ldots + y_r. \tag{50}$$

One of the reasons results become simpler for the Gaussian case is that there $y_1, \ldots, y_r$ are independent. Since $Exx' = M = \Sigma \lambda_j P_j$,

$$\begin{aligned} Ey_k y_\ell' &= 0, \qquad \ell \neq k, \qquad Ey_j y_j' = \lambda_j P_j, \\ Ey_\ell' y_k &= 0, \qquad (\ell \neq k), \qquad Ey_j' y_j = \lambda_j q_j. \end{aligned} \tag{51}$$

Thus (41) may be rewritten as

$$n^{1/2}(\bar{\lambda}_j - \lambda_j) \sim \frac{n^{1/2}}{q_j} \text{trace} \left(\frac{1}{n} \sum_{i=1}^{n} y_{ji} y_{ji}' - \lambda_j P_j\right),$$

$$= \frac{n^{1/2}}{q_j} \left(\frac{1}{n} \sum_{i=1}^{n} y_{ji}' y_{ji} - \lambda_j q_j\right), \tag{52}$$

so that by (51) and the Central Limit Theorem

$$Ln^{1/2}(\bar{\lambda}_j - \lambda_j) \to G_1(0, \text{var}\,(y_j' y_j) q_j^{-2}), \tag{53}$$

where L stands for 'probability law of' and where $G_q(\mu, Z)$ stands for the Gaussian distribution in q dimensions with mean vector μ and covariance matrix Z. Similarly (41) can be written as

$$n^{1/2}(\hat{P}_j - P_j) \sim n^{1/2} \sum_{i=1}^{n} \sum_{k \neq j} \frac{y_{ki} y_{ji}' + y_{ji} y_{ki}'}{\lambda_j - \lambda_k}. \tag{54}$$

If $Lx = G_q(0, M)$, $y_1, y_2, \ldots, y_r$ are independent and $Ly_j' y_j \lambda_j^{-1} = \chi^2_{q_j}$ so that var $(y_j' y_j) = \lambda_j^2 2q_j$. Then (53) reads:

$$Ln^{1/2}(\bar{\lambda}_j - \lambda_j) \to G_1(0, 2\lambda_j^2/q_j).$$

Hence

$$Ln^{1/2}(\log(\bar{\lambda}_j/\lambda_j) - 1) \to G_1(0, 2/q_j), \tag{55}$$

giving the variance stabilizing transformation. Moreover, in this Gaussian case the $n^{1/2}(\bar{\lambda}_j - \lambda_j)$ or $n^{1/2}(\log(\bar{\lambda}_j/\lambda_j) - 1)$, $j = 1, \ldots, r$ are asymptotically independent, a simplification result which is not true in general. Under no circumstances could it be expected that the $\hat{P}_j$ would be independent since

$$\sum_{j=1}^{r} \hat{P}_j = I_q.$$

With this introduction, the compact paper by Tyler (1981) may be read for more details on $\hat{P}_j$. He also gives tests. For the special case of $r = 2$ and distributions restricted to Ω_q, see Watson (1983a). If an additional assumption is made that the distribution of x depends only upon $\|y_1\|, \ldots, \|y_r\|$ more results may be derived – see Watson (1983b).

4 Direct approach to large-sample theory of cross-product matrices

The eigenvalues of M_n are the roots $\hat{\lambda}$ of

$$|M_n - \lambda I| = |M - \lambda I + \frac{1}{\sqrt{n}} G_n| = 0 \tag{56}$$

where, as in Section 3,

$$M = \sum_{1}^{r} \lambda_j P_j, \; G_n = \sqrt{n}\,(M_n - M).$$

Suppose orthonormal eigenvectors of M are selected to span each of the invariant subspaces V_j and arranged as column vectors to form a $q \times q$ orthogonal matrix H. Let the first q_1 columns correspond to V_1, the next q_2 columns to V_2, etc., and write it in partitioned form

$$H = [H_1, \ldots, H_r] \; . \tag{57}$$

Then since $H'H = HH' = I_q$, we have

$$\begin{gathered} H'_a H_b = 0 \; (a \neq b), \qquad H'_a H_a = I_{q_a}, \\ H_1 H'_1 + \ldots + H_r H'_r = I_q, \\ H_a H'_a = P_a, \qquad a = 1, \ldots, r, \end{gathered} \tag{58}$$

and

$$H'MH = D(\lambda_j I_{q_j}), \tag{59}$$

a matrix partitioned so all r^2 submatrices are zero except for the multiples of identity matrices on the diagonal.

If H is applied to (56), it takes the partitioned form,

$$|(\lambda_i - \lambda) I_{q_i} \delta_{ij} + n^{-1/2} H'_i G_n H_j| = 0 \tag{60}$$

since $n \to \infty$, we seek the $0(1)$ and $0(n^{-1/2})$ terms only in the expansion of (60). Applying the formula

$$\begin{vmatrix} A & C \\ B & D \end{vmatrix} = |A|\ |D - BA^{-1}C|$$

when A is the leading submatrix of (60), it is seen that $BA^{-1}C$ is $0(n^{-1})$ and so negligible. Hence we may repeat the procedure to find that equation (60) and hence (56) is, to this order

$$\prod_{j=1}^{r} |(\lambda_j - \lambda)I_{q_j} + n^{-1/2}H_j'G_nH_j| = 0 \ . \tag{61}$$

This shows that the eigenvalues of M_n, for large n, form clusters about the r distinct roots λ_j of M. Expanding the jth factor in (61) to $0(n^{-1/2})$, we only need the product of the diagonal terms and find the equation

$$(\lambda_j - \lambda)^{q_j}(1 + n^{1/2}\ \frac{\text{trace } H_j'G_nH_j}{\lambda_j - \lambda}) = 0 \ . \tag{62}$$

Since trace $H_j'G_nH_j$ = trace $H_jH_j'G_n$ = trace P_jG_n by (58) the q_j roots of (62) tend to λ_j as $n \to \infty$ and the leading terms of the polynomial (degree q_j) equation for λ are

$$\lambda^q - \{q_j\lambda_j + n^{-1/2} \text{ trace } P_jG_n\}\lambda^{q-1} + \ldots = 0 \tag{63}$$

so that if the roots of this equation are denoted by $\hat{\lambda}$,

$$\Sigma\, \hat{\lambda} = q_j\lambda_j + n^{-1/2} \text{ trace } P_jG_n, \tag{64}$$

as we found in (32) and (42). But one cannot expect to obtain the roots in the cluster for λ_j from (62) (it gives them to be $\lambda_j(q - 1$ times), $\lambda_j + n^{-1/2}$ trace P_jG_n (once)) because when λ is within $n^{-1/2}$ of λ *all* the terms in the matrix in (61) are of order $n^{-1/2}$. However, (63) does give the correct coefficient for λ^{q-1} in (61).

Since the eigenvalues of M_n will in general be distinct, the approximations made above are inadequate to discuss e.g. the joint distribution of the eigenvalues in a cluster.

The following direct derivation of the analogue of (30) or (41) is harder to justify. Write

$$\hat{P}_j = P_j + n^{-1/2}\Delta, \qquad \Delta = n^{1/2}(\hat{P}_j - P_j) \tag{65}$$

and, because the roots in the cluster are within n^{-1} of λ_j, set

$$M_n\hat{P}_j = (\lambda_j + n^{-1/2}\delta)\hat{P}_j \tag{66}$$

i.e.,

$$(M + n^{-1/2}G_n)(P_j + n^{-1/2}\Delta) = (\lambda_j + n^{-1/2}\delta)(P_j + n^{-1/2}\Delta)$$

so that the terms in $n^{-1/2}$ yield the equation

$$G_nP_j + M\Delta = \lambda_j\Delta + \delta P_j$$

or

$$(M - \lambda_j I)\Delta = -G_n P_j + \delta P_j \ . \tag{67}$$

But

$$M - \lambda_j I = \sum_{k \neq j} (\lambda_k - \lambda_j) P_k$$

so that we could replace Δ by $\Delta - P_j X$ and still satisfy (67). Thus (67) is solved by multiplication by $\Sigma\ (\lambda_k - \lambda_j)^{-1} P_k$ and adding $P_j X$ so that

$$\Delta = \sum_{k \neq j} (\lambda_j - \lambda_k)^{-1} P_k G_n P_j + P_j X.$$

However, from (65) we see that Δ must be symmetric and this determines X. Thus

$$\Delta = n^{1/2}(\hat{P}_j - P_j) = \sum_{k \neq j} \frac{P_k G_n P_j + P_j G_n P_k}{\lambda_j - \lambda_k} \tag{68}$$

which is the desired result. However, without the results of Section 3, (65) and (66) are merely intuitions unless they were proved by a different method.

5 Additional remarks

(i) Suppose (x_i, y_i) for $i = 1, \ldots, n$ are independent copies of a pair of random vectors (x, y), $x \in \mathbb{R}^q$, $y \in \mathbb{R}^p$. Define the estimator of $N = \mathrm{E}xy'$,

$$N_n = n^{-1} \sum_1^n x_i y_i',$$

and assume that the Central Limit Theorem holds so that

$$n^{1/2}(N_n - N) \xrightarrow{d} F \ . \tag{69}$$

One may wish to estimate the singular values of N so one would find the non-zero eigenvalues of $N_n N_n'$ or $N_n' N_n$, whichever is the smaller. But using (69),

$$N_n' N_n \sim N'N + n^{-1/2}(F'N + N'F) \tag{70}$$

so that the previous theory is applicable.

(ii) Suppose that $x_1, \ldots, x_n$ is a sample from one q-dimensional distribution, $x_1^*, \ldots, x_m^*$ a sample from another distribution in $\mathbb{R}^q$ and let $M_n = n^{-1} \Sigma\, x_i x_i'$, $M_m^* = m^{-1} \Sigma\, x_i^* x_i^{*\prime}$. Then we often need to study the solutions of

$$(M_n - \lambda M_m{}^*)v = 0\ . \tag{71}$$

Anderson (1958) gives examples and calls λ and v the eigenvalues and vectors of M_n in the metric of $M_m{}^*$. To study them in large samples we suppose that the Central Limit Theorem applies in both cases so that as $m, n \to \infty$,

$$\begin{aligned} M_n &\sim M + n^{-1/2}G, \\ M_m &\sim M^* + m^{-1/2}G^*. \end{aligned} \tag{72}$$

The eigenvalues are those of $M_m{}^{*-1/2}M_nM_m{}^{*-1/2}$, which by (72) are those of

$$\begin{aligned} M^{*-1/2}\Big(I_q - \frac{m^{-1/2}}{2}G^*M^{*-1}\Big)&(M + n^{-1/2}G)\Big(I_q - \frac{m^{-1/2}}{2}M^{*-1}G^*\Big)M^{*-1/2} \\ &= M^{*-1/2}MM^{*-1/2} + n^{-1/2}M^{*-1/2}GM^{*-1/2} \\ &\quad - \frac{m^{-1/2}}{2}M^{*-1/2}G^*M^{*-1}MM^{*-1/2} \\ &\quad - \frac{m^{-1/2}}{2}M^{*-1/2}MM^{*-1}G^*M^{*-1/2}\ . \end{aligned} \tag{73}$$

If we set $n = \alpha\ell$, $m = \beta\ell$ with $\alpha, \beta > 0$ and $\ell \to \infty$ (73) has the form of a symmetric fixed matrix plus $\ell^{-1/2}$ times a symmetric Gaussian matrix so that the earlier theory is applicable.

(iii) A common statistical problem that does *not* fall into the categories we have discussed is the following. Suppose an ergodic finite Markov chain is observed for n successive times and that $\hat{p}_{ij}$ is the proportion of transitions from state i to state j. Then $\hat{p}_{ij}$ tends to p_{ij}, the transition probability, and we may write

$$[p_{ij}] = [\hat{p}_{ij}] + n^{-1/2}\{n^{1/2}[\hat{p}_{ij} - p_{ij}]\} \tag{74}$$

where the expression in braces becomes Gaussian. Here, however, the matrices are not symmetric. The spectral decomposition of non-symmetric matrices is well known to be more complicated than that for symmetric matrices. Kato, of course, gives a detailed account of it and of its perturbation and this theory might well be used to study (74) as $n \to \infty$.

(iv) Returning to the results of Section 3, suppose that one of the eigenvalues, λ_j say, has multiplicity one, so that its invariant subspace is one dimensional and defined by an eigenvector v_j so estimates of both are defined by $M_n\hat{v}_j = \hat{\lambda}_j\hat{v}_j$ and $\hat{P}_j = \hat{v}_j\hat{v}_j'$. To make v_j and $\hat{v}_j$ uniquely defined, choose them so that their first non-zero components are positive. The asymptotic properties of $\hat{v}_j$ must follow from (41). Since $\hat{v}_j'v_j \to 1$,

$$\hat{v}_j - v_j \xrightarrow{d} \sum_{k \neq j} \frac{P_kGv_j}{\lambda_j - \lambda_k}, \qquad \text{as } n \to \infty. \tag{75}$$

This formula and its application are discussed further in Watson (1984).

(v) More generally the use of (41) and (42) depends upon knowing, or being able to estimate, the covariance matrix of G. Thus one must know or be able to estimate fourth moments of the components of the random vectors x. If x is assumed to be Gaussian, fourth moments depend upon second moments and this is one reason why the results then simplify greatly; other reasons were given in Section 3. If n is not Gaussian, simulation or bootstrapping might be used – instead of direct estimation of fourth moments.

Appendix

In Section 2 we put aside the problem of showing that the error terms in (30) and (32) are in fact $0(x^2)$, as they would seem to be on using (14).

The series

$$\sum_{0}^{\infty} (-x)^p A^p$$

for $(I + xA)^{-1}$ is convergent if $|x|\ \|A\| < 1$ so that the difference

$$(I + xA)^{-1} - (I - xA) = \sum_{2}^{\infty}(-x)^p A^p \tag{A1}$$

has a norm which is less than or equal to

$$\begin{aligned} \sum^{\infty} |x|^p \|A\|^p &= x^2\|A\|^2(1 - |x|\|A\|)^{-1}, \\ &\leq 2x^2\|A\|^2, \qquad \text{if } |x|\|A\| < \tfrac{1}{2}. \end{aligned}$$

Thus we may write, for $|x| \to 0$,

$$(I + xA)^{-1} = I - xA + 0(|x|^2\|A\|^2) \tag{A2}$$

The key error to estimate is that in (17). To get it we use (A2) with $A = T_1R_0(\delta)$. Thus this error is x^2 times a matrix quantity of order

$$\int_{C_j} R_0(\delta)\|T_1R_0(\delta)\|^2 \, d\delta$$

where C_j can be taken as a circle about λ_j of radius r which encloses no other eigenvalue of T_0 and $R_0(\delta) = (T_0 - \delta I_q)^{-1}$. Since

$$\|T_1R_0(\delta)\| \leq \|T_1\|^2\|R_0(\delta)\|^2,$$

and we are using the matrix norm ($\|A\|^2 = \text{trace } A\bar{A}'$), the error is of order $x^2\|T_1\|^2$ times a quantity

$$\int_{C_j} R_0 \|R_0\|^2 \, d\delta = \int_{C_j} \left(\Sigma \frac{P_i}{\lambda_i - \delta}\right) \left(\Sigma \frac{q_k}{|\lambda_k - \delta|^2}\right) d\delta. \tag{A3}$$

Imagining that r is small we may examine the various integrals in (A3). The largest is $0(r^{-2})$. If r is fixed, then the remainder is indeed $0(x^2)$ as $x \to 0$. If one wants r to tend to zero as x tends to zero, and sets $r = x^{(1-\delta)/2}$, $0 < \delta < 1$, then $x/r^2 \to 0$ as $x \to 0$. Then the error should be written $0(x^2/r^2)$ and $0(x)$ as $x \to 0$.

References

Anderson, T.W. (1958), *An Introduction to Multivariate Analysis*, New York: Wiley.

Anderson, T.W. (1963), Asymptotic Theory for Principal Components, *Annals of Mathematical Statistics*, 34, 122-48.

Davis, A.W. (1977), 'Asymptotic Theory for Principal Components Analysis-non-normal case', *Australian Journal of Statistics*, 19, 206-13.

Kato, T. (1976), *Perturbation Theory for Linear Operators*, New York: Springer-Verlag (second edition, 1980).

Kim, K.M. (1978), 'Orientation Shift Model on the Sphere', unpublished Ph.D. Thesis, University of California, Berkeley.

Muirhead, R.J. (1982), *Aspects of Multivariate Statistical Theory*, New York: Wiley.

Tyler, D.E. (1979), 'Redundancy Analysis and Associated Asymptotic Distribution Theory', unpublished Ph.D. Thesis, Princeton University.

Tyler, D.E. (1981), 'Asymptotic Inference for Eigenvectors', *Annals of Statistics*, 9, 725-36.

Watson, G.S. (1983a), 'Large Sample Theory for Distribution on the Hypersphere with Rotational Symmetries', *Annals of the Institute of Mathematical Statistics*, 35, 303-19.

Watson, G.S. (1983b), 'Distribution in $\mathbb{R}^q$ with Rotational Symmetries', *Australian Journal of Statistics*, 25, 389-94.

Watson, G.S. (1983c), *Statistics on Spheres*, New York: Wiley.

Watson, G.S. (1984), 'The Calculation of Confidence Regions for Eigenvectors', *Australian Journal of Statistics*, 26, 272-6.

12 Bayesian prediction with random regressors

*Arnold Zellner and Soo-Bin Park**

1 Introduction

In this article we analyse the problem of prediction from regression equations with random independent variables. For example, in predicting electricity sales using a regression equation, the independent variables usually include, among others, income, price, and weather variables. To obtain predictions of the dependent variable, predictions of the independent variables are required. Further, inferences about future values of the dependent variable should reflect uncertainty about the future values of the independent variables. Some work on this problem from the sampling theory point of view is reported in Feldstein (1971). Herein we analyse this prediction problem with random independent variables from the Bayesian point of view.

We first review the general derivation of the predictive probability density function (pdf) for future values of the dependent variable given future values of the independent variables, the so-called conditional case. This case is treated in many Bayesian works including Raiffa and Schlaifer (1961), Zellner (1971), Box and Tiao (1973), Aitchison and Dunsmore (1975), and Leamer (1978). Then we indicate how to take account of uncertainty regarding the future values of the independent variables in obtaining the predictive pdf for future values of the dependent variable, the unconditional case. With the complete predictive pdf available for the unconditional case, it can be used to obtain optimal point predictions and unconditional predictive intervals. Next, the general Bayesian analysis is specialized to apply to simple and multiple regressions. After analysing the normal regression case, we provide results relevant for a wide range of data and prior distributions. Finally, the Bayesian prediction methods are applied using stock market data. Prediction results conditional upon given values of an independent variable are contrasted with those associated with unconditional prediction.

*Research financed by the National Science Foundation and by income from the H.G.B. Alexander Endowment Fund, Graduate School of Business, University of Chicago. Soo-Bin Park received support from the Social Sciences and Humanities Research Council of Canada during his visit to the University of Chicago.

The plan of the paper is as follows. In Section 2, general principles of Bayesian prediction are reviewed. Section 3 provides prediction results for simple and multiple regression while in Section 4 the results are applied using the market model of financial economics. Some concluding remarks are provided in Section 5.

2 General Bayesian prediction principles[1]

Let (y, x) denote given data relating to a dependent variable, y and to an independent variable or variables, x with likelihood function $p(y|x, \theta_1)p(x|\theta_2)$ where θ_1 and θ_2 are parameter vectors and $p(\cdot)$ is a generic symbol denoting a probability density function (pdf). Assume that $p(\theta_1, \theta_2|I)$ is the prior pdf for θ_1 and θ_2 based on initial information I. Then the posterior pdf for θ_1 and θ_2 is given by

$$p(\theta_1, \theta_2|D) = cp(\theta_1, \theta_2|I)p(y|x, \theta_1)p(x|\theta_2) \tag{1}$$

where $D \equiv (y, x, I)$, the sample and prior information and c is a normalizing constant. Now let the future, unknown values of the dependent and independent variables be denoted by (y_f, x_f) and have pdf given by $p(y_f|x_f, \theta_1)p(x_f|\theta_2)$. Then the joint predictive pdf for (y_f, x_f) is

$$p(y_f, x_f|D) = \int\int p(y_f|x_f, \theta_1)p(x_f|\theta_2)p(\theta_1, \theta_2|D)\, d\theta_1\, d\theta_2 \tag{2}$$

where $\theta_1 \subset \Theta_1$ and $\theta_2 \subset \Theta_2$. Finally, the marginal predictive pdf or unconditional predictive pdf for y_f is

$$\begin{aligned} p(y_f|D) &= \int p(y_f, x_f|D)\, dx_f \\ &= \int p(y_f|x_f, D)p(x_f|D)\, dx_f \end{aligned} \tag{3}$$

where $x_f \subset R_{x_f}$. Note that the second line of (3) expresses the marginal predictive pdf for y_f as an average of the conditional pdf, $p(y_f|x_f, D)$ with the marginal predictive pdf for x_f, $p(x_f|D)$ serving as the weight function. $p(y_f|x_f, D)$ is employed to make *conditional* predictive inferences given x_f, while $p(y_f|D)$ is employed to make *unconditional* predictive inferences.

In the case that θ_1 and θ_2 are a priori independent, that is $p(\theta_1, \theta_2|I) = p(\theta_1|I_1)p(\theta_2|I_2)$, then from (1), θ_1 and θ_2 are a posteriori independent assuming θ_1 and θ_2 have no common elements, that is $p(\theta_1, \theta_2|D) = p(\theta_1|D_1)p(\theta_2|D_2)$ with

$$p(\theta_1|D_1) = c_1p(\theta_1|I_1)p(y|x, \theta_1) \tag{4}$$

and

$$p(\theta_2|D_2) = c_2p(\theta_2|I_2)p(x|\theta_2) \tag{5}$$

where $D_1 \equiv (I_1, y, x)$ and $D_2 \equiv (I_2, x)$. Further the conditional predictive pdf for y_f given x_f is given by

$$p(y_f|x_f, D_1) = \int p(y_f|x_f, \theta_1)p(\theta_1|D_1)\, d\theta_1 \tag{6}$$

while the predictive pdf for x_f is given by:

$$p(x_f|D_2) = \int p(x_f|\theta_2)p(\theta_2|D_2)\, d\theta_2. \tag{7}$$

Then the joint predictive pdf for y_f and x_f is $p(y_f|x_f, D_1) \times p(x_f|D_2)$ and the marginal or unconditional predictive for y_f is

$$p(y_f|D) = \int p(y_f|x_f, D_1)p(x_f|D_2)\, dx_f \tag{8}$$

where $D = (D_1, D_2)$, the sample and prior information.

In the next section, we apply these general results to some specific regression problems.

3 Analysis of specific and general regression prediction problems

3.1 Simple regression model

The first problem that we consider is that of prediction for a simple regression with a single random independent variable. Our simple regression model is

$$y_i = \mu + \beta(x_i - \bar{x}) + \varepsilon_i \qquad i = 1, 2, \ldots n \tag{9}$$

where the ε_i's are assumed independently drawn from a normal distribution with mean zero and variance σ_1^2 and

$$\bar{x} = \sum_{i=1}^{n} x_i/n.$$

Further, we assume

$$x_i = \eta + v_i \qquad i = 1, 2, \ldots, n \tag{10}$$

where the v_i's are independently drawn from a normal distribution with zero mean and variance σ_2^2. Writing $y' = (y_1, y_2, \ldots, y_n)$, $x' = (x_1, x_2, \ldots, x_n)$ and $i' = (1, 1, \ldots, 1)$, the likelihood function for $\theta_1' = (\mu, \beta, \sigma_1)$ and $\theta_2' = (\eta, \sigma_2)$ is $p(y|x, \theta_1)p(x|\theta_2)$ with

$$p(y|x, \theta_1) \propto \sigma_1^{-n}\exp\{-[y - \mu i - \beta(x - \bar{x}i)]'[y - \mu i - \beta(x - \bar{x}i)]/2\sigma_1^2\} \tag{11}$$

and

$$p(x|\theta_2) \propto \sigma_2^{-n}\exp\{-(x - \eta i)'(x - \eta i)/2\sigma_2^2\}. \tag{12}$$

As regards a prior pdf for the parameters, we shall employ the following diffuse prior,

$$p(\mu, \beta, \eta, \sigma_1, \sigma_2) \propto 1/\sigma_1\sigma_2, \tag{13}$$

that is, the parameters μ, β, η, log σ_1, and log σ_2 are independently and uniformly distributed.[2] With this prior the parameters $\theta_1' = (\mu, \beta, \sigma_1)$ and $\theta_2' = (\eta, \sigma_2)$ are independent and thus the general results in (4)-(8) apply, that is

$$p(\theta_1|D_1) \propto \sigma_1^{-(n+1)}\exp\{-[\nu_2 s_{y\cdot x}^2 + n(\mu - \bar{y})^2 + m_{xx}(\beta - \hat{\beta})^2]/2\sigma_1^2\} \tag{14}$$

and

$$p(\theta_2|D_2) \propto \sigma_2^{-(n+1)}\exp\{-[\nu_1 s_x^2 + n(\eta - \bar{x})^2]/2\sigma_2^2\} \tag{15}$$

where $D_1 \equiv (y, x, I_1)$, $D_2 \equiv (x, I_2)$, I_1 and I_2 denote the diffuse prior information given by (13), $m_{xx} = (x - \bar{x}i)'(x - \bar{x}i)$, $\bar{y} = i'y/n$, $\hat{\beta} = (x - \bar{x}i)'(y - \bar{y}i)/m_{xx}$, $\nu_2 s_{y\cdot x}^2 = [y - \bar{y}i - \hat{\beta}(x - \bar{x}i)]'[y - \bar{y}i - \hat{\beta}(x - \bar{x}i)]$, $\nu_2 = n - 2$, $\nu_1 s_x^2 = m_{xx}$ and $\nu_1 = n - 1$.

From (14), it is seen that the conditional posterior pdf for (μ, β) given σ_1^2 is bivariate normal with mean $(\bar{y}, \hat{\beta})$ and diagonal covariance matrix with elements σ_1^2/n and σ_1^2/m_{xx}. Also, the marginal posterior pdf for σ_1 is $p(\sigma_1|D_1) \propto \sigma_1^{-(\nu_2+1)} \times \exp\{-\nu_2 s_{y\cdot x}^2/2\sigma_1^2\}$, obtained by integrating (14) with respect to μ and β. Now a future value of y, y_f is assumed generated by

$$y_f = \mu + \beta(x_f - \bar{x}) + \varepsilon_f \tag{16}$$

where x_f is a future value of x and ε_f is $N(0, \sigma_1^2)$ and is independent of the ε_i's in (9).[3] Then given x_f, σ_1 and D_1, y_f is normally distributed with conditional mean $\hat{y}_f = \bar{y} + \hat{\beta}(x_f - \bar{x})$ and conditional variance $[1 + 1/n + (x_f - \bar{x})^2/m_{xx}]\sigma_1^2$, that is

$$p(y_f|x_f, \sigma_1, D_1) \propto g_1^{-1/2}\sigma_1^{-1}\exp\{-(y_f - \hat{y}_f)^2/2g_1\sigma_1^2\} \tag{17}$$

where $g_1 \equiv 1 + 1/n + (x_f - \bar{x})^2/m_{xx}$. On multiplying this last expression by $p(\sigma_1|D_1)$, the marginal posterior pdf for σ_1, and integrating over σ_1, the resulting conditional predictive pdf for y_f given x_f and D_1 is

$$p(y_f|x_f, D_1) \propto g_1^{-1/2}[\nu_2 s_{y\cdot x}^2 + (y_f - \hat{y}_f)^2/g_1]^{-(\nu_2+1)/2} \tag{18}$$

a pdf in the univariate Student-*t* form with $\nu_2 = n - 2$ degrees of freedom. This is the conditional predictive pdf for y_f given x_f that has mean $\hat{y}_f = \bar{y} + \hat{\beta}(x_f - \bar{x})$ and variance, $V(y_f|x_f, D_1) = [1 + 1/n + (x_f - x)^2/m_{xx}]\nu_2 s_{y\cdot x}^2/(\nu_2 - 2)$ for $\nu_2 > 2$.

To obtain the unconditional predictive pdf for y_f, we need the predictive pdf for x_f, assumed generated by $x_f = \eta + v_f$, where v_f is $N(0, \sigma_2^2)$ and is independent of the previous v_i's. Then from (15) x_f given D_2 and σ_2 is normal with mean $\bar{x}$ and conditional variance $(1 + 1/n)\sigma_2^2$, that is $p(x_f|\sigma_2, D_2) \propto \sigma_2^{-1} \times \exp\{-(x_f - \bar{x})^2/2\sigma_2^2(1 + 1/n)\}$. From (15), the marginal posterior pdf of σ_2 is $p(\sigma_2|D_2) \propto \sigma_2^{-(\nu_1+1)}\exp\{-\nu_1 s_x^2/2\sigma_2^2\}$ and the joint pdf $p(x_f|\sigma_2, D_2)p(\sigma_2|D_2)$ can be integrated with respect to σ_2 to yield the marginal predictive pdf for x_f, namely

$$p(x_f|D) \propto \{\nu_1 s_x^2 + (x_f - \bar{x})^2/(1 + 1/n)\}^{-(\nu_1+1)/2} \tag{19}$$

which is in the univariate Student-t form with $\nu_1 = n - 1$ degrees of freedom, mean $\bar{x}$ and variance $(1 + 1/n)\nu_1 s_x^2/(\nu_1 - 2)$ for $\nu_1 > 2$.

Then the marginal pdf for y_f is obtained by integrating the joint pdf $p(y_f|x_f, D_1)p(x_f|D_2)$ with respect to x_f, that is

$$p(y_f|D) = \int_{-\infty}^{\infty} p(y_f|x_f, D_1)p(x_f|D_2)\, \mathrm{d}x_f \tag{20}$$

with $D = (D_1, D_2)$, $p(y_f|x_f, D_1)$ given in (18) and $p(x_f|D_2)$ given in (19). This integral can be evaluated numerically. However, the mean and variance of (20) can be obtained analytically from (19) in conjunction with the conditional moments of (18) to obtain

$$\begin{aligned} \mathrm{E}(y_f|D) &= \bar{y} + \hat{\beta}(\mathrm{E}x_f|D_2 - \bar{x}) \\ &= \bar{y} \end{aligned} \tag{21}$$

since $\mathrm{E}x_f|D_2 = \bar{x}$ from (19) and

$$\mathrm{V}(y_f|D) = [(\nu_1 - 1)/(\nu_2 - 2)](1 + 1/n)m_{yy}/(\nu_1 - 2) \tag{22}$$

where $m_{yy} = (y - \bar{y}i)'(y - \bar{y}i)$. For comparison with (22), the conditional variance of y_f given x_f, shown below (18) can be expressed as

$$\mathrm{V}(y_f|x_f, D) = [1 + 1/n + (x_f - \bar{x})^2/m_{xx}](1 - r_{xy}^2)m_{yy}/(\nu_2 - 2) \tag{23}$$

where $r_{xy}^2 = m_{xy}^2/m_{xx}m_{yy}$, the squared sample correlation coefficient with $m_{xy} = (x - \bar{x}i)'(y - \bar{y}i)$. If $x_f = \bar{x}$ in (23), $\mathrm{V}(y_f|x_f = \bar{x}, D) = (1 + 1/n)(1 - r_{xy}^2)m_{yy}/(\nu_2 - 2)$ and $\mathrm{V}(y_f|x_f = \bar{x}, D)/\mathrm{V}(y_f|D) = (1 - r_{xy}^2)(\nu_1 - 2)/(\nu_1 - 1) < 1$. It is the case that this ratio can be much smaller than one.

A different derivation of the above results with a slightly different diffuse prior distribution can be done by letting $y_{1i} \equiv y_i$ and $y_{2i} \equiv x_i$ and writing

$$(y_{1i}, y_{2i}) = (\mu_1, \mu_2) + (u_{1i}, u_{2i}) \qquad i = 1, 2, \ldots, n \tag{24}$$

where the vectors (y_{1i}, y_{2i}) are assumed independently drawn from a normal distribution with mean vector $\mu' = (\mu_1, \mu_2)$ and 2×2 positive definite symmetric covariance matrix Σ. In matrix notation, (24) can be written as

$$\underset{n\times 2}{Y} = \underset{n\times 1}{i}\ \underset{1\times 2}{\mu'} + \underset{n\times 2}{U} \tag{25}$$

and the likelihood function is

$$\begin{aligned} p(Y|\mu, \Sigma) &\propto |\Sigma|^{-n/2}\exp\{-\tfrac{1}{2}\mathrm{tr}(Y - i\mu')'(Y - i\mu')\Sigma^{-1}\} \\ &\propto |\Sigma|^{-n/2}\exp\{-\tfrac{1}{2}\mathrm{tr}[S + n(\mu' - \bar{y}')'(\mu' - \bar{y}')]\Sigma^{-1}\} \end{aligned}$$

where $\bar{y} = (\bar{y}_1, \bar{y}_2)$, with $\bar{y}_1$ and $\bar{y}_2$ sample means and $S = \{s_{ij}\}$ with $s_{ij} = (y_i - \bar{y}_i i)'(y_j - \bar{y}_j i)$, $i, j = 1, 2$.

As regards a diffuse prior for the parameters μ and Σ, we shall use the following Jeffreys' prior,[4]

$$p(\mu, \Sigma) \propto |\Sigma|^{-3/2} \tag{26}$$

Then the posterior pdf for μ and Σ is

$$p(\mu, \Sigma|D) \propto |\Sigma|^{-(n+3)/2}\exp\{-\tfrac{1}{2}\mathrm{tr}[S + n(\mu' - \bar{y}')'(\mu' - \bar{y}')]\Sigma^{-1}\} \tag{27}$$

where D denotes the sample and prior information. From (27), we have

$$p(\mu|\Sigma, D) \sim \mathrm{BN}(\bar{y}, \Sigma/n) \tag{28}$$

and

$$p(\Sigma|D) \propto |\Sigma|^{-\nu/2}\exp\{-\tfrac{1}{2}\mathrm{tr}\ S\Sigma^{-1}\} \tag{29}$$

where $\mathrm{BN}(\bar{y}, \Sigma/n)$ denotes a bivariate normal pdf with mean vector $\bar{y}' = (\bar{y}_1, \bar{y}_2)$ and covariance matrix Σ/n. In (29), we give the marginal pdf for Σ which is in the inverted Wishart form with $\nu = n + 2$ degrees of freedom – see e.g. Zellner (1971, p. 227 and p. 395).

Let $y_f' = (y_{1f}, y_{2f})$, a vector of future values be given by

$$y_f' = \mu' + u_f'$$

where $y_f' = (y_{1f}, y_{2f})$ and y_f' has a $\mathrm{BN}(\mu', \Sigma)$ pdf and is independent of Y. Then $p(y_f|\Sigma, D)$ is bivariate normal with mean $\bar{y}' = (\bar{y}_1, \bar{y}_2)$ and covariance matrix $(1 + 1/n)\Sigma$ and the marginal predictive pdf for y_f is[5]

$$\begin{aligned} p(y_f|D) &\propto \int p(y_f|\Sigma, D)p(\Sigma|D)\,\mathrm{d}\Sigma \\ &\propto |S + (y_f' - \bar{y}')'(y_f' - \bar{y}')/(1 + 1/n)|^{-n/2} \\ &\propto \{1 + (y_f - \bar{y})'S^{-1}(y_f - \bar{y})/(1 + 1/n)\}^{-(\nu_2+2)/2} \end{aligned} \tag{30}$$

where $p(\Sigma|D)$ is given in (29) and $\nu_2 = n - 2$. From the third line of (30), it is seen that $y_f' = (y_{1f}, y_{2f})$ has a bivariate Student-t pdf with

$$\mathrm{E}(y_f|D) = \bar{y} \qquad \nu_2 > 1 \tag{31}$$

and

$$\mathrm{V}(y_f|D) = (1 + 1/n)S/(\nu_2 - 2) \qquad \nu_2 > 2 \tag{32}$$

Further, from properties of the bivariate Student-t pdf, the marginal predictive pdfs for y_{1f} and for y_{2f} are univariate Student-t pdfs $p(y_{jf}|D) \propto [1 + (y_{jf} - \bar{y}_j)^2/s_{jj}(1 + 1/n)]^{-(\nu_2+1)/2}$ for $j = 1, 2$. Note that the degrees of freedom for this marginal pdf is $\nu_2 = n - 2$; there is a loss of one degree of freedom associated with integrating out σ_{12} in (30). Finally, from (30), we can write

$$\begin{aligned} p(y_f|D) \propto \{1 &+ (y_{1f} - \hat{y}_{1f})^2/s_{1\cdot2}^2(1 + 1/n) \\ &+ (y_{2f} - \bar{y}_2)^2/s_{22}(1 + 1/n)\}^{-(\nu_2+2)/2} \end{aligned}$$

where $\hat{y}_{1f} = \bar{y}_1 + \hat{\beta}(y_{2f} - \bar{y}_2)$, $\hat{\beta} = s_{12}/s_{22}$, $s_{1\cdot2}^2 = (1 - r_{12}^2)s_{11}$, and $r_{12}^2 = s_{12}^2/s_{11}s_{22}$, and the conditional predictive pdf for y_{1f} given y_{2f}

$$p(y_{1f}|y_{2f}, D) \propto \{1 + (y_{1f} - \hat{y}_{1f})^2 a^2\}^{-(\nu_1+1)/2} \tag{33}$$

where $\nu_1 = n - 1$ and $a^2 = s_{1\cdot2}^2(1 + 1/n)[1 + (y_{2f} - \bar{y}_2)^2/s_{22}(1 + 1/n)]$. From (33), the conditional moments of y_{1f} given y_{2f} and D are

$$E(y_{1f}|y_{2f}, D) = \hat{y}_{1f} = \bar{y}_1 + \hat{\beta}(y_{2f} - \bar{y}_2) \qquad \nu_1 > 1 \tag{34}$$

and

$$V(y_{1f}|y_{2f}, D) = a^2/(\nu_1 - 2) = \frac{s_{1\cdot2}^2}{(\nu_1 - 2)}[1 + 1/n + (y_{2f} - \bar{y}_2)^2/s_{22}] \qquad \nu_1 > 2 \tag{35}$$

where s_{ij}, $i, j = 1, 2$ are elements of $S = (Y - i\bar{y}')'(Y - i\bar{y}')$ and $s_{1\cdot2}^2 = s_{11} - s_{12}^2/s_{22}$. The conditional variance in (35) can be compared with the unconditional variance of y_{1f}, $V(y_{1f}|D) = (1 + 1/n)s_{11}/(\nu_2 - 2)$, obtained from (32).

3.2 Multiple regression case

Here we consider p variables rather than just two and obtain their marginal and conditional predictive pdfs. Let the observations satisfy

$$(y_{1i}, y_{2i} \ldots y_{pi}) = (\mu_1, \mu_2 \ldots \mu_p) + (u_{1i}, u_{2i} \ldots u_{pi}) \quad i = 1, 2, \ldots, n \tag{36}$$

where the vectors $(y_{1i}, y_{2i} \ldots y_{pi})$ have been independently drawn from a multivariate normal distribution with mean vector $\mu' = (\mu_1, \mu_2, \ldots, \mu_p)$ and $p \times p$ positive definite symmetric covariance matrix Σ. Then in matrix terms, $Y = i\mu' + U$ where Y is $n \times p$, i is $n \times 1$, μ' is $1 \times p$ and U is $n \times p$, and the likelihood function is

$$p(Y|\mu, \Sigma) \propto |\Sigma|^{-n/2}\exp\{-\tfrac{1}{2}\text{tr}\,(Y - i\mu')'(Y - i\mu')\Sigma^{-1}\} \tag{37}$$

Here, as in the previous section, we shall employ a Jeffreys' diffuse prior,

$$p(\mu, \Sigma) \propto |\Sigma|^{-(p+1)/2} \tag{38}$$

and the posterior pdf is

$$\begin{aligned} p(\mu, \Sigma|D) &\propto |\Sigma|^{-(p+n+1)/2}\exp\{-\tfrac{1}{2}\text{tr}\,(Y - i\mu')'(Y - i\mu')\Sigma^{-1}\} \\ &\propto |\Sigma|^{-(p+n+1)/2}\exp\{-\tfrac{1}{2}\text{tr}\,[S + n(\mu' - \bar{y}')'(\mu' - \bar{y}')]\Sigma^{-1}\} \end{aligned} \tag{39}$$

where D denotes the data and prior assumptions, $\bar{y}' = (\bar{y}_1, \bar{y}_2, \ldots, \bar{y}_p)$, a vector of sample means and

$$S = (Y - i\bar{y}')'(Y - i\bar{y}') \tag{40}$$

a $p \times p$ matrix proportional to the sample covariance matrix.

From (39), the conditional posterior pdf for μ given Σ is multivariate normal with mean $\bar{y}$ and covariance matrix Σ/n, i.e. MVN($\bar{y}$, Σ/n). On integrating (39) with respect to the p elements of μ, the marginal posterior pdf of Σ is in the following inverted Wishart form,

$$p(\Sigma|D) \propto |\Sigma|^{-\nu/2}\exp\{-\tfrac{1}{2} \text{ tr } S\Sigma^{-1}\} \tag{41}$$

with $\nu = n + p$.

Now let a future vector, $y'_f = (y_{1f}, y_{2f}, \ldots, y_{pf})$, independent of the sample observations be normal with mean μ' and covariance matrix Σ, that is

$$y'_f = \mu' + u'_f \tag{42}$$

with $E(y'_f|\mu') = \mu'$ and $V(y'_f|\mu, \Sigma) = \Sigma$. Given Σ and D, y'_f has a normal distribution with mean $\bar{y}$ and covariance matrix, $(1 + 1/n)\Sigma$, that is

$$p(y_f|\Sigma, D) \propto |\Sigma|^{-1/2}\exp\{-\tfrac{1}{2} \text{ tr } (y'_f - \bar{y}')'(y'_f - \bar{y}')\Sigma^{-1}/(1 + 1/n)\}. \tag{43}$$

Then the marginal predictive pdf for y_f is

$$\begin{aligned} p(y_f|D) &\propto \int p(y_f|\Sigma, D)p(\Sigma|D)\, d\Sigma \\ &\propto |S + (y'_f - \bar{y}')'(y'_f - \bar{y}')/(1 + 1/n)|^{-n/2} \\ &\propto \{1 + (y_f - \bar{y})'S^{-1}(y_f - y)/(1 + 1/n)\}^{-(\nu_p+p)/2} \end{aligned} \tag{44}$$

where $\nu_p = n - p$. From (44), it is seen that the predictive pdf for y_f is in the multivariate Student-t form with ν_p degrees of freedom. From properties of this distribution,

$$E(y_f|D) = \bar{y} \qquad \nu_p > 1 \tag{45}$$

and

$$V(y_f|D) = S(1 + 1/n)/(\nu_p - 2) \qquad \nu_p > 2 \tag{46}$$

Further, individual elements of y_f have a univariate Student-t marginal pdf; that is, $(y_{jf} - \bar{y}_j)/[s_{jj}(1 + 1/n)/\nu_p]^{1/2}$ has a univariate Student-t pdf with ν_p degrees of freedom.

From (44), the conditional predictive pdf for y_{1f} given $y'_{0f} = (y_{2f}, y_{3f}, \ldots, y_{pf})$ is given by

$$\begin{aligned} p(y_{1f}|y_{0f}, D) \propto \{1 + (y_{1f} - \hat{y}_{1f})^2/[1 \\ + 1/n + (y_{0f} - \bar{y}_0)'S_{00}^{-1}(y_{0f} - \bar{y}_0)s^2_{1\cdot 0}]\}^{-(\nu_1+1)/2} \end{aligned} \tag{47}$$

where $\nu_1 = n - 1$, $\bar{y}'_0 = (\bar{y}_2, \bar{y}_3, \ldots, \bar{y}_p)$,

$$\begin{aligned} \hat{y}_{1f} &= \bar{y}_1 + \hat{\beta}'_{1\cdot 0}(y_{0f} - \bar{y}_0) \\ \hat{\beta}_{1\cdot 0} &= S_{00}^{-1}s_{12} \\ s^2_{1\cdot 0} &= s_{11} - s'_{12}S_{00}^{-1}s_{12} \end{aligned}$$

with s_{11}, s_{12} and S_{00} submatrices of S in (40), that is

$$\underset{p \times p}{S} = \begin{bmatrix} \overset{1}{s_{11}} & \overset{p-1}{s'_{12}} \\ s_{12} & S_{00} \end{bmatrix} \begin{matrix} 1 \\ p-1 \end{matrix}$$

From the conditional pdf in (47), we have

$$E(y_{1f}|y_{0f}, D) = \hat{y}_{1f} = \bar{y}_1 + \hat{\beta}'_{1 \cdot 0}(y_{0f} - \bar{y}_0) \qquad (48)$$

and

$$V(y_{1f}|y_{0f}, D) = [1 + 1/n + (y_{0f} - \bar{y}_0)'S_{00}^{-1}(y_{0f} - \bar{y}_0)]s_{1 \cdot 0}^2/(\nu_1 - 2). \quad (49)$$

Since $s_{1 \cdot 0}^2 = (1 + R^2)s_{11}$, where R is the multiple correlation coefficient, a direct comparison of the conditional variance of y_{1f} in (49) with the unconditional variance in (46), namely $s_{11}(1 + 1/n)/(\nu_p - 2)$, with $\nu_p = n - p$, can be made.

In closing this sub-section, we note that from (44), the conditional predictive pdf of a $p_1 \times 1$ sub-vector of y_f, say y_{1f}, given the remaining elements of y_f, say y_{2f} a $p_2 \times 1$ vector with $p_1 + p_2 = p$, can be obtained by using standard properties of the multivariate Student-t pdf – see e.g. Zellner (1971, pp. 383ff). The result is a p_1-dimensional multivariate Student-t pdf. Also, using the results in Zellner and Chetty (1965), Geisser (1965), and Zellner (1971), the marginal predictive pdf for a $q \times p$ matrix of future values, Y_f, can be derived and is in the matrix Student-t form. Then, too, instead of using a diffuse prior pdf, these problems can be analysed employing a natural conjugate prior pdf in the multivariate normal form for μ given Σ with a marginal prior pdf for Σ in the inverted Wishart form.

3.3 General predictive results for regression models

Above predictive results for independent and identically normally distributed observations were obtained. Since often this distributional assumption is inappropriate, for example independent variables may be autocorrelated and/or non-normal, we now derive the moments of general predictive pdfs. To compute these moments, a posterior pdf for the regression model's parameters and a predictive pdf for the independent variables are required. These pdfs can be derived using either diffuse or informative prior pdfs and appropriate data distributional assumptions. As will be seen, the moments of the unconditional predictive pdf for the dependent variable can be expressed in terms of moments of the posterior pdf for regression parameters and of the predictive pdf for the independent variables.

3.3.1 Simple regression model

Let a simple regression model be given by $y_i = \mu + \beta(x_i - \bar{x}) + \varepsilon_i$, $i = 1, 2,$

. . ., n, where y_i is the dependent variable, μ and β are regression parameters with unknown values, x_i is a scalar independent variable,

$$\bar{x} = \sum_{i=1}^{n} x_i/n,$$

and the ε_i's are error terms assumed independently drawn from a distribution with zero mean and variance σ^2. Given the sample observations (y_i, x_i), $i = 1, 2, \ldots, n$, let a future as yet unobserved value of the dependent variable, say $y \equiv y_f$ be generated by

$$\begin{aligned} y &= \mu + \beta(x - \bar{x}) + \varepsilon \\ &= \mu + \beta z + \varepsilon \end{aligned} \tag{50}$$

where $x \equiv x_f$, $z \equiv x - \bar{x}$ and $\varepsilon \equiv \varepsilon_f$ is assumed drawn independently from the same distribution from which the ε_i's were drawn. In (50), y, z and ε are random variables with (μ, β), z and ε mutually independent.

To compute Ey, we assume that a joint pdf for μ, β and z of the form $p(\mu, \beta|D_1)p(z|D_2)$ is available, where $p(\mu, \beta|D_1)$ is a posterior pdf for μ and β based on sample and prior information denoted by D_1 and $p(z|D_2)$ is a predictive pdf for z based on sample and prior information denoted by D_2. Under these assumptions, the predictive mean of y in (50) is given by:

$$\mathrm{E}y = \bar{\mu} + \bar{\beta}\bar{z} \tag{51}$$

where $\bar{\mu} = \mathrm{E}\mu$ and $\bar{\beta} = \mathrm{E}\beta$ are posterior means, $\bar{z} = \mathrm{E}z$ is the predictive mean of z and $\mathrm{E}\varepsilon = 0$ has been used.

From (50) and (51), we have,

$$\begin{aligned} e \equiv y - \mathrm{E}y &= \mu - \bar{\mu} + \beta z - \bar{\beta}\bar{z} + \varepsilon \\ &= \mu - \bar{\mu} + (\beta - \bar{\beta})\bar{z} + (z - \bar{z})\bar{\beta} + (\beta - \bar{\beta})(z - \bar{z}) + \varepsilon. \end{aligned} \tag{52}$$

From the second line of (52), it is seen that e is a linear combination of $\mu - \bar{\mu}$, $\beta - \bar{\beta}$, $z - \bar{z}$, and ε plus a non-linear term, $(\beta - \bar{\beta})(z - \bar{z})$. In prediction conditional upon $z = \bar{z}$, $e = \mu - \bar{\mu} + (\beta - \bar{\beta})\bar{z} + \varepsilon$, a linear form in $\mu - \bar{\mu}$ $\beta - \bar{\beta}$ and ε. If in this last expression, $\bar{z} = \mathrm{E}x - \bar{x} = 0$ or $\mathrm{E}x = \bar{x}$, then $e = \mu - \bar{\mu} + \varepsilon$, the case of prediction with a non-stochastic x set equal to $\bar{x}$, the sample mean of the x_i's.

The unconditional predictive variance of y is

$$\mathrm{E}e^2 = \sigma_\mu^2 + \bar{\beta}^2\sigma_z^2 + \bar{z}^2\sigma_\beta^2 + 2\bar{z}\sigma_{\mu\beta} + \sigma_\beta^2\sigma_z^2 + \bar{\sigma}^2 \tag{53}$$

where $\sigma_\mu^2 = \mathrm{E}(\mu - \bar{\mu})^2$, $\sigma_\beta^2 = \mathrm{E}(\beta - \bar{\beta})^2$ and $\sigma_{\mu\beta} = \mathrm{E}(\mu - \bar{\mu})(\beta - \bar{\beta})$ are posterior moments, $\sigma_z^2 = \mathrm{E}(z - \bar{z})^2$ is the variance of the predictive pdf for z, and $\bar{\sigma}^2$ is the posterior mean of $\sigma^2 = \mathrm{E}\varepsilon^2$.

In connection with (53), write

$$e = w + \varepsilon \tag{54}$$

where $w = \mu - \bar{\mu} + (\beta - \bar{\beta})\bar{z} + (z - \bar{z})\bar{\beta} + (\beta - \bar{\beta})(z - \bar{z})$ from (52). Then $\mathrm{E}e^2 = \mathrm{E}w^2 + \mathrm{E}\varepsilon^2$ given that w and ε are independent. On evaluating $\mathrm{E}w^2$, the result is as shown above. We shall refer to w as the *signal component* of e and $\mathrm{E}w^2/\mathrm{E}\varepsilon^2$ as the signal to noise variance ratio. Also, note that if z is fixed at $\bar{z}$, $\sigma_z^2 = 0$ and $\mathrm{E}e^2 = \sigma_\mu^2 + \bar{z}^2\sigma_\beta^2 + 2\bar{z}\sigma_{\mu\beta} + \bar{\sigma}^2$, a result for conditional prediction given $z = \bar{z}$. If in this conditional result $\bar{z} = 0$, then $\mathrm{E}e^2 = \sigma_\mu^2 + \bar{\sigma}^2$ since $z = \bar{z} = 0$ leads to (50) being $y = \mu + \varepsilon$. Finally, from (53) if z is random with $\bar{z} = 0$, then $\mathrm{E}e^2 = \sigma_\mu^2 + \bar{\beta}^2\sigma_z^2 + \sigma_\beta^2\sigma_z^2 + \bar{\sigma}^2$.

The third central moment of y using (54) is

$$\mathrm{E}e^3 = \mathrm{E}(w + \varepsilon)^3 = \mathrm{E}w^3 + \mathrm{E}\varepsilon^3.$$

On evaluating $\mathrm{E}w^3$ under the assumption that the third-order moments of $\mu - \bar{\mu}$, $\beta - \bar{\beta}$ and $z - \bar{z}$ are all zero, the result is:

$$\mathrm{E}e^3 = 6\bar{\beta}\sigma_z^2[\bar{z}\sigma_\beta^2 + \sigma_{\mu\beta}] + \mathrm{E}\varepsilon^3. \tag{55}$$

Thus generally the pdf for $e = y - \mathrm{E}y$ will be skewed. If $\mathrm{E}\varepsilon^3 = 0$ and $\bar{\beta} > 0$, the pdf will exhibit positive (negative) skewness if $\bar{z}\sigma_\beta^2 + \sigma_{\mu\beta} > 0$ (< 0) and no skewness if $\bar{z}\sigma_\beta^2 + \sigma_{\mu\beta} = 0$, a condition that is satisfied, for example, if $\bar{z} = 0$ and $\sigma_{\mu\beta} = 0$. Further, if $\mathrm{E}\varepsilon^3 = 0$ and z is fixed, then $\sigma_z^2 = 0$ and $\mathrm{E}e^3 = 0$, that is the third central moment of y is zero.

The fourth central moment of y is

$$\begin{aligned}\mathrm{E}e^4 = {} & \mathrm{E}w_1^4 + 6\mathrm{E}w_1^2\mathrm{E}w_2^2 + \mathrm{E}w_2^4 + \mathrm{E}(\beta - \bar{\beta})^4\mathrm{E}(z - \bar{z})^4 \\ & + 6[\sigma_z^2\mathrm{E}(\mu - \bar{\mu})^2(\beta - \bar{\beta})^2 + \bar{\beta}^2\sigma_\beta^2\mathrm{E}(z - \bar{z})^4 + \bar{\sigma}^2\sigma_\beta^2\sigma_z^2]\end{aligned} \tag{56}$$

with $w_1 = \mu - \bar{\mu} + (\beta - \bar{\beta})\bar{z}$ and $w_2 = (z - \bar{z})\bar{\beta} + \varepsilon$. Note that w_1 and w_2 are independent. In the derivation, all third-order moments of $\mu - \bar{\mu}$, $\beta - \bar{\beta}$ and $z - \bar{z}$ have been assumed equal to zero. More insight into the kurtosis of the distribution of e can be gained by using $e = w + \varepsilon$ from (54). Then $\mathrm{E}e^4 = \mathrm{E}w^4 + 6\mathrm{E}w^2\mathrm{E}\varepsilon^2 + \mathrm{E}\varepsilon^4$, $\mathrm{E}e^2 = \mathrm{E}w^2 + \mathrm{E}\varepsilon^2$ and

$$\gamma = \frac{\mathrm{E}e^4}{(\mathrm{E}e^2)^2} = 3[1 + (\gamma_w\phi + \gamma_\varepsilon/\phi)/6]/[1 + (\phi + 1/\phi)/2] \tag{57}$$

where $\gamma_w = \mathrm{E}w^4/(\mathrm{E}w^2)^2$, $\gamma_\varepsilon = \mathrm{E}\varepsilon^4/(\mathrm{E}\varepsilon^2)^2$, and $\phi = \mathrm{E}w^2/\mathrm{E}\varepsilon^2$, the 'signal-noise variance ratio.' In (57), if $\gamma_w = \gamma_\varepsilon = 3$ and $\phi = 1$, then $\gamma = 3$. A more general condition for $\gamma = 3$ is $(\gamma_w\phi + \gamma_\varepsilon/\phi)/6 = (\phi + 1/\phi)/2$ or $\phi^2 = -(\gamma_\varepsilon - 3)/(\gamma_w - 3) > 0$.

Given that the first four moments of y are available, a Pearson curve can be employed to approximate its distribution. Alternatively, given that the predictive pdf for y is given by

$$p(y|D) = \int p(y|z, \theta)p(\theta|D_1)p(z|D_2)\, \mathrm{d}\theta\, \mathrm{d}z \tag{58}$$

where $\theta' = (\mu, \beta, \sigma)$, $p(\theta|D_1)$ is the posterior pdf for θ given sample and prior information D_1, $p(z|D_2)$ is the predictive pdf for z given sample and prior information D_2 and $D = (D_1, D_2)$, $p(y|D)$ and its moments can be calculated using numerical integration techniques. This approach will be convenient when it is difficult to evaluate posterior moments of θ and predictive moments of z analytically.

3.3.2 Multiple regression model

Let our model for a future observation, y be:

$$y = \mu + z'\beta + \varepsilon \tag{59}$$

with $z = x - \bar{x}$, where $\bar{x}$ is a vector of sample means of the independent variables and ε is a future error term. Then the predictive mean of y is

$$\mathrm{E}y = \bar{\mu} + \bar{z}'\bar{\beta} \tag{60}$$

where $\bar{\mu} = \mathrm{E}\mu$ and $\bar{\beta} = \mathrm{E}\beta$ are posterior means and $\bar{z} = \mathrm{E}z = \mathrm{Ex} - \bar{\mathrm{x}}$ is the mean of the predictive pdf for z.

Then

$$\begin{aligned} e = y - \mathrm{E}y &= \mu - \bar{\mu} + z'\beta - \bar{z}'\bar{\beta} + \varepsilon \\ &= \mu - \bar{\mu} + (\beta - \bar{\beta})'\bar{z} + (z - \bar{z})'\bar{\beta} + (z - \bar{z})'(\beta - \bar{\beta}) + \varepsilon. \end{aligned} \tag{61}$$

Further, assume ε, z and (μ, β) are mutually independent. If we write

$$e = \ell'\delta + (z - \bar{z})'(\beta - \bar{\beta}) + \varepsilon \tag{62}$$

where $\ell' = (1, \bar{z}', \bar{\beta}')$ and $\delta' = \{(\mu - \bar{\mu}), (\beta - \bar{\beta}), (z - \bar{z})\}$, then with $\mathrm{E}\varepsilon^2 = \bar{\sigma}^2$, the posterior mean of σ^2,

$$\mathrm{E}e^2 = \ell'\mathrm{E}\delta\delta'\ell + \mathrm{E}(z - \bar{z})'(\beta - \bar{\beta})(\beta - \bar{\beta})'(z - \bar{z}) + \bar{\sigma}^2$$

since $2\mathrm{E}\ell'\delta(z - \bar{z})'(\beta - \bar{\beta}) = 0$, or

$$\mathrm{E}e^2 = \ell_1'V_1\ell_1 + \bar{\beta}'V_z\bar{\beta} + \mathrm{tr}\ V_\beta V_z + \bar{\sigma}^2 \tag{63}$$

where $\ell_1' = (1\ \bar{z}')$, V_1 is the posterior covariance matrix of (μ, β), V_z is the predictive covariance matrix of z and V_β is the posterior covariance matrix of β. If μ and β are uncorrelated, then (63) becomes

$$\mathrm{E}e^2 = \sigma_\mu^2 + \bar{z}'V_\beta\bar{z} + \bar{\beta}'V_z\bar{\beta} + \mathrm{tr}\ V_\beta V_z + \bar{\sigma}^2 \tag{64}$$

If z is fixed at $\bar{z}$, $V_z = 0$ and (64) becomes $\mathrm{E}e^2 + \sigma_\mu^2 + \bar{z}'V_\beta\bar{z} + \bar{\sigma}^2$, the result for conditional prediction when $\mathrm{E}(\mu - \bar{\mu})(\beta - \bar{\beta}) = 0$.

If in (62), we write $e = w + \varepsilon$, where $w = \ell'\delta + (z - \bar{z})'(\beta - \bar{\beta})$, then on evaluation $\mathrm{E}e^3 = \mathrm{E}(w + \varepsilon)^3$ assuming all third-order moments of the elements of $\mu - \bar{\mu}$, $\beta - \bar{\beta}$, and $z - \bar{z}$ are zero, the result is:

$$\mathrm{E}e^3 = 6[\bar{z}'V_\beta V_z\bar{\beta} + (\mu - \bar{\mu})(\beta - \bar{\beta})'V_z\bar{\beta}] + \mathrm{E}\varepsilon^3. \tag{65}$$

If in (65), $\mathrm{E}\varepsilon^3 = 0$ and $V_z = 0$, appropriate if z is fixed, then $\mathrm{E}e^3 = 0$. Also if in (65), $\mathrm{E}\varepsilon^3 = 0$, $\bar{z} = 0$ and $\mathrm{E}(\mu - \bar{\mu})(\beta - \bar{\beta}) = 0$, then $\mathrm{E}e^3 = 0$.

From $e = w + \varepsilon$, where $w = \ell'\delta + (z - \bar{z})'(\beta - \bar{\beta})$, we have $\mathrm{E}e^2 = \mathrm{E}w^2 + \mathrm{E}\varepsilon^2$ and $\mathrm{E}(w + \varepsilon)^4 = \mathrm{E}w^4 + 6\mathrm{E}w^2\mathrm{E}\varepsilon^2 + \mathrm{E}\varepsilon^4$ and thus $\mathrm{E}e^4/(\mathrm{E}e^2)$ can be brought into the form of (57) with $\phi = \mathrm{E}w^2/\mathrm{E}\varepsilon^2$. Finally, under our assumptions about the third-order moments,

$$\begin{aligned} \mathrm{E}e^4 &= \mathrm{E}(w + \varepsilon)^4 \\ &= \mathrm{E}w^4 + 6\mathrm{E}w^2\mathrm{E}\varepsilon^2 + \mathrm{E}\varepsilon^4 \end{aligned} \tag{66}$$

which can be evaluated further to yield a more explicit expression for the fourth central moment of y.

As noted above, the first four moments of e can be employed to fit a Pearson Curve to approximate the pdf for y. Alternatively, a numerical integration approach, mentioned in connection with (58) can be applied here to yield the predictive pdf for y and its moments. That is, $p(y|D) = \int p(y|z, \theta, D_1)p(\theta|z, D_1)p(z|D_2)\, \mathrm{d}\theta\, \mathrm{d}z$, where $\theta' = (\delta', \sigma)$, and the moments of $p(y|D)$ can be computed using numerical integration techniques given the forms of $p(y|z, \theta, D_1)$, $p(\theta|z, D_1)$, and $p(z|D_2)$.

4 Application of results

In this section we analyse monthly stock return data, January 1977–December 1979 ($n = 36$) relating to five US corporations: Westinghouse, General Electric, Standard Oil of Indiana, IBM and Sears. These data and a series of monthly value-weighted New York Stock Exchange market returns are utilized in our analyses. In Table 1 sample means and standard deviations of returns are presented.

The 'market model' of financial economics posits that the j'th corporation's return in month t, y_{jt}, is linearly related to the market return in month t, x_t, and a white noise error term, ε_{jt} that is assumed normally distributed. The x_t's, the market returns, are assumed independently drawn from a normal distribution with mean η and constant variance. Thus for each corporation, the following is the model for the observations, $t = 1, 2, \ldots, 36$,

$$x_t = \eta + v_t \tag{67}$$

$$y_{jt} = \alpha_j + \beta_j x_t + \varepsilon_{jt} \tag{68}$$

with v_t and ε_{jt} independent normal errors with zero means and variances σ_v^2 and $\sigma_{j\cdot x}^2$, respectively. In Table 2 the results of simple regressions of company stock returns on the market return are presented. With a diffuse prior pdf for the parameters, the least squares parameter estimates are posterior means of the regression intercepts and slope coefficients. The squared correlations range from 0.274 to 0.555 and can be interpreted as approximate posterior means of the corresponding population squared correlation coefficients. The reported Durbin-Watson statistics provide no evidence of serious serial correlation.

Table 1 *Sample mean returns and sample standard deviations of returns, Jan. 1977-Dec. 1979 (n = 36)*[a]

	Sample mean	Sample standard deviation
	(percent per month)	
Value Wtd. NYSE	.690	4.043
Westinghouse	1.153	8.534
General Electric	.260	4.810
Standard Oil (Ind.)	1.355	5.404
IBM	.252	4.987
Sears	−1.195	5.969

[a]Data are from the Monthly Stock Returns File of the Center for Research in Security Prices, Graduate School of Business, U. of Chicago. Monthly returns, r_t, are given by

$$r_t = (s_t p_t - p_{t-1} + d_t)/p_{t-1} \times 100$$

where p_t = closing price at end of month t, s_t = correction for stock splits during month t, d_t = dividends paid in month t. The value weighted New York Stock Exchange (NYSE) returns are weighted averages of monthly returns of all NYSE stocks with the weights being end-of-month values of outstanding shares.

Table 2 *Simple regressions of monthly company stock returns*[a] *on monthly value-weighted NYSE market return,*[a] *Jan. 1977-Dec. 1979 (n = 36)*[b]

Company	Intercept	Slope	R^2	D.W.
1 Westinghouse	.191	1.39	.436	2.08
	(1.10)	(.272)		
2 General Electric	−.352	.886	.555	2.14
	(.551)	(.136)		
3 Standard Oil	.872	.700	.274	1.73
	(.790)	(.195)		
4 IBM	−.283	.774	.394	1.83
	(.666)	(.165)		
5 Sears	−1.92	1.05	.508	2.48
	(.719)	(.178)		

[a]Percent per month.
[b]Figures in parentheses are conventional standard errors. Figures in the last column of the table are computed values of the Durbin-Watson statistic.

From (67) and (68), we have $x_t = \eta + v_t$ and $y_{jt} = \mu_j + u_{jt}$, where η and μ_j are means and the errors (v_t, u_{jt}) have a bivariate normal distribution with zero mean vector and 2 × 2 positive definite symmetric covariance matrix, Σ, and are independently distributed. Thus the analysis of Section 3.1 can be applied to yield the unconditional predictive moments of a future value of y_{jt}, denoted by y_{jf} which are presented in Table 3. From the results in Table 3, it is seen that unconditional predictive variances are much larger than the corresponding conditional predictive variances, the latter computed by setting the future value of x equal to its mean. In addition, the figures in Table 3 exhibit the difficulty in predicting stock returns for individual firms. For example, Westinghouse's point prediction is 1.153% per month with an unconditional predictive variance equal to 81.87 or an unconditional standard deviation equal to 9.05, approximately *nine* times the point prediction.

5 Concluding remarks

In this paper the importance of taking proper account of random independent regressors in making predictive inferences about a dependent variable has been emphasized. General and specific Bayesian procedures for treating this problem have been described. In an application, it was shown that unconditional predictive variances are about two times as large as conditional predictive variances and very large in an absolute sense. Thus, in general, conditional prediction provides spuriously precise predictive inferences and hence can be misleading. This conclusion applies not only to simple and multiple regression but also to prediction in structural econometric models with exogenous variables whose values must be predicted in order to predict values of the endogenous variables.

Table 3 *Predictive means and variances for stock returns of five corporations*[a]

Corporation	Mean, $Ey_{jf} = \bar{y}_j$	Predictive Variances Unconditional	Conditional[b]
	(% per month)		
Westinghouse	1.153	81.9	44.8
General Electric	0.2601	26.0	11.2
Standard Oil (Ind.)	1.355	32.8	23.1
IBM	.2519	28.0	16.4
Sears	−1.195	40.0	19.1

[a]Predictive moments were computed based on n = 36 monthly observations, January 1977-December 1979 and a diffuse prior for the parameters.
[b]Predictive variance conditional on the market return set equal to its sample mean.

While we have emphasized simple and multiple regression in this paper, the principles and procedures are applicable to multivariate regression and simultaneous equation models. For the multivariate regression problem, marginal and conditional predictive pdfs can be readily obtained from the joint predictive pdf for the dependent variable vector as noted in the text. Also, it is possible to obtain unconditional predictive pdfs for a matrix of future values of the dependent variables – see, e.g., Zellner (1971, Chapter 8) for analysis relating to this problem. With a diffuse prior or a natural conjugate prior, this predictive pdf will be in the matrix Student-t form. These and related problems will receive attention in future work.

Notes

1 See Aitchison and Dunsmore (1975) for additional consideration of Bayesian prediction analysis and extensive references to the literature.
2 Other prior distributions, including natural conjugate prior distributions, can also be incorporated in the analysis.
3 Note that if we write $y_i = \beta_0 + \beta x_i + \varepsilon_i$, then from $y_i = \mu + \beta(x - \bar{x}) + \varepsilon_i$, $\mu = \beta_0 + \beta\bar{x}$ and (16) can alternatively be expressed as $y_f = \beta_0 + \beta x_f + \varepsilon_f$.
4 See, e.g. Zellner (1971, Chapter 8) where this prior pdf is discussed and employed in analyses of multivariate regression problems. Note that (25) can be viewed as a special case of a regression system with just intercepts in each equation.
5 For details regarding the integration over the distinct elements of Σ, see e.g. Zellner (1971, p. 229). In going from the second to the third line of (29), the algebraic result $|I + bb'| = 1 + b'b$, where b is a column vector, has been employed.

References

Aitchison, J. and Dunsmore, I.R. (1975), *Statistical Prediction Analysis*, London: Cambridge University Press.
Box, G.E.P. and Tiao, G.C. (1973), *Bayesian Inference in Statistical Analysis*, Reading, Mass.: Addison-Wesley.
Feldstein, M.S. (1971), 'The Error of Forecast in Econometric Models when the Forecast-Period Exogenous Variables are Stochastic', *Econometrica*, 39, 53-60.
Geisser, S. (1965), 'Bayesian Estimation in Multivariate Analysis', *Annals of Mathematical Statistics*, 36, 150-9.
Leamer, E.E. (1978), *Specification Searches*, New York: Wiley.
Raiffa, H.A. and Schlaifer, R.S. (1961), *Applied Statistical Decision Theory*, Boston: Graduate School of Business Administration, Harvard University.
Zellner, A. (1971), *An Introduction to Bayesian Inference in Econometrics*, New York: Wiley.
Zellner, A. and Chetty, V.K. (1965), 'Prediction and Decision Problems in Regression Models from the Bayesian Point of View', *Journal of the American Statistical Association*, 60, 608-16.

Part IV
Applications

13 How accurate are the British national accounts?

Richard Stone

1 Introduction

In a recent paper (Stone (1984)) I gave the results of an attempt at balancing a simple version of the British national accounts for the years 1969 through 1979. By this I mean adjusting the entries so that the accounts balance without the introduction of residual errors, unidentified items and other balancing entries. The technique I used is the old one of adjusting conditioned observations by the method of least squares and involves the simple task of formulating a matrix of independent constraints and the more difficult task of estimating the elements in a variance matrix of the initial entries in the accounts. The idea of adjusting the national accounts in this way was proposed in Stone, Champernowne and Meade (1942) but for a variety of reasons, discussed in Stone (1975), was never put to practical use until the last few years. Recently Byron (1978) presented an alternative formulation which makes it possible to balance very large accounting matrices without incurring prohibitive costs; and more recently still, further work in this direction has been done by my friend and colleague F. van der Ploeg (Ploeg (1982)), to whom I am indebted for carrying out the calculations in the present paper.

In order to balance the accounts we need to know the relative but not the absolute errors of the entries. My aim in this paper is to see what can be said about their absolute accuracy both before and after the accounts have been balanced. I shall start by giving a summary of the adjustment procedure described in Stone (1984) and then suggest a means of measuring accuracy.

2 The adjustment procedure

Let x, of type $\nu \times 1$, denote a vector of true values of the unknowns, the entries in the accounts, which are subject to μ independent linear constraints given by

$$Gx = h \tag{1}$$

where G, the constraint matrix, is of type $\mu \times \nu$ and rank μ; and h, a vector of known constants, is of type $\mu \times 1$. Let x^* denote a vector of unbiased estimates of the elements of x; let V^*, of order ν and rank not less than μ, denote the variance matrix of the elements of x^*; and assume that any constraints satisfied by x^* are linearly independent of (1). In what follows I assume that the elements of x^* are estimated independently, so that in this example V^* is a diagonal matrix with the variances in the diagonal and no covariances.

The best linear unbiased estimator, x^{**} say, of x is given by

$$x^{**} = x^* - V^*G'(GV^*G')^{-1}(Gx^* - h) \tag{2}$$

and V^{**}, the variance matrix of x^{**}, is given by

$$V^{**} = V^* - V^*G'(GV^*G')^{-1}GV^*. \tag{3}$$

The elements of V^* are based on given assessments of the reliability of the elements of x^* and might be termed the *a priori* variance estimates. The elements of V^{**} depend on the constraints as well as on the elements of V^* and might be termed the *a posteriori* variance estimates. The adjustments to the initial estimates can be made with the help of V^* but, as can be seen from (2), they depend only on the relative and not on the absolute size of the elements of V^*.

3 Measuring the absolute accuracy of the entries

In Stone (1984) the initial estimates, the x^*, were derived from the 1980 *Blue Book* (UK, CSO (1950-)) complemented by the 1981 edition of *Economic Trends Annual Supplement* (UK, CSO (1975-)). Their variances, the elements of V^*, were based on the CSO's reliability ratings given in the 1968 version of *Sources and Methods* (UK, CSO (1968)) and calculated on the assumption that they are proportional to the square of the product of the reliability rating and the initial estimate.

Thus if the reliability rating of item j is denoted by r_j^* and if the initial estimate itself is denoted by x_j^*, then the margin of error, as I shall call it, of item j is given by their product. If this is interpreted as a standard error, s_j^* say, then

$$s_j^* = r_j^* x_j^* \tag{4}$$

and the corresponding variance, v_j^*, the jth element in the diagonal of V^*, is

$$v_j^* = s_j^{*2}.$$

If we were right in interpreting the s_j^* as standard errors, we should expect the adjustments to the initial estimates, the a_j^* say, where

$$a_j^* = x_j^{**} - x_j^*,$$

to be of the same order of magnitude as the corresponding s_j^*. In practice the a_j^* tend to be altogether smaller. Since the accounts can be balanced by making comparatively small adjustments, it seems likely that the margins of error and variances suggested by the CSO's ratings are too pessimistic and should be scaled down. The scaling method I shall use, which was first proposed in Stone, Champernowne and Meade (1942, Section IV), can be described as follows.

Since the initial entries, the x_j^*, are assumed to have been estimated independently, the sum of the squares of the standardized adjustments, that is

$$\sum_j (a_j^{*2} v_j^{*-1}),$$

is distributed as χ^2 with $(\nu - \mu - 1)$ degrees of freedom; and the break-even point, that is the value which is as likely as not to be exceeded by χ^2, is approximately equal to the number of degrees of freedom. Accordingly, the appropriate scaling factor, α say, is given by

$$\alpha = (\nu - \mu - 1)^{-1} \sum_j (a_j^{*2} v_j^{*-1}) \tag{5}$$

Thus we obtain the variance matrix we are looking for, $\tilde{V}^*$ say, as

$$\tilde{V}^* = \alpha V^* \tag{6}$$

and the corresponding standard error for entry j, $\tilde{s}_j^*$ say, as

$$\tilde{s}_j^* = \alpha^{1/2} s_j^*. \tag{7}$$

The scaled *a posteriori* variance matrix, $\tilde{V}^{**}$ say, can be obtained by substituting $\tilde{V}^*$ for V^* in (3); and the corresponding standard error for entry j, $\tilde{s}_j^{**}$ say, is

$$\tilde{s}_j^{**} = \tilde{v}_j^{**1/2}.$$

The results of the calculations described in this and the preceding section are exemplified numerically in the next three sections.

4 The accounts before and after adjustment

A version of the British national accounts before and after adjustment is shown in Table 1. The entries are arranged in pairs, the upper figure (in roman type) representing the initial estimate, the x_j^*, and the lower (in italics) representing the final, adjusted one, the x_j^{**}. I have chosen 1969 for my example because it is the year closest to that in which the CSO's reliability ratings were published.

Only fourteen of the accounts in Table 1 are accounts proper: the thirteen numbered accounts and the account marked D. The fifteenth, marked E, simply brings together in the row all the errors in the *Blue Book*, which disappear in the adjusted version. The only constraints in this system are accounting constraints; and so, since the system is closed and contains fourteen accounts, there are thirteen independent constraints. The initial totals are not independently measured but are obtained by adding up the entries, and so there are no arithmetic constraints requiring that components should sum to totals; and no entry is measured in more than one way, and so there are no single-value constraints requiring the reconciliation of alternative measurements.

Row and column 1 contain the consolidated production account of Britain, with incomings in the row and outgoings in the column. All the initial estimates in this account are measured directly but they do not balance without the inclusion of the residual error, in column 1 and row E, which in 1969 was −£350 million. The adjusted entries balance without error.

The second account is the consolidated production account of the rest of the world, with British imports in the row and, in the column, British exports and the rest of the world's balance of trade with Britain. In the *Blue Book*, imports and exports are measured directly but the balance of trade is a residual. As with other residuals, I have assigned to it a variance equal to the sum of the variances of the other items in the account.

Accounts 3 through 7 are the income and outlay accounts of the four domestic sectors and the rest of the world; and account D is a dummy account for dividends and interest transfers for which the *Blue Book* provides sectoral detail about either the recipient or the payer but not about both. For instance, the £3864 million in row 3 and column D represents the dividends and interest received by the personal sector from the other domestic sectors. In the case of the rest of the world, however, payments to each of the domestic sectors can be allocated to the appropriate recipients, and vice versa.

Accounts 8 through 12 are the capital accounts of the four domestic sectors and the rest of the world. Items 8.3, 9.4, 10.5 and 11.6 are the savings of the domestic sectors. Item 12.7 is the balance of payments, that is the saving placed at the disposal of Britain by the rest of the world; in 1969 this was negative, which means that in that year, according to the *Blue Book*, Britain lent £471 million to the rest of the world.

The *Blue Book* figures for saving by persons, companies and the rest of the world are the residuals of the income and outlay accounts of those sectors and I have treated them therefore as unmeasured items, like the balance of trade. But the savings of the two public sectors, items 10.5 and 11.6, I have treated as measured items since all the public sector entries are based on detailed accounting data and the concept of residual estimation seems out of place; consequently, items 10.5 and 11.6 were assigned the relatively small variances suggested by the CSO. Item 12.7 was not assigned a variance but was estimated simply from the accounting constraint governing account 7.

Finally, rows 13 and E contain net acquisitions of financial assets. In the

Blue Book these are divided into identified items, which are measured directly, and unidentified ones, which are obtained as residuals and not given a reliability rating. In principle each of the measured items (shown in row 13) should be assigned a variance based on the CSO's rating; and each of their unmeasured counterparts (shown in row E, columns 8 to 12) should be assigned a variance equal to the sum of the variances of the other entries in the relevant account. In practice only the acquisitions by the two private sectors, 13.8/E.8 and 13.9/E.9, were treated like this; the public sectors' acquisitions, both measured and unmeasured, were all assigned the same variance based on the CSO's ratings for the measured items. The final figures for the four domestic sectors in row 13, columns 8 to 11, are the sums of identified and unidentified items after adjustment. The rest of the world's acquisitions, 13.12/E.12, were estimated, on the same principle as the balance of payments, from the accounting constraint governing account 12.

To sum up. Given my assumptions, there are seven unmeasured entries in the accounts of Table 1: the balance of trade, 7.2; the saving of the two private sectors, 8.3 and 9.4; the balance of payments, 12.7; and the unidentified net acquisitions of financial assets by the two private sectors and the rest of the world, E.8, E.9 and E.12 respectively. Only five of these, namely 7.2, 8.3, 9.4, E.8 and E.9, enter into the adjustment procedure through the application of sum variances. I have used eleven constraints to balance accounts 1 to 6, D, and 8 to 11, and the remaining two to estimate 12.7 and 13.12 + E.12 so as to balance accounts 7 and 12.

5 Reliability ratings, variances and margins of error

The CSO distinguish three categories of reliability: A or 'good', B or 'fair' and C or 'poor'. The percentage margins of error in the three categories lie in the ranges < 3, 3-10 and > 10. My reading of the CSO's assessments suggests for the aggregates given in Table 1 the ratings set out in Table 2.

In order to use these ratings we must convert them into numbers. I have put A = 0.015, B = 0.065 and C = 0.150. These correspond to the r_j^* for measured items in (4) above. Thus for instance, the variance of the initial estimate of British imports, $x_{2.1}^*$, is

$$\begin{aligned} v_{2.1}^* &= (0.015)^2(9930)^2 \\ &= 22186. \end{aligned}$$

Similarly, the variance of the initial estimate of British exports, $x_{1.2}^*$, is

$$\begin{aligned} v_{1.2}^* &= (0.015)^2(10109)^2 \\ &= 22993. \end{aligned}$$

Therefore the variance of the initial estimate of the unmeasured balance of trade, $x_{7.2}^*$, is

Table 1 *A version of the British national accounts with the errors shown explicitly: initial and finally adjusted estimates for 1969 (£ million)*

		1	2	3	4	5	6	7	D	8	9	10	11	12	13	E	Totals
Production	1 Britain		10109	29233			7997			1297	4167	1414	2286				56503
			10117	*29286*			*7999*			*1316*	*4320*	*1414*	*2286*				*56738*
	2 Rest of the world	9930															9930
		9922															*9922*
Income and outlay	3 Persons	31290			35		3937	341	3864								39467
		31230			*35*		*3936*	*341*	*3864*								*39406*
	4 Companies	3815						1161	1619								6595
		3798						*1164*	*1619*								*6581*
	5 Public corporations	445						15	80								540
		445						*15*	*80*								*540*
	6 General government	7488		7420	1131	610		203	176								17028
		7487		*7422*	*1131*	*610*		*203*	*176*								*17029*
	7 Rest of the world		−179	416	458		554										1249
			−195	*415*	*458*		*554*										*1232*
	D Dividends and interest n.e.s.			761	3306	120	1552										5739
				761	*3306*	*120*	*1552*										*5739*

Capital transactions	8 Persons	812		1637									186				2635
		804		*1522*									*186*				*2512*
	9 Companies	1553			1665								606				3824
		1532			*1651*								*606*				*3789*
	10 Public corporations	1024				−190				6	14		50				904
		1024				*−190*				*6*	*14*		*50*				*904*
	11 General government	496					2988			577	48	0					4109
		496					*2988*			*577*	*48*	*0*					*4109*
	12 Rest of the world							−471					0				−471
								−491					*0*				*−491*
	13 Net acquisitions of fin. assets									1810	−1407	−514	975	−864			0
										613	*−593*	*−510*	*981*	*−491*			*0*
	E Errors	−350								−1055	1002	4	6	393			0
		0								*0*	*0*	*0*	*0*	*0*			*0*
	Totals	56503	9930	39467	6595	540	17028	1249	5739	2635	3824	904	4109	−471	0	0	
		56735	*9922*	*39406*	*6581*	*540*	*17029*	*1232*	*5739*	*2512*	*3789*	*904*	*4109*	*−491*	*0*	*0*	

Note. The noughts in cells 11.10 and 12.11 refer respectively to net capital transfers to general government from public corporations and net capital transfers abroad from general government. In 1969 these items happened to be zero but this is not always the case.

Table 2 *Reliability ratings of the initial estimates*

	1	2	3	4	5	6	7	D	8	9	10	11	12	13	E
1		A	A			A			C	C	A	A			
2	A														
3	A			C		A	B	B							
4	B						B	B							
5	A						A	A							
6	A		A	A	A		A	A							
7		Z	B	B		A									
D			B	B	A	A									
8	C		Z									A			
9	C			Z								A			
10	C				A				A	A		A			
11	C					A			A	A	A				
12							(Z)					A			
13									C	B	A	A	(C)		
E									Z	Z	A	A	(Z)		

Note. The five ratings denoted by Z refer to unmeasured items which were assigned variances equal to the sum of the variances of the other entries in accounts 2, 3, 4, 8 and 9 respectively. The ratings in brackets were not used in the adjustment procedure, the items to which they refer being estimated from the constraints governing accounts 7 and 12.

$$\begin{aligned} v^*_{7.2} &= 22186 + 22993 \\ &= 45179. \end{aligned}$$

The square roots of the above elements of V^* are

$$\begin{aligned} s^*_{2.1} &= 149 \\ s^*_{1.2} &= 152 \\ s^*_{7.2} &= 213. \end{aligned}$$

These figures seem very large in comparison with the adjustments, the a^*_j, which can be obtained from (2) and are

$$\begin{aligned} a^*_{2.1} &= \ -7.9 \\ a^*_{1.2} &= \ \ \ 8.2 \\ a^*_{7.2} &= -16.1. \end{aligned}$$

If we use α as in (5) to scale the elements of V^* and the s^*_j, we find, since $(\nu - \mu - 1) = (59 - 11 - 1) = 47$ and

$\sum_j (a_j^{*2} v_j^{*-1}) = 0.24895$, that in (6) and (7)

$$\alpha = 0.0052967$$

and

$$\alpha^{1/2} = 0.072779.$$

Thus

$$\tilde{s}^*_{2.1} = 10.8$$
$$\tilde{s}^*_{1.2} = 11.0$$
$$\tilde{s}^*_{7.2} = 15.5$$

which are of the same order or magnitude as the adjustments.

The corresponding unscaled variances of the final estimates, the elements of V^{**}, are obtained from (3) and work out at

$$v^{**}_{2.1} = 16489$$
$$v^{**}_{1.2} = 16874$$
$$v^{**}_{7.2} = 21553$$

and the scaled margins of error are

$$\tilde{s}^{**}_{2.1} = 9.3$$
$$\tilde{s}^{**}_{1.2} = 9.5$$
$$\tilde{s}^{**}_{7.2} = 10.7.$$

6 A summary of the results

The principal series which emerge from the calculations described in Sections 2 and 3 are brought together in Table 3. Column 1 shows my interpretation of the CSO's reliability ratings of the measured items and the implied ratings of the unmeasured ones, r^*. Columns 2 and 3 contain the unscaled variances of the initial and final estimates, v^* and v^{**}. Columns 4 to 8 contain the initial estimates, x^*, their scaled margins of error, $\tilde{s}^*$, the adjustments, a^*, the scaled margins of error of the final estimates, $\tilde{s}^{**}$, and the final estimates themselves, x^{**}.

Perhaps the most striking feature of Table 3 is the smallness of the adjustments needed to balance the accounts, as shown in column 6. This feature is not peculiar to 1969 but, *mutatis mutandis*, is found in every year of the period 1969-79 to which I applied the calculations. As a consequence, the margins of error based on the CSO's reliability ratings are greatly reduced. The reduction varies from year to year but the value of α for 1969, namely 0.0053, is close to the average for the eleven-year period. Thus on the whole it would appear that the measured items are quite accurate and that although fairly large errors occur in the unmeasured items, these are generally much reduced by adjustment.

7 Concluding remarks

According to the argument of this paper, the fact that the necessary adjustments are so small leads us to revise downwards substantially the initial margins of error ascribed to the estimates. In itself this might seem a desirable result were it not that it disagrees not only with the CSO ratings but also with the revisions given in successive *Blue Books*, which in many cases imply much larger margins of error than the $\bar{s}_j^*$ and $\bar{s}_j^{**}$ shown in Table 3.

As regards the CSO ratings, the discrepancy is not very disturbing since these ratings are pretty rough anyway and, furthermore, in the absence of better information I was forced to treat them in a very simplistic fashion in that I ascribed to each of them only a single value. With the A rating, which lies in the range of < 3 percentage points, this may not lead to excessive inaccuracy; but with the B rating, which spans a range of 3 to 10 per cent, and *a fortiori* with the C rating, which may indicate an error of anything above 10 per cent, a single value can be very misleading. The only remedy is to seek an improvement in the initial reliability measures.

For instance, we can see from the *Blue Book* revisions that while the figures for the more recent years continue for some time to be heavily dependent on provisional data, those for earlier years tend to settle down until they hardly change at all. It should not be impossible to give different ratings to the different 'vintages', grading them according to the degree of firmness they have reached. Also, the reliability of different items and their components depends on their source, and it would be interesting to regroup the entries by source and rate them accordingly. But these are refinements which only the compilers of the statistics can bring about.

As regards the discrepancy with the margins of error implied by the *Blue Book* revisions, some light might be thrown on the matter by adjusting the estimates for a single year as given in successive *Blue Books*. If, for instance, I had adjusted the 1969 figures as given in the 1970 as opposed to the 1980 *Blue Book*, the adjustments might have come out much larger. And by repeating the exercise with each of the intervening revisions we might find the successive adjusted values converging to something that might be considered the true values.

There are a number of other steps that could be taken to improve the accuracy of the method. Thus, I have not introduced covariances in the variance matrix, as should be done whenever the estimates are interdependent. For instance, the estimates of gross investment by the two private sectors taken together are given by the CSO a higher rating than either of their component parts. To some extent, therefore, the adjustments to the component parts should offset each other, but this would become apparent only through the introduction of covariances.

Table 3 *The British national accounts for 1969: inputs and outputs of the adjustment procedure*

	1	2	3	4	5	6	7	8
	r^*	v^*	v^{**}	x^*	$\tilde{s}^*$	$x^{**} - x^* = a^*$	$\tilde{s}^{**}$	x^{**}
Production a/c: Britain								
2.1 Imports	0.015	22186	16489	9930	10.8	−7.9	9.3	9922.1
3.1 Factor incomes paid to persons	0.015	220290	140780	31290	34.2	−60.4	27.3	31229.6
4.1 Factor incomes paid to companies	0.065	61492	42307	3815	18.0	−17.0	15.0	3798.0
5.1 Factor incomes paid to public corps.	0.015	45	30	445	0.5	0.0	0.4	445.0
6.1 Indirect taxes (net)	0.015	12616	9100	7488	8.2	−1.3	6.9	7486.7
8.1 Depreciation: persons	0.150	14835	14384	812	8.9	−7.5	8.7	804.5
9.1 Depreciation: companies	0.150	54266	49751	1553	17.0	−21.2	16.2	1531.8
10.1 Depreciation: public corps.	0.150	23593	506	1024	11.2	0.0	1.6	1024.0
11.1 Depreciation: general govt.	0.150	5535	4511	496	5.4	0.1	4.9	495.9
E.1 Residual error				−350		350.0		0.0
Production a/c: rest of the world								
1.2 Imports from Britain (British exports)	0.015	22993	16874	10109	11.0	8.2	9.5	10117.2
7.2 Balance of trade with Britain	1.188	45179	21553	−179	15.5	−16.1	10.7	−195.1
Income & outlay a/c: persons								
1.3 Consumers' expenditure	0.015	192280	131700	29233	31.9	52.7	26.4	29285.7
6.3 Income taxes & nat. insurance contributions	0.015	12388	8926	7420	8.1	2.1	6.9	7422.1
7.3 Current transfers abroad	0.065	731	730	416	2.0	−0.3	2.0	415.7
D.3 Dividends & interest n.e.s. paid out	0.065	2447	2391	761	3.6	0.0	3.6	761.0
8.3 Saving	0.430	495220	125910	1637	51.2	−115.3	25.8	1521.7

continued

Table 3 continued

		1	2	3	4	5	6	7	8
		r^*	v^*	v^{**}	x^*	$\tilde{s}^*$	$x^{**} - x^* = a^*$	$\tilde{s}^{**}$	x^{**}
Income & outlay a/c: companies									
3.4	Gifts to charities	0.150	28	28	35	0.4	0.0	0.4	35.0
6.4	Income taxes	0.015	288	286	1131	1.2	−0.1	1.2	1131.1
7.4	Profits (before tax) due abroad	0.065	886	882	458	2.2	−0.4	2.2	457.6
D.4	Dividends & interest n.e.s. paid out	0.065	46178	25397	3306	15.6	0.1	11.6	3306.1
9.4	Saving	0.213	125640	51390	1665	25.8	−14.3	16.5	1650.7
Income & outlay a/c: public corps.									
6.5	Income taxes	0.015	84	34	610	0.7	0.0	0.4	610.0
D.5	Dividends & interest n.e.s. paid out	0.015	3	3	120	0.1	0.0	0.1	120.0
10.5	Saving	0.015	8	8	−190	0.2	0.0	0.2	−190.0
Income & outlay a/c: general govt.									
1.6	Consumers' expenditure	0.015	14389	9815	7997	8.7	1.5	7.2	7998.5
3.6	Current transfers to persons	0.015	3488	3213	3937	4.3	−0.6	4.1	3936.4
7.6	Current transfers abroad	0.015	69	69	554	0.6	0.0	0.6	554.0
D.6	Dividends & interest n.e.s. paid out	0.015	542	533	1552	1.7	−0.1	1.7	1551.9
11.6	Saving	0.015	2009	1797	2988	3.3	0.2	3.1	2988.2
Income & outlay a/c: rest of the world									
3.7	Current transfers from abroad to persons	0.065	491	491	341	1.6	0.2	1.6	341.2
4.7	Property income from abroad to companies	0.065	5695	5516	1161	5.5	2.5	5.4	1163.5
5.7	Property income from abroad to public corps.	0.015	1	1	15	0.0	0.0	0.1	15.0
6.7	Current transfers from abroad to general govt.	0.015	9	9	203	0.2	0.0	0.2	203.0
12.7	Balance of payments	(0.065)	(937)	(937)	−471	(2.2)	−19.5	(2.2)	−490.5

Income & outlay a/c: dividends & interest n.e.s.								
3.D Dividends & interest n.e.s. paid to persons	0.065	63081	25902	3864	18.3	0.0	11.7	3864.0
4.D Property income n.e.s. paid to companies	0.065	11074	9879	1619	7.7	0.0	7.2	1619.0
5.D Property income n.e.s. paid to public corps.	0.015	1	1	80	0.1	0.0	0.1	80.0
6.D Dividends & interest n.e.s. paid to gen. govt.	0.015	7	7	176	0.2	0.0	0.2	176.0
Capital a/c: persons								
1.8 Gross investment	0.150	37850	34915	1297	14.2	19.2	13.6	1316.2
10.8 Capital transfers to public corps.	0.015	0	0	6	0.0	0.0	0.0	6.0
11.8 Taxes on capital	0.015	75	75	577	0.6	0.0	0.6	577.0
13.8 Identified net acquisitions of fin. assets	0.150	73712	67280	1810	19.8	−15.1	18.9	1794.9
E.8 Unidentified net acquisitions of fin. assets	0.747	621700	164130	−1055	57.4	−127.0	29.5	−1182.0
Capital a/c: companies								
1.9 Gross investment	0.150	390690	156680	4167	45.5	152.7	28.8	4319.7
10.9 Capital transfers to public corps.	0.015	0	0	14	0.0	0.0	0.0	14.0
11.9 Taxes on capital	0.015	1	1	48	0.1	0.0	0.1	48.0
13.9 Identified net acquisitions of fin. assets	0.065	8364	8271	−1407	6.7	−2.7	6.6	−1409.7
E.9 Unidentified net acquisitions of fin. assets	0.759	579040	132390	1002	55.4	−185.6	26.5	816.4
Capital a/c: public corps.								
1.10 Gross investment	0.015	450	441	1414	1.5	0.0	1.5	1414.0
11.10 Capital transfers to general govt.	0.015	0	0	0	0.0	0.0	0.0	0.0
13.10 Identified net acquisitions of fin. assets	0.015	59	59	−514	0.6	0.0	0.6	−514.0
E.10 Unidentified net acquistiions of fin. assets	0.015	0	0	4	0.0	0.0	0.0	4.0
Capital a/c: general govt.								
1.11 Gross investment	0.065	22079	5783	2286	10.8	0.3	5.5	2286.3
8.11 Capital transfers to persons	0.015	8	8	186	0.2	0.0	0.2	186.0
9.11 Capital transfers to companies	0.015	83	82	606	0.7	0.0	0.7	606.0
10.11 Capital transfers to public corps.	0.015	1	1	50	0.1	0.0	0.1	50.0
12.11 Capital transfers abroad	0.015	0	0	0	0.0	0.0	0.0	0.0
13.11 Identified net acquisitions of fin. assets	0.015	214	212	975	1.1	−0.1	1.1	974.9
E.11 Unidentified net acquisitions of fin. assets	0.015	0	0	6	0.0	0.0	0.0	6.0

continued

Table 3 continued

	1	2	3	4	5	6	7	8
	r^*	v^*	v^{**}	x^*	$\tilde{s}^*$	$x^{**} - x^* = a^*$	$\tilde{s}^{**}$	x^{**}
Capital a/c: rest of the world								
13.12 Identified net acquisitions of fin. assets	(0.150)	(16796)	(16796)	−864	(9.4)	373.5	(9.4)	−490.5
E.12 Unidentified net acquisitions of fin. assets	(0.150)	(3475)	(3475)	393	(4.3)	−393.0	(4.3)	0.0

Note: The figures in brackets indicate ratings, variances and margins of error that were not used in the adjustment procedure.

Further, there is no doubt that the errors in the initial estimates are not all random, and allowance should be made for this by adjusting several years simultaneously. I have not tried to do this though it would certainly produce a better specification of the errors in the series to which it were applicable.

And at the end of it all there still remains the problem of the unmeasured residual items. I am well aware that my use of sum variances is far from solving it.

But we are only at the beginning of applying adjustment methods to economic measurements and more experience is needed to build up reliable procedures.

References

Byron, R.P. (1978), 'The Estimation of Large Social Account Matrices', *Journal of the Royal Statistical Society* A 141, 359-67.

Ploeg, F. van der (1982), 'Reliability and the Adjustment of Sequences of Large Economic Accounting Matrices' (With Discussion), *Journal of the Royal Statistical Society* A 145, 169-94.

Stone, J.R.N. (1975), 'Direct and Indirect Constraints in the Adjustment of Observations', in *Nasjonalregnskap, Modeller og Analyse* (Essays in Honour of Odd Aukrust), Oslo: Statistik Sentralbyra, 42-61.

Stone, J.R.N. (1984), 'Balancing the National Accounts: The Adjustment of Initial Estimates – A Neglected Stage in Measurement', in *Demand, Trade and Equilibrium*, (Essays in Honour of Ivor F. Pearce), eds A. Ingham and A.M. Ulph, London: Macmillan, 191-212.

Stone, J.R.N., Champernowne, D.G. and Meade, J.E. (1942), 'The Precision of National Income Estimates', *Review of Economic Studies*, 9, 111-25.

United Kingdom, Central Statistical Office (1952-), *National Income and Expenditure*, London: Her Majesty's Stationery Office.

United Kingdom, Central Statistical Office (1968), *National Accounts Statistics: Sources and Methods*, London: Her Majesty's Stationery Office.

United Kingdom, Central Statistical Office (1975-), *Economic Trends, Annual Supplement*, London: Her Majesty's Stationery Office.

14 The pattern of financial asset holdings in Australia

*Kenneth W. Clements and John C. Taylor**

1 Introduction

An understanding of the determinants of holdings of financial assets is of crucial importance for a number of macroeconomic issues. The growth of non-bank financial intermediaries, the substitutability between money and other assets, the determination of interest rates and so on are all related to the pattern of financial asset holdings. The most popular approach to modelling holdings of financial assets is the multivariate stock adjustment model due to Brainard and Tobin (1968). This has the distinct advantage over single equation approaches that the balance sheet constraints are built in, so that the asset demands sum to total wealth. The Brainard-Tobin model does, however, suffer from the problem that there is a large number of unconstrained parameters to be estimated, with the result that many applications are characterized by statistical imprecision of a substantial proportion of the estimates.[1] The source of the problem is that interest rates are highly collinear, so that the data cannot determine such a large number of free parameters.

In this paper, we review and extend our recent work on alternative approaches to modelling holdings of financial assets by households. In Section 2 we present a new portfolio model in the Brainard-Tobin tradition, but which has fewer free parameters. The model is estimated and then used (i) to decompose changes in asset holdings into effects due to wealth and interest rate movements; (ii) to measure the welfare cost of interest rate movements; and (iii) in an out-of-sample forecasting exercise. Section 3 contains a Markov change analysis of the evolution of asset holdings, together with an application of a logistic model.

2 A system-wide portfolio model

In this section, we set out a simple portfolio allocation model which explains asset holdings in terms of wealth and interest rates. The model is applied to quarterly Australian data over the 1970s and then used for a number of applications. The results of this section are an extension of Clements and Taylor (1981) and Taylor and Clements (1981, 1983).

2.1 The model

We write A_i for the nominal value of (financial) asset i ($i = 1, \ldots, n$), $a_i = A_i/P$ for the real value of asset i (P = CPI),

$$W = \sum_{i=1}^{n} a_i$$

for total real wealth, $s_i = a_i/W$ for the ith portfolio share and r_i for the interest rate on asset i. We postulate that the demand for asset i takes the following form:

$$s_i = \alpha_i + \beta_i \log W + \sum_{j=1}^{n} \pi_{ij} r_j. \tag{1}$$

The first part of (1), $s_i = \alpha_i + \beta_i \log W$, is the Working (1943) – Leser (1963) Engel curve model from consumption theory. This model is very flexible and robust in consumer demand applications[2] and there is a presumption that it would probably also be satisfactory for asset demand. The coefficient β_i represents 100 times the effect on s_i of a 1 per cent increase in wealth, all interest rates remaining constant. Equation (1) is linear in the levels of interest rate variables, which is a specification corresponding closely to the widely used Cagan (1956) form of the demand for money equation. The coefficient π_{ij} gives the effect on s_i of a 1 percentage point increase in r_j (other things equal). Finally, (1) is very similar to Deaton and Muellbauer's (1980) consumer demand model AIDS (the almost ideal demand system), which possesses a number of desirable aggregation and flexibility properties.

Weath and interest rate elasticities for asset i are

$$\partial \log a_i/\partial \log W = 1 + \beta_i/s_i \qquad \partial \log a_i/\partial \log r_j = r_j\pi_{ij}/s_i.$$

Thus, an asset with positive (negative) β_i has a wealth elasticity larger (smaller) than unity.

The balance sheet restrictions can be derived by summing equation (1) over $i = 1, \ldots, n$. Since the asset shares sum to unity this gives

$$1 = \sum_i \alpha_i + \sum_i \beta_i \log W + \sum_i \sum_j \pi_{ij} r_j.$$

For this equality to hold for all values of the variables on the right, the coefficients must satisfy the following constraints:

$$\sum_i \alpha_i = 1 \qquad \sum_i \beta_i = 0 \qquad \sum_i \pi_{ij} = 0.$$

With these restrictions, equation (1) satisfies the balance sheet constraint

$$(\sum_i a_i = W \text{ or } \sum_i s_i = 1).$$

The interest rate coefficients of (1) are subject to homogeneity and Slutsky symmetry restrictions.[3] Homogeneity means that it is only changes in relative rates of return which matter. With specification (1), the homogeneity condition is formulated in terms of equal percentage point changes, not equi-proportionate changes. Homogeneity implies

$$\sum_j \pi_{ij} = 0 \qquad i = 1, \ldots, n.$$

Slutsky symmetry means that interest rate substitution effects are symmetric,

$$\pi_{ij} = \pi_{ji} \qquad i, j = 1, \ldots, n.$$

These restrictions are linear in the coefficients and can thus be easily tested and then imposed.

2.2 The data

We use quarterly Australian data from March 1970-June 1979 and distinguish $n = 4$ assets, (i) fixed deposits, (ii) total savings bank deposits, (iii) permanent building society deposits and (iv) special bonds plus Australian savings bonds (hereafter, bonds). Financial wealth is defined as the sum of the holdings of these assets. The data are given in Tables 1 and 2; see Taylor and Clements (1981) for full definitions and sources.

2.3 Results

Initial results suggest that savings bonds are qualitatively different to special bonds. We model this quality change by allowing the wealth coefficients to be different before and after the introduction of savings bonds. This allows the wealth elasticities to change with the introduction of the new asset. Our estimating equation becomes

$$s_i = \alpha_i + \beta_i D.\log W + \beta_i^*(1 - D).\log W + \sum_{j=1}^{n} \pi_{ij} r_j,$$

where $D = 1$ before the introduction of savings bonds in 1976, 0 afterwards.
The homogeneity – and symmetry-constrained FIML results are given in

Table 3.[4] As can be seen, all the wealth coefficients are significant except for fixed deposits, implying that these have an elasticity insignificantly different from unity. All own-interest rate coefficients are significantly positive, as they should be. With the exception of π_{24}, which is not significantly different from zero, all the off-diagonal π_{ij}'s are negative and significant. This indicates that the assets are pairwise substitutes, which is reasonable as they all play a similar store-of-value role. Building society deposits are a strong luxury (wealth elasticity greater than unity), while the other three assets are necessities.

In Taylor and Clements (1981) the results of Table 3 are compared with the unrestricted estimates. The homogeneity and symmetry restrictions are formally rejected by a likelihood ratio test; the observed value of the test statistic is $-2 \log \lambda = 19.1$, which is greater than the critical value of $\chi^2(6)$ at the 5 per cent level of 12.6. However, there is marked improvement in the signs and significance of the interest rate coefficients when the restrictions are imposed, so that there are good economic grounds for accepting the restricted model.

2.4 A decomposition of the change in the portfolio share

In this sub-section we use the model to decompose the change in each portfolio share into its components. In Table 4 we summarize the wealth, interest rates and residual components of the change in each of the shares, Δs_i.

Over the 1970s, one of the most dramatic changes in the Australian financial sector has been the growth of building societies at the expense of the savings bank. The share of wealth held in the form of savings bank deposits fell by 18 percentage points over this period (from 72 to 54 per cent; see Table 1), while building societies grew by 14 percentage points (from 9 to 23 per cent). The major reason for the growth of building societies is the increase in wealth. This accounts for 13.8 percentage points of the 14.2 total. This is consistent with the high wealth elasticity for this asset given in Table 3. The effect of increases in the interest rates on building society deposits is to increase the share by 3.4 points, but this is almost totally offset by increases in the other three rates; the effect of all interest rate changes is to *decrease* the share by 0.2 points. For a further analysis, see Clements and Taylor (1981).

2.5 The welfare cost of interest rate movements

In this sub-section we give a brief analysis of the effects of inflation on financial markets. The effect we focus on is that in an inflationary environment, not all interest rates are free to instantaneously adjust upwards in a uniform manner. Some rates adjust fully while others adjust only partially, so that there is a change in the structure of relative rates of interest. In this case, inflation can be said to distort relative interest rates, which can be expected to have the usual welfare cost as funds leave those assets whose relative rates have fallen and go to those yielding higher rates.

We obtain an upper estimate of the welfare cost of this distortion by attributing all observed changes in relative interest rates to inflation. The observed rates need to be compared with a base; for this base we use sample means, which amounts to assuming that on average over the 1970s the returns on these assets were not distorted by inflation. Writing r_i^* for the deviation of r_i from its sample mean (given in Table 2), the welfare cost can be expressed as (Harberger (1964)):

$$L = \frac{1}{2} \sum_{i=1}^{4} \sum_{j=1}^{4} r_i^* S_{ij} r_j^*,$$

where $S_{ij} = \partial a_i/\partial r_j$ is the effect on holdings of asset i of a change in r_j, real wealth remaining constant. From (1), $\partial a_i/\partial r_j = W\pi_{ij}$, so that the cost can be formulated as a fraction of wealth as

$$\frac{L}{W} = \frac{1}{2} \sum_{i=1}^{4} \sum_{j=1}^{4} r_i^* \pi_{ij} r_j^*.$$

It should be noted that demand homogeneity

$$(\sum_j \pi_{ij} = 0)$$

implies that the loss is zero when all rates increase by the same percentage point amount. We evaluate this expression with the data given in Table 2 and the estimates of π_{ij} given in Table 3.

The welfare cost and the rate of inflation are given in Table 5. As can be seen the losses are not trivial; the average loss is 1 per cent of GDP, which is quite substantial by the usual standards. Furthermore, there is a clear tendency for the loss to rise with inflation (in the mid-1970s in particular) but then decline. This latter decline coincides with a general move to greater interest rate flexibility.

It should, however, be repeated that these welfare costs represent upper bounds. In further work it may be worthwhile to extend this analysis to decompose changes in relative interest rates into effects due to (i) inflation and (ii) other factors. It would then be interesting to see by how much the welfare cost falls when the analysis is applied solely to the inflation component of changes in relative rates.

2.6 An out-of-sample test

We now use the model to predict asset holdings for the ten quarters following the estimation period. The data are given in Tables 6 and 7, while the forecasts are presented in Table 8. As can be seen, there is a tendency for the forecast errors to grow over time and, with the exception of fixed deposits and bonds, most are significant.[5] However, it should be stressed that this represents a stringent test of the model for the following reasons. (i) In contrast to standard practice, these forecasts are entirely 'hands off' in that no 'ad hoc' adjustments are made. (ii) There is more variability of relative interest rates over this period than over the estimation period. In part this is due to the deregulation of bank interest rates in December 1980.

3 Other approaches

We now use basically the same data as before to explore the applicability of two alternative approaches to modelling asset holdings. The first is the Markov chain model, which is based on and extends Anderson and Clements (1982). The second approach is an application of the logistic growth model to one of the assets; this is based on Broadbent, Clements and Johnson (1981).

3.1 A Markov chain analysis

Consider $1 of financial wealth which can be held in any of *n* assets. The Markov chain model is a stochastic process describing where this $1 will be held, with the probability of it being held in a certain asset depending only on where it was last held. Thus, the Markov model specifies that where the wealth was held before the previous period is irrelevant for the current placement of the $1.

Let $p_{ij} \geq 0$ be the probability that the $1 will be held in the form of asset *j* given that it was previously in asset *i*; we shall refer to p_{ij} as the (i, j)th transition probability. We assume that the $1 will continue to be held in the form of one of the assets, implying

$$\sum_{j=1}^{n} p_{ij} = 1 \quad (i = 1, \ldots, n).$$

Writing s_{i0} for the initial proportion of wealth held in i, $s_{i0}p_{ij}$ if this goes to asset *j* next period. The total proportion of wealth in *j* next period is the sum of this over *i*,

$$s_{j1} = \sum_i s_{i0} p_{ij},$$

which we write in vector form as

$$s_1' = s_0' P, \tag{2}$$

where $s_t = [s_{it}]$ is the tth asset distribution ($t = 0, 1$) and $P = [p_{ij}]$ is the transition matrix. For the subsequent period we have $s_2' = s_1'P = s_0'P^2$ (from (2)). Repeated application of this procedure yields $s_t' = s_0'P^t$. The (i, j)th element of P^t is thus the probability of moving \$1 from asset i to j in t steps (periods).

If P^t for some t consists exclusively of non-zero elements (implying that any transition can be made in at most t steps), then the Markov chain is said to be *regular*. In this case, it can be shown (Theil (1972, Chapter 5)) that no matter what initial distribution s_0, there is always convergence to the same steady-state distribution $\pi = [\pi_i]$ as $t \to \infty$,

$$\lim_{t \to \infty} s_0' P^t = \pi'.$$

Furthermore, the steady-state proportions π_i sum to one and are all positive. The vector π is the steady-state distribution in the sense that once it is attained, the system will stay there: $\pi' = \pi' P$. This does not mean that there is no movement of wealth between assets in the steady state, but that movements cancel each other out to keep the asset distribution constant.

We apply the Markov model to the Australian asset data with savings bank deposits disaggregated into (i) investment accounts and (ii) ordinary accounts. No information is available about the micro transitions from one asset to another, so that we need to apply regression-type techniques to (2) to estimate the p_{ij}'s; see Lee *et al.* (1970). The ML estimates of the transition probabilities are given in Table 9. Each row of the table gives the probability of moving in one quarter \$1 previously held in the asset at the left of the row (asset i) into each of the five assets (asset j). According to the first row, for \$1 previously in a fixed deposit, the probability of continuing to hold it in that form is 0.73. The probability of moving it into a savings bank investment account is zero; to a savings bank ordinary account 0.17; to a building society 0.10; and there is a zero probability of moving it into bonds. As the wealth must go somewhere, these probabilities sum to one.

For a given row, the diagonal probability is always much larger than any of the other elements. This means that for each asset, the most likely one quarter 'move' is no move; i.e. wealth is most likely to stay where it was previously. Thus, there is a good deal of inertia in holdings of these assets. There is nonetheless a number of substantial off-diagonal elements which reflect the (one quarter) interrelationships between assets. There are large cross-probabilities for fixed deposits to savings bank ordinary accounts (p_{13}), fixed deposits to building societies (p_{14}), building societies to fixed deposits (p_{41}) and bonds to building societies (p_{54}).

It can be shown that $1/(1 - p_{jj})$ is the average time that wealth stays in asset j. Thus, the average time wealth spends in each asset is (3.7, 11.5, 10.9, 6.1, 3.7) quarters (in the same order as Table 9). As can be seen, the turnover of the two types of savings bank deposits is half (or less) that of the other three assets. This corresponds with the notion that very little 'smart money' is held in these low interest bearing forms; people who hold money in savings banks are not concerned with actively managing their wealth.

The steady-state asset distribution corresponding to the transition matrix is $\pi' = (0.141, 0.203, 0.332, 0.235, 0.087)$. Thus in the steady-state, fixed deposits make up 14 per cent of financial wealth, savings bank investment accounts 20 per cent, savings bank ordinary accounts 33 per cent, building society deposits 24 per cent, with the remaining 9 per cent in bonds. It is of interest that the system is very close to the steady state by the end of the sample period (June 1979) when the observed asset distribution is (0.140, 0.209, 0.334, 0.231, 0.087). This is to be expected if the data are generated by a process which can be well-approximated by a Markov chain; i.e. as we move through time, the observed asset distribution should get closer to the steady state.

As an illustrative application of the model, we analyse the convergence of the process to the steady state after an exogenous increase in wealth. Before the shock let the system be in the steady state, so that $s = \pi$. Then let wealth increase from W_0 to W_1, with all the increase held initially in asset j. In this case, the initial distribution is

$$s_0'(j) = (1/W_1)[W_0\pi_1, \ldots, W_0\pi_j + W_1 - W_0, \ldots, W_0\pi_5],$$

and the evolution of the system can be simulated as

$$s_t'(j) = s_0'(j)P^t.$$

We assume that wealth increases by 2 per cent from the actual value in June 1979 and that it is all held first in asset 1, then all in asset 2 and so on. In Figures 1-5, we plot the percentage deviation of the dollar holdings of each asset from the old steady state,

$$z_{it}(j) = 100\,\frac{W_1 s_{it}(j) - W_0\pi_i}{W_0\pi_i} \qquad i, j = 1, \ldots, 5,$$

where $s_{it}(j)$ is the ith element of $s_t(j)$.[6] As the steady state is independent of where the additional wealth was initially held, we have

$$\lim_{t\to\infty} s_{it}(j) = \pi_i$$

and it follows that $z_{it}(j)$ converges to $100(W_1 - W_0)/W_0 = 2$ per cent for all i and j. In words, holdings of each asset increase by 2 per cent in the steady state; this follows from the constancy of the steady-state asset distribution. As can be seen from the graphs, the system approaches the steady state quite rapidly, except when the wealth is initially held in savings bank ordinary accounts.

3.2 A logistic growth model

The rate of adoption of new products and technology has been extensively analysed with the logistic model (see, e.g. Fitzroy (1976), Griliches (1957)). The objective is to estimate the rate of adoption, the saturation level and sometimes the responsiveness of the saturation level to economic variables. Savings bank investment accounts (SIAs) were first introduced in Australia in December 1969. In this sub-section we show that the growth of this new asset is similar to that of other new products in that the evolution of SIAs can be explained very well in terms of a logistic model. This type of growth of a new asset can be understood in terms of a learning process whereby people perceive SIAs as becoming less risky over time.

In Figure 6, we plot against time the percentage of total financial wealth (as defined in Section 2) held in SIAs. As can be seen, it does have a distinct *S*-shape, with the slope first increasing and then decreasing as the percentage tends to an upper asymptote. We use Oliver's (1969) generalized logistic function,

$$p_t = \gamma + \frac{\varkappa_t}{1 + \exp(\alpha_1 - \alpha_2 t)} + \varepsilon_t,$$

where p_t is the percentage of wealth held in SIAs at time t; $\varkappa_t = \varkappa_1 + \varkappa_2 \bar{r}_t$ where $\bar{r}$ is the relative rate of return on SIAs;[7] γ and $\gamma + \varkappa_t$ are lower and upper asymptotes (for a fixed value of $\bar{r}$); and ε is an AR1 disturbance, $\varepsilon_t = \varrho\varepsilon_{t-1} + e_t$ with e_t white noise.

Using the quarterly Australian data from December 1969 to June 1979 we obtain the following ML estimates (asymptotic *t*-values errors are given in parentheses);

$\hat{\gamma} = 2.65\ (11.0)$	$\hat{\alpha}_1 = 6.70\ (12.9)$	$R^2 = 0.998$
$\hat{\varkappa}_1 = 17.33\ (32.7)$	$\hat{\alpha}_2 = 0.363\ (12.5)$	S.E. $= 0.432$
$\hat{\varkappa}_2 = 1.62\ (2.9)$	$\hat{\varrho} = 0.669\ (5.0)$	D.W. $= 1.72.$

As can be seen, all estimates are highly significant and the model fits the data well, with the coefficient of determination (R^2) equal to 0.998 and the standard deviation of the residuals (S.E.) being 0.43 per cent. The interest elasticity of holdings is $\varkappa_2\bar{r}/p[1 + \exp(\alpha_1 - \alpha_2 t)] = 0.07$ at sample means. This agrees well with the system-wide elasticity given in Table 3 for all savings bank deposits.

The conclusion which emerges from this analysis is that the evolution of holdings of SIAs conforms well with the logistic process.

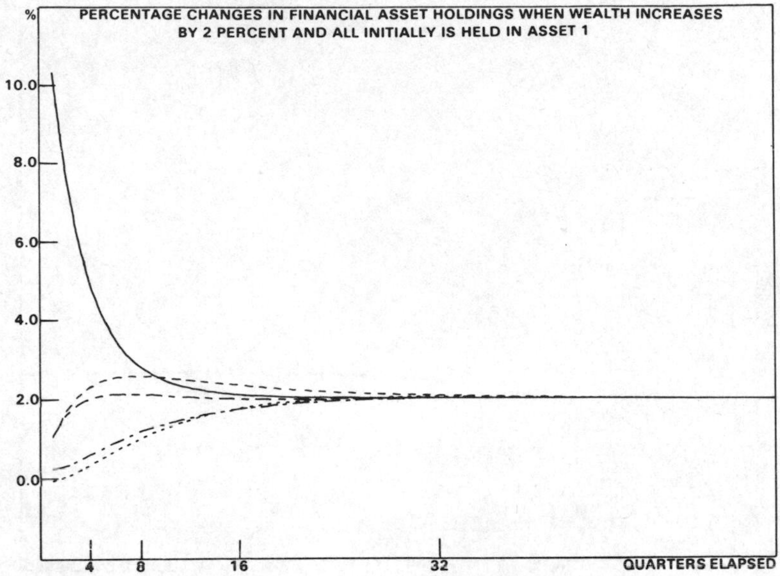

Figure 1

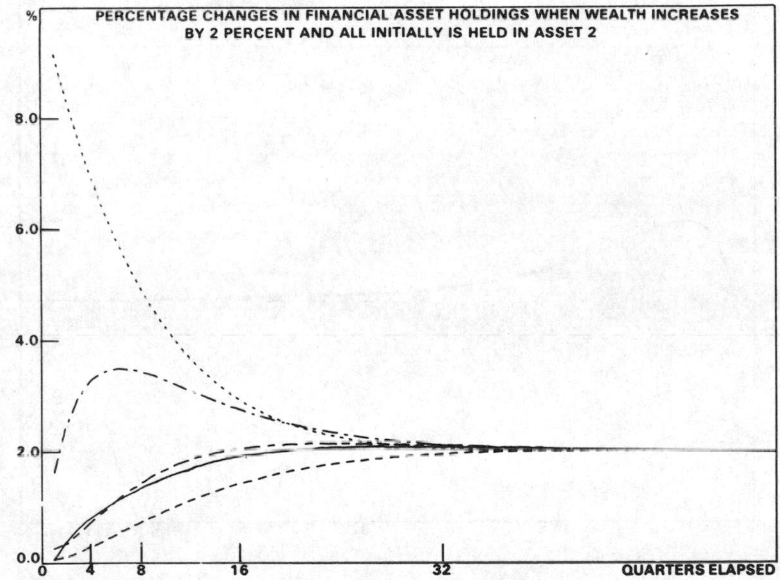

Figure 2

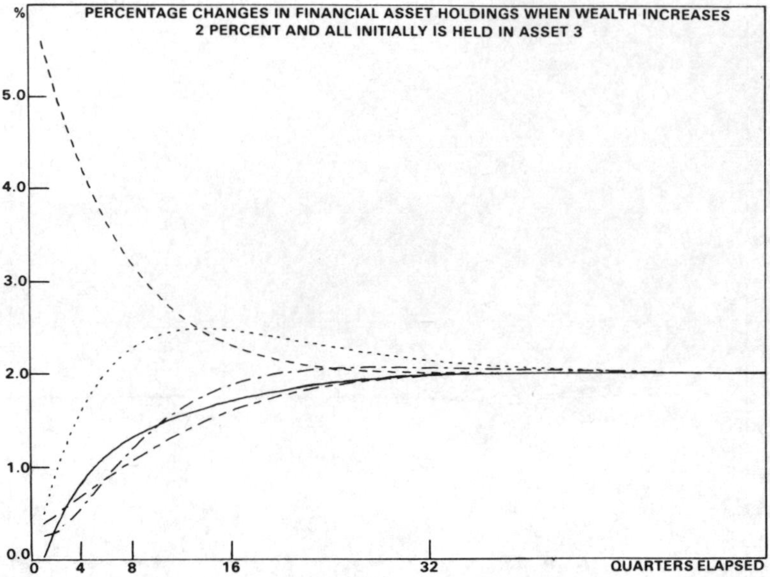

Figure 3

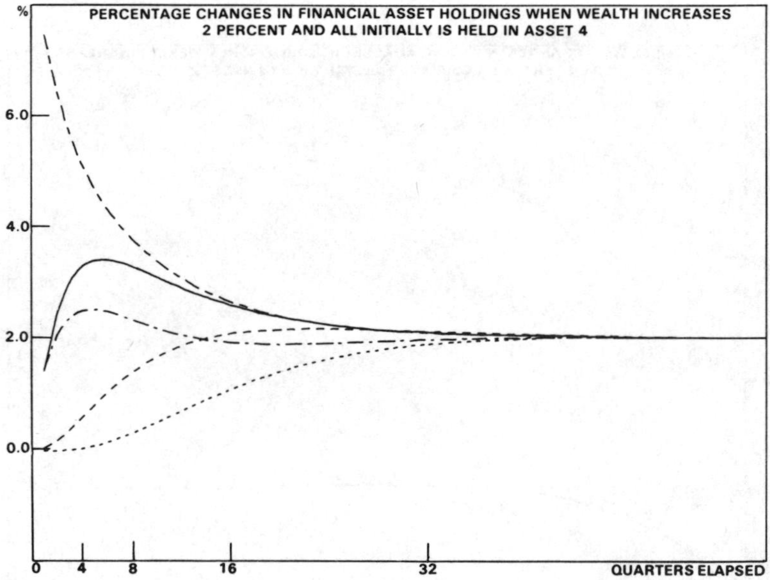

Figure 4

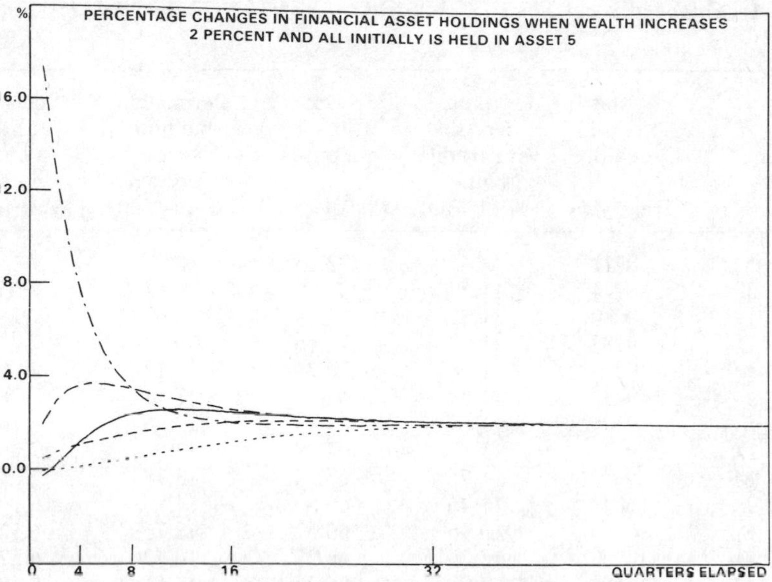

KEY

———	Asset 1: Fixed deposits
········	Asset 2: Savings bank investment accounts
-----------	Asset 3: Savings bank ordinary accounts
- - - - -	Asset 4: Permanent building society deposits
-·-·-·-	Asset 5: Special/Australian savings bonds

Figure 5

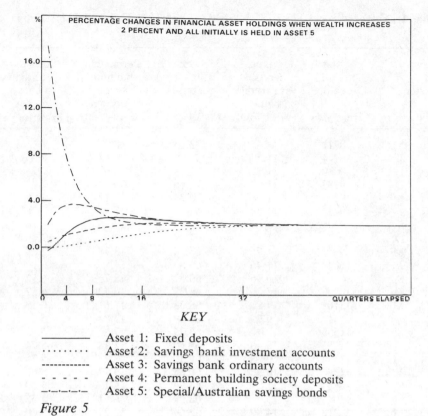

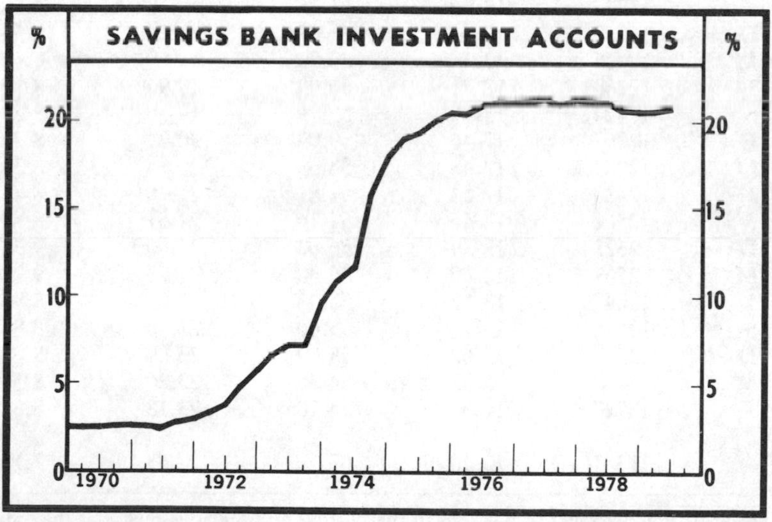

Figure 6

Table 1 *Financial asset holdings: Australia, March 1970-June 1979 (seasonally adjusted)*

Year and quarter		Total financial wealth (real $M)	Fixed deposits with trading banks (% of total)	Savings bank deposits (% of total)	Permanent building society deposits (% of total)	Special/ Australian savings bonds (% of total)
1970	M	8911	11.68	72.15	8.99	7.18
	J	8974	11.82	71.60	9.54	7.05
	S	9080	11.72	71.04	10.00	7.24
	D	9187	11.37	70.66	10.53	7.44
1971	M	9290	11.26	70.24	11.12	7.38
	J	9432	11.54	69.41	11.77	7.28
	S	9605	11.82	68.45	12.36	7.36
	D	9732	11.87	67.69	12.96	7.48
1972	M	9837	11.75	67.24	13.78	7.24
	J	10046	11.46	66.85	14.80	6.90
	S	10366	10.96	66.52	15.76	6.77
	D	10768	10.35	66.37	16.72	6.57
1973	M	11165	9.87	66.33	17.61	6.19
	J	11414	9.79	66.49	17.84	5.88
	S	11556	10.12	66.29	17.86	5.73
	D	11553	10.48	65.60	18.18	5.74
1974	M	11494	10.38	65.10	18.77	5.75
	J	11394	10.30	64.85	19.17	5.68
	S	11137	11.39	63.84	19.15	5.63
	D	11045	13.12	62.99	18.51	5.38
1975	M	11212	14.09	62.69	18.22	5.00
	J	11440	14.19	62.19	18.92	4.70
	S	11777	13.96	61.76	19.70	4.58
	D	11923	13.64	61.58	20.24	4.55
1976	M	12025	13.12	60.79	19.69	6.40
	J	12260	12.71	60.03	18.96	8.30
	S	12404	12.56	59.79	19.36	8.29
	D	12367	12.46	59.02	20.22	8.31
1977	M	12283	12.48	58.33	20.84	8.34
	J	12430	12.54	57.81	21.25	8.41
	S	12561	12.46	57.16	21.51	8.88
	D	12622	12.39	56.62	21.60	9.39
1978	M	12769	12.70	56.30	21.73	9.27
	J	13047	13.12	55.97	22.03	8.88
	S	13178	13.10	55.60	22.46	8.84
	D	13213	13.02	55.00	23.09	8.89
1979	M	13487	13.82	54.35	23.26	8.56
	J	13727	14.34	54.10	23.18	8.38
Mean		11334	12.10	63.13	17.68	7.10

Stocks are arithmetic averages of holdings in the current and previous quarters; they are thus interpreted as at mid-quarter. Total financial wealth is the sum of holdings of the four assets and the CPI (=1 in 1966/67) is used as the deflator for real wealth. Deposits with savings banks are ordinary and investment accounts plus deposits stock.

Table 2 *Interest Rates: Australia, March 1970-June 1979 (seasonally adjusted; per cent p.a.)*

Year and quarter		Fixed deposits with trading banks	Savings bank deposits	Permanent building society deposits	Special/ Australian savings bonds
1970	M	5.15	3.78	6.00	5.20
	J	5.30	3.79	6.00	5.80
	S	5.30	3.80	6.00	6.40
	D	5.30	3.80	6.30	6.40
1971	M	5.30	3.80	6.60	6.40
	J	5.30	3.80	6.60	6.40
	S	5.30	3.81	6.60	6.40
	D	5.30	3.82	6.60	6.10
1972	M	4.90	3.82	6.60	5.60
	J	4.50	3.82	6.55	5.40
	S	4.50	3.83	6.50	5.40
	D	4.50	3.85	6.50	5.40
1973	M	4.50	3.87	6.50	5.40
	J	4.50	3.88	6.35	5.60
	S	4.50	3.89	6.40	6.00
	D	5.75	4.06	7.20	7.10
1974	M	7.25	4.26	7.85	8.00
	J	7.50	4.32	8.90	8.00
	S	8.50	4.71	9.90	8.60
	D	9.50	5.15	9.90	9.20
1975	M	9.50	5.14	9.95	9.10
	J	9.50	5.08	9.70	9.00
	S	9.50	5.12	9.35	9.10
	D	9.25	5.14	9.10	9.20
1976	M	8.75	5.18	9.00	9.85
	J	8.63	5.24	9.10	9.85
	S	8.75	5.27	9.10	9.70
	D	8.75	5.27	9.15	9.60
1977	M	8.88	5.29	9.20	10.00
	J	9.00	5.33	9.20	10.00
	S	9.00	5.34	9.15	10.00
	D	9.00	5.33	9.10	9.63
1978	M	9.00	5.26	8.95	9.13
	J	9.00	5.19	8.80	9.00
	S	9.00	5.18	8.80	9.00
	D	8.75	5.11	8.50	8.88
1979	M	8.50	5.07	8.25	8.75
	J	8.50	5.11	8.30	9.00
Mean		7.21	4.57	7.96	7.82

Interest rates are arithmetic averages of the current and previous quarter's rates; they are thus lined up with the asset holdings given in Table 1.

Table 3 *Asset demand equations: Australia, March 1970-June 1979*

Equation	Parameters							Elasticities						
	α_i	β_i	β^*_i	π_{i1}	π_{i2}	π_{i3}	π_{i4}	W	W^*	r_1	r_2	r_3	r_4	R^2
1 Fixed deposits	.2720	−.0169	−.0165	.0135	−.0044	−.0042	−.0049	.86	.86	.81	−.17	−.28	−.32	.73
	(2.0)	(1.2)	(1.2)	(8.2)	(3.2)	(2.8)	(3.3)							
2 Savings bank deposits	3.0722	−.2572	−.2612		.0097	−.0072	.0019	.59	.59	−.05	.07	−.09	.02	.96
	(15.0)	(11.5)	(11.8)		(4.6)	(5.3)	(1.4)							
3 Permanent building society deposits	−2.8247	.3187	.3189			.0146	−.0032	2.80	2.80	−.17	−.18	.66	−.14	.99
	(27.6)	(28.3)	(28.8)			(6.3)	(2.0)							
4 Special/Australian savings bonds	.4805	−.0446	−.0412				.0062	.37	.42	−.50	.12	−.35	.68	.83
	(4.1)	(3.4)	(3.2)				(3.0)							

Asymptotic *t*-values are given in parentheses. R^2 is the squared correlation coefficient between the actual and predicted value of the dependent variable. Elasticities are evaluated at sample means. Wealth elasticities before the introduction of savings bonds in 1976 are given in the column headed W and those after the introduction in the column headed W^*.

Table 4 *Decomposition of change in portfolio shares Australia, March 1970-June 1979*

Asset i		Change in share of wealth in asset i	Components of Δs_i						
			Wealth	Interest rates					Residual
			$\beta_i D.\Delta\log W + \beta_i^*(1-D).\Delta\log W$	$\pi_{i1}\Delta r_1$	$\pi_{i2}\Delta r_2$	$\pi_{i3}\Delta r_3$	$\pi_{i4}\Delta r_4$	$\sum_{j=1}^{4} \pi_{ij}\Delta r_j$	
		(1)	(2)	(3)	(4)	(5)	(6)	(7)	(8)
s_1	Sum	2.66	−0.72	4.52	−0.59	−0.97	−1.86	1.11	2.28
	Mean	0.07	−0.02	0.12	−0.02	−0.03	−0.05	0.03	0.06
s_2	Sum	−18.05	−11.17	−1.47	1.29	−1.66	0.72	−1.12	−5.76
	Mean	−0.49	−0.30	−0.04	0.03	−0.04	0.02	−0.03	−0.16
s_3	Sum	14.19	13.77	−1.41	−0.96	3.36	−1.22	−0.22	0.64
	Mean	0.38	0.37	−0.04	−0.03	0.09	−0.03	−0.01	0.02
s_4	Sum	1.20	−1.88	−1.64	0.25	−0.74	2.36	0.23	2.85
	Mean	0.03	−0.05	−0.04	0.01	−0.02	0.06	0.01	0.08

Column (1) = (2) + (3) + (4) + (5) + (6) + (8). All entries are to be divided by 100.

Table 5 *Welfare cost of interest rate changes and the rate of inflation: Australia, March 1970-June 1979*

Year and quarter		Welfare cost as a percentage of wealth	Welfare cost in millions of 1966/67 dollars	Welfare cost as a percentage of real GDP	Rate of inflation (per cent p.a.)
1970	M	.68	61	.90	3.20
	J	.65	58	.82	3.73
	S	.87	79	1.11	3.80
	D	.62	57	.80	4.88
1971	M	.50	46	.63	4.92
	J	.50	47	.65	5.40
	S	.50	49	.65	6.70
	D	.44	42	.56	7.19
1972	M	.78	76	1.01	7.12
	J	1.28	128	1.68	6.23
	S	1.27	132	1.72	5.70
	D	1.29	139	1.77	4.50
1973	M	1.31	147	1.83	5.67
	J	1.36	155	1.94	8.19
	S	1.55	179	2.18	10.62
	D	.46	53	.64	13.23
1974	M	.04	5	.06	13.57
	J	.73	84	1.02	14.40
	S	1.78	198	2.41	16.05
	D	1.52	168	2.00	16.25
1975	M	1.67	187	2.25	17.56
	J	1.61	184	2.16	16.94
	S	1.29	152	1.79	12.10
	D	.81	97	1.16	14.04
1976	M	.33	40	.46	13.38
	J	.26	32	.37	12.32
	S	.23	28	.32	13.93
	D	.23	28	.32	14.40
1977	M	.34	41	.47	13.63
	J	.37	46	.52	13.44
	S	.37	47	.53	13.15
	D	.34	43	.49	9.26
1978	M	.47	60	.67	8.20
	J	.59	77	.86	7.88
	S	.59	78	.85	7.86
	D	.51	67	.72	7.76
1979	M	.45	60	.64	8.20
	J	.41	56	.60	8.84
Mean		.76	85	1.04	9.85

Real GDP is in terms of 1966/67 prices and is seasonally adjusted. Source: Australian Bureau of Statistics, 'Historical Series of Quarterly Estimates of National Income and Expenditure, Australia, September Quarter 1959 to June Quarter 1980', cat. no. 5207.0. The rate of inflation is the quarter-on-quarter percentage change of the Consumer Price Index (weighted average of six state capital cities).

Source: ABS, 'Consumer Price Index, Australia', cat. no. 6401.0, various issues.

Table 6 *Financial asset holdings: Australia, September 1979-December 1981 (seasonally adjusted)*

Year and quarter		Total financial wealth (real $M)	Fixed deposits with trading banks (% of total)	Savings bank deposits (% of total)	Permanent building society deposits (% of total)	Special/ Australian savings bonds (% of total)
1979	S	13723	14.29	53.65	23.38	8.68
	D	13682	14.31	52.87	23.88	8.94
1980	M	13699	14.07	52.60	24.55	8.78
	J	13725	14.00	52.59	25.07	8.35
	S	13688	14.35	52.28	25.36	8.01
	D	13825	14.91	51.92	25.49	7.68
1981	M	13980	15.83	51.80	25.31	7.06
	J	14064	17.00	51.46	24.94	6.60
	S	14019	17.81	50.79	24.97	6.44
	D	13803	18.05	50.60	25.23	6.12
Mean		13821	15.46	52.06	24.82	7.67

See notes to Table 1.

Table 7 *Interest rates: Australia, September 1979-December 1981 (seasonally unadjusted; per cent p.a.)*

Year and quarter		Fixed deposits with trading banks	Savings bank deposits	Permanent building society deposits	Special/ Australian savings bonds
1979	S	8.50	5.11	8.35	9.25
	D	8.75	5.08	8.40	9.25
1980	M	9.00	5.14	8.40	9.50
	J	9.50	5.30	8.45	9.75
	S	10.00	5.61	8.55	10.00
	D	10.75	5.83	8.60	10.88
1981	M	11.75	6.13	8.55	11.88
	J	12.13	6.42	8.60	12.25
	S	12.63	6.75	9.10	12.25
	D	13.00	7.09	9.60	12.25
Mean		10.60	5.85	8.66	10.73

See notes to Table 2.

Table 8 *Out-of-sample forecasts of financial asset holdings: Australia, September 1979-December 1981 (seasonally adjusted)*

Year and quarter	Fixed deposits with trading banks (% of total)		Savings bank deposits (% of total)		Permanent building society deposits (% of total)		Special/Australian savings bonds (% of total)	
	Forecast	Forecast error	Forecast	Forecast error	Forecast	Forecast error	Forecast	Forecast error
1979 S	12.67	1.62(2.6)	55.31	−1.66(1.8)	23.35	.03 (.1)	8.67	.00 (.0)
D	12.99	1.32(2.2)	55.22	2.35(2.5)	23.24	.64(1.4)	8.55	.39 (.7)
1980 M	13.19	.88(1.4)	55.17	−2.57(2.8)	23.05	1.50(3.1)	8.59	.20 (.4)
J	13.64	.36 (.6)	55.08	−2.49(2.7)	22.78	2.29(4.6)	8.51	−.16 (.3)
S	14.03	.32 (.5)	55.19	−2.91(3.1)	22.33	3.03(5.9)	8.45	−.44 (.8)
D	14.48	.43 (.7)	54.94	−3.02(3.2)	21.97	3.52(6.1)	8.61	−.93(1.6)
1981 M	15.21	.62 (.9)	54.73	−2.93(3.0)	21.30	4.01(5.8)	8.76	−1.70(2.6)
J	15.38	1.62(2.2)	54.73	−3.27(3.3)	21.06	3.88(5.3)	8.83	−2.22(3.3)
S	15.71	2.10(2.9)	54.56	−3.77(3.8)	21.24	3.73(5.3)	8.50	−2.06(3.1)
D	15.88	2.17(3.0)	54.76	−4.16(4.2)	21.08	4.15(6.1)	8.28	−2.16(3.4)
Mean	14.32	1.14	54.97	−2.91	22.14	2.68	8.58	−.91

The forecast error is actual minus forecast. Asymptotic *t*-values are given in parentheses. See notes to Table 1.

Table 9 *Maximum likelihood estimates of transition probabilities: Australia, September 1973-June 1979*

Previous asset (i of p_{ij})	Current asset (j of p_{ij})				
	1	2	3	4	5
1 Fixed deposits	.733	0	.166	.102	0
2 Savings bank investments accounts	.022	.913	.004	.003	.058
3 Savings bank ordinary accounts	.020	.053	.908	.019	0
4 Permanent building society deposits	.113	0	0	.837	.050
5 Special/Australian savings bonds	0	0	.073	.200	.727

Notes

* We would like to thank Peter Goldschmidt and Kal Stening for excellent research assistance; and John Anderson and Henri Theil for helpful comments.
1 See Evans (1979) for a recent survey in which this conclusion emerges very clearly.
2 See, e.g. Clements and Theil (1979), Izan and Clements (1979) and Leser (1963).
3 See Taylor and Clements (1983) for a discussion of the rational behaviour lying behind the demand equations, homogeneity and Slutsky symmetry.
4 We use Wymer's (1978) RESIMUL program.
5 We use Salkever's (1976) dummy variable technique to obtain the forecast error variances.
6 We are grateful to John Anderson for providing us with these graphs which were produced with his program MATGRAF (Anderson (1981)).
7 The variable $\bar{r}$ is defined as the rate of return on SIAs less a weighted average of the rate on the five assets listed in Table 12, where the weights are current period shares of the assets in the total.

References

Anderson, J.S. and Clements, K.W. (1982), 'Holdings of Financial Assets: A Markov Chain Analysis', *Statistics and Probability Letters*, 1, 36-40.

Brainard, W.C. and Tobin, J. (1968), 'Pitfalls in Financial Model Building', *American Economic Review*, 58, 99-122.

Broadbent, J., Clements, K.W. and Johnson, L.W. (1981), 'Growth in Holdings of a New Financial Asset: A Logistic Analysis', *Australian Journal of Management*, 6, 1-6.

Cagan, P. (1956), 'The Monetary Dynamics of Hyperinflation', M. Friedman, ed., Chicago: University of Chicago Press.

Clements, K.W. and Taylor, J.C. (1981), 'The Determinants of Holdings of Financial Assets in Australia', *Australian Journal of Management*, 6, 17-25.

Clements, K.W. and Theil, H. (1979), 'A Cross-Country Analysis of Consumption Patterns', Report 7924 of the Center for Mathematical Studies in Business and Economics, The University of Chicago.

Deaton, A. and Muellbauer, J. (1980), 'An Almost Ideal Demand System', *American Economic Review*, 70, 312-26.

Evans, W.H. (1979), 'Financial Modelling in Australia', Research Discussion Paper 7902, Reserve Bank of Australia, Sydney.

Fitzroy, P.T. (1976), *Analytical Methods for Marketing Management*, London: McGraw-Hill.

Griliches, Z. (1957), 'Hybrid Corn: An Exploration in the Economics of Technical Change', *Econometrica*, 25, 501-22.

Harberger, A.C. (1964), 'Taxation, Resource Allocation and Welfare', in *The Role of Direct and Indirect Taxes in the Federal Reserve System*, Princeton: Princeton University Press for the NBER and the Brookings Institute. Reprinted in A.C. Harberger (1974) *Taxation and Welfare*, Chicago: The University of Chicago Press.

Izan, H.Y. and Clements, K.W. (1979), 'A Cross-Cross-Section Analysis of

Consumption Patterns', *Economics Letters*, 4, 83-6.
Lee, T.C., Judge, G.G. and Zellner, A. (1970), *Estimating the Parameters of the Markov Probability Model from Aggregate Time Series Data*, Amsterdam: North-Holland.
Leser, C.E.V. (1963), 'Forms of Engel Functions', *Econometrica*, 31, 694-703.
Oliver, F.R. (1969), 'Another Generalisation of the Logistic Growth Function', *Econometrica*, 37, 144-7.
Salkever, D.S. (1976), 'The Use of Dummy Variables to Compute Predictions, Prediction Errors and Confidence Intervals', *Journal of Econometrics*, 4, 393-7.
Taylor, J.C. and Clements, K.W. (1981), 'A Simple Portfolio Allocation Model of Financial Wealth', mimeographed, Perth: the University of Western Australia.
Taylor, J.C. and Clements, K.W. (1983), 'A Simple Portfolio Allocation Model of Financial Wealth', *European Economic Review*, 23, 241-51.
Theil, H. (1972), *Statistical Decomposition Analysis with Applications in the Social and Administrative Sciences*, Amsterdam: North-Holland.
Working, H. (1943), 'Statistical Laws of Family Expenditure', *Journal of the American Statistical Association*, 38, 43-56.
Wymer, C.R. (1978), 'Computer Programs: RESIMUL Manual', mimeographed, Washington: International Monetary Fund.

15 Dwelling commencements in Australia: lags and autocorrelation

*Ross A. Williams**

1 Introduction

In the NIF-10 model[1] of the Australian economy, dwelling commencements react quite slowly to housing loans and general liquidity. The nature of the data is such as to suggest that the estimated lags are unrealistically long, at least for housing loans. This paper examines the issue, paying attention to the relationships between lags and error structure. The explanatory variables are initially confined to the two used in NIF-10. A competing model is then introduced in which the explanatory variables used are the asset price of existing dwellings and the cost of construction of new dwellings.

The difficulty of disentangling lagged behaviour in economic variables (termed systematic dynamics by Mizon (1977)) from autocorrelated error terms (error dynamics) has long been recognized in applied econometrics. Important contributions to the debate have been made by Griliches (1961), Sargan (1964), Mizon (1977), Hendry and Mizon (1978) and Sargan (1980). The last three papers have emphasized the need to commence with a very general specification and then test for tighter specification. But there is always need for tests of mis-specification, if only because of the difficulty of determining the order of the maximum lag lengths. Furthermore, for dwelling commencements the NIF-10 equation exists and can be treated as the maintained hypothesis.

The NIF-10 model is outlined in Section 2 of the paper and empirical estimates of it are discussed in Section 3. In Section 4 a less restricted version of the model is estimated and an attempt is made to separate systematic dynamics from error dynamics. A new preferred equation is chosen and the results compared in Section 5 with the NIF-10 equation. Section 6 contains results obtained using the alternative set of explanatory variables. An overview of the findings is presented in Section 7.

2 The NIF-10 equation for dwelling commencements

In the NIF-10 model developed by the ABS and Treasury, the target or desired level of dwelling commencements (S^*) is specified to be a function of the level of mortgage approvals for new dwellings for owner occupation (*LN*) and the four-quarter change in private sector liquid assets as measured by *M*4 (*M*3 plus all deposits and shareholders funds with permanent building societies). Actual commencements (*S*) are assumed to adjust exponentially to the target level. Thus the model may be written:

$$S^* = \gamma_0 + \gamma_1 LN + \gamma_2 \Delta_4 M4$$
$$\Delta S = \lambda(S^* - S_{-1})$$

which gives the estimating equation:

$$S = \beta_0 + \beta_1 LN + \beta_2 \Delta_4 M4 + \beta_3 S_{-1} \tag{1}$$

Total lending for owner occupation is determined in the monetary sector of NIF-10 and is basically supply determined. However, the *proportion* of total lending which is for the purchase or construction of new dwellings is demand determined.[2] The *M*4 variable is used as a general measure of liquidity available to households.

3 Empirical estimates: NIF-10

Ordinary least squares estimates of equation (1) are first presented in Table 1 using quarterly seasonally adjusted data for the period 1967(3) to 1979(2), as in NIF-10 (1981). The dependent variable is the real value of commencements, including alterations and additions valued at over $10,000. The empirical estimates are close to but not identical with those presented in NIF-10 (1981, p. 228) owing to subsequent changes in the implicit price index for investment in dwellings which is used to convert all variables to real values.[3] The explanatory power of the equation is high ($R^2 = 0.930$), although there is evidence of third-order autocorrelation in the residuals. (Throughout the paper the test used for autocorrelation is the generalization of Durbin's *h*-statistic as set out in Breusch and Pagan (1980, p. 244). The test statistics h_i, where i is the order of the autocorrelation, are distributed as the unit normal.)

The results obtained by extending the data period to 1981(2) are given as equation [ii] in Table 1. The eight extra observations lower the explanatory power of the model and raise the size of the coefficient on the lagged dependent variable, but the errors appear to be independent.

Two features of the results require comment. Firstly, the long-run coefficient on loans for new dwellings, *LN*, is always close to unity. This is true for the reported equations ([i] and [ii]) and for recursive estimates of the coefficients. This result might be interpreted as implying that eventually all loans for new dwellings result in commencements. The difficulty with this interpretation is that loans for new dwellings can be either for construction

Table 1 *Dwelling commencements: NIF-10 equation and extensions*

Period of estimation 1967(3) to 1979(2)

[i] $S = \underset{(24.8)}{112.1} + \underset{(0.067)}{0.288}\, LN + \underset{(0.0022)}{0.0085}\, \Delta_4 M4 + \underset{(0.056)}{0.676}\, S_{-1}$

$R^2 = 0.9296,\ s = 24.61,\ h_1 = 1.21,\ h_2 = 0.42,\ h_3 = 1.98,\ h_4 = -1.60,\ h_5 = 0.41$

Period of estimation 1967(3) to 1981(2)

[ii] $S = \underset{(29.6)}{64.1} + \underset{(0.091)}{0.231}\, LN + \underset{(0.0034)}{0.0093}\, \Delta_4 M_4 + \underset{(0.060)}{0.787}\, S_{-1}$

$R^2 = 0.8874,\ s = 37.74,\ h_1 = 1.88,\ h_2 = -1.13,\ h_3 = 1.56,\ h_4 = 0.36,\ h_5 = -1.11$

[iii(a)] $S = \underset{(34.9)}{54.2} + \underset{(0.184)}{0.253}\, LN - \underset{(0.194)}{0.047}\, LN_{-1} + \underset{(0.0079)}{0.0121}\, \Delta_4 M4 - \underset{(0.0074)}{0.0030}\, \Delta_4 M4_{-1} + \underset{(0.079)}{0.815}\, S_{-1}$

$R^2 = 0.8881,\ s = 38.37,\ h_1 = 1.84,\ h_2 = -1.46,\ h_3 = 1.49,\ h_4 = 0.39,\ h_5 = -1.24$

[iii(b)] $S = \underset{(52.1)}{382.2} + \underset{(0.201)}{0.359}\, LN + \underset{(0.0082)}{0.0113}\, \Delta_4 M4 + \underset{(0.037)}{0.991}\, \hat{u}_{-1}$

$R^2 = 0.8444,\ s = 44.36,\ h_1 = 2.23,\ h_2 = -1.10,\ h_3 = 0.66,\ h_4 = -0.56,\ h_5 = -2.58$

[iv(a)] $S = \underset{(57.9)}{9.9} + \underset{(0.192)}{0.212}\, LN + \underset{(0.198)}{0.015}\, LN_{-1} + \underset{(0.0119)}{0.0224}\, M4 - \underset{(0.0121)}{0.0200}\, M4_{-1} + \underset{(0.097)}{0.757}\, S_{-1}$

$R^2 = 0.8810,\ s = 39.57,\ h_1 = 2.66,\ h_2 = -0.69\ \ h_3 = 1.32,\ h_4 = 0.11,\ h_5 = -1.78$

[iv(b)] $S = \underset{(145.7)}{-186.5} + \underset{(0.178)}{0.255}\, LN + \underset{(0.0054)}{0.0237}\, M4 + \underset{(0.093)}{0.775}\, \hat{u}_{-1}$

$R^2 = 0.8746,\ s = 39.83,\ h_1 = 2.60,\ h_2 = -1.26,\ h_3 = 0.54,\ h_4 = -0.56,\ h_5 = -2.49$

[v] $S = \underset{(132.0)}{59.1} + \underset{(0.157)}{0.228}\, LN + \underset{(0.160)}{0.202}\, LN_{-1} + \underset{(0.162)}{0.176}\, LN_{-2} + \underset{(0.0062)}{0.0127}\, M4_{-1} + \underset{(0.139)}{1.049}\, \hat{u}_{-1} - \underset{(0.187)}{0.525}\, \hat{u}_{-2} + \underset{(0.205)}{0.573}\, \hat{u}_{-3} - \underset{(0.168)}{0.508}\, \hat{u}_{-4}$

$R^2 = 0.9149,\ s = 34.51,\ h_1 = -0.56,\ h_2 = -0.60,\ h_3 = -0.42,\ h_4 = -0.32,\ h_5 = 0.93$

NOTES: S = real value of commencements; LN = real value of loans for new dwellings; $M4$ = real value of $M3$ plus building society deposits and shareholders funds. The unit of measurement is 1974-75 \$M. Both S and LN include alterations and additions. All data are seasonally adjusted. The mean of the dependent variable for equations (ii)-(v) is 644. Standard errors are given in parentheses. s = standard error of estimate. h_i = test statistic for ith-order serial correlation. Where residuals, $\hat{u}$, are included the equation has been estimated nonlinearly using Adrian Pagan's AUT program.

or for purchase. Since 1976-7, when the relevant data first became available,[4] the percentage of advances granted for the purchase of new dwellings has fluctuated between 40 and 50 per cent of total loans for new dwellings. It follows that some loans for new dwellings will relate to commencements in the *preceding* quarter or quarters.

The second, and related, feature of the results is the extremely long lags. Equation [ii] in Table 1, for example, implies that the average lag between the approval of a loan for construction or purchase of a new dwelling and actual commencement of the dwelling is nearly a year. Given the institutional features mentioned above this is unacceptable.

4 Autocorrelation and lags

The explanation for the NIF results would seem to be that the coefficient of the lagged dependent variable is measuring not the reaction time path but autocorrelation in the error.[5] Almon lag estimates confirmed this view. Autocorrelated errors are to be expected in a housing equation which does not contain cyclically moving real variables. As the NIF equation contains the dependent variable lagged one period, it is natural to look first at a first-order autoregressive error structure.

4.1 First-order autoregressive error

To illustrate the issues,[6] consider the following dynamic equation:

$$y_t = \beta_1 x_t + \beta_2 x_{t-1} + \beta_3 z_t + \beta_4 z_{t-1} + \beta_5 y_{t-1} + e_t \qquad (2)$$

where x and z are exogenous variables and e is a classically distributed error term. Equation (2) reduces to a static model with a first-order autoregressive error term, i.e.

$$y_t = \beta_1 x_t + \beta_3 z_t + u_t, \qquad u_t = \beta_5 u_{t-1} + e_t \qquad (3)$$

if the following restrictions hold:

$$\beta_2 + \beta_1\beta_5 = 0 \qquad \text{and} \qquad \beta_4 + \beta_3\beta_5 = 0. \qquad (4)$$

The coefficient of the first-order autoregressive error term in (3) is the coefficient on the lagged dependent variable in (2). Of course the reduction is just the inverse of the usual Cochrane-Orcutt transformation.

If equation (2) is solved for y in terms of current and lagged values of x and z then the successive weights, w_i, on x lagged i periods are: $w_0 = \beta_1$, $w_1 = \beta_2 + \beta_1\beta_5$, $w_i = \beta_5^{i-1}w_1$ ($i = 2, 3, \ldots$). The restriction $\beta_2 + \beta_1\beta_5 = 0$ is thus clearly seen to imply that the weights on x fall to zero after the current period. Similarly, the restriction $\beta_4 + \beta_3\beta_5 = 0$ implies that the weights on lagged z are zero.[7]

Now the NIF equation for housing commencements is not exactly in the form (2) because LN enters without a lag and $M4$ enters as the difference between the current value and a four-quarter lagged value. The 'omitted' variables such as LN_{-1} may, however, have been apparently 'of the wrong sign' or insignificantly different from zero when the unrestricted form was estimated. It also follows that the estimated coefficient of the lagged dependent variable will be a biased estimate of the autoregressive error coefficient insofar as the omitted variables are correlated with the included variables.[8]

The most obvious choices for the x and z variables are either LN and $\Delta_4 M4$ or LN and $M4$ (although the 'true' model could contain lagged values of these variables in equation (3)). The results obtained by including these variables are given in Table 1 as equations [iii(a)] and [iii(b)] (LN and $\Delta_4 M4$) and equations [iv(a)] and [iv(b)] (LN and $M4$), where the (a)-equations are the unrestricted ones.

As expected, the coefficients on the lagged values of the financial variables (the 'omitted' variables) tend to be 'of the wrong sign' unless considered in the context of an autoregressive error term. The appropriateness of the restrictions (4) may be tested conveniently using the likelihood ratio test. The values of the statistic (distributed as χ^2_2) are 18.46 for equation [iii] and 2.91 for equation [iv]. The restrictions would therefore appear to be valid for equation [iv] but not for equation [iii]. The results, however, are indicative rather than exact owing to the presence of some serial correlation in the error terms.

The coefficient on $\hat{u}_1$ (and its standard error) in equation [iv(b)] is almost identical to that on S_{-1} in equation [iv(a)]. The explanatory power of equation [iv(b)] is similar to that of the NIF equation; it is the interpretation which differs. In [iv(b)] the short and long run responses to liquidity variables are the same and factors external to the model, as measured by $\hat{u}_{-1}$, are important. In the NIF-10 model, as represented by equation [ii] in Table 1, the long-run effects are nearly five times the short-run effects; liquidity variables are asserted to explain most of the variation in dwelling commencements.

The results give grounds for believing that autocorrelation is important, but its exact form has not been determined. It is not appropriate to replace S_{-1} in the NIF-10 equation by $\hat{u}_{-1}$, and respecifying the lag pattern (such as in equation [iv]) always produced autocorrelated residuals (other results are not reported). It appears that the error structure is more complex than first-order. This raises the question of whether the term $\Delta_4 M4$ is reflecting a higher-order error process.

4.2 Fourth-order autoregressive error

To investigate further, the equation for new dwelling commencements was re-estimated with all variables (LN, $M4$, S_{-1}) lagged up to four quarters, i.e.

$$S = \alpha + \sum_{i=0}^{4} \beta_i LN_{-i} + \sum_{i=0}^{4} \gamma_i M4_{-i} + \sum_{i=1}^{4} \delta_i S_{-i} + e \qquad (5)$$

The empirical estimates of (5) are given in Table 2. Three interesting results emerge. Firstly, all the coefficients on the lagged dependent variables are significant at the 5 per cent level (the errors pass the test for independence). Secondly, these coefficients alternate in sign and the coefficients on LN and $M4$ exhibit a strong tendency to do likewise. Thirdly, the coefficient on the current value of $M4$ is extremely small, negative, and has a t-value of only -0.19.

In total, the results strongly suggest the presence of a fourth-order autoregressive error process and weights on LN and $M4_{-1}$ which decline at a much faster rate than in the NIF-10 equation.[9] Experimenting with lags (while keeping the fourth-order error process) showed the coefficient on LN to be very small and highly insignificant after two quarters, and for $M4$ the only significant coefficient was on $M4_{-1}$. The preferred model is thus:

$$S = \beta_0 + \beta_1 LN + \beta_2 LN_{-1} + \beta_3 LN_{-2} + \beta_4 M4_{-1} + u \qquad (6)$$
$$u = \varrho_1 u_{-1} + \varrho_2 u_{-2} + \varrho_3 u_{-3} + \varrho_4 u_{-4} + e$$

Before discussing the parameter estimates it is appropriate to comment on an alternative parameterization, namely, the rational distributed lag.

Table 2 *Unrestricted equation for commencements*

Variable	Lag 0	1	2	3	4
LN	0.254	−0.013	0.233	−0.309	−0.130
	(0.170)	(0.224)	(0.227)	(0.234)	(0.210)
$M4$	−0.003	0.019	−0.024	0.022	−0.006
	(0.014)	(0.026)	(0.027)	(0.025)	(0.014)
S		0.925	−0.467	0.585	−0.414
		(0.145)	(0.194)	(0.219)	(0.164)

$\alpha = -48.2$ (62.6), $R^2 = 0.9251$, $s = 34.68$, $h_1 = -1.00$, $h_2 = -1.93$, $h_3 = -0.92$, $h_4 = -0.87$, $h_5 = 0.31$

4.3 *Rational distributed lags*

The rational distributed lag model is given by:

$$y_t = \frac{A(L)}{B(L)} x_t + e_t \tag{7}$$

where $A(L)$ and $B(L)$ are polynomials in the lag operator L. Rearranging (7) gives

$$B(L)y_t = A(L)x_t + B(L)e_t \tag{8}$$

Now equation (8) is of the same type as equation (5) but with the imposition of a moving-average error term. Since the tests used for the estimated equation (5) showed no serial correlation in the error term, equation (8) would appear to be inappropriate. As a check, however, equations of type (8) were estimated, both with and without the implied restrictions between the coefficients of lagged values of y and e.[10] In the unrestricted equations no coefficients on the moving-average error terms were significant and restricting the coefficients produced a relatively poor fit and re-introduced serial correlation into the residuals.

If the significant coefficients on the lagged values of S are indicating a finite rational distributed lag (Pagan (1978)) on LN and $M4$ then regressions of S on current and lagged values of LN and $M4$ should yield uncorrelated errors. This did not occur, confirming the results obtained using Almon lags where errors always exhibited strong autocorrelation. Finally, combinations of the dependent variable lagged i periods and an autoregressive error structure of order $(4 - i)$ produced estimated equations with higher values of s than for equation [v] and parameter estimates (including those for the error term) which were not consistent with those obtained from regressing S on current and lagged values of LN and $M4$ only.

As was the case with only one lagged S, the four lagged values of S in Table 2 appear to be picking up serial correlation and not distributed lags on the explanatory variables.

5 Empirical results: NIF-10 versus autoregressive error model (6)

Empirical estimates of (6) are given as equation [v] in Table 1.[11] The error terms are uncorrelated: the first 14 autocorrelation coefficients were calculated from $\hat{e}$ and all were less than 0.05 in absolute magnitude; the values of the Lagrange multiplier test statistic (again for 14 lags) were always less than unity in absolute magnitude. There is much less serial correlation in equation [v] than in equation [ii]. The restrictions which (6) imposes on a general equation (with explanatory variables LN, LN_{-1}, . . ., LN_{-6}; $M4_{-1}$, . . ., $M4_{-5}$;S_{-1}, . . ., S_{-4}) are easily satisfied by the likelihood ratio test: $\chi_8^2 = 8.93$ compared with a critical value at the 5 per cent level of 15.51. The standard error of estimate, s, is smaller for equation [v] than for equation [ii] and the Akaike Information Criterion also favours equation [v].

In equation [v] (autoregressive errors) the long-term effect on new commencements of an increase in loans for new dwellings is 0.606 (with a standard error of 0.286) and occurs in 3 quarters (current period plus two lags). This roughly corresponds to the proportion of loans granted for the *construction* of new dwellings. The NIF-10 equation [ii] implies a similar response after three periods but further lagged responses raise the long-term effect to around unity. In equation [v] the relatively large standard errors on the coefficients of the LN terms means that the division of the total effect between quarters has not been determined with precision. This reflects in part the correlation between successive values of LN and in part changes in the proportion of loans which are for construction.

The role of general liquidity differs appreciably in the two models. The fourth differencing on $M4$ in equation [ii] seems to be reflecting the autoregressive error structure. Equation [v] suggests that it is the general level of liquidity in the preceding quarter which influences commencements. The elasticity of commencements with respect to $M4_{-1}$ is estimated to be 0.62 (evaluated at sample means).

The strength of the autoregressive error process in equation [v] indicates the need to use other variables in the model. This conclusion is supported by the failure of equation [ii] to pass the CUSUMSQ test for stability over time.

The error structure is perhaps best interpreted as a parsimonious representation of a moving average. Solving for u in terms of e yields, for equation [v],

$$u_t = e_t + 1.049e_{t-1} + 0.575e_{t-2} + 0.626e_{t-3} + 0.448e_{t-4} + \dots$$

with the weights becoming smaller after four lags. External shocks to the model have relatively long-lasting effects on activity in the housing industry.

Re-estimating the model using a fourth-order moving average confirmed these results:

$$\underset{(133.44)}{S = 20.46} + \underset{(0.153)}{0.244LN} + \underset{(0.153)}{0.271LN_{-1}} + \underset{(0.159)}{0.207LN_{-2}} + \underset{(0.0062)}{0.0129M4_{-1}} + u$$

$$u = e + \underset{(0.162)}{1.068e_{-1}} + \underset{(0.249)}{0.546e_{-2}} + \underset{(0.251)}{0.605e_{-3}} + \underset{(0.181)}{0.346e_{-4}}$$

$$R^2 = 0.9108, \quad s = 35.34, \quad h_1 = 0.68, \quad h_2 = 0.68,$$
$$h_3 = -0.02, \quad h_4 = 0.74, \quad h_5 = -0.23$$

These estimates are very similar to those of equation [v] in Table 1. The only change of note is an increase in the sum of the coefficients on the *LN* terms from 0.61 in equation [v] to 0.72. The reproduction of results using a moving average provides an additional check on whether the global maximum of the likelihood function has been found.[12]

6 Alternative model

In recent years an increasing proportion of dwelling construction in Australia has been undertaken by investors and speculative builders. This has been recognized by the Treasury in *Budget Statement Number 2, 1982-83* (pp. 17-18). They cite rapid growth in three types of housing: retirement housing, housing associated with resource projects, and accommodation in resort areas. To this list should be added inner-city apartments, particularly in Sydney. It follows that the relationship between total dwelling activity and loans for owner-occupation has weakened over time.

Speculative builders and investors can be expected to increase their level of building activity when the asset price of the existing stock rises relative to the construction cost of new dwellings. Owner-occupiers will also be influenced to some extent by this ratio in deciding whether to purchase an existing or a new dwelling.

Thus an alternative to the NIF-10 model was estimated in which financial variables were replaced by the real price of existing dwellings including land, p^h, and the real cost of construction, C. The nominal price series was constructed partly from sales data for capital cities (excluding Perth) supplied to the Department of Housing and Construction and partly from sales data collected by Philip Shrapnel (see Williams (1983)). The nominal cost series is the implicit deflator for private dwelling investment from the national accounts. The implicit deflator for non-durable personal consumption expenditure was used to convert the nominal series to indexes in real terms (1974-5 = 1000). The dependent variable was again the (seasonally adjusted) real value of commencements and the estimation period 1967(3) to 1981(2).

The empirical results paralleled those obtained using financial variables in that a fourth-order autoregressive error term was found to be significant. In this case no lags were required on the economic variables. The preferred equation is:

$$\begin{aligned} S = {} & \underset{(191.2)}{776.1} + \underset{(0.156)}{1.093}p^h - \underset{(0.313)}{1.214}C + \underset{(0.123)}{1.092}\hat{u}_{-1} - \underset{(0.186)}{0.583}\hat{u}_{-2} \\ & + \underset{(0.208)}{0.621}\hat{u}_{-3} - \underset{(0.145)}{0.622}\hat{u}_{-4} \end{aligned}$$

$$R^2 = 0.8999, \quad s = 36.66, \quad h_1 = -0.18, \quad h_2 = -0.86,$$
$$h_3 = -1.13, \quad h_4 = -1.56, \quad h_5 = 0.58$$

The coefficients on the autoregressive error structure are remarkably like those in equation [v] in Table 1. The coefficient of determination and standard error of estimate are only a little less than those in equation [v]. The two price coefficients are each significant at the 5 per cent level and have the expected opposite signs. The implied elasticities are very similar in absolute magnitude: 1.5 for the asset price of the existing stock and −1.7 for construction costs of new dwellings. Functional form is not important: the same elasticity estimates were obtained using a double logarithmic model.

The pattern of autocorrelation remained when the asset price variables were combined with the NIF-10 explanatory variables and when the period of estimation (for both the asset price model and NIF-10) was reduced to 1973(4)-1981(2).[13] Of course, the appropriate combined model would be one in which loans to owner-occupiers for *new construction* was added as a variable to the asset price model of this section. Unfortunately such data exist only from 1976.

It is likely that the cost-of-construction variable, C, does not take sufficient account of the holding costs faced by builders. A more appropriate measure of cost may be $C^* = (1 + kr)C$, where r is the annual rate of interest charged to builders by finance companies and k is a conversion factor encompassing the period of the loan and the extent to which financial costs are already included in C. With the addition of the rate of interest the preferred equation is in logarithmic form:

$$\underset{}{\ln S} = \underset{(0.42)}{7.62} + \underset{(0.24)}{1.61} \ln p^h - \underset{(0.57)}{1.04} \ln C - \underset{(0.15)}{0.41} \ln r + \underset{(0.079)}{0.955}\hat{u}_{-1} - \underset{(0.093)}{0.343}\hat{u}_{-4}$$

$$R^2 = 0.9027, \quad s = 0.0554, \quad h_1 = 0.78, \quad h_2 = -1.96,$$
$$h_3 = 1.10, \quad h_4 = -0.98, \quad h_5 = -0.33$$

where the cost term is written as $(rC)^\alpha C^\beta = r^\alpha C^\gamma$ and r is a beginning of period rate.

The coefficient on the rate of interest is significant at the 5 per cent level. The point estimates imply that the level of commencements would be little affected by an equi-proportional increase in p^h, C and r. The error structure is less complex than in other equations. (The t-values on $\hat{u}_{-2}$ and $\hat{u}_{-3}$, when included, were less than 2.0 in absolute value.) This is a hopeful sign, but more work is required to further reduce the importance of the error term.

7 Conclusions

In the NIF-10 model of the Australian economy dwelling commencements are assumed to be a function of loans to owner-occupiers for new dwellings and general liquidity. Staying within this framework it has been shown that these monetary variables are quicker acting than is suggested by NIF findings. The lagged dependent variable in the NIF-10 equation is really acting as a proxy for autocorrelated errors and, indirectly, omitted variables. A methodological point to note is that although an equation which contains a lagged dependent variable may satisfy the standard significance and diagnostic tests the implicit lag pattern should be consistent with estimates obtained by regressing the dependent variable on current and lagged values of the exogenous variables only.

Autocorrelation remained important in an alternative model in which the explanatory variables were the asset price of existing dwellings and construction costs for new dwellings. Only current values of the exogenous variables were significant in this model.

In all the equations considered in this paper the goodness of fit is critically dependent on the inclusion of either a lagged dependent variable or lagged residuals. Forecasts for more than a few quarters ahead are likely to be seriously deficient.[14] Medium-term forecasts of private dwelling activity require attention to be paid to a wider list of variables than those considered in this paper. In particular, a measure of demand-supply imbalance would seem to be needed. Looker and Carland (1980, p. 70) have already noted the importance of stocks of unsold dwellings held by speculative builders.

Notes

*The paper was written while on leave from the University of Melbourne. Jenny Anderssen provided valuable research assistance. I am indebted to Michael McAleer and Deane Terrell for comments on an earlier draft. The paper would not have been possible without the openness of the ABS-Treasury NIF team in providing clear documentation of their model and data.

1 See Department of Treasury (1981) and Looker and Carland (1980).
2 Explanatory variables are the ratio of income to repayment commitments, the price of new dwellings relative to rental prices, the per capita stock of dwellings, and changes in *M*4 relative to loans for all dwellings. A major omission is the asset price of the existing stock relative to the construction cost of new buildings.
3 The September 1981 version of the National Accounts is used.
4 See ABS, *Housing Finance for Owner Occupation, Australia* (5609.0).
5 Griliches (1961) was one of the first to spell out the relationship between a partial adjustment model and a static model with autoregressive errors.
6 For a more general discussion see Mizon (1977), Hendry and Mizon (1978), and Hendry, Pagan and Sargan (1984).
7 The restrictions are of the type which, by taking out a common factor (in this case $(1 - \beta_5 L)$, where L is the lag operator), convert an infinite rational distributed lag $(\beta_1 + \beta_2 L)/(1 - \beta_5 L)$ into a finite lag. See Pagan (1978).
8 Griliches (1961) looks at this bias from another viewpoint, namely, an equation in which the lagged dependent variable is incorrectly included and the lagged error

term is incorrectly omitted, i.e. 'true' equation is $y = \beta_1 x + \beta_3 z + \beta_5 \hat{u}_{-1}$; estimated equation is $y = \beta_1' x + \beta_3' z + \beta_5' y_{-1}$.

9 The latter point may be illustrated by reference to the simple model $y_t = \beta_1 x_t + \beta_2 x_{t-1} + u_t$, $u_t = \varrho u_{t-1} + e_t$. For positive ϱ, the coefficient on x_{t-1} in the unrestricted form is negative only if $\beta_2 < \varrho\beta_1$.

10 The possibility of different lags on *LN* and *M*4 was allowed for by estimating models of the form $S = A_1(L)LN + A_2(L)M4 + B_1(L)S_{-1} + B(L)e_t$. As before, the longest lag on *S* was restricted to four periods.

11 As a check, a fifth-order autoregressive error structure was tried but was found to be unnecessary: the coefficient on $\hat{u}_{-5}$ was 0.115 with a standard error of 0.217; the other coefficients were little affected.

12 A potential weakness of the likelihood ratio tests used in this paper is that only a local maximum is reached. In the NIF equations and equations [iii] and [iv] in Table 1, the moving average process is essentially being approximated by one with weights declining exponentially at a slow rate.

13 Figures on the dependent variable are published on a consistent basis from 1973(4). When seasonally unadjusted data for the dependent variable is used the fourth-order autoregressive error structure persists, suggesting that it is not caused by the seasonal adjustment procedure per se, although any changes in the timing of recording data on commencements (such as occurred in 1981(3)) might cause problems.

14 Using the NIF equation [i] of Table 1 to project 8 quarters ahead gives an average under prediction of 6.3 per cent if all values of S_{-1} are assumed known and 15.4 per cent if only the initial value is given.

References

Breusch, T.S. and Pagan, A.R. (1980), 'The Lagrange Multiplier Test and its Application to Model Specification in Econometrics', *Review of Economic Studies*, 47, 239-54.

Department of the Treasury (1981), *The NIF-10 Model of the Australian Economy*, Canberra: AGPS.

Griliches, Z. (1961), 'A Note on Serial Correlation Bias in Estimates of Distributed Lags', *Econometrica*, 29, 65-73.

Hendry, D.F. and Mizon, G.E. (1978), 'Serial Correlation as a Convenient Simplification, Not a Nuisance: A Comment on a Study of the Demand for Money by the Bank of England', *Economic Journal*, 88, 549-63.

Hendry, D.F., Pagan, A.R. and Sargan, J.D. (1984), 'Dynamic Specification', in *Handbook of Econometrics*, 2, eds Z. Griliches and M. Intriligator, Amsterdam: North-Holland.

Looker, J.C. and Carland, D.J. (1980), 'The Housing Sector Model in the National Income Forecasting Model', in Department of Housing and Construction, *Housing Economics*, Canberra: AGPS.

Mizon, G.E. (1977), 'Model Selection Procedures', in *Studies in Modern Economic Analysis*, eds. M.J. Artis and A.R. Nobay, Oxford: Blackwell.

Pagan, A.R. (1978), 'Rational and Polynomial Lags: The Finite Connection', *Journal of Econometrics*, 8, 247-54.

Sargan, J.D. (1964), 'Wages and Prices in the United Kingdom: A Study in Econometric Methodology', in *Econometric Analysis for National Economic Planning*, eds. P.E. Hart, G. Mills and J.K. Whitaker, London: Butterworths.

Sargan, J.D. (1980), 'Some Tests of Dynamic Specification for a Single Equation', *Econometrica*, 48, 879-98.
Williams, R.A. (1983), 'Ownership of Dwellings and Personal Wealth in Australia', *Australian Economic Review*, 62, 55-62.

Notes on contributors

Murray BEATTIE holds a degree from Monash University, where he was also a Tutor in the Department of Econometrics and Operations Research. He is a Member of the Institute of Actuaries, and is employed by a Life Office. He has published in the area of applied econometrics.

Kenneth W. CLEMENTS is Professor of Economics at the University of Western Australia. Prior to taking up the Chair in 1981 he was Research Economist at the Reserve Bank of Australia. He was educated at Monash University and the University of Chicago, where he was later Assistant Professor of Economics and International Business in the Graduate School of Business, and Associate Director of the Centre for Mathematical Studies in Business and Economics. In 1980 he was Associate Director of the Centre for Studies in Money, Banking and Finance at Macquarie University. His publications cover a number of areas of economics and econometrics.

Donald COCHRANE was Dean of Economics and Politics at Monash University until 1981. He was previously Professor of Economics at Monash, and was Sidney Myer Professor of Commerce at the University of Melbourne from 1955 to 1961. His various appointments included that of Economist with the United Nations, and a SEATO Travelling Professorship. He was educated at the Universities of Melbourne and Cambridge and, in addition to his academic writings, he served on or chaired numerous government committees.

Russel J. COOPER is Senior Lecturer in the School of Economic and Financial Studies at Macquarie University. He was educated at Macquarie University, the Australian National University, and Monash University where he held a Lectureship in the Department of Econometrics and Operations Research. He spent two years at the Reserve Bank of Australia and he has published in the areas of intertemporal optimization and applied economic modelling.

David E.A. GILES is Professor of Economics at the University of Canterbury, where he was educated. He previously worked as a Research

Officer at the Reserve Bank of New Zealand before taking up a Lectureship and later the Chair of Econometrics at Monash University. He has held a visiting appointment at the University of Western Ontario and has published widely in both applied and theoretical econometrics.

Edward J. HANNAN is Professor of Statistics in the Institute of Advanced Studies at the Australian National University. He was educated at the University of Melbourne and is a Fellow of the Australian Academy of Science, of the Academy of Social Sciences in Australia, and of the Econometric Society. He has held a number of visiting appointments and has authored three books and numerous articles in various areas of probability theory and mathematical statistics, especially time-series analysis.

Grant H. HILLIER is Senior Lecturer in the Department of Econometrics and Operations Research at Monash University. He was educated at the University of Adelaide and the University of Pennsylvania, and previously held a Lectureship in Economics at the University of Reading. He has published in econometrics and statistics journals.

Maxwell L. KING is Professor of Econometrics at Monash University where he previously held a Lectureship in the Department of Econometrics and Operations Research. He holds degrees from the University of Canterbury and worked as a Research Officer at the Reserve Bank of New Zealand. His special interest is hypothesis testing and he has published widely in economics, econometrics and statistics journals.

Michael McALEER is Lecturer in the Department of Statistics, Faculty of Economics at the Australian National University. He was educated at Monash University and Queen's University, Canada. He has published in economics, econometrics and statistics journals, especially in the area of model specification and testing.

Keith R. McLAREN is Senior Lecturer in the Department of Econometrics and Operations Research and the Department of Economics at Monash University. He was educated at Monash University and Northwestern University, and has held visiting appointments at Northwestern and at the University of California (San Diego). His publications reflect his interests in duality theory and intertemporal optimization.

Lonnie J. MAGEE is Assistant Professor of Economics at McMaster University. He is a graduate of the University of Waterloo, and received his PhD from the University of Western Ontario. His special interest is finite-sample distribution theory.

Guy H. ORCUTT is Professor of Economics and Statistics and in the Institution for Social and Policy Studies at Yale University. He was educated at the University of Michigan, has held appointments at MIT, Cambridge University, Harvard University, the University of Wisconsin, the International Monetary Fund, and the World Bank, and has held a number of visiting positions. He is a Fellow and former Vice President of the American Statistical Association, Fellow and former Council Member of the Econometric Society, and has served on the Executive Committee of the American Economic Association. He has published several books and numerous articles on various aspects of economic modelling.

Soo-Bin PARK is Professor of Economics at Carleton University. He was educated at Seoul National University and Indiana University. He has held visiting appointments at the University of Chicago and has published in the areas of theoretical and applied econometrics.

Peter D. PRAETZ is Associate Professor in the Department of Econometrics and Operations Research and the Department of Accounting and Finance at Monash University. He was educated at the Universities of Melbourne and Adelaide and has held positions at the Commonwealth Scientific and Industrial Research Organisation, the University of Adelaide, and as a consulting actuary. He is a Fellow of the Institute of Actuaries, and his publications have been in the areas of econometrics, statistics, finance, and actuarial science.

J. Denis SARGAN was Tooke Professor of Economic Science and Statistics at the London School of Economics and Political Science prior to his retirement in 1984. Previously he was Professor of Econometrics at the LSE, and held positions at Leeds University. He was educated at the University of Cambridge, is a Fellow of the British Academy and a Fellow and Past President of the Econometric Society. His numerous articles on such topics as finite sample theory, time series, and nonlinear modelling have appeared in the leading econometrics and statistics journals.

Virendra K. SRIVASTAVA is Professor of Statistics at Lucknow University. He was educated at Lucknow University and the Indian Statistical Institute and previously held positions at the Banaras Hindu University and at the Planning Research and Action Institute. He has held visiting appointments at Concordia University and Monash University. He has published numerous articles in statistics and econometrics, especially in the area of finite-sample distribution theory.

Sir Richard STONE was the P.D. Leake Professor of Finance and

Accounting at the University of Cambridge until his retirement in 1980, and is a Fellow of King's College, Cambridge, the Econometric Society and the British Academy, and an Honorary Fellow of Gonville and Caius College, Cambridge. He was educated at the University of Cambridge and holds honorary doctorates from the Universities of Oslo, Brussels, Geneva, Warwick, Paris and Bristol. His positions included that of director of the Department of Applied Economics at Cambridge from 1945 to 1955, and he is a former President of the Econometric Society and the Royal Economic Society. He has authored several important books and has published widely in the areas of social accounting and econometrics. In recognition of his pioneering contributions, especially in the field of National Income accounting, Sir Richard was named as Nobel Laureate in Economic Science in 1984.

John C. TAYLOR is Research Economist at the Reserve Bank of Australia. He was educated at the University of New South Wales.

Aman ULLAH is Professor of Economics at the University of Western Ontario. He was educated at Lucknow and Delhi Universities and previously taught at the Delhi School of Economics, Southern Methodist University, and Lucknow University. He has held visiting appointments at the Australian National University, Monash University, Erasmus University and the Catholic University of Louvain. He has co-authored two books and published widely in econometrics and statistics.

Geoffrey S. WATSON is Professor of Statistics at Princeton University. He has degrees from the University of Melbourne and North Carolina State University, and has held positions at the Commonwealth Scientific and Industrial Research Organisation, the Universities of Melbourne and Toronto, Princeton University, the John Hopkins University, and the Australian National University. He has held a number of awards and visiting Professorships; is a Fellow and former Council Member of the Institute of Mathematical Statistics; and is a Fellow of the International Statistical Institute, the Royal Statistical Society, the American Association for the Advancement of Science, and the American Statistical Association. He has authored or co-authored many books and numerous articles in many areas of mathematical statistics.

Ross A. WILLIAMS is Professor of Econometrics at the University of Melbourne. He was educated at the University of Melbourne and the London School of Economics and has held positions at Monash University, the World Bank and the Australian National University. He has co-authored two books and published a number of articles in economics and applied econometrics, especially in the area of consumer demand analysis.

Arnold ZELLNER is the H.G.B. Alexander Professor of Economics and Statistics, Graduate School of Business at the University of Chicago. He has previously held appointments at the University of Washington and the University of Wisconsin. He has held visiting positions at Yale University, the Netherlands School of Economics and the Econometric Institute (Rotterdam), Stanford University, the University of California (Berkeley) and Monash University, and is a founding co-editor of the *Journal of Econometrics* and the founding editor of the *Journal of Business and Economic Statistics*. He is a Fellow of the American Statistical Association, the American Academy of Arts and Sciences, the American Association for the Advancement of Science and a Fellow and former Council member of the Econometric Society. He has authored and edited a number of books, and his many published contributions span a wide range of interests in economics, econometrics and statistics, most notably in connection with Bayesian inference.

Appendix 1
Application of least squares regression to relationships containing auto-correlated error terms*

D. Cochrane and G.H. Orcutt

We point out that autocorrelated error terms require modification of the usual methods of estimation and prediction; and we present evidence showing that the error terms involved in most current formulations of economic relations are highly postively autocorrelated. In doing this we demonstrate that when estimates of autoregressive properties of error terms are based on calculated residuals there is a large bias towards randomness. We demonstrate how much efficiency may be lost by current methods of estimation and prediction; and we give a tentative method of procedure for regaining the lost efficiency.

Introduction

Three major complications may be distinguished in the statistical measurement of relationships between economic time series:

1. The existence of simultaneous relationships between the variables.
2. The presence of auto-correlated error terms. This has been less exactly called the time-series complication.
3. The presence of errors of observation in each of the variables.

The first complication was forcefully brought to the attention of economists by Frisch [1] and Haavelmo [2]; and much work has since been done by Koopmans [3] and others, [4] in finding the structural parameters when the economic variables are described by a system of simultaneous equations. This approach is very promising but the time-series complication has been assumed away by the specification that the error terms which enter into each equation are independent in successive periods of time.

A considerable amount of work has also been devoted to problems relating to the second complication. The rather extensive literature connected with the variate difference method, conveniently summarized by

* We wish to express our thanks for the considerable assistance we have received from Richard Stone.

Tintner [5], and also the general analysis of economic time trends may be included under this heading. More directly related to the problem are the studies which examine the distribution of correlations between autocorrelated series, [6] the major proportion of which are devoted to tests for the null hypothesis. Of those papers which are concerned with the measurement of functional relationships between series, few make it clear that the significant factor in the analysis is the autocorrelation of the error term and not the autocorrelation of the time series themselves. This fact has been well expressed by Aitken [7], but its importance seems to have escaped the attention of economists. We should also refer to a paper by Champernowne [8] which became available after this study was essentially complete. Champernowne's paper recovers much of the ground developed by Aitken and is an exceedingly useful study, carrying the problem into the field of statistical estimation and sampling theory.

The third complication arises when the assumption that the explanatory variables are measured free from error cannot be maintained, and may therefore be a problem of some importance when considering economic data. In the absence of a complete knowledge of the correlation matrix of the errors, simplifying assumptions that the errors in each of the variables are random and uncorrelated both with the systematic part of each variable and with the errors in the other variables must be made. The problems involved have received consideration in the work of Frisch [9], Koopmans [10], Tintner [11], Reiersøl [12] and Geary [13].

The objects of this paper are four-fold. First, we wish to focus the attention of economists on the fact that the presence of autocorrelated error terms requires some modification of the usual least squares method of estimation; and secondly, we wish to show that there is strong evidence in favour of the view that the error terms involved in most current formulations of economic relations are highly positively autocorrelated. In doing this we demonstrate the presence of a large bias towards randomness in estimates of the autoregressive properties of error terms which are based on calculated residuals. Third we indicate roughly how much efficiency is lost by current methods of estimation and prediction if error terms are highly autocorrelated; and finally present a tentative method of procedure.

In arriving at our conclusions we have placed considerable reliance on results obtained from a number of sampling experiments. We recognize that results arrived at by this procedure may not have the elegance or all of the utility of results obtained deductively from the same assumptions; nevertheless this method of approach is a legitimate one and frequently makes it possible to obtain useful answers to problems which have proved stubborn to mathematical statisticians. In this connection it might be noticed that there are a large number of important questions in the field of statistics which in principle could be answered deductively but which have till the present time proved too difficult. Most of these questions could be answered by sampling experiments and it is to be hoped that, as improved calculating equipment becomes available, more attention will be given to this approach.

In order to concentrate on the problem of auto-correlated errors, we have ignored the difficulties arising from the simultaneous equations complication and the errors in the variables complication. However, it should be obvious that for the purpose of estimating structural parameters it is necessary to find a method of dealing simultaneously with all three complications, or at least some indication of their relative importances. A consideration of some aspects of the difficulties to be experienced in analysing relationships when more than one of these complications are present is contained in a following paper [14].

Regression analysis with autocorrelated error terms of known autoregressive properties

It may be helpful to restate briefly the assumptions underlying the method of least squares. Suppose a single linear relationship exists between the variables $x_{1t}, x_{2t}, \ldots x_{kt}$ of the form

$$x_{1t} = a + \sum_{j=2}^{k} b_{1j}x_{jt} + u_t \tag{2.1}$$

where u_t is a random error term with constant variance, while the a and the b's are constants to be determined. Provided the $x_{2t} \ldots x_{kt}$ are independent of the random error term u_t, then the best linear unbiassed estimates of these coefficients are given by the method of least squares, best estimates meaning those estimates which have a minimum variance. This is true even if the independent variables are autocorrelated, provided we can consider them as fixed in repeated samples [15]. If in addition the error term is normally distributed then the least squares estimates are maximum likelihood estimates [16].

In many economic relationships it is an oversimplification to assume that error terms are independent in time. If we have a relationship in which the error term is autocorrelated, it has been shown by Aitken [17] that the method of least squares still yields the best linear unbiassed estimates of the regression coefficients provided the lack of independence in the error series is taken into account. One method of overcoming this lack of independence is to make the error term random by transforming all the variables according to the autoregressive structure of the error term. Suppose we have a linear relationship given by

$$y_t = a_0 + a_1x_t + u_t \tag{2.2}$$

where u_t is generated by the Markoff scheme

$$u_t = \beta u_{t-1} + \varepsilon_t \tag{2.3}$$

with random disturbances ε_t and a known autoregression coefficient β. We may substitute for u_t in equation (2.2) and obtain

$$y'_t = a'_0 + a_1 x'_t + \varepsilon_t \tag{2.4}$$

where

$$y'_t = y_t - \beta y_{t-1} \quad \text{and} \tag{2.5}$$

$$x'_t = x_t - \beta x_{t-1} \tag{2.6}$$

and the application of least squares to equation (2.4) will produce best linear unbiassed estimates of the regression coefficients a'_0 and a_1.*

It is also possible to improve on the ordinary methods of prediction when the error terms are autocorrelated. If we wish to estimate y_t from a given x_t it can be seen that equation (2.2) is not the most efficient form in which to make this estimation. A more appropriate form would be to use the relation

$$y_t = a'_0 + a_1(x_t - \beta x_{t-1}) + \beta y_{t-1} \tag{2.7}$$

where a'_0 and a_1 are estimated from (2.4). In a later section we shall illustrate the gain to be achieved by using this relation in problems of estimation.

In the discussion which follows it is convenient to restrict the meaning of error term to the true series of errors in a relationship, that is the series of errors which would be obtained if the *true* values of the regression parameters were applied in the relationship. To distinguish the discrepancies actually obtained from the true errors we shall call them residuals. In addition, we shall limit the word disturbance to describe the random elements in an autoregressive equation.

Autocorrelation of error terms and residuals of economic and constructed relationships

In this section we develop the argument that the error terms in many if not most current formulations of economic relations are highly positively autocorrelated, but it should be stressed that we are not trying to prove that this must be so in every case or that it is impossible to formulate relations in which the error terms are random. Since the autocorrelation properties of economic time series will frequently arise in this section, we should first like to refer to a study by Orcutt [18] in which it is shown that the fifty-two series used in Tinbergen's [19] model of the economic system of the United States might be considered to have been obtained by drawings from a single

* A more complete statement of this solution is to be found in Section 6.

population of linear stochastic series having the same underlying autoregressive structure. The underlying autoregressive equation was estimated to be of the form

$$x_{t+1} = x_t + 0.3(x_t - x_{t-1}) + \varepsilon_{t+1} \tag{3.1}$$

where the ε's are random disturbances. The high positive autocorrelation of economic time series which (3.1) implies is a feature which should not be overlooked.

Turning to the error terms, let us investigate their sources and see if there is reason to believe that the error terms also are likely to be highly positively autocorrelated. We can examine their sources under three main headings.

(1.) Systematic errors may arise from a faulty choice of the form of relationship assumed to exist between economic variables. Since the economic variables are positively autocorrelated, then in general errors of this type will be positively autocorrelated. Further the shortness of most available time series makes the statistical results meaningless if very complicated relationships are adopted, so that errors of this type are inevitable.

(2.) Error terms may arise owing to the omission of variables, both economic and non-economic, from the analysis. Important variables may be omitted either because they are not available or because their importance is not realized. Furthermore, because of the brevity of available time series, it is also frequently necessary to neglect variables which individually have but a small influence. Nevertheless, it is evident that the total influence of a number of such variables may be very substantial and highly positively autocorrelated.* Now, as already indicated, there is strong evidence in favour of believing that most economic time series are highly positively autocorrelated. Therefore, in so far as the omitted variables are economic time series, we may expect the resulting error terms to be highly positively autocorrelated.

Consider also the case of non-economic variables which are likely to

* This may be shown as follows. If we have two unrelated autocorrelated series x_t and y_t whose first autocorrelations are given by

$$\frac{\operatorname{cov}(x_t, x_{t-1})}{\operatorname{var}(x)} \text{ and } \frac{\operatorname{cov}(y_t, y_{t-1})}{\operatorname{var}(y)}$$

then if $z_t = x_t + y_t$ the first autocorrelation of z_t is given by

$$\frac{\operatorname{cov}(x_t, x_{t-1}) + \operatorname{cov}(y_t, y_{t-1})}{\operatorname{var}(x) + \operatorname{var}(y)}$$

This result may be generalized to show that the sum of any number of autocorrelated series is also autocorrelated with its first autocorrelation equal to the sum of the first lag covariances of the individual series divided by the sum of the individual variances.

influence economic behaviour but which are generally omitted. Some of those that more readily come to mind are population and its age, sex and spatial distribution, changes in cultural patterns, technological developments, exploitation and exhaustion of mineral resources including changes in soil fertility, and climatic conditions. Most of the above series have very high positive autocorrelations but even where the autocorrelations are not high, as in the case of at least certain climatic conditions, it is evident that their impact on the economic system is still likely to be autocorrelated. Thus even if rainfall was really a random series, the water level in the soil, being the result of rainfall over several years, would be positively autocorrelated. We might recall in this respect the correlograms given by Wold [20] of the average yearly rainfall during the period 1867 to 1936 of four cities in or near the drainage basin of Lake Väner and the average annual water level (obtained from quarterly observations) of Lake Väner from 1867 to 1936. The correlogram of the yearly rainfall indicated a random series while that of the level of the lake indicated a positively autocorrelated series showing that, whilst the occurrence of certain meteorological factors may be random, their general influence over time may be systematic.

Now it may be reasonably argued that the economic behaviour of individuals is not completely dependent on economic variables or non-economic variables of the type we have mentioned, and that, even if an explanation incorporated in the correct manner as many as necessary of these variables, it would still not yield perfectly correct predictions.* No doubt this is true, and the explanatory variables needed to complete the explanation may be of an approximately random character since they relate to such things as the physiological processes of each individual. However, it would be a mistake to infer from this that economic time series contain a significant random component, for what will obviously happen when the behaviour of a large number of individuals is averaged is that those actions of individuals which are positively correlated with the actions of others will dominate the average while those actions which are random for each individual and uncorrelated as between individuals will be averaged out.

(3.) The series of data used may not measure exactly what is required for the particular analysis. In so far as the discrepancy is one of coverage, it seems reasonable to believe that the error term involved will have much the same autoregressive properties as economic series in general. In so far as the discrepancy is more nearly what might perhaps be called a pure error of observation, it would appear more difficult to say anything about whether or not it is autocorrelated. However, on the basis of discussions with economists engaged in the construction of basic economic data, we have formed a very strong impression that, if an error is committed one year, it

* See for example T. Haavelmo, 'The Probability Approach in Econometrics', *op. cit.* Section 11.

will very likely be committed again the next year and that most errors of observation are positively autocorrelated.

Let us now see whether our theory is plausible by making a brief examination of the autocorrelations of the residuals obtained in several econometric studies. These are two papers by Lawrence R. Klein, 'The Use of Econometric Models as a Guide to Economic Policy' [21], and 'Economic Fluctuations in the United States 1921-1941' [22]; a paper by M.A. Girshick and Trygve Haavelmo [23] and a paper by Richard Stone [24]. The measure of autocorrelation used is the ratio of the mean square successive difference to the variance of the residuals. This ratio is generally denoted by δ^2/s^2 [25] where δ^2 and s^2 are defined by

$$\delta^2 = \frac{1}{N-1}\sum_{t=1}^{N-1}(x_{t+1} - x_t)^2, \qquad (3.2)$$

$$s^2 = \frac{1}{N}\sum_{t=1}^{N}(x_t - \bar{x})^2, \qquad (3.3)$$

where $\bar{x} = \frac{1}{N}\sum_{t=1}^{N} x_t.$

This ratio has been calculated by Klein for the residuals in his two papers and we have computed the ratios for the residuals in the other two papers [26]. Two ratios in each of Klein's papers have been omitted as they refer to first differences of the economic series and are not comparable for our purposes. It should be mentioned that the residuals given in Klein's paper in *Econometrica* and the residuals given by Girshick and Haavelmo were calculated by the reduced-form method which presupposes that it is possible to solve for each of a number of jointly dependent variables in terms of exogenous variables and random error terms and these random error terms are simply linear combinations of the error terms given in the original system of equations [27]. The residuals obtained from Klein's mimeographed paper and from Stone's paper were calculated by ordinary least squares method of regression. The total number of series considered is 43 and Table 1 shows them classified according to source and number of parameters used in each equation. The individual values of δ^2/s^2 are illustrated on the scatter diagrams of Figures 1-4.

The probability distribution of δ^2/s^2 for a random series has been tabulated [28] for various N, where N is the number of items. This distribution is symmetrical around $2N/N - 1$ so that for $N = 20$ the expected value of δ^2/s^2 for a random series is 2.11. This is the horizontal dotted line shown on the diagrams. In view of the high positive autocorrelation of economic time series and the reasons given for expecting error terms to be autocorrelated, there seems little chance of obtaining a value of δ^2/s^2 around the upper tail

Table 1 *Summary of values of δ^2/s^2 obtained for various residuals*

Source of residuals	Number of years	Number of parameters				Total
		3	4	5	6	
Klein – Econometrica	22	2	7	2	1	12
Klein – Mimeographed study	20	1	7	1	—	9
Girshick and Haavelmo	20	2	2	1	—	5
Stone	19	4	6	6	1	17
Total		9	22	10	2	43
$P(\delta^2/s^2 < 1.24) = 0.025$		7	5	4	—	16
$P(\delta^2/s^2 < 1.37) = 0.05$		8	10	4	—	22

of the distribution and, since we wish to minimize the risk of failing to reject a value of δ^2/s^2 as coming from a random population, the appropriate test would seem to involve the use of the value of δ^2/s^2 corresponding to the 5 per cent significant level, from the lower tail only. Since all our series are of approximately the same length, this value is 1.37 for $N = 20$. The value of δ^2/s^2 (=1.24) corresponding to the 5 per cent significance level which includes both tails has also been added.* Out of the 43 series, 16 are significantly different from a random series at the 2½ per cent level, while 22 are significant at the 5 per cent level. These results indicate that in many cases the assumption of random error terms is not a very good approximation to the truth.

The sloping lines on Figures 1-4 correspond to the average of twenty estimates of δ^2/s^2 obtained from constructed relationships, described in subsequent paragraphs, in which the error terms were first summations of random series. It would seem more reasonable to consider that the values of δ^2/s^2 are distributed around a line of this nature rather than around the horizontal random line. This suggestion is supported by the decreasing proportion of residuals which are significantly different from random series as the number of parameters in the relationship increases. From Table 1 it can be seen that the proportions which are significantly different from random are 8/9, 10/22, 4/10 and 0/2 for 3, 4, 5 and 6 parameters respectively.

* Klein has taken the 5 per cent level of significance to include both tails of the distribution (*Econometrica, op. cit.*, p. 114).

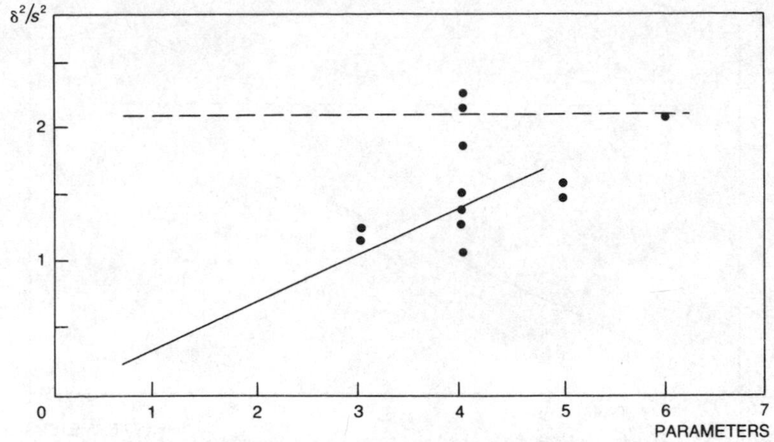

Figure 1 Autocorrelation of residuals estimates by Klein-Econometrica.

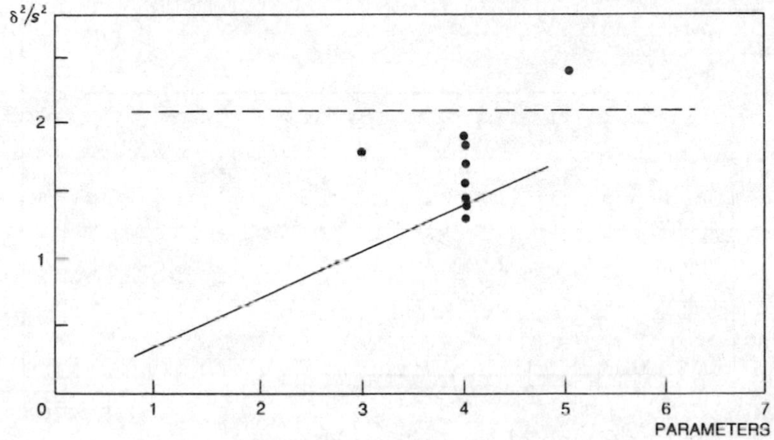

Figure 2 Autocorrelation of residuals estimates by Klein-Mimeographed study.

Construction of an experimental model

The examination of the residuals obtained from actual economic relationships fails to reject the hypothesis that error terms are highly positively autocorrelated in a number of economic relationships. Little is known about the behaviour of relationships possessing autocorrelated error terms, so it was decided to construct several relationships of this type from artificial

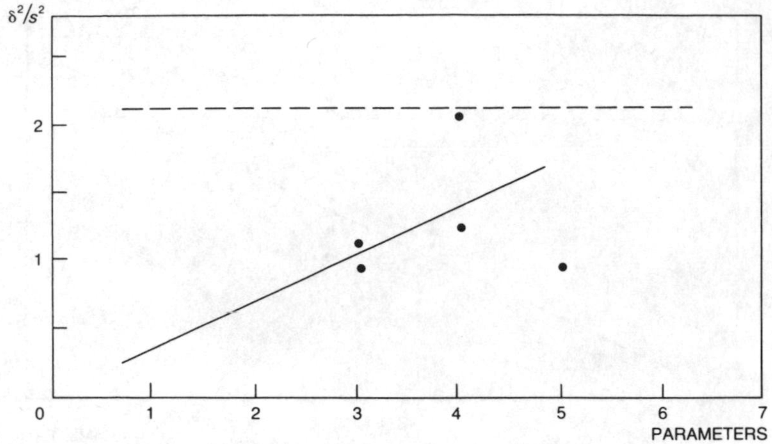

Figure 3 Autocorrelation of residuals estimates by Girshick and Haavelmo.

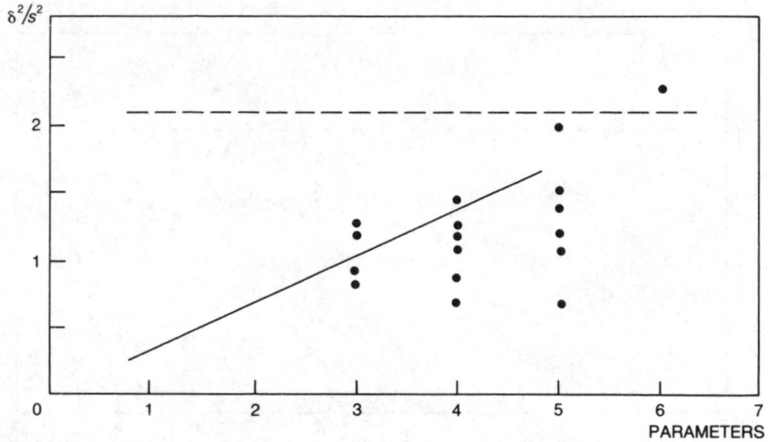

Figure 4 Autocorrelation of residuals estimates by Stone.

series and observe the results of applying least squares regression. The general form of the relationship adopted was –

$$X_1 = k + b_{12.3t}X_2 + b_{13.2t}X_3 + b_{1t.23}t + u \qquad (3.4)$$

where X_2, X_3 and u were independently constructed series all possessing the same autoregressive structure, t represented a linear time trend and the true values of the constants were $k = 0$, $b_{12.3t} = 2$, $b_{13.2t} = 1$ and $b_{1t.23} = 0$. Thus the actual equation used for the construction was –

$$X_1 = 2X_2 + X_3 + u. \tag{3.5}$$

Five sets of relationships of this form were constructed with different autoregressive structures, each set containing 20 equations. The series used were generated according to the following formulae:–

$$\begin{aligned} &A. \quad x_{t+1} = x_t + 0.3(x_t - x_{t-1}) + \varepsilon_{t+1} \\ &B. \quad x_{t+1} = x_t + \varepsilon_{t+1} \\ &C. \quad x_{t+1} = 0.3x_t + \varepsilon_{t+1} \\ &D. \quad x_{t+1} = \varepsilon_{t+1} \\ &E. \quad x_{t+1} = \varepsilon_{t+1} - \varepsilon_t \end{aligned} \tag{3.6}$$

where the ε's denote series of random disturbances. Instead of stating the precise form of the autoregressive equation each time a series is referred to we shall use the letters A, B, C, D and E as a convenient notation.

The random elements were obtained from Tables of Random Sampling Numbers [29]. Two figure numbers were extracted, ignoring the number 00, so that they ranged from 1 to 99. The number 50 was then subtracted throughout so that we possessed a rectangular distribution ranging from +49 to −49 with a true mean of zero. We then formed 60 independent series of these random elements, each one 20 items in length, omitting a few numbers between each series so that we could later extrapolate for forecasting. The application of these series in groups of three to the relation (3.5) gave us the 20 equations of set D. The other transformations were then formed from this basic set. For example, the set of first summations, series B, was formed by making the first-term of each series zero and summing progressively over each item of the random set. Simplifications of the calculations involved were made by using the fact that C is the first difference of A, while B, D and E are respectively the first summation of a random series, a random series, and the first difference of a random series. It can be easily seen that there were 21 items in series A and B, 20 in C and D and 19 in E. They are therefore analogous in length to most available economic time series.

In each set a regression analysis was carried out with one explanatory variable (in this case the error term became $(X_3 + u)$), in several of the sets the analysis was extended to two explanatory variables and in the case of set B to three explanatory variables. In addition, the statistic δ^2/s^2 was calculated for the actual error terms and for the residuals. A complete summary of these calculations is contained in Table 2.

Bias introduced in estimating the autocorrelations of residuals

Given a set of equations in which the explanatory variables and the error terms possess the same autoregressive structure, can we say anything about

Table 2 *Summary of statistics calculated for five transformations involving relationships in which the explanatory variables and error term possess the same autoregressive structure*

Equation No.	Generating Properties of		Values of δ^2/s^2				Regression parameters								Correlation coefficient		
	Explanatory variable	Error term	Actual error series		Estimated residuals		Constant term k		Regression coefficients						Calculated value		True value for infinite series
									b_{12}		b_{13}		b_{1t}				
			Mean	Variance	Mean	Variance	Mean	Standard deviation	Mean	Variance	Mean	Variance	Mean	Variance	Mean	Variance	
1	A	A	0.310	0.128	0.490	0.165	16.832	155.89	2.053	0.927	—	—	—	—	0.754	0.067	0.817
2	A	A	0.310	0.128	0.790	0.153	−5.560	169.15	2.290	0.766	—	—	−1.430	339.60	0.926	0.006	0.817
3	B	B	0.450	0.223	0.685	0.279	−7.663	105.18	2.079	0.755	—	—	—	—	0.769	0.049	0.817
4	B	B	0.450	0.223	1.081	0.283	−16.809	112.95	2.260	0.517	—	—	−1.005	168.91	0.917	0.004	0.817
5	B	B	0.309	0.071	1.058	0.320	2.527	63.59	2.160	0.335	0.930	0.478	—	—	0.927	0.012	0.913
6	B	B	0.309	0.071	1.396	0.311	−10.074	86.35	2.174	0.220	1.062	0.157	−1.202	101.30	0.970	0.0005	0.913
7	B	B	N.C.	—	N.C.	—	N.C.	—	—	—	1.242	1.919	—	—	0.440	0.181	0.408
8	C	C	1.494	0.260	1.559	0.258	−1.260	13.484	2.185	0.175	—	—	—	—	0.839	0.005	0.817
9	D	D	1.982	0.264	2.007	0.264	−1.069	9.84	2.140	0.111	—	—	—	—	0.838	0.0056	0.817
10	D	D	2.138	0.228	2.153	0.171	0.102	7.46	2.120	0.075	0.973	0.051	—	—	0.930	0.0004	0.913
11	D	D	N.C.	—	N.C.	—	N.C.	—	—	—	0.963	0.305	—	—	0.381	0.044	0.408
12	E	E	2.996	0.115	3.011	0.147	0.303	2.35	2.075	0.127	—	—	—	—	0.839	0.0079	0.817
							(0)		(2.075)	(0.128)	—	—	—	—	(0.844)	(0.008)	
13	E	E	3.047	0.070	2.934	0.064	0.072	1.72	2.060	0.088	0.898	0.100	—	—	0.929	0.001	0.913
							(0)	—	(2.060)	(0.088)	(0.898)	(0.100)	—	—	(0.929)	(0.001)	
14	E	E	N.C.	—	N.C.	—	N.C.	—	—	—	0.820	0.403	—	—	0.341	0.062	0.408

* Figures in parentheses were calculated assuming a mean of zero.
N.C. indicates that certain statistics were not calculated.

the way in which the autocorrelations of the residuals vary as the number of explanatory variables is increased? Figure 5 presents this information with each set labelled according to its autoregressive structure. The number of parameters includes the constant term so that we have one parameter when only the mean is estimated. Straight lines have been fitted visually to the points for each set using as additional points, except for *D*, the true values of δ^2/s^2 which are zero for *A* and *B*, 1.4 for *C* and 3.0 for *E*. The sets, *A*, *B* and *C* show a marked bias upwards as the number of parameters is increased. It is not expected that this linearity would continue indefinitely but would flatten out as more than four parameters are used and approach nearer and nearer to the value of δ^2/s^2 expected for a random series. The random set *D* merely shows a distribution around the horizontal straight line and when we pass to the series of first differences of random numbers *E* there is only very slight evidence of a downward movement in the values of δ^2/s^2 with increasing parameters.*

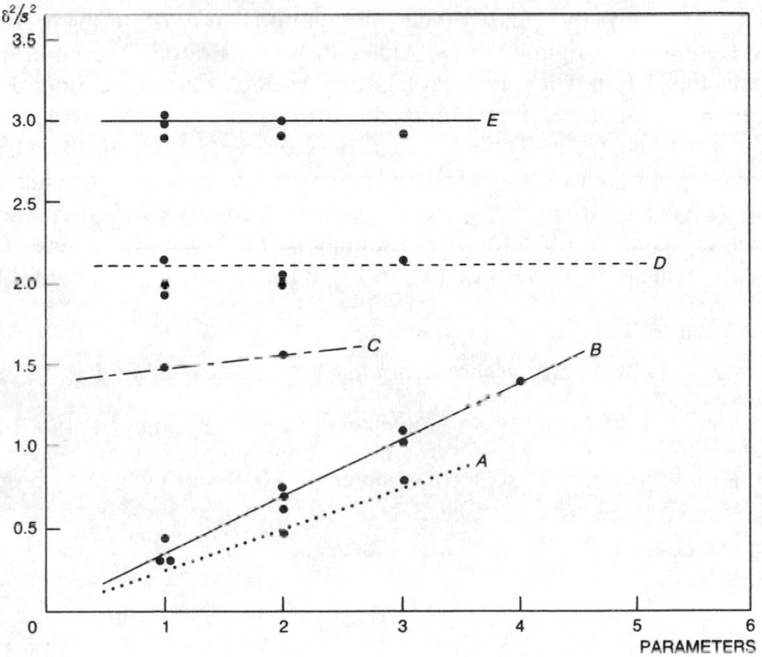

Figure 5 Autocorrelation of residuals obtained from constructed relationships.

* The first autocorrelation of the first differences of a random series is $r_1 = -0.5$ or $\delta^2/s^2 = 3.0$.

Another way of illustrating the bias in the estimated autocorrelations of the residuals as more variables are introduced is to apply our previous test of significance to the individual values of δ^2/s^2 obtained in set *B*. This has been done in Table 3. As the number of parameters increases the proportion of residuals which yield a value of δ^2/s^2 significantly different from that expected for a random series at the 5 per cent level grows smaller; from 19/20 when only the mean is estimated to only 10/20 when four parameters are used. This is a similar result to that found for the residuals of actual economic relationships.

The amount of variance to be explained in an economic time series can be regarded as composed of two parts, the first due to the smooth movements of the autoregressive structure of the series and the second due to the random disturbances. What is important for a real explanation is that a proportion of the variance due to the disturbances should be explained as well as that due to the general movement of the series. Now quite high correlations between autocorrelated series may be obtained purely by chance* and when this happens what is largely explained is the variance due to the regular movements through time. The residuals of such a relationship will be essentially the year-to-year fluctuations and of a more random character than the original series. This can be illustrated by comparing the two cases in set *B* in which two explanatory variables are used, one of which includes a linear time trend and the other two real variables. From equations (4) and (5) in Table 2 it can be seen that, while the inclusion of time adds an amount of 0.026 less to the explanation of the variance of the dependent variable than the inclusion of the second explanatory variable, the average value of δ^2/s^2 for the residuals is 0.023 greater. These are the two points which are close together in Figure 5 for three parameters and it

Table 3 *Significance tests applied to residuals of set B*

Explanation	Number of parameters	Number different from random at significance levels of: 2½ per cent	5 per cent	Total number of residuals
Actual error term	1	19	20	20
	1	19	19	20
One explanatory variable	2	17	18	20
One explanatory variable + time	3	13	15	20
Two explanatory variables	3	11	14	20
Two explanatory variables + time	4	7	10	20

* See G.U. Yule *op. cit.* and Orcutt and James *op. cit.*

can be seen that the addition of a linear time trend in the explanation produced approximately the same bias as the inclusion of a real explanatory variable. This is confirmed by the average value of δ^2/s^2 obtained when X_2, X_3 and t are the explanatory variables.

Since the inclusion of the bogus variable time had about the same effect in biasing the residuals towards randomness as the inclusion of real explanatory variables, we were curious about the effect of including other types of non-related series in the explanation. We therefore correlated two unrelated series, X_2 and X_3, of set B. With X_2 as the dependent variable it was found that the average amount of the variance explained was 0.32, while the mean value of δ^2/s^2 for the residuals was 0.74. This latter value is slightly higher than that obtained for equation (3) of Table 2 where the average explained variance is 0.64 with a mean value of $\delta^2/s^2 = 0.69$ for the autocorrelation of the residuals. This suggests that if error terms are autocorrelated then it would frequently be a mistake to attempt to justify the statistical requirements of randomness by adding more explanatory variables or by experimenting with different combinations of the variables. Owing to the shortness of economic time series, high accidental correlations may be obtained between the variables added and the error term due to their autoregressive structures and since the residuals obtained from the least squares method of regression are orthogonal to the explanatory variables they will tend to be biassed towards a random series.

Estimation of regression coefficients and prediction by least squares for relationships containing autocorrelated error terms

Our objectives in this section are to show that the usual application of the method of least squares to relationships containing highly positively autocorrelated error terms results in an extremely inefficient use of data and that it is only necessary to apply a transformation which will make the error term approximately random in order to regain most of this efficiency.

The complete information is contained in Table 2 but in order to illustrate the position more clearly we have set out some of the more relevant calculations in Tables 4 and 5.

The decline in the variances of both the correlation coefficient and the regression coefficient as the error term becomes random is very marked. In the case of one explanatory variable the variance of the correlation coefficient when the error term is of form A is approximately 11 times the variance when the error term is random, while the ratio of the corresponding variances of the regression coefficient is approximately 9 to 1. As we introduce more determining variables into the explanation, we can see from Table 5 that the variances of the regression coefficients decrease until in the limiting case all the variation in the variable to be determined is

Table 4 *Variances of regression parameters under different transformations using one explanatory variable*

Generating properties of		Values of δ^2/s^2 for		Variance of	
Explanatory variable	Error term	Error term	Residuals	Correlation coefficient	Regression coefficient
A	A	0.31	0.49	0.067	0.927
B	B	0.45	0.69	0.049	0.755
C	C	1.49	1.56	0.005	0.175
D	D	1.98	2.00	0.0056	0.111
E	E	3.00	3.01	0.008	0.127

Table 5 *Variances of regression parameters under different transformations using two explanatory variables*

Generating properties		Values of δ^2/s^2		Variance of		
Explanatory variable	Error term	Error terms	Residuals	Multiple correlation coefficient	Regression coefficients b_{12}	b_{13}
B	B	0.31	1.06	0.012	0.34	0.48
D	D	2.14	2.15	0.0004	0.08	0.05
E	E	3.05	2.93	0.001	0.09	0.10

explained and there is a complete set. This limiting case is of course very rarely approached in practice and if we consider the set B, where for three explanatory variables the mean multiple correlation coefficient is as high as 0.97 (see Table 2, equation 6), we find the variances of the regression coefficients are 0.22 and 0.16 for b_{12} and b_{13} respectively, which from Table 5 can be seen to be three times the variances of the regression coefficients calculated in the random transformation even though the mean multiple correlation coefficient in this form is only 0.93.

In Table 4 we can see that fluctuations in the variances of the regression parameters are very small for reasonably large movements of δ^2/s^2 around the random value, given by the results for C, D and E. The true values of the autocorrelation coefficients of the error terms vary from $r_1 = 0.3$ to $r_1 = -0.5$ in these cases. This relative stability of the variances indicates that a transformation which makes the error term approximately random will have regained most of the improvement in the efficiency possible.

Similar results would also appear to be true for the case of two explanatory variables.

In our model there is no real trend, yet the introduction of a linear trend to sets *A* and *B* improves their explanation and reduces the variance of the regression coefficients. This would seem to be due to the fact already considered that the trend factor reduces the amount of autocorrelation in the residuals and can be regarded as one method of transforming the error term. In these circumstances the introduction of a polynomial trend may be a useful device in obtaining more accurate results, but it is difficult to attach an economic meaning to the coefficients of time.

In order to obtain some idea of the accuracy of estimation of regression parameters under other possible types of relationships and to illustrate once more the importance of having the error term random, we constructed from the series already calculated two sets of relationships in which the autoregressive structure of the explanatory variable and the error term were different. The form of the relationship was –

$$X_1 = k + b_{12}X_2 + v \tag{4.1}$$

where X_2 was of form *A* in both sets and v adopted first form *B* and second form *D*. The true values of the constants were $k = 0$ and $b_{12} = 2$ while the error term was taken from our previous sets with $v = X_3 + u$. The first differences of each set were calculated and then a further correction was made to randomize the explanatory variable. This latter process produced error terms generated by the following formulae –

$$\begin{aligned} &F. \quad x_{t+1} = \varepsilon_{t+1} - 0.3\varepsilon_t \\ &G. \quad x_{t+1} = (\varepsilon_{t+1} - \varepsilon_t) - 0.3(\varepsilon_t - \varepsilon_{t-1}) \end{aligned} \tag{4.2}$$

where the ε's denote a series of random disturbances. The results of the calculations are set out in Table 6 and the values of δ^2/s^2 provide additional points for Figure 5. In each set it can be seen that a considerable gain is to be obtained in the efficiency of the estimates of the correlation coefficients and regression coefficients when the error term is random. If error terms are really random as postulated by many economists, there is nothing to be gained from making any transformation, even though the original series possess high positive autocorrelation. It can also be seen from the mean values of the regression coefficients of Tables 2 and 6 that the least squares estimates are not biassed when the error term is autocorrelated even though they are not the best estimates.

Tests of significance

It is well recognized that the ordinary test of significance for the null hypothesis can be applied to the correlation between two series provided

Table 6 *Summary of statistics calculated for various transformations when the explanatory variable and error term possess different autoregressive structures*

Equation no.	Generating properties of		Values of δ^2/s^2				Regression parameters				Correlation coefficient	
	Explanatory variable	Error term	Actual error series		Estimated residuals		Constant term		Regression coefficient			
			Mean	Variance	Mean	Variance	Mean	Standard deviation	Mean	Variance	Mean	Variance
	First relationship											
15	A	B	0.450	0.222	0.661	0.274	−26.233	165.16	2.070	0.485	0.844	0.025
15	C	D	N.C.		N.C.		−1.090	9.68	2.163	0.124	0.846	0.0057
17	D	F	N.C.		N.C.		−0.807	7.95	2.124	0.141	0.805	0.011
	Second relationship											
18	A	D	1.971	0.195	2.047	0.179	−1.533	68.50	2.021	0.022	0.938	0.003
19	C	E	2.913	0.150	2.921	0.156	−0.284	5.13	2.114	0.189	0.736	0.018
20	D	G	N.C.		N.C.		−1.123	3.89	2.069	0.364	0.670	0.028

N.C. indicates that certain statistics were not calculated.

one of them is random.* This can be seen to be equivalent to making the error term random in the special case of a zero regression coefficient. To apply confidence limits it is necessary that the dependent variable is distributed normally and randomly around a linear function of the explanatory variable. This is true even if the explanatory variable is not random.† If economic time series possess the properties which we are suggesting, then the transformation to make the error terms random will put them in a form in which it will be possible to apply confidence limits and test the significance of regression parameters in the ordinary way.

Prediction

Prediction is one of the primary reasons for undertaking statistical analysis. In Table 7 we present some material derived from our constructed relations which emphasizes the huge improvement that it is possible to make if one is dealing with a formulation involving error terms which are a first summation of random elements. This table also indicates how misleading the variance of the residuals may be in such a case.

The fact that the items in column IV are smaller than those in column V is, of course, to be expected, since the regression parameters have been chosen to minimize the mean square of the residuals and the true errors are those obtained by use of the true values of the regression parameters. In the cases of random error terms, rows 2 and 5, this downward bias is small and could, if desired, be easily compensated by taking account of the number of parameters fitted. In the cases of error terms which are the first summation of random numbers, the downward bias is exceedingly large for series of this length and should emphasize the caution needed in interpreting standard errors of estimate if the error terms are likely to be highly positively autocorrelated. Column VI gives the variance of the errors of prediction one item beyond the parts of the series utilized for estimating the regression parameters. That is, each of the series involved in each set of twenty equations was extended one item and the dependent variable then predicted with a knowledge of the regression coefficients previously calculated. Column VI again illustrates in a rather simple way how misleading the variance of residuals may be when the error terms are autocorrelated, as in rows 1, 3 and 4. It should of course be realized that the much smaller variances obtained in rows 2 and 5 are due both to the fact that better estimates of the regression parameters have been obtained and used in these

* See M.S. Bartlett, 'Some Aspects of the Time-Correlation Problem in regard to Tests of Significance', *Journal of the Royal Statistical Society*, Vol. 98, 1935, pp. 536-43.

† See R.A. Fisher, 'The Goodness of Fit of Regression Formulae and the Distribution of Regression Coefficients', *Journal of the Royal Statistical Society*, Vol. 85, 1922, pp. 597-612, and H. Cramer, 'Mathematical Methods of Statistics', *op. cit.*, pp. 548-55.

Table 7 *A comparison of the variances of residuals, true errors and predictions obtained from several transformations of the constructed relations*

No.	Generating properties of: Explanatory variable	Generating properties of: Error term	Number of explanatory variables	Mean variance of residuals	Mean variance of true errors	Variance of errors of predictions one item beyond sample
	I	II	III	IV	V	VI
1	B	B	1	5142	7725	7479
2	D	D	1	1375	1466	933
3	B	B	2 + time	784	4386	7127
4	B	B	2	1690	4386	3991
5	D	D	2	634	749	774

cases and also that the prediction formula makes use of the fact that the errors involved in rows 1, 3 and 4 are the first summation of random numbers. Thus, whereas in row 1 the estimating formula was

$$X_{1,n+1} = a_1 + b_{12}X_{2,n+1}, \tag{4.3}$$

in row 2, the estimating formula was

$$X_{1,n+1} = a'_1 + b'_{12}(X_{2,n+1} - X_{2n}) + X_{1n}. \tag{4.4}$$

The errors involved in the prediction formula (4.4) are therefore random in time whereas those in (4.3) are first summations of random terms.

A tentative method of procedure

Having recognized that the error terms implicit in many current formulations of economic relations are highly positively autocorrelated, and also having recognized the importance of carrying out estimation and prediction by means of relations involving random error terms, how shall we proceed when faced with a practical situation? One way of evading this problem would be to change some of the variables, add additional variables, or modify the form of the relation until a relationship involving what appear to be random error terms is found. However, while this may possibly be a satisfactory way out in some cases, it obviously does not help much if by some means or other one has arrived at what is believed to be the most reasonable choice of variables and form of relation. This choice of variables and form of relation usually does not involve any specification of whether or not the errors are autocorrelated and what is required is the best method of estimating the parameters and various standard errors of the chosen relation, and not some other relation. In this situation the objective, of course, is to make an autoregressive transformation of the dependent and independent variables such that the error term becomes random. If the autoregressive properties of the error term were known, then it would simply be a matter of making the indicated autoregressive transformation as illustrated in section 2. The real problem arises when the autoregressive properties of the error term are not known but must be estimated. Except for the fact, which our experiments demonstrate, that nearly optimum results can be achieved if the error term is only a rough approximation to a random series, solution of the problem would seem rather hopeless for series of only twenty items.

One fairly obvious procedure, which we are inclined to rule out because of the large biases demonstrated in section 3, would be the following iterative process. First estimate the desired regression coefficients by ordinary least squares and obtain the resulting series of residuals. Then estimate from those residuals by least squares the autoregressive parameters of a one or two lag difference equation. Use these autoregressive parameters to make an autoregressive transformation of the observed series aimed at randomizing the error term, and re-estimate the desired regression coefficients. Put these revised estimates back in the original equation, obtain the resulting series of residuals and estimate their autoregressive parameters. Use these to make a new autoregressive transformation of the original series and so on until estimates of the desired regression coefficients are obtained which are consistent with estimates of the autoregressive parameters of the residuals in the sense that no further adjustments are necessary. Since it is only necessary to make the error term approximately random it is unlikely that much would be gained by carrying the above process more than one or two rounds. The real difficulty with this procedure is that the series of residuals will, as shown in section 3, be strongly biassed towards randomness and therefore the autoregressive transformation based in the above way on the residuals may not in fact go far enough in randomizing the error term.

An alternative procedure which appears more promising to us is that of selecting an autoregressive transformation of the series involved such that the autocorrelations of the series of residuals are approximately equal to the expected values of autocorrelations of random series of the same length. We have not worked out an efficient procedure for doing this; but, if one is willing to approximate the autoregressive properties of the error term by a one or even two lag linear difference equation, it is fairly easy after one or two trials to choose an autoregressive transformation which will result in residuals that are sufficiently random. Furthermore, if our evidence that many error terms appear to be approximately first summations of random term is accepted, then the obvious procedure is to work with first differences of the series used. Thus, given a relation between ordinary economic variables

$$X_{1t} = a_1 + b_{12}X_{2t} + b_{13}X_{3t} \tag{5.1}$$

we suggest as a first approximation estimation and prediction in the form

$$(X_{1t} - X_{1,t-1}) = b_{12}(X_{2t} - X_{2,t-1}) + b_{13}(X_{3t} - X_{3,t-1}). \tag{5.2}$$

If (5.1) had contained a linear trend then (5.2) would have contained a constant term. The residuals from (5.2) can be obtained and tested for randomness.

If we prove to be right about the nature of most error terms in current formulations of economic relations, then the residuals of the first difference transformation will turn out to be sufficiently random and no further steps will be necessary. If the residuals in this form do not turn out to be sufficiently random, then a new transformation can be devised on the basis of their autocorrelations. The main advantages of this procedure are, first, that in many cases it will result immediately in the correct transformation and, secondly, that when it does not it will usually result in residuals that are not highly positively autocorrelated and thereby reduce the amount of bias towards randomness which is present in this case. This will be a help in devising successive autoregressive transformations.

On the basis of this study Richard Stone* has recalculated a number of demand studies for the United Kingdom 1920-38. The general results will be published by Stone, but he has kindly made available to us the material presented in Table 8. We present this material as further evidence that in many cases the use of first differences does result in essentially random series. It also seems reassuring, in so far as Stone's work is concerned, and rather remarkable, that in most cases the multiple correlations for the relations in first difference form remained very high.

Appendix to section 2

It is of interest to compare the simple solution presented in section 2 with the general solution given by Aitken [30]. We shall not repeat his elegant and rigorous proofs but shall merely illustrate his approach and deduce the special case where the error series follows a simple Markoff scheme. For this it is necessary to follow his generality of notation and employ matrices and vectors, using P' and y' to denote the matrix or vector obtained by transposing P or y and P^{-1} as the inverse matrix of P.

Consider first the simple case of least squares with non-autocorrelated errors. Let the approximate representation of the column vector of data

$$y = \{y_1 y_2 \ . \ . \ . \ y_n\} \tag{6.1}$$

* These studies were originally given in his paper on 'Analysis of Demand', *op. cit.*, but the recalculations were made on the basis of revised estimates of the data.

Table 8 *Values of δ^2/s^2 for a number of demand studies for the United Kingdom 1920-38*

Commodity	Number of parameters	Value of δ^2/s^2 for residuals		Adjusted multiple correlation coefficient	
		Original data	First differences	Original data	First differences
Beer	3	1.28	1.86	0.989	0.962
	4	1.13 }	2.01	0.989 }	0.977
	4 + time	1.23 }		0.993 }	
Spirits	3 + time	1.26	2.63	0.992	0.875
Telegrams	3	1.24	1.61	0.985	0.967
	4 + time	1.10	1.65	0.987	0.966
Imported wine	4	1.49	1.84	0.893	0.754
Communication services	3 + time	0.71	2.05	0.996	0.834
	4 + time	0.70	2.11	0.996	0.822
Lard	3 + time	0.90	2.06	0.838	0.864
Margarine	4	1.26 }	1.80	0.959 }	0.748
	4 + time	2.02 }		0.969 }	
	5 + time	2.31	2.31	0.976	0.756
Mean value of δ^2/s^2		1.28	1.99		

by the column vector

$$z = \{z_1 z_2 \ . \ . \ . \ z_n\} \tag{6.2}$$

be linear in terms of a set of $(k + 1)$ prescribed functions

$$1, x_{1t}, x_{2t}, \ . \ . \ ., x_{kt} \qquad (t = 1, \ . \ . \ . \ n). \tag{6.3}$$

Let P denote the matrix of these functional values so that the ith row of P is the row vector

$$[1, x_{1i}, x_{2i} \ . \ . \ . \ x_{ki}]. \tag{6.4}$$

Then P is of order $n \times (k + 1)$ and with the restriction of linear independence over the n values $x_{i1}, \ . \ . \ ., x_{in}$, it is of rank $(k + 1)$. Let a denote a column vector of $(k + 1)$ coefficients

$$a = \{a_0 a_1 a_2 \ . \ . \ . \ a_k\}. \tag{6.5}$$

Then the set of values z_i is the vector

$$z = Pa. \tag{6.6}$$

If the data y are independent then the principle of least squares minimizes the sum of the squared residuals. This is the vector product

$$s^2 = (y - Pa)'(y - Pa) \tag{6.7}$$

and for the minimal conditions $\partial s^2/\partial a = 0$ we obtain the set of normal equations

$$P'Pa = P'y. \tag{6.8}$$

Having established this general result for least squares, Aitken extends the argument to the case of autocorrelated errors. If the set of errors be arranged according to their variances and covariances by the elements of a symmetric matrix U of order $n \times n$, then the least squares estimates are obtained by minimizing

$$(y - Pa)'U^{-1}(y - Pa). \tag{6.9}$$

Differentiating in the manner above, we obtain the set of more general normal equations

$$P'U^{-1}Pa = P'U^{-1}y. \tag{6.10}$$

Let us now apply these general results to a simple specific example. Suppose we have a linear relation

$$Y_t = \alpha_0 + \alpha_1 X_t + u_t \qquad (t = 1 \ldots n) \tag{6.11}$$

where u_t is defined by the simple Markoff process

$$u_t = \beta u_{t-1} + \varepsilon_t \qquad (\beta < 1) \tag{6.12}$$

where β is a known constant and ε_t a random disturbance. Our variance, covariance matrix of error may be defined by the symmetric matrix of order $n \times n$ where we have assumed unit variance of ε_t for simplicity, although the final result would not be altered if we did not.

$$U = \frac{1}{1-\beta^2}\begin{bmatrix} 1 & \beta & \beta^2 & . & \beta^n \\ \beta & 1 & \beta & . & \beta^{n-1} \\ \beta^2 & \beta & 1 & . & \beta^{n-2} \\ . & . & . & . & . \\ \beta^n & \beta^{n-1} & \beta^{n-2} & . & 1 \end{bmatrix} \tag{6.13}$$

from which we obtain the symmetric inverse matrix

$$U^{-1} = \begin{bmatrix} 1 & -\beta & 0 & .. & 0 \\ -\beta & 1+\beta^2 & -\beta & .. & 0 \\ 0 & -\beta & 1+\beta^2 & .. & 0 \\ . & . & . & .. & . \\ . & . & . & .1+\beta^2 & -\beta \\ 0 & 0 & 0 & .-\beta & 1 \end{bmatrix}. \tag{6.14}$$

The matrix P is of order $n \times 2$ where the ith row is

$$[1 \ X_i] \tag{6.15}$$

while the vector of coefficients becomes the column vector

$$\begin{bmatrix} \alpha_0 \\ \alpha_1 \end{bmatrix}. \tag{6.16}$$

Applying these components to the general normal equations (6.10) and expanding we obtain the estimate of α_1 as

$$\hat{\alpha}_1 = \frac{\sum_1^n x_t y_t - \beta \sum_2^n x_t y_{t-1} - \beta \sum_2^n x_{t-1} y_t + \beta^2 \sum_3^n x_{t-1} y_{t-1}}{\sum_1^n x_t^2 - 2\beta \sum_2^n x_t x_{t-1} + \beta^2 \sum_3^n x_{t-1}^2} \tag{6.17}$$

where x_t, y_t are in terms of deviations from their means which are given by

$$\bar{x} = \frac{1}{n - \beta(n-2)} \left(\sum_1^n X_t - \beta \sum_2^{n-1} X_t \right). \tag{6.18}$$

These are completely general results for error terms of the simple type considered and do not involve any assumptions about the distribution of the random disturbances ε_t. If ε_t are normally distributed then we have a maximum likelihood solution.

Comparing the estimate (6.17) with that obtained by our modified transformation procedure of section 2 we have from (6.11) and (6.12)

$$Y_t - \beta Y_{t-1} = \alpha_0' + \alpha_1(X_t - \beta X_{t-1}) + \varepsilon_t \tag{6.19}$$

where the least squares estimate of α_1 is

$$\hat{\hat{\alpha}}_1 = \frac{\sum_2^n x_t y_t - \beta \sum_2^n x_t y_{t-1} - \beta \sum_2^n x_{t-1} y_t + \beta^2 \sum_2^n x_{t-1} y_{t-1}}{\sum_2^n x_t^2 - 2\beta \sum_2^n x_t x_{t-1} + \beta^2 \sum_2^n x_{t-1}^2} \tag{6.20}$$

where the means are calculated by

$$\frac{1}{n-1} \sum_2^n X_t \quad \text{and} \quad \frac{1}{n-1} \sum_2^n X_{t-1}. \tag{6.21}$$

If we represent the numerator and denominator of (6.20) by A and B respectively we obtain

$$\hat{\hat{\alpha}}_1 = \frac{A}{B} \tag{6.22}$$

so that the estimator given by (6.17) is

$$\hat{\alpha}_1 = \frac{A + x_1 y_1(1 - \beta^2)}{B + x_1^2(1 - \beta^2)}. \tag{6.23}$$

The reason for this difference is that $\hat{\alpha}_1$ ignores the possibility of making use of the first error term u_1, and estimates the regression coefficients using only $(n - 1)$ transformed terms. The sum of squares of the $(n - 1)$ terms is

$$\sum_2^n \varepsilon_t^2 = \sum_2^n (u_t - \beta u_{t-1})^2. \tag{6.24}$$

The first term may be introduced by using the fact that the expected value of ε_1^2 given u_1 is

$$E(\varepsilon_1^2) = (1 - \beta^2)u_1^2 \tag{6.25}$$

so that

$$s^2 = \sum_1^n \varepsilon_t^2 = \sum_2^n (u_t - \beta u_{t-1})^2 + (1 - \beta^2)u_1^2. \tag{6.26}$$

If we substitute for the u's in terms of x and y from (6.11) and minimize in the ordinary way with respect to α_0 and α_1, we again obtain the solutions (6.17) and (6.18). It can be seen therefore that $\hat{\hat{\alpha}}_1$ is an unbiased estimate of α_1 but by ignoring the first term a maximum of one degree of freedom is lost in the transformation procedure as β approaches zero. As β approaches unity the difference between $\hat{\alpha}_1$ and $\hat{\hat{\alpha}}_1$ approaches zero and when $\beta = 1$ the solutions (6.17) and (6.20) are identical and the obvious course is to make a first difference transformation.

In the case of multivariate regression the procedure of transforming the variables and applying ordinary least squares analysis provides a much simpler solution than the method indicated by (6.17). The transformation procedure also provides a simpler solution in the case where the autoregressive structure of the error term comprises a linear stochastic difference equation involving two or more lagged terms.

References

1 R. Frisch, *Statistical Confluence Analysis by means of Complete Regression Systems*, Oslo 1934.

2 T. Haavelmo, 'The Probability Approach in Econometrics', *Econometrica*, Vol. 12 Supplement, July 1944, and 'The Statistical Implications of a System of Simultaneous Equations', *Econometrica*, Vol. 11, 1943, pp. 1-12.

3 T. Koopmans, 'Statistical Estimation of Simultaneous Economic Relations', *Journal of the American Statistical Association*, Vol. 40, 1945, pp.448-66, and 'Statistical Methods of Measuring Economic Relationships', *Cowles Commission Discussion Papers*, Statistics No. 310. (Mimeographed copy of lectures delivered at the University of Chicago 1947.)

4 See for example M.A. Girshick and T. Haavelmo, 'Statistical Analysis of the Demand for Food: Examples of Simultaneous Estimation of Structural Equations', *Econometrica*, Vol. 15, 1947, pp. 79-110; J. Marshak and W.H. Andrews, 'Random Simultaneous Equations and the Theory of Production', *Econometrica*, Vol. 12, pp. 143-205; for a mathematical treatment, T.W. Anderson and H. Rubin, 'Estimation of the Parameters of a Single Stochastic Difference Equation in a Complete System', to be published in *Annals of Mathematical Statistics*.

5 G. Tintner, 'The Variate Difference Method', Cowles Commission Monograph No. 5, 1940.

6 G.U. Yule, 'Why do we sometimes get nonsense correlations between time-series etc.?', *Journal of the Royal Statistical Society*, Vol. 89, 1926, pp. 1-64; M.S. Bartlett, 'Some Aspects of the Time-Correlation problem in regard to Tests of Significance', *Journal of the Royal Statistical Society*, Vol. 98, 1935, pp. 536-43, and 'On the Theoretical Specification and Sampling Properties of Autocorrelated Time Series', *Journal of the Royal Statistical Society*, Vol. 8, 1946, pp. 27-41; Galvenius and H. Wold, 'Statistical Tests of H. Alfven's Theory of Sunspots', *Arkiv for Matematik*, Astronomi Ochfysik Band 34A No. 24, pp. 1-9; G.H. Orcutt and S.F. James, 'Testing the Significance of Correlation between Time Series', *Biometrika*, Vol. 35, 1948, pp. 1-17.

7 A.C. Aitken, 'On Least Squares and Linear Combinations of Observations', *Proceedings of Royal Society Edinburgh*, Vol. 55, 1934/5, pp. 42-8.

8 D.G. Champernowne, 'Sampling Theory applied to Autoregressive Sequences', to be published in *Journal of the Royal Statistical Society*. Series B Vol. 10, 1948.

9 R. Frisch, *op. cit*.

10 T. Koopmans, 'Linear Regression Analysis of Economic Time Series', Netherlands Economic Institute Haarlem 1937.

11 G. Tintner, 'Some Applications of Multivariate Analysis to Economic Data', *Journal of the American Statistical Association*, Vol. 41, 1946, pp. 472-500.

12 O. Reiersøl, 'Confluence Analysis by Means of Instrumental Sets of Variables', *Arkiv for Matematik, Astronomi Och Fysik*, Band 32A, No. 4, 1945.

13 R.C. Geary, 'Determination of Unbiased Linear Relations between the Systematic Parts of Variables with Errors of Observation', *Econometrica*, vol. 17, 1949.

14 G.H. Orcutt and D. Cochrane, 'A Sampling Study of the Merits of Certain Transformations in Regression Analysis', to be published.

15 For a general proof, see F.N. David and J. Neyman, 'Extension of the Markoff Theorem on Least Squares', *Statistical Research Memoirs*, Vol. II, London, 1938, pp. 105-16; also C.R. Rao, 'Generalisation of Markoff's Theorem and Tests of Linear Hypothesis', *Sankhya*, Vol. 7, 1945, pp. 9-16.

16 H. Cramer, *Mathematical Methods of Statistics*, Princeton 1946, pp.548-55, and M.S. Bartlett, 'On the Theory of Statistical Regression', *Proceedings of Royal Society Edinburgh*, Vol. 53, 1933, pp. 260-83.

17 A.C. Aitken, *op. cit*.

18 G.H. Orcutt, 'A Study of the Autoregressive Nature of the Time Series used for Tinbergen's Model of the Economic System of the United States 1919-32', *Journal of the Royal Statistical Society*, Vol. 10, Series B, 1948, pp. 1-53.

19 J. Tinbergen, 'Statistical Testing of Business-Cycle Theories Vol. II; Business Cycles in the United States of America 1919-32', League of Nations, Geneva, 1939.

20 Herman Wold, 'A Study in the Analysis of Stationary Time Series', Uppsala 1938, pp. 171-4.

21 *Econometrica*, Vol. 15, 1947, pp. 111-51.
22 Mimeographed paper distributed by the author and the Cowles Commission for Research in Economics, Chicago.
23 *Op. cit.*
24 Richard Stone, 'The Analysis of Market Demand', *Journal of the Royal Statistical society*, Vol. 108, 1945, pp. 286-391.
25 The relationship between the ratio of the mean square successive difference to the variance and the serial or autocorrelation coefficient for an infinite series is given by

$$r_1 = 1 - \tfrac{1}{2}\delta^2/s^2$$

where r_1 is the first autocorrelation. It can be seen that as r_1 moves from +1 to −1 the ratio δ^2/s^2 moves from 0 to 4.
26 The actual residuals were not published in the paper by Richard Stone but he has very kindly let us have the calculated residuals for 17 equations which include some revised estimates and a few additional relationships (see Table 8).
27 For a more detailed discussion of reduced form methods see Girshick and Haavelmo, *op. cit.*, especially p. 85.
28 J. von Neumann, 'Distribution of the Ratio of the Mean Square Successive Difference to the Variance', *Annals of Mathematical Statistics*, Vol. 12, pp. 367-95; B.S. Hart and J. von Neumann, 'Tabulation of the Probabilities for the Ratio of the Mean Square Successive Differences to the Variance', *Annals of Mathematical Statistics*, Vol. 13, pp. 207-14.
29 M.G. Kendall and B. Babington Smith, *Tracts for Computers No. 24*, Cambridge University Press, 1939.
30 A.C. Aitken, 'On Least Squares and Linear Combinations of Observations', *op. cit.*

(Reprinted from *Journal of the American Statistical Association*, 1949, vol. 44, 32-61, with the permission of the American Statistical Association).

Appendix 2
A sampling study of the merits of autoregressive and reduced form transformations in regression analysis

Guy H. Orcutt and Donald Cochrane

This paper is concerned with some aspects of regression analysis when the error terms are autocorrelated and there exists more than one relationship between the variables. In particular, we investigate the merits of autoregressive transformations and the reduced form transformation in dealing with these complications.

An important result is that, unless it is possible to specify something about the intercorrelation of the error terms in a set of relations and to choose approximately the correct autoregressive transformation, a certain amount of scepticism is justified concerning the possibility of estimating structural parameters from aggregative time series of only twenty observations.

1 Introduction

The statistical estimation of the various parameters which enter into theoretical formulations of economic relationships is one of the main objectives of econometrics and the most common statistical technique used is multivariate regression analysis. The classical method of least squares regression has been shown to give best linear unbiassed estimates of the coefficients when certain well known conditions are fulfilled. If a linear relationship exists between the dependent variable x_{1t} and a set of independent variables $x_2 \ldots x_p$ of the form

$$x_{1t} = b_0 + \sum_{j=2}^{p} b_{1j}x_{jt} + u_t \tag{1}$$

these conditions are satisfied if among other things[1]

(i) the error term is non-autocorrelated, so that the expected value $E(U_t \cdot U_{t-h}) = 0$ for $h \neq 0$;

(ii) each of the determining variables x_{jt} $(j = 2, \ldots, p)$ is independent of the error term U_t, i.e., $E(x_{jt}U_t) = 0$ $(j = 2, \ldots, p)$.

The formidable complications which have arisen in estimating the structural parameters of economic relationships have their origin, in so far as they are purely statistical in nature, in the fact that these two conditions are not realistic and have to be relaxed in most applications to economic data. The major complications which have arisen may be classified as follows:

(a) the auto-correlated error complication;
(b) the errors in variables complication;
(c) the simultaneous equations complication.

The first of these complications arises when condition (i), that the errors are independently distributed in time, does not hold while condition (ii), that the determining variables are independent of the error term, cannot be maintained when the other two complications are present.

The simultaneous equations approach

The data used in most formulations of economic relationships are obtained from historical time processes and not from conducted experiments, and as a consequence are the results of the solution of a system of simultaneous relations corresponding to the economic processes involved. In order to obtain accurate estimates of the structural parameters of any single equation it may therefore be necessary to take account of the whole system of simultaneous equations in which it occurs. Consider a simple illustration of this problem. The consumption and price of a commodity enter into both a demand and a supply relation so that if we attempt to find the demand relation by considering only the regression of the quantity consumed on the price of the commodity we are ignoring the fact that price is not an independent variable but will depend on the nature of the supply relation. Haavelmo[2] suggested that in such cases the variables should be considered in a joint normal probability distribution which should be studied to clarify the stochastical relationship which the system of equations implies. Such a method assumes that the errors in the equations are non-autocorrelated and normally distributed and that there are no errors of observation in the variables.

It has been shown that for large samples the parameters estimated by the method of maximum likelihood from this joint probability distribution have certain optimal properties. They are asymptotically unbiassed estimates and are also efficient statistics.[3] One method of estimating these parameters is to rewrite the system of equations in the reduced form and solve for each of the endogenous variables in terms of the lagged values of the endogenous variables and the exogenous variables which appear in the system. These solutions will be in terms of linear equations and the method of least squares can then be applied by considering each endogenous variable in turn as the dependent variable. The coefficients in this form possess the properties of best unbiassed estimates for large samples. The structural parameters of the original equations can then be derived from these coefficients but it should be mentioned that it may not always be possible to identify the structural parameters of the original relations from the coefficients of the equations estimated in the reduced form. The problem of identification is a very important one for the method discussed and a careful analysis of the system of equations that is being considered should be made before attempting any statistical application.[4] The estimates obtained from the reduced form method are maximum likelihood solutions for an exactly identified system.

Autocorrelated error terms

In an earlier paper[5] we showed that the error terms involved in many current formulations of economic relationships are highly positively autocorrelated. In doing so, we demonstrated that under these circumstances the application of least squares regression to the original data produced very inefficient estimates of the parameters to be measured and suggested that this efficiency could be recovered by applying an autoregressive transformation to the variables which would make the error term approximately random.

Objects of this paper

In this paper we are concerned with the problem of carrying out regression analysis when the error terms are autocorrelated and there exists more than one relationship between the variables. In particular we investigate the merits of autoregressive transformations and the reduced form transformation in dealing with these complications. It is assumed that there are no errors of observation in the variables.

The problems with which we are dealing are essentially deductive in nature and the ideal solution to them is one reached by purely deductive steps from stated premises. However, since it has not been possible as yet to obtain such a solution, and considering the problems of some importance, we have resorted to the method of sampling experiments. That is, we embody our assumptions in experimental models, use these models to generate sets of time series and investigate empirically the results of various estimating procedures on the series generated. Up to the present only large sample properties of the parameters derived by the simultaneous estimation of structural relations have been demonstrated. Since economic data rarely comprise series of more than 20 years, these large sample properties would seem to require more careful investigation and the sampling experiment approach provides a convenient and legitimate method of making such an investigation. In addition it might be mentioned that the use of such methods might also provide the answers to many problems which have proved intractable to mathematical statistics and the improvements in calculating equipment are very welcome for these purposes.

2 Construction of the experimental models

In order to reduce the computational burden as much as possible we worked with the simplest types of systems which seemed at all reasonable from the standpoint of applying any conclusions to economic studies. Two models were adopted and are explained as follows. The original series of Model I were generated by a recursive system of equations

$$x_t = a_0 + a_1 y_t + (u_{1t} + u_{2t}) \tag{2}$$

$$y_t = b_0 + b_1 x_{t-1} + u_{3t} \tag{3}$$

where x_t and y_t are the series to be considered and u_{it} $(i = 1, 2, 3)$ are the error terms involved in the two relations. These error terms were generated by the autoregressive equations

$$u_{it} = u_{i,t-1} + \varepsilon_{it} \qquad (i = 1, 2, 3) \tag{4}$$

where the ε_{it} denote series of random disturbances. The values of the parameters in (2) and (3) were chosen to be

$$\begin{cases} a_0 = b_0 = 0 \\ a_1 = 1.0 \\ b_1 = 0.4 \end{cases} \tag{5}$$

The ε_{it} $(i = 1, 2, 3)$ are independently distributed single digit random numbers. They were extracted from *Tables of Random Sampling Numbers*,[6] ignoring zeros so that they ranged from 1 to 9. Subtracting the number 5 from each we obtained three random series ε_{it}, possessing rectangular distributions with ranges of +4 to −4 and an expected value of zero. The three series u_{it} were then generated by applying equations (4) with initial values of zero, so that we had three independent series of first summations of random elements each comprising over 500 terms. Taking x_0 as zero and making use of the properties of the system given by (2) and (3), we then generated long series of x_t and y_t, from the three error series u_{it}. The first five items of the series of x_t and y_t were discarded and the remaining long series were each divided into 20 segments of 21 items with 5 items omitted between segments. One of these items was later used for prediction. By this procedure we obtained a sample of 20 pairs of series generated by the same underlying autoregressive structure but involving different samples of random disturbances.

For Model II the original series were generated by the same process as just described for Model I except that instead of being independent the error terms were now highly intercorrelated. This result was achieved by using the same series of u_{1t} *and* u_{2t} as before but replacing the series u_{3t} by u_{2t} so that the true correlation between the error terms was 0.71. The recursive system therefore became

$$x'_t = a_0 + a_1 y'_t + (u_{1t} + u_{2t}) \tag{6}$$
$$y'_t = b_0 + b_1 x'_{t-1} + u_{2t} \tag{7}$$

where the constants remained the same as given in (5). The same procedure was used to obtain the individual sets of x_t and y_t as explained for Model I.

Choice of parameters

Our choice of the autoregressive properties of the error series u_{it} was based upon the evidence presented in our previous paper[7] and the reasonableness of assuming that error terms are first summations of random elements has been further supported from the results obtained by Stone for a number of demand studies in the United Kingdom.[8] Our choice of the product $a_1 b_1$ was made so that x_t and y_t would have approximately the same autoregressive structures as claimed by Orcutt[9] for the series used in Tinbergen's[10] model of the economic system of the United States. For instance in the case of independent error terms we can see from (2) and (3) that the autoregressive structures of the two series are

$$x_t = x_{t-1} + 0.4(x_{t-1} - x_{t-2}) + \eta_{1t} \tag{8}$$
$$y_t = y_{t-1} + 0.4(y_{t-1} - y_{t-2}) + \eta_{2t} \tag{9}$$

where η_{1t} and η_{2t} are random disturbances defined in terms of ε_{it} ($i = 1$, 2, 3).

Having made the decision as to the product $a_1 b_1$, only one more significant decision remains to be made about the general structure of the model. This is the correlation between either pair of variables x_t and y_t or y_t and x_{t-1}. For n approaching infinity this may be more clearly seen as follows. We may express our model in the form

$$x_t = a y_t + v_{1t} \tag{10}$$
$$y_t = b x_{t-1} + v_{2t} \tag{11}$$

where x_t and y_t are in terms of deviations from their means and v_{1t}, v_{2t} are random error series. Expressing x_t and y_t in autoregressive forms, we can derive the following relations:

$$\frac{\mathrm{E}(x_t^2)}{\mathrm{E}(v_{1t}^2)} = \frac{1}{1 - \varrho^2}\left(1 + a^2 \frac{\mathrm{E}(v_{2t}^2)}{\mathrm{E}(v_{1t}^2)}\right) = R_1 \tag{12}$$

$$\frac{\mathrm{E}(y_t^2)}{\mathrm{E}(v_{2t}^2)} = \frac{1}{1 - \varrho^2}\left(\frac{\varrho^2}{a^2}\frac{\mathrm{E}(v_{1t}^2)}{\mathrm{E}(v_{2t}^2)} + 1\right) = R_2 \tag{13}$$

where

$$ab = \varrho, \quad R_1 = \frac{1}{1 - r^2_{x_t y_t}} \quad \text{and} \quad R_2 = \frac{1}{1 - r^2_{y_t x_{t-1}}}.$$

It can be readily seen that, having decided the correlation between say x_t and y_t, we have R_1 and since the term

$$a^2 \frac{\mathrm{E}(v^2_{2t})}{\mathrm{E}(v^2_{1t})}$$

appears in both (12) and (13), then R_2 is a function of ϱ and R_1 which are both known and is automatically determined. All we have left to decide is the weights to be assigned to the coefficient a and the relative variances of the error terms. We made the relative variances

$$\mathrm{E}(v^2_{2t})/\mathrm{E}(v^2_{1t}) = \tfrac{1}{2},$$

so that for $r^2_{x_t y_t} = 0.44$ we have $a = a_1 = 1$. The resulting form provides an intermediate and reasonable model of a simplified economic system. On the basis of the calculations needed for this study, it is possible to work out the extreme cases in which either of the error terms has zero variance. This is done in the next section.

3 Calculations involved and some special cases

The results of the calculations carried out are contained in Tables 1 to 5. The equations referred to in these tables are:

Model I.

$$\begin{aligned} \text{I.} \quad & x_t = a_0 + a_1 y_t + (u_{1t} + u_{2t}) \\ \text{II.} \quad & y_t = b_0 + b_1 x_{t-1} + u_{3t} \\ \text{III.} \quad & x_t = \varrho_0 + \varrho_1 x_{t-1} + (u_{1t} + u_{2t} + a_1 u_{3t}). \end{aligned} \tag{14}$$

Model II.

$$\begin{aligned} \text{IV.} \quad & x'_t = a_0 + a_1 y'_t + (u_{1t} + u_{2t}) \\ \text{V.} \quad & y'_t = b_0 + b_1 x_{t-1} + u_{2t} \\ \text{VI.} \quad & x'_t = \varrho_0 + \varrho_1 x'_{t-1} + (u_{1t} + (1 + a_1) u_{2t}). \end{aligned} \tag{15}$$

Both these systems are exactly identified. Equations I and IV were calculated by the direct application of least squares regression. Equations II and V are already in the reduced form so that the use of least squares is the appropriate procedure. The reduced forms of equations I and IV are equations III and VI respectively, so that the reduced form estimates of a_1 and a_0 are given by

$$a'_1 = \varrho_1 / b_1 \tag{16}$$

$$a'_0 = \varrho_0 - b_0 a'_1 = \bar{x}_t - a'_1 \bar{y}_t \tag{17}$$

where $\bar{x}_t$, and $\bar{y}_t$ are the means of the two series x_t and y_t. The calculations relating to these estimates are given by equations IA and IVA in Model I and Model II respectively. For each of the equations we have made first and second difference transformations and the regression parameters have been estimated in the three forms. The original relations and the autoregressive transformations are denoted by the letters O, F.D. and S.D. in the tables.

Special cases

At the end of section 2 we pointed out that it is possible to derive the cases where the variance of either one of the error terms is equal to zero. In both these cases the least squares estimates and the reduced form estimates lead to identical results. Rewriting the simple system of (10) and (11)

$$x_t = ay_t + v_{1t} \tag{18}$$

$$y_t = bx_{t-1} + v_{2t} \tag{19}$$

where v_{1t}, v_{2t} are random elements so that the reduced form of x_t is

$$x_t = \varrho x_{t-1} + v_{1t} + av_{2t} \qquad (\varrho = ab) \tag{20}$$

we can say that when (19) is an exact relation then the single equation least squares estimates and the reduced form estimates of a are the same and proportional to the estimate of the autoregressive coefficient obtained in (20). When (18) is an exact relation then the single equation least squares and the reduced form estimates of a are both exact. These equalities may be more clearly seen as follows:

First assumption $E(v_{2t}^2) = 0$

so that our system becomes

$$x_t = ay_t + v_{1t} \tag{21}$$

$$y_t = bx_{t-1} \tag{22}$$

$$x_t = \varrho x_{t-1} + v_{1t} \tag{23}$$

and the least squares estimate of b is exact.

The single equation least squares estimate of a is given by

$$\hat{a} = \frac{\Sigma\, x_t y_t}{\Sigma\, y_t^2} = \frac{1}{b}\frac{\Sigma\, x_t x_{t-1}}{\Sigma\, x_{t-1}^2} = \frac{\hat{\varrho}}{b} \tag{24}$$

where $\hat{\varrho}$ is the least squares estimate of ϱ. The reduced form estimate of a is therefore

$$\tilde{a} = \frac{\hat{\varrho}}{b} = \hat{a}. \tag{25}$$

Second assumption $E(v_{1t}^2) = 0$
so that our system is now

$$x_t = ay_t \tag{26}$$

$$y_t = bx_{t-1} + v_{2t} \tag{27}$$

$$x_t = \varrho x_{t-1} + av_{2t} \tag{28}$$

and the single equation least squares estimate of a is exact. Now (27) and (28) are identical except for a scalar multiplier a, therefore the reduced form estimates of a are $\hat{\varrho}/\hat{b}$ and will also be exact.

4 General results

In the ensuing discussion we shall be content to point out the general and more important features of the calculations and if the reader desires further information it may be obtained from the tables which are presented in detail.

Structural parameters

It has been proved by Mann and Wald[11] that for large samples a linear stochastic difference equation may be treated as a classical regression problem in which the lagged values of the series appear as independent variables. However, the adequacy of the ordinary least squares regression has not been demonstrated for small samples, particularly of the size usually considered by economists, and in fact Koopmans[12] has mentioned that for a sample of 3 items a bias will be present in the least squares estimates of the parameters of a single lag autoregressive equation. Orcutt[13] has pointed out that this bias is probably due partly to the necessity of using the sample means of the time series instead of the true means and partly to the skewness of the distribution of sample estimates even when the true means are used. His empirical evidence shows that this bias is very substantial for series having only a weak central tendency. If we look at equations III and VI in Table 1 we find, for the first difference transformation, examples of single lag autoregressive equations. In these cases the means of the estimated regression coefficients are given, and it can be seen that the biasses are 2.3 and 2.8 times the standard error of the means of twenty estimates. This indicates that even for low values of the autoregressive coefficient the bias is still rather large. When we estimate the coefficients assuming a true mean of zero we find from equations III and VI in Table 2 that the bias is considerably reduced but is still far from negligible.

The question naturally arises as to whether a similar sort of small sample bias is to be expected in single equation least squares and reduced form estimates of the parameters of a system of recursive equations. In the previous section we showed that when either one of the equations was exact the estimates of both methods were the same. They were exact in one case and possessed the same bias and variance as the coefficient of a single lag autoregressive equation of the type just considered in the other. It is therefore of interest to examine first our Model I which corresponds to an intermediate case from the two extremes and second our Model II which adds the complication due to intercorrelated error terms and accordingly a further bias to the single equation estimates by the direct correlation between the independent variable and the error series.

First look at the single equation estimates of the regression coefficients given in Table 1, by the sets of equations I and IV. The estimates based on the original series are badly biassed and have large variances in both methods. As expected the bias is greater in Model II where the error terms are intercorrelated. The mean of the variances of the regression coefficients estimated from each equation separately (see column 11) does not reflect the true position and is only a fraction of what it should be. When we make a first difference transformation the estimates of the regression coefficient in Model I possess very little bias while the mean of the estimated variances of the regression coefficients also appears to be reasonable. However, in Model II there is still a large bias due to the correlation of the independent variable and the error term of equation IV.

Turning to the reduced form estimates given by equations IA and IVA we see that they are badly biassed for both the original series and first differences of both models. In the case of the original series the biasses are in the same direction as the single equation biasses but are much larger, in the first difference transformation the bias is downwards in both models and is due to the short series bias previously considered.

So far we have considered the coefficients obtained when we estimated the means in each transformation. It is therefore of interest to see the bias in the estimates of the first difference transformation when we make use of the fact that the true mean of the series is zero. This is equivalent to assuming that there is no trend in the original relationships. The results for the first difference transformation of both models are given in Table 2. In the case of Model I the estimates obtained by the single equation least squares regression are not biassed but the same bias as previously obtained is present in the case of equation IV for Model II. The reduced form estimates are still biassed in both models, although they show an improvement over the estimates obtained when the means are estimated.

Our calculations may be used to see whether the means of the reduced form estimates are significantly biassed from the true values in the first difference transformations. When we calculate the coefficient using estimated means we find from Table 1 that the values 0.62 from equation IA

Table 1 *Regression parameters*

Equation	Autoregressive transformation		Constant term (True value zero)			Regression coefficient					Mean of estimated variance	Correlation coefficient			Estimated mean variance of error
	Single equation	Reduced form	Mean	Standard error of mean	Variance	True value	Mean	Standard error of mean	Variance: Using mean	Variance: Using true value		Mean	Standard error of mean	Variance	
	(1)	(2)	(3)	(4)	(5)	(6)	(7)	(8)	(9)	(10)	(11)	(12)	(13)	(14)	(15)
Model I															
I	O		−25.75	13.62	3712.	1.0	1.27	0.11	0.223	0.283	0.038	0.84	0.05	0.057	20.6
	F.D.		−0.18	0.16	0.54	1.0	0.97	0.05	0.053	0.052	0.082	0.62	0.03	0.014	14.1
	S.D.		−0.04	0.08	0.11	1.0	0.61	0.07	0.094	0.239	0.129	0.40	0.03	0.021	28.2
IA		O	35.11	116.91	298030.	1.0	2.10	0.48	4.502	5.494	—	—	—	—	83.4
		F.D.	−0.63	1.05	30.11	1.0	0.62	0.15	0.432	0.551	—	—	—	—	18.1
		S.D.	0.18	0.69	10.15	1.0	−1.82	0.66	8.605	16.104	—	—	—	—	198.3
II	O		−10.57	9.55	1824.	0.4	0.59	0.05	0.058	0.091	0.007	0.82	0.05	0.045	11.4
	F.D.		−0.25	0.15	0.43	0.4	0.36	0.03	0.014	0.015	0.017	0.54	0.03	0.018	6.8
	S.D.		−0.07	0.03	0.02	0.4	0.20	0.03	0.021	0.061	0.023	0.29	0.04	0.037	12.3
III	O		−18.36	4.71	444.	0.4	0.90	0.02	0.008	0.255	0.013	0.88	0.02	0.006	22.8
	F.D.		−0.57	0.24	1.19	0.4	0.26	0.06	0.062	0.079	0.050	0.25	0.05	0.057	21.4
	S.D.		0.01	0.09	0.15	0.4	−0.27	0.05	0.050	0.490	0.053	−0.27	0.05	0.049	30.3

Model II

IV	O	−14.28	7.77	1206.	1.0	1.48	0.06	0.079	0.301	0.016	0.94	0.01	0.004	13.3
	F.D.	−0.07	0.10	0.183	1.0	1.51	0.03	0.020	0.276	0.054	0.83	0.02	0.005	11.2
	S.D.	−0.03	0.07	0.097	1.0	1.53	0.03	0.072	0.345	0.140	0.70	0.02	0.006	28.2
IVA	O	−8.23	9.59	1839.	1.0	1.52	0.08	0.114	0.378	—	—	—	—	14.4
	F.D.	−0.54	0.26	1.334	1.0	0.52	0.18	0.668	0.863	—	—	—	—	24.2
	S.D.	3.03	2.04	83.038	1.0	5.23	7.85	1226.5	1883.1	—	—	—	—	17470.1
V	O	−8.07	5.94	760.	0.4	0.59	0.03	0.018	0.055	0.004	0.89	0.02	0.007	10.0
	F.D.	−0.13	0.12	0.279	0.4	0.33	0.02	0.011	0.014	0.011	0.59	0.03	0.020	7.4
	S.D.	−0.06	0.05	0.042	0.4	0.09	0.02	0.006	0.099	0.012	0.19	0.03	0.020	11.7
VI	O	−28.13	5.34	570.	0.4	0.86	0.02	0.009	0.224	0.014	0.86	0.02	0.005	36.2
	F.D.	−0.33	0.23	1.082	0.4	0.23	0.06	0.062	0.086	0.050	0.23	0.06	0.061	34.9
	S.D.	−0.15	0.11	0.249	0.4	−0.34	0.04	0.036	0.583	0.051	−0.34	0.04	0.034	47.7

and 0.52 from equation IVA are both significantly different from the true value of the regression coefficient at the 5 per cent. level,[14] using the standard error of the mean calculated from the variance around the estimated mean. In fact they are significantly different from the true value of the coefficient at the 2 per cent level. When we assume that the true means of the series are zero only the mean of the reduced form estimates for Model II is significantly biassed. From Table 2 it can be seen that the value of 0.79 for equation IA is not significant at the 5 per cent. level but the value of 0.66 for equation IVA is significant at the 2 per cent. level.

Consider now the efficiency of the least squares and reduced form estimates. In Table 1 we find that the variances of the reduced form estimates compare very unfavourably in all cases with the variances of the single equation estimates. This may be illustrated by the ratios of the reduced form variances to the single equation variances. Even when we include the effect of the bias on the estimates by calculating the variance around the true value of the regression coefficient, the ratios still remain very high for Model I and although they fall slightly in Model II they are still greater than unity. For the cases where we assume a knowledge of the true mean, Table 2 shows that the ratio of the variances of the reduced form estimates to the variances of the single equation estimates around the estimated means and the true value are 7 : 1 and 8 : 1 respectively for

Table 2 *Regression parameters calculated by assuming true mean of zero (First Difference Transformation)*

Equation	Regression coefficient					Correlation coefficient		
	True value	Mean	Standard error of mean	Variance: Using mean	Variance: Using true value	Mean	Standard error of mean	Variance
	(1)	(2)	(3)	(4)	(5)	(6)	(7)	(8)
Model I								
I	1.0	1.00	0.05	0.041	0.039	0.66	0.03	0.014
IA	1.0	0.79	0.12	0.290	0.319	—	—	—
II	0.4	0.39	0.03	0.015	0.014	0.58	0.03	0.017
III	0.4	0.33	0.05	0.059	0.061	0.33	0.05	0.056
Model II								
IV	1.0	1.50	0.03	0.021	0.271	0.84	0.01	0.004
IVA	1.0	0.66	0.13	0.352	0.446	—	—	—
V	0.4	0.35	0.02	0.009	0.011	0.61	0.03	0.017
VI	0.4	0.27	0.05	0.056	0.070	0.27	0.05	0.055

Model I and 17 : 1 and 1½ : 1 for Model II. These are still very high ratios and are surprising results.

	Ratios of variances regression estimates	
	Using estimated mean	Using true value
Model I		
Original series	20 : 1	19 : 1
First differences	8 : 1	11 : 1
Model II		
Original series	1½ : 1	1¼ : 1
First differences	30 : 1	3 : 1

In Model I, where the error terms are random and independent, the single equation estimates would be the maximum likelihood solutions for large samples and normally distributed error terms[15] and we therefore expected the single equation approach to produce better estimates than those obtained by the reduced form method. However, where the error terms are random and intercorrelated the reduced form estimates are the maximum likelihood solutions for large samples if the correlation between the unlagged error terms is unknown. This is the case of Model II and we should therefore have expected the results of Model I to be reversed, but the discussion of the last few paragraphs has shown that these expectations have been far from realised.

Autocorrelation of residuals

The autocorrelations of the true error terms and the estimated residuals are presented in Table 3. The measure of autocorrelation used is the ratio of the mean square successive difference to the variance. This statistic is usually denoted by δ^2/s^2 and for a random series it is symmetrically distributed around a mean of $2n/n - 1$ where n is the number of items in the series.[16] In a previous paper[17] we showed that highly positively autocorrelated error terms become strongly biassed towards randomness as the number of parameters in the estimation relationship increases. This result is again illustrated in Table 3.

Further it should be noted that not only are the residuals biassed when the single equation least squares method of estimation is used, but this bias appears to be approximately the same as can be seen from (column 7) Table 3, when the reduced form method of estimation is used.

There is also an additional bias in the residuals caused by the application of biassed estimates of the regression coefficients. This may be seen in the residuals of the first difference transformation in equation IV, Table 3

Table 3 *Autocorrelation of residuals*

Equation	Autocorrelation transformation		Values of δ^2/s^2						
				Actual error series			Estimated residuals		
	Single equation	Reduced form	Values for infinite series	Mean	Standard error of mean	Variance	Mean	Standard error of mean	Variance
	(1)	(2)	(4)	(5)	(5)	(6)	(7)	(8)	(9)
Model I									
I	O		0.0	0.61	0.09	0.14	1.00	0.10	0.22
	F.D.		2.0	2.16	0.10	0.20	2.21	0.10	0.21
	S.D.		3.0	—	—	—	—	—	—
IA		O	0.0	0.61	0.09	0.14	1.07	0.10	0.19
		F.D.	2.0	2.16	0.10	0.20	1.93	0.09	0.18
		S.D.	3.0	—	—	—	—	—	—
II	O		0.0	0.43	0.06	0.08	0.97	0.11	0.22
	F.D.		2.0	2.05	0.09	0.17	2.00	0.08	0.14
	S.D.		3.0	—	—	—	—	—	—
III	O		0.0	—	—	—	1.49	0.10	0.21
	F.D.		2.0	—	—	—	1.87	0.05	0.04
	S.D.		3.0	—	—	—	—	—	—
Model II									
IV	O		0.0	0.61	0.09	0.14	1.10	0.13	0.34
	F.D.		2.0	2.16	0.10	0.20	2.50	0.10	0.20
	S.D.		3.0	—	—	—	—	—	—
IVA		O	0.0	0.61	0.09	0.14	1.04	0.11	0.24
		F.D.	2.0	2.16	0.10	0.20	2.07	0.11	0.24
		S.D.	3.0	—	—	—	—	—	—
V	O		0.0	0.51	0.06	0.08	1.17	0.10	0.18
	F.D.		2.0	2.17	0.09	0.17	2.01	0.08	0.11
	S.D.		3.0	—	—	—	—	—	—
VI	O		0.0	—	—	—	1.47	0.11	0.22
	F.D.		2.0	—	—	—	1.92	0.06	0.06
	S.D.		3.0	—	—	—	—	—	—

(column 7). It can be easily shown that the application of biassed coefficients in this equation will produce negatively autocorrelated error terms and this is illustrated in the result obtained. A final interesting feature of the autocorrelation of the residuals is to be seen in equations III and VI. In the first difference transformation we are estimating the coefficient of a single lag autoregressive equation with random disturbance but it is noticeable that because of the downward bias in the estimate of the coefficient the residuals are not completely randomized.

Prediction

In each equation we forecasted the dependent variable for the next period from a knowledge of the independent variable and using the regression coefficients calculated from the series up to that period. The forecasts were then compared with the actual value of the dependent variable obtained from our constructed series as explained in section 2, and the variances of error are shown in Table 4. The forecasts based directly upon the single equation estimates of the parameters have a smaller variance of error than those based on the direct use of the reduced form estimates of the parameters in the set of structural equations IA and IVA. This is true for both models and each autoregressive transformation. In both models the smallest variance of error of forecast is given when using single equation estimates in the first difference transformation.

We also calculated the variance of forecast for the two main equations of both models in first difference transformation using the knowledge that the true means of the series were zero. Table 5 shows that these results do not change the general impression and the single equation least squares estimates still provide the smallest variances of the errors of forecast.

5 Conclusions

Care must be taken when drawing general conclusions from sampling experiments of the type considered in this paper but the results appear to us to be of a striking and significant nature. They indicate that unless it is possible to specify with some degree of accuracy the intercorrelation between the error terms of a set of relations and unless it is possible to choose approximately the correct autoregressive transformation so as to randomize the error terms, then a certain amount of scepticism is justified concerning the possibility of estimating structural parameters from aggregative time series of only twenty observations when generated by systems analogous to those examined in this paper. This scepticism will be

Table 4 *Errors of forecast*

Equation	Autoregressive transformation		Actual errors of forecast			Estimated mean variance of	
	Single equation	Reduced form	Mean	Standard errors of mean	Variance	Error	Individual forecast
	(1)	(2)	(3)	(4)	(5)	(6)	(7)
Model I							
I	O		2.45	1.09	23.8	20.6	24.0
	F.D.		−0.03	0.65	8.6	14.1	16.2
	S.D.		−1.52	1.10	24.3	28.2	31.3
IA		O	6.19	4.57	417.1	83.4	—
		F.D.	−1.03	0.76	11.5	18.1	—
		S.D.	−5.86	3.43	235.7	198.3	—
II	O		−1.27	1.04	21.6	11.4	13.8
	F.D.		−1.06	0.67	9.0	6.8	7.6
	S.D.		−1.12	0.68	9.2	12.3	13.9
III	O		0.63	1.35	36.6	22.8	26.7
	F.D.		−1.18	1.04	21.9	21.4	23.8
	S.D.		−2.30	1.18	27.8	30.3	34.0
Model II							
IV	O		1.92	1.09	25.6	13.3	15.4
	F.D.		−0.66	0.59	7.0	11.2	12.4
	S.D.		−1.22	1.19	28.2	28.2	31.0
IVA		O	1.65	1.14	26.0	14.4	—
		F.D.	0.38	0.91	16.4	24.2	—
		S.D.	40.56	34.39	23654.	17470.	—
V	O		0.38	0.74	10.9	10.0	11.6
	F.D.		0.02	0.53	5.6	7.4	8.3
	S.D.		−0.77	0.68	9.2	11.7	13.1
VI	O		2.10	1.07	23.0	36.2	41.4
	F.D.		0.31	1.03	21.0	34.9	38.9
	S.D.		−1.96	1.24	30.7	47.7	53.9

considerably increased if it is also attempted to make a choice of variables and time lags from the same data.

If the error terms are independent or nearly independent between equations, the results obtained justify the use of single equation least squares estimation, in which case the main problem lies in making the correct autoregressive transformation. This would seem to be the situation

Table 5 *Errors of forecast assuming true mean of zero (First Difference Transformation)*

Equation	Actual errors of forecast		
	Mean	Standard error of mean	Variance
Model I			
I	−0.10	0.58	6.66
IA	0.36	0.66	8.64
Model II			
IV	0.41	0.54	5.82
IVA	−0.69	0.90	16.15

as regards many demand relationships, particularly those which are in terms of current variables and those relating to agricultural products.

For short run prediction we would appear to be in a somewhat more favourable position since the estimated variance of errors of individual forecasts obtained from single equation regression analysis seem to be in line with the actual errors and as small as could be expected even in the absence of a simultaneous equations complication. However, it must be remembered that such predictions assume that the same system will continue.

Notes

1 For a complete statement of the conditions under which least squares give 'best unbiassed' estimates, see F.N. David and J. Neyman, 'Extension of the Markoff Theorem on Least Squares', *Statistical Research Memoirs*, Vol. II, London 1938.

2 T. Haavelmo, 'The Probability Approach in Econometrics', Supplement to *Econometrica*, Vol. 12, July 1944.

3 A more complete discussion can be found in T. Koopmans, 'Statistical Methods of Measuring Economic Relationships', *Cowles Commission Discussion Papers* Statistics No. 310 (mimeographed copy of lectures delivered at the University of Chicago 1947) and T. Haavelmo, 'Methods of Measuring the Marginal Propensity to Consume', *Journal of the American Statistical Association*, Vol. 42, 1947, pp. 105-22.

4 See Koopmans, 'Statistical Methods of Measuring Economic Relationships', *op. cit*. A very good description of the practical procedure is contained in M.A. Girshick and T. Haavelmo, 'Statistical Analysis of the Demand for Food: Examples of Simultaneous Estimation of Structural Equations', *Econometrica*, Vol. 15, 1947, pp. 79-110. Further references may be found in the various articles to which we have referred.

5 D. Cochrane and G.H. Orcutt, 'Application of Least Squares Regression to Relationships containing Autocorrelated Error Terms', *Journal of the American Statistical Association*, Vol. 44, 1949, pp. 32-61.
6 M.G. Kendall and B. Babington-Smith, 'Tables of Random Sampling Numbers', *Tracts for Computers No. 24*, Cambridge University Press 1939.
7 D. Cochrane and G. Orcutt, *op. cit.*
8 Richard Stone, 'The Analysis of Market Demand: An Outline of Methods and Results' read before a meeting of the European section of the Econometric Society at The Hague, September 1948, and to be published in *The Review of the International Statistical Institute*.
9 G.H. Orcutt, 'A Study of the Autoregressive Nature of the Time Series Used for Tinbergen's Model of the Economic System of the United States 1919-32', *Journal of the Royal Statistical Society*, Vol. X, Series B, 1948, pp. 1-53.
10 J. Tinbergen, 'Statistical Testing of Business-Cycle Theories Vol. II; Business Cycles in the United States of America 1919-32', League of Nations, Geneva, 1939.
11 H.B. Mann and H. Wald, 'On the Statistical Treatment of Linear Stochastic Difference Equations', *Econometrica*, Vol. 11, 1943, pp. 173-220.
12 T. Koopmans, 'Serial Correlation and Quadratic Forms in Normal Variables', *Annals of Mathematical Statistics*, Vol. 13, 1942, pp. 14-33.
13 G.H. Orcutt, *op. cit.*
14 Using the t tables for 20 degrees of freedom. We are using both tails of the distribution but a case can be made for using only one tail. This would halve the levels of signficance.
15 R. Bentzel and H. Wold, 'On Statistical Demand Analysis from the viewpoint of Simultaneous Equations', *Skandinavisk Aktuarietidskrift*, Vol. 29, 1946, pp. 95-114.
16 The probability distribution of this statistic has been tabulated; see B.S. Hart and J. von Neumann, 'Tabulation of the Probabilities for the Ratio of the Mean Square Successive Difference to the Variance', *Annals of Mathematical Statistics*, vol. 13, pp. 207-214.
17 D. Cochrane and G. Orcutt, *op. cit.*

(Reprinted from *Journal of the American Statistical Association*, 1949, vol. 44, 356-72, with the permission of the American Statistical Association.)

Appendix 3
The method of iterative maximization

J.D. Sargan

Consider the general method of maximizing a function $f(a, b)$ which is a function of two vectors a and b by the following iterative procedure. First maximize with respect to b keeping a constant, and then maximize with respect to a keeping b constant, and iterate. Although the procedure may not be very efficient, it converges to a local maximum in a very wide class of cases.

Basic assumptions

(i) For some c the set of points $f(a, b) > c$ is bounded.
(ii) The function is continuous throughout this region.

Take as arbitrary starting point some point within the region, and label the successive points obtained by the iteration (a_i, b_i) and the successive values of the function f_i, $i = 1, 2, 3, \ldots$

Since the function cannot decrease at any stage, the points must stay within the bounded region. Since f_i is a positive monotonic sequence with an upper bound (since the function is continuous on a closed set) the sequence converges to its upper bound f^*. Also since the sequence (a_i, b_i) is bounded it possesses limit points. Consider any limit point (a^*, b^*). Since there is a sub-sequence of points, denoted by (a_i^*, b_i^*), which converges to the limit point and the function is continuous, $f(a^*, b^*) = f^*$.

There are three possibilities to be considered. Either all except a finite number of the sub-sequence are obtained by maximizing with respect to a, when the limit point is called of type a, or all except a finite number are obtained by maximizing with respect to b, when the limit point is of type b, or the sub-sequence has an infinite number of points of both types when the limit point is of type ab. We suppose that the limit point is of type a or ab; the limit point of type b can be considered by interchanging a and b in the following argument.

Suppose $f(a, b^*)$ had not a maximum at $a = a^*$. Then there exists a^{**} such that $f(a^{**}, b^*) > f(a^*, b^*) = f^*$. By continuity there exists δ_1 such that $f(a^{**}, b) > f^*$ if $|b - b^*| < \delta_1$. Now since the sub-sequence (a_i^*, b_i^*) tends to the limit point of type a or ab there exists a point of this sub-sequence obtained by maximizing with respect to a, such that $|b_i^* - b^*| < \delta_1$. And then $f(a^{**}, b_i^*) > f^* \geqslant f(a_i^*, b_i^*)$. But a_i^* was obtained by maximizing $f(a, b_i^*)$ with respect to a.

This is a contradiction showing that $f(a^*, b^*) \geqslant f(a, b^*)$ for all a.

Suppose now that $f(a^*, b)$ had not a maximum at $b = b^*$, so that there exists b^{**} such that $f(a^*, b^{**}) > f^*$. There exists δ_2 such that $f(a^*, b^{**}) > f^*$ if $|a - a^*| < \delta_2$ from continuity. We can find a point of the sub-sequence obtained by maximizing with respect to a such that $|a_i^* - a^*| < \delta_2$. At the next stage of the iteration we choose b so as to maximize $f(a_i^*, b)$. If we take $b = b^{**}$ we obtain $f(a_i^*, b^{**}) > f^*$. This contradicts the definition of f^* as an upper bound of the sequence. Thus $f(a^*, b^*) \geqslant f(a^*, b)$ for all values of b. From these two results it follows that if $f(a, b)$ has all first-order derivatives at (a^*, b^*) this is a stationary point of the function.

Since the presence of more than one limit point would require that the function had several stationary points of this type each with a value of the function equal to f^*, in general there will only be one limit point. Indeed it can be shown that the stationary points must satisfy further very restrictive conditions. It must be possible to link the points in a cyclic chain so that each pair in the chain differs only in the value of one of the vectors a or b. In practice only the presence of a single limit point need be considered and in this case the sequence of points converges to this limit point. Thus the original sequence will converge to one of the stationary values in the region. Furthermore only maxima or saddle points need be considered.

However, the likelihood of the limit point being a saddlepoint is low. Suppose that the limit point were a saddlepoint and that at some stage of the iteration the current point had been obtained by maximizing with respect to b. The linear space $b = b_i$ must not intersect the region where $f > f^*$ for then the sequence would obviously not converge to the saddlepoint. This condition is unlikely to be fulfilled for all i.

In particular if the vector b has only one component, as in the case considered in the body of the paper, convergence to a saddlepoint is extremely unlikely. If there is a direction through the saddlepoint (α, β) such that $f(a^* + k\alpha, b^* + k\beta) > f^*$ for all $|k| < \delta$, and this condition is certainly satisfied if the function has continuous second-order derivatives at the saddlepoint, then we can find a point of the sequence obtained by maximizing with respect to b which lies within a distance $\delta\beta$ of the limit point. If this point is (a_i, b_i) take $k = (b_i - b^*)/\beta$. The corresponding point on the line defined above could be taken as the next point in the iteration, and unless $k = 0$, $f_{i+1} > f^*$. This is a contradiction showing that the sequence does not converge to the saddlepoint. The only case where the sequence does converge to the saddlepoint is where for some finite i, $b_i = b^*$. In this case the next point in the sequence is the saddlepoint, and so are all subsequent points. This case, however, occurs with probability zero.

(Reprinted, with permission, from Vol. XVI of the Colston Papers, being the Proceedings of the Sixteenth Symposium of the Colston Research Society, 1964, published by Butterworths Scientific Publications, London.)

Index